Favorite Brand Name™

GRILLING

and More

Publications International, Ltd.

Favorite Brand Name Recipes at www.fbnr.com

Microwave Cooking: Microwave ovens vary in wattage. Use the cooking times as guidelines and check for doneness before adding more time.

Preparation/Cooking Times: Preparation times are based on the approximate amount of time required to assemble the recipe before cooking, baking, chilling or serving. These times include preparation steps such as measuring, chopping and mixing. The fact that some preparations and cooking can be done simultaneously is taken into account. Preparation of optional ingredients and serving suggestions is not included.

CONTENTS

124

232

368

INTRODUCTION

Grill cookery is more than just tailgate barbecuing for Saturday's college football game. It is a method of cooking with a history directly linked to how food gets cooked and a future closely correlated to its popularity. A dry-heat cooking method employing direct flame heat, grilling is similar to broiling in that both lend definitive flavors by sealing foods' natural juices and caramelizing surface sugars. Grilling is easily identified on a cooked product because, unlike broiling, it leaves its mark, literally.

Grilling first evolved in the West Indies. Due to the extreme heat of the region, Caribbean cultures began smoking meats over racks to preserve them as well as to eliminate insect infestations. Spanish explorers eventually tried their hand at it with imported pigs and cattle. The natives referred to this cooking process as "barbacoa," commonly believed to be the origins of the English word "barbecue." The European settlers eventually developed smoke houses and pits. Shortly thereafter, the grill itself began to take shape. Its designer is not known, but it took the form of a low table: a wrought-iron grilltop with legs. Early models included a sandwich-type basket that compressed food between two grill sides, usually used for smaller cuts of meat that might be difficult to turn on an open grill.

Aside from grill design, little has changed the face of grilling over the years since. Modern tools are evident in the professional kitchen as well as in backyards across the country; there seems to be a new gadget every day. Professionals welcome grilling as a way to add variety, specific flavor and particular appearance, while home chefs similarly perfect it, though on a much smaller scale. A common practice for both the professional and the novice is to add water-soaked wood chips to hot coals to impart smoky flavors to cooked products.

The future of grilling means different things to different people. The professional kitchen is rooted in classical methods, which are not apt to change. There are several indoor grilling options and the home cook is constantly being presented with variations, new inventions and new gimmicks. There are coated grill pans lined with non-stick materials complete with built-in ridges that allow for the "grill effect." Grilling appliances are also available and perform admirably.

Ask any grilling enthusiast worth their "kiss the cook" apron and they'll swear by the outdoor method. There's just nothing like being out in the backyard, dabbing some sauce on a rack of ribs, flipping burgers and rotating corn cobs.

Commonly grilled foods include fatty fish (which hold together better than leaner fish), tender and well-marbled cuts of beef, poultry and a variety of vegetables. The heat source is often high, higher than smoking but slightly less than broiling. The size of the cooked product is normally individual portions, although larger cuts of meat can be grilled and sliced for service. Vegetables are usually skewered, but some may be done right on the grill, zucchini for instance.

To check temperature of coals, cautiously hold the palm of your hand at grid level—over the coals for direct heat and over the drip pan for indirect heat—and count the number of seconds you can hold your hand in that position before the heat forces you to pull it away.

2 Seconds:
  hot, about 375°F or more

3 Seconds:
  medium-hot, about 350°F to 375°F

4 Seconds:
  medium, about 300°F to 350°F

5 Seconds:
  low, about 200°F to 300°F

Direct vs. Indirect Grilling

• For direct cooking, arrange the coals in a single layer directly under the food. Use this method for quick-cooking foods, such as hamburgers, steaks and fish.

• For indirect cooking, arrange coals to one side of the grill. Place a drip pan under the food at the other side. For more heat, divide the coals on either side of the drip pan. Use this method for slow-cooking foods, such as roasts and whole chicken.

FIRIN' UP
THE GRILL

Start the grilling season off right and get your taste buds ready for some of the best grilled starters ever. This is just the beginning, so don't eat too much.

Grilled Quesadilla Snacks

1½ cups (6 ounces) shredded
    Monterey Jack cheese
½ red or yellow bell pepper,
    chopped
2 ounces sliced smoked ham,
    cut into thin strips
2 ounces sliced smoked
    turkey, cut into thin strips
¼ cup finely chopped green
    onions
⅓ cup *French's*® Classic Yellow®
    Mustard
2 teaspoons ground cumin
10 flour tortillas (6 inch)

1. Combine cheese, bell pepper, ham, turkey and onions in medium bowl. Combine mustard and cumin in small bowl; mix well.

2. Place 5 tortillas on sheet of waxed paper. Spread 1 rounded teaspoon mustard mixture over each tortilla. Sprinkle cheese mixture evenly over mustard mixture. Top with another tortilla, pressing down firmly to form quesadilla.

3. Place quesadillas on oiled grid. Grill over medium heat 2 minutes or until cheese is melted and heated through, turning once. Cut each quesadilla into quarters. Serve with salsa and cilantro, if desired. *Makes 10 servings*

Prep Time: 30 minutes
Cook Time: 2 minutes

Grilled Quesadilla Snacks

Hawaiian Ribs

1 can (8 ounces) crushed
    pineapple in juice,
    undrained
⅓ cup apricot jam
3 tablespoons *French's*®
    Classic Yellow® Mustard
1 tablespoon red wine vinegar
2 teaspoons grated peeled
    fresh ginger
1 clove garlic, minced
3 to 4 pounds pork baby back
    ribs*

Or, if baby back ribs are not available, substitute 4 pounds pork spareribs, cut in half lengthwise. Cut spareribs into 3- to 4-rib portions. Cook 20 minutes in enough boiling water to cover. Grill ribs 30 to 40 minutes or until no longer pink near bone, brushing with portion of pineapple mixture during last 10 minutes.

1. Combine crushed pineapple with juice, apricot jam, mustard, vinegar, ginger and garlic in blender or food processor. Cover and process until very smooth.

2. Place ribs on oiled grid. Grill ribs over medium heat 40 minutes or until ribs are no longer pink near bone. Brush ribs with portion of pineapple sauce mixture during last 10 minutes of cooking. Cut into individual ribs to serve. Serve remaining sauce for dipping.

Makes 8 servings (1½ cups sauce)

Note: Try mixing 2 tablespoons *French's*® Mustard, any flavor, with ¾ cup peach-apricot sweet 'n' sour sauce to create a delicious luau fruit dip. Serve with assorted cut-up fresh fruit.

Prep Time: 10 minutes
Cook Time: 40 minutes

Grilled Turkey Ham Quesadillas

Nonstick cooking spray
¼ cup salsa
4 (7-inch) flour tortillas
½ cup shredded reduced-
    sodium reduced-fat
    Monterey Jack cheese
¼ cup finely chopped turkey
    ham
1 can (4 ounces) diced green
    chilies, drained
Additional salsa (optional)
Fat-free sour cream
    (optional)

1. To prevent sticking, spray grid with cooking spray. Prepare coals for grilling.

2. Spread 1 tablespoon salsa onto each tortilla. Sprinkle cheese, turkey ham and chilies equally over half of each tortilla; fold over uncovered half to make "sandwich"; spray tops and bottoms of tortilla "sandwiches" with cooking spray.

3. Grill quesadillas on uncovered grill over medium coals 1½ minutes per side or until cheese is melted and tortillas are golden brown, turning once. Quarter each quesadilla and serve with additional salsa and sour cream, if desired.

Makes 8 servings

Hawaiian Ribs

Greek-Style Grilled Feta

1 package (8 ounces) feta
    cheese, sliced in half
    horizontally
24 (¼-inch) slices small onion
½ green bell pepper, thinly
    sliced
½ red bell pepper, thinly sliced
½ teaspoon dried oregano
    leaves
¼ teaspoon garlic pepper or
    black pepper
24 (½-inch) slices French bread

1. Spray 14-inch-long sheet of foil with nonstick cooking spray. Cut feta into 24 slices. Place onion slices in center of foil and top with feta slices. Sprinkle with bell pepper slices, oregano and garlic pepper.

2. Seal foil using Drugstore Wrap technique.* Place foil packet on grid upside down and grill on covered grill over hot coals 15 minutes. Turn packet over; grill on covered grill 15 minutes more.

3. Open packet carefully and serve immediately with slices of French bread.   *Makes 8 servings*

*Place the food in the center of an oblong piece of heavy-duty foil, leaving at least a two-inch border around the food. Bring the two long sides together above the food; fold down in a series of locked folds, allowing for heat circulation and expansion. Fold the short ends up and over again. Press folds firmly to seal the foil packet.

Spicy Wings

16 chicken wings
½ cup olive or vegetable oil
¼ cup balsamic vinegar
¼ cup honey
2 tablespoons brown sugar
2 tablespoons cane syrup or
    dark corn syrup
1 tablespoon TABASCO®
    brand Pepper Sauce
1 teaspoon soy sauce
½ teaspoon dried thyme leaves
¼ teaspoon ground nutmeg
¼ teaspoon Worcestershire
    sauce

Cut off and discard bony wing tips. Cut remaining wings in half. Combine remaining ingredients in large bowl until well blended; add wings. Cover and marinate in refrigerator 1 hour.

Prepare grill. Place wings on grid. Grill 15 to 20 minutes over medium coals, turning frequently.   *Makes 32 appetizers*

Greek-Style Grilled Feta

Wingin' It on the Grill—Buffalo Style

2½ **pounds chicken wings**
  ½ **cup *Frank's® RedHot®*
    Cayenne Pepper Sauce**
  ⅓ **cup butter or margarine,
    melted**
  **Prepared blue cheese salad
    dressing**
  Celery sticks

Cut off wing tips from chicken wings; discard. Cut wings in half between remaining joint to make two pieces. Place wing pieces on grid. Grill over medium-high coals 30 minutes or until thoroughly cooked and crispy, turning often. Place in large bowl.

Combine *Frank's RedHot* Sauce and butter. Pour over wings; toss well to coat evenly. Serve wings with blue cheese dressing and celery sticks.

Makes 6 servings

Shanghai Red Wings: Cook wings as directed. Combine ¼ cup soy sauce, 3 tablespoons *Frank's RedHot* Sauce, 3 tablespoons honey, 2 tablespoons peanut oil, 1 teaspoon grated peeled fresh ginger and 1 teaspoon minced garlic in small bowl; mix well. Pour over wings; toss well to coat evenly. Serve as directed.

Cajun Wings: Cook wings as directed. Combine ⅓ cup *Frank's RedHot* Sauce, ⅓ cup ketchup, ¼ cup (½ stick) melted butter or margarine and 2 teaspoons Cajun seasoning blend in small bowl; mix well. Pour over wings; toss well to coat evenly. Serve as directed.

Santa Fe Wings: Cook wings as directed. Combine ¼ cup *Frank's RedHot*, ¼ cup (½ stick) melted butter or margarine, ¼ cup chili sauce and 1 teaspoon chili powder in small bowl; mix well. Pour over wings; toss well to coat evenly. Serve as directed.

Prep Time: 10 minutes
Cook Time: 30 minutes

Grilled Corn Soup

4 ears Grilled Corn-on-the-Cob
   (recipe follows)
5 green onions
4 cups chicken broth, divided
   Salt and black pepper

Cut kernels from cobs to make 2 to 2½ cups. Slice green onions, separating the white part from the green. Place corn, white part of onions and 2 cups chicken broth in blender or food processor; process until mixture is slightly lumpy. Place corn mixture in large saucepan; add remaining chicken broth. Simmer gently 15 minutes. Stir in sliced green onion tops; season to taste with salt and pepper.

Makes 4 to 6 servings

Grilled Corn-on-the-Cob: Turn back corn husks; do not remove. Remove silks with stiff brush; rinse corn under cold running water. Smooth husks back into position. Grill ears, on a covered grill, over medium-hot KINGSFORD® briquets, about 25 minutes or until tender, turning corn often. Remove husks and serve.

FOOD FACT

Corn is a native American food. When the English arrived in America, they called this yellow grain of the Indians "corn" because it was their generic term for grain or things that were small. The settlers soon learned to make a variety of tasty corn dishes, including bread and pudding. To the Pilgrims, fresh corn pudding served with maple syrup was the equivalent of today's premium ice cream--and eaten as frequently.

Grilled Antipasto Platter

16 medium scallops

16 medium shrimp, shelled and deveined

12 mushrooms (about 1 inch diameter)

3 ounces thinly sliced prosciutto or deli-style ham

16 slender asparagus spears

1 jar (6½ ounces) marinated artichoke hearts, drained

2 medium zucchini, cut lengthwise into slices

1 large *or* 2 small red bell peppers, cored, seeded and cut into 1-inch-wide strips

1 head radicchio, cut lengthwise into quarters (optional)

Lemon Baste (recipe page 49)

Lemon wedges

Soak 12 long bamboo skewers in water for at least 20 minutes to keep them from burning. Thread 4 scallops on each of 4 skewers and 4 shrimp on each of another 4 skewers. Thread 6 mushrooms on each of 2 more skewers. Cut prosciutto into 2×1-inch strips. Wrap 2 asparagus spears together with 2 strips of prosciutto; secure with a toothpick. Repeat with remaining asparagus spears. Wrap each artichoke heart in 1 strip of prosciutto; thread on 2 remaining skewers. Place ingredients except radicchio and lemon wedges on a baking sheet. Reserve ¼ cup Lemon Baste. Brush remaining Lemon Baste liberally over ingredients on baking sheet.

Spread medium KINGSFORD® Briquets in a wide single layer over the bed of the grill. Oil hot grid to help prevent sticking. Grill skewers, asparagus bundles, zucchini and red peppers, on an uncovered grill, 7 to 12 minutes until vegetables are tender, seafood firms up and turns opaque and prosciutto around wrapped vegetables is crisp, turning once or twice. Remove each item from grill to a large serving platter as it is done. Pour remaining baste over all. Serve hot or at room temperature. Garnish with radicchio, if desired, and lemon wedges.

Makes 4 main-dish servings or 8 appetizer servings

Grilled Antipasto Platter

California Quesadillas

1 small ripe avocado
2 packages (3 ounces each)
    cream cheese, softened
3 tablespoons *Frank's®*
    RedHot® Cayenne Pepper
    Sauce
¼ cup minced fresh cilantro
    leaves
16 (6-inch) flour tortillas
    (2 packages)
1 cup (4 ounces) shredded
    Cheddar or Monterey
    Jack cheese
½ cup finely chopped green
    onions
    Sour cream (optional)

Halve avocado and remove pit. Scoop out flesh into food processor or bowl of electric mixer. Add cream cheese and *Frank's RedHot* Sauce. Cover and process, or beat, until smooth. Add cilantro; process, or beat, until well blended. Spread rounded tablespoon avocado mixture onto each tortilla. Sprinkle half the tortillas with cheese and onions, dividing evenly. Top with remaining tortillas; press gently.

Place tortillas on oiled grid. Grill over medium coals 5 minutes or until cheese melts and tortillas are lightly browned, turning once. Cut into triangles. Serve with sour cream, if desired. Garnish as desired.   *Makes 8 appetizer servings*

Note: You may serve avocado mixture as a dip with tortilla chips.

Prep Time: 20 minutes
Cook Time: 5 minutes

FOOD FACT

Quesadillas are one of Mexico's most popular snacks. They are made from flour tortillas topped with shredded cheese, such as Monterey Jack or Chihuahua. Then they are folded into half moons and toasted on a griddle or in a skillet until the cheese melts. An alternate method is to place the filling ingredients on a large tortilla. The filling is then topped with a second tortilla, and the quesadilla is toasted on a griddle. This large quesadilla is cut into wedges to serve. Usually served as an appetizer or entrée, quesadillas may be garnished with guacamole and salsa. Other popular fillings include refried beans, chorizo, chicken and vegetables.

California Quesadillas

Grilled Lobster, Shrimp and Calamari Seviche

¾ cup fresh orange juice

⅓ cup fresh lime juice

2 tablespoons tequila

2 jalapeño peppers,* seeded and minced

2 tablespoons chopped fresh cilantro, chives or green onion tops

1 teaspoon honey

1 teaspoon ground cumin

1 teaspoon olive oil

10 squid, cleaned and cut into rings and tentacles

½ pound medium shrimp, peeled, deveined and tails removed

2 lobster tails (8 ounces each), meat removed and shells discarded

Jalapeño peppers can sting and irritate the skin; wear rubber gloves when handling peppers and do not touch eyes. Wash hands after handling peppers.

1. To make marinade, combine orange juice, lime juice, tequila, jalapeños, cilantro and honey in medium glass bowl.

2. Measure ¼ cup marinade into small glass bowl; stir in cumin and oil. Set aside. Refrigerate remaining marinade.

3. Prepare grill for direct grilling.

4. Bring 1 quart water in 2-quart saucepan to a boil over high heat. Add squid; cook 30 seconds or until opaque. Drain. Rinse under cold water; drain. Add squid to refrigerated marinade.

5. Thread shrimp onto 1 metal skewer. Brush shrimp and lobster with reserved ¼ cup marinade.

6. Place shrimp on grid. Grill shrimp, on uncovered grill, over medium-hot coals 2 to 3 minutes per side or until shrimp turn pink and opaque. Remove shrimp from skewers and add to squid. Place lobster on grid. Grill 5 minutes per side or until meat turns opaque and is cooked through. Slice lobster meat into ¼-inch-thick slices; add to squid.

7. Refrigerate at least 2 hours or overnight.

Makes 6 appetizer servings

Grilled Lobster, Shrimp and Calamari Seviche

Sausage-Bacon-Apricot Kabobs

1 package BOB EVANS®
   Italian Grillin' Sausage
   (approximately 5 links)
1 cup dried apricot halves
8 slices bacon
3 tablespoons apricot
   preserves
3 tablespoons lemon juice
1 tablespoon Dijon mustard
1 teaspoon Worcestershire
   sauce

Precook sausage 10 minutes in gently boiling water. Drain and cut into ¾-inch slices. Alternate sausage and apricots on 8 wooden skewers,* weaving bacon back and forth in ribbonlike fashion between them. Grill or broil over medium-high heat 3 to 4 minutes on each side. Combine preserves, lemon juice, mustard and Worcestershire in small bowl. Brush preserves mixture on kabobs; continue grilling, turning and basting frequently, until bacon is cooked through. Refrigerate leftovers. *Makes 8 kabobs*

Soak wooden skewers in water 30 minutes before use to prevent burning.

Grilled Stuffed Mushrooms

24 large 2-inch mushrooms,
   wiped clean
3 tablespoons olive oil,
   divided
1 red bell pepper, seeded and
   chopped
½ cup minced fresh Italian
   parsley
2 tablespoons *French's®*
   Worcestershire Sauce
1 teaspoon garlic powder
1⅓ cups *French's®* French Fried
   Onions, divided
½ cup grated Parmesan cheese

Remove stems from mushrooms. Finely chop stems; set aside. Brush mushrooms caps with 1 tablespoon oil. Place caps on a tray.

Heat remaining 2 tablespoons oil in large nonstick skillet over medium-high heat. Add chopped stems and pepper; cook and stir until tender. Stir in parsley, Worcestershire and garlic powder. Cook until liquid is evaporated, stirring often. Stir in ⅔ *cup* French Fried Onions and cheese.

Spoon about 1 tablespoon mushroom mixture into each mushroom cap. Place mushroom caps on vegetable grilling rack or basket. Place on grid. Grill over medium-high coals 15 minutes or until mushrooms are tender. Sprinkle with remaining ⅔ *cup* onions. Grill 1 minute or until onions are golden. Serve warm.

Makes 6 appetizer servings

Prep Time: 30 minutes
Cook Time: 25 minutes

Sausage-Bacon-Apricot Kabobs

Turkey Ham Quesadillas

¼ **cup picante sauce or salsa**

4 **(7-inch) regular or whole wheat flour tortillas**

½ **cup shredded reduced-fat reduced-sodium Monterey Jack cheese**

¼ **cup finely chopped turkey-ham or lean ham**

¼ **cup canned diced green chilies, drained *or* 1 to 2 tablespoons chopped jalapeño peppers***

Nonstick cooking spray

Additional picante sauce or salsa for dipping (optional)

Fat-free or low-fat sour cream (optional)

*Jalapeño peppers can sting and irritate the skin; wear rubber gloves when handling peppers and do not touch eyes. Wash hands after handling.

1. Spread 1 tablespoon picante sauce on each tortilla.

2. Sprinkle cheese, turkey ham and chilies equally over half of each tortilla. Fold over uncovered half to make quesadilla; spray tops and bottoms of quesadillas with cooking spray.

3. Grill on uncovered grill over medium coals 1½ minutes per side or until cheese is melted and tortillas are golden brown, turning once. Quarter each quesadilla and serve with additional picante sauce and fat-free sour cream, if desired.

Makes 8 appetizer servings

FOOD FACT

A tortilla is a round, thin unleavened Mexican bread that is baked on a griddle. It can be made of either corn or wheat flour, water and a little salt. Traditionally the dough is shaped and flattened by hand and cooked on both sides on a hot griddle until dry and flecked with brown. Tortillas are a staple of Mexican and Tex-Mex cooking. They can be eaten plain or used as a base for tacos, burritos, enchiladas and many other dishes. Both corn and flour tortillas are available in supermarkets and Mexican markets either shelf stable or refrigerated. The word tortilla in Spain refers to a thin omelet. Tortilla Española is a popular example. It consists of thinly sliced potatoes and onions cooked in an egg mixture in a skillet. It may be served hot or at room temperature.

Red Hot Pepper Wings

28 chicken wing drumettes
    (2¼ to 3 pounds)
2 tablespoons olive oil
    Salt and black pepper
2 tablespoons melted butter
1 teaspoon sugar
¼ to ½ cup hot pepper sauce

Brush chicken with oil; sprinkle with salt and pepper. Grill chicken on covered grill over medium KINGSFORD® Briquets about 20 minutes until juices run clear, turning every 5 minutes. Combine butter, sugar and pepper sauce in large bowl; add chicken and toss to coat. Serve hot or cold.

Makes 7 servings

Cheesy Mushroom Crostini

4 tablespoons prepared garlic
    butter,* divided
12 slices sourdough French
    bread, cut diagonally
1 package (10 ounces)
    mushrooms, wiped clean
    and sliced
1 red onion, chopped
1 jar (4 ounces) chopped
    pimiento, drained
½ cup (4 ounces) crumbled
    Gorgonzola or blue
    cheese, divided
¼ cup chopped fresh basil
2 tablespoons *French's*® Napa
    Valley Style Dijon
    Mustard
1 tablespoon balsamic or red
    wine vinegar

Or, if prepared garlic butter is not available, substitute ¼ cup melted butter mixed with ¼ teaspoon garlic powder.

1. Divide 2 tablespoons garlic butter evenly between bread slices. Brush butter on one side of bread. Place bread, buttered-side up, on oiled grid. Grill over medium-high heat 3 minutes or until golden, turning once. Transfer to serving platter.

2. Heat remaining garlic butter in large skillet over medium-high heat. Add mushrooms and onion; cook and stir 5 to 8 minutes or until mushrooms are golden. Add pimiento, ¼ cup cheese, basil, mustard and vinegar; cook and stir 3 minutes or until liquid is evaporated.

3. Spoon mushroom mixture evenly over bread slices. Top with remaining cheese. Serve warm.

Makes 12 servings

Prep Time: 25 minutes
Cook Time: 15 minutes

Grilled Chicken Tostados

1 pound boneless skinless
chicken breast halves
1 teaspoon ground cumin
¼ cup orange juice
¼ cup plus 2 tablespoons
salsa, divided
1 tablespoon plus
2 teaspoons vegetable oil,
divided
2 cloves garlic, minced
8 green onions
1 can (16 ounces) refried
beans
4 (10-inch) *or* 8 (6- to 7-inch)
flour tortillas
2 cups chopped romaine
lettuce
1½ cups (6 ounces) shredded
Monterey Jack cheese
with jalapeño peppers
1 ripe medium avocado, diced
(optional)
1 medium tomato, seeded
and diced (optional)
Chopped fresh cilantro and
sour cream (optional)

Place chicken in single layer in shallow glass dish; sprinkle with cumin. Combine orange juice, ¼ cup salsa, 1 tablespoon oil and garlic in small bowl; pour over chicken. Cover; marinate in refrigerator at least 2 hours or up to 8 hours, stirring mixture occasionally.

Prepare grill for direct cooking.

Drain chicken; reserve marinade. Brush green onions with remaining 2 teaspoons oil. Place chicken and green onions on grid. Grill, covered, over medium-high heat 5 minutes. Brush tops of chicken with half of reserved marinade; turn and brush with remaining marinade. Turn onions. Continue to grill, covered, 5 minutes or until chicken is no longer pink in center and onions are tender. (If onions are browning too quickly, remove before chicken is done.)

Meanwhile, combine beans and remaining 2 tablespoons salsa in small saucepan; cook, stirring occasionally, over medium heat until hot.

Place tortillas in single layer on grid. Grill, uncovered, 1 to 2 minutes per side or until golden brown. (If tortillas puff up, pierce with tip of knife or flatten by pressing with spatula.)

Transfer chicken and onions to cutting board. Slice chicken crosswise into ½-inch strips. Cut onions crosswise into 1-inch-long pieces. Spread tortillas with bean mixture; top with lettuce, chicken, onions, cheese, avocado and tomato, if desired. Sprinkle with cilantro and serve with sour cream, if desired. *Makes 4 servings*

Grilled Chicken Tostada

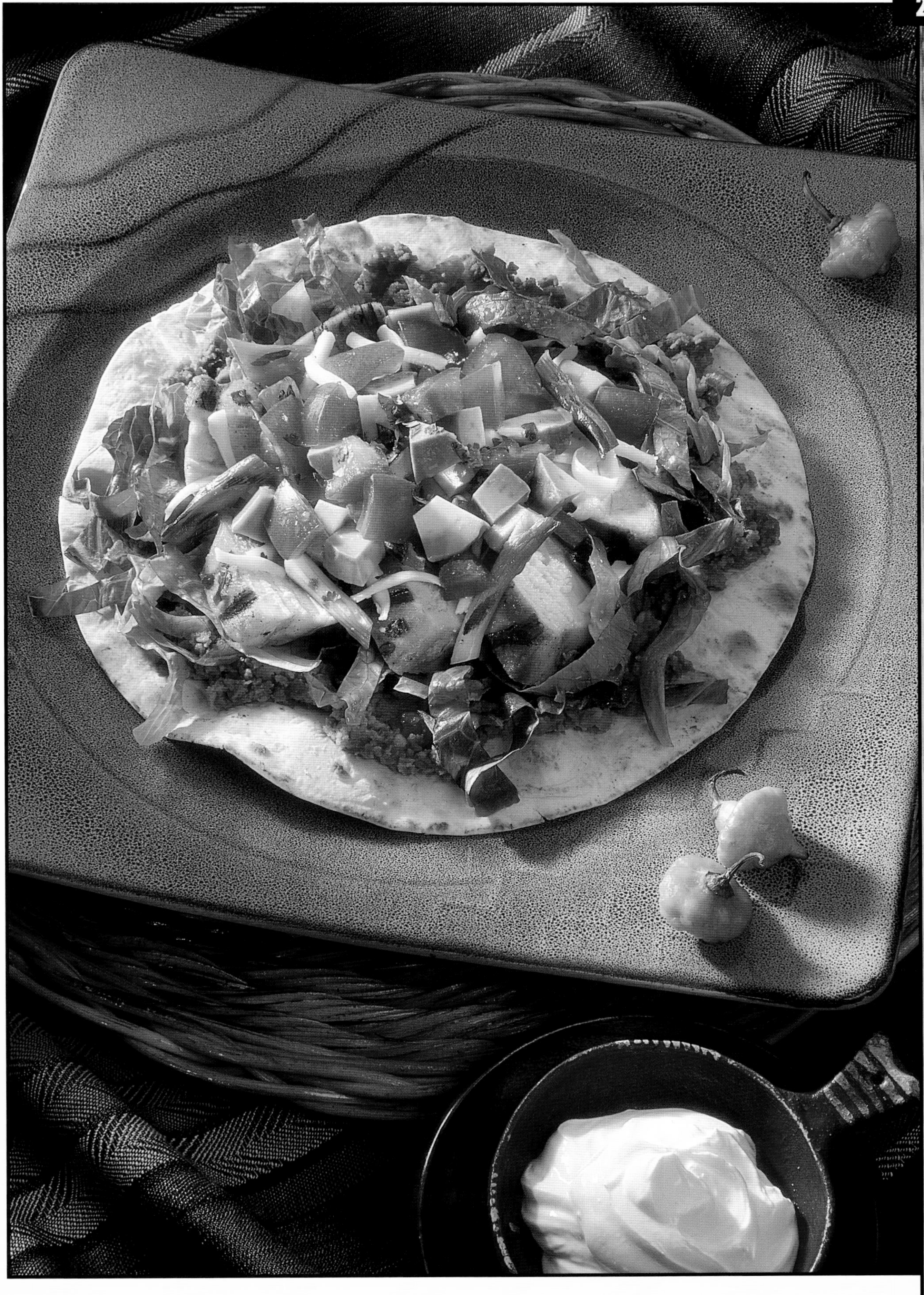

Grilled Red Bell Pepper Dip

1 red bell pepper, stemmed, seeded and halved

1 cup fat-free or reduced-fat ricotta cheese

4 ounces fat-free cream cheese

¼ cup grated Parmesan cheese

1 clove garlic, minced *or*
   1 clove Grilled Garlic (recipe follows)

½ teaspoon Dijon mustard

¼ teaspoon salt

¼ teaspoon herbes de Provence*

Mini pita pockets, Melba toast, pretzels or fresh vegetables

Substitute ¼ teaspoon each rubbed sage, crushed dried rosemary, thyme, oregano, marjoram and basil leaves for herbes de Provence.

1. Grill bell pepper halves skin-side down on covered grill over medium coals 15 to 25 minutes or until skin is charred, without turning. Remove from grill and immediately place in bowl; cover and let stand 15 to 20 minutes. Remove and discard skin with paring knife.

2. Place bell pepper in food processor. Add cheeses, garlic, mustard, salt and herbes de Provence; process until smooth. Serve with mini pita pockets or vegetables for dipping.

Makes about 2 cups

Grilled Garlic

2 cloves garlic
Nonstick cooking spray

Thread garlic cloves onto water-soaked wooden or bamboo skewer. Spray with cooking spray. Grill on covered or uncovered grill over medium coals about 8 minutes or until browned and tender. Or, place 2 garlic cloves on sheet of foil; lightly spray with cooking spray and carefully seal foil packet. Finish grilling as directed.

FOOD FACT

All peppers should be firm, crisp and feel heavy for their size. They should be shiny and brightly colored and their stems should be green and hard. Avoid peppers that have wrinkles, soft spots or bruises. If you plan to stuff or peel peppers, purchase round, blocky peppers rather than oddly-shaped peppers.

Grilled Red Bell Pepper Dip

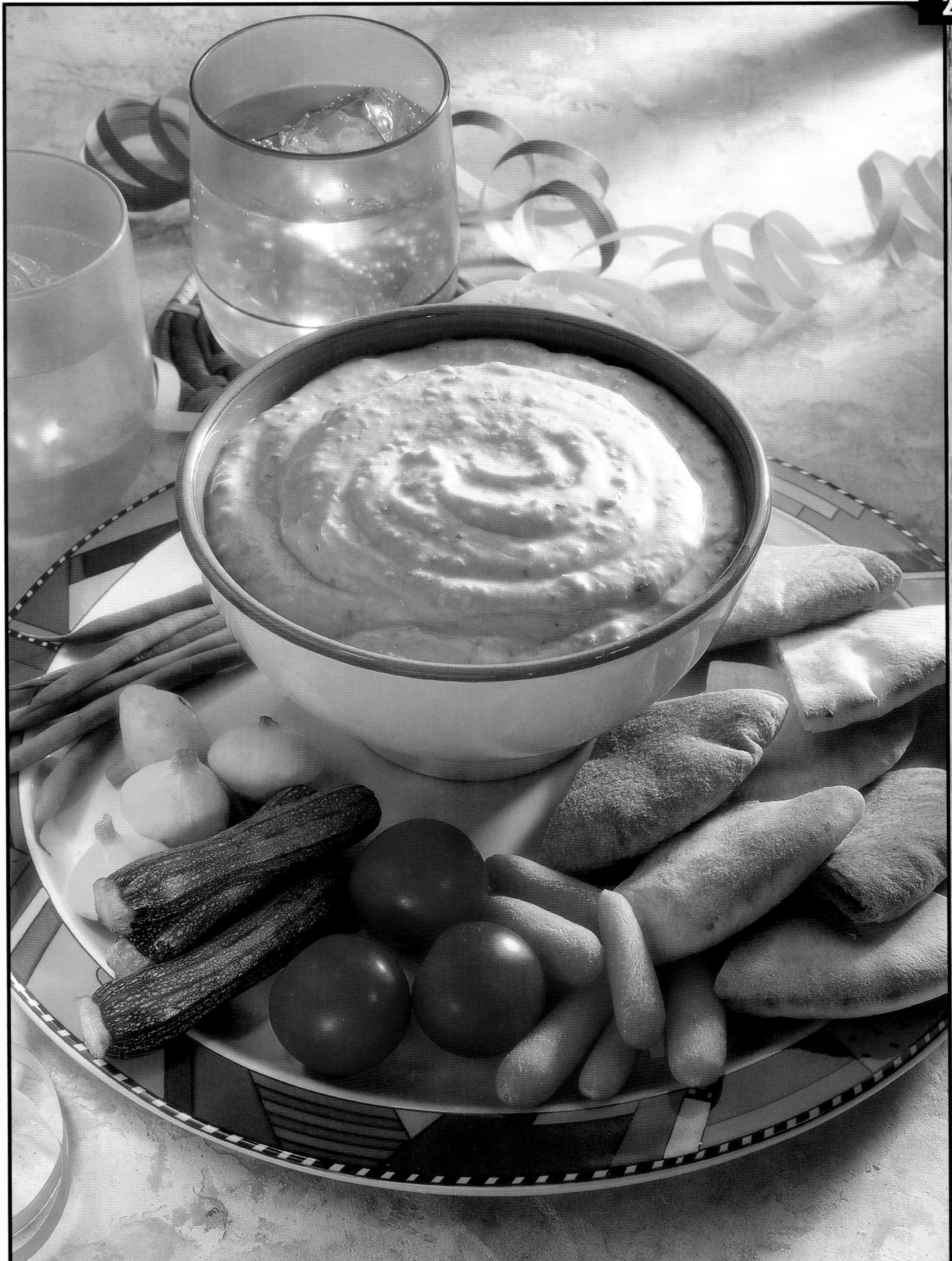

Grilled Orange Chicken Skewers with Cranberry Plum Sauce

6 chicken thighs, skinned and boned
24 bamboo skewers, soaked in water for 30 minutes
1 red bell pepper, cubed
1 green bell pepper, cubed
½ cup fresh-squeezed orange juice
2 tablespoons olive oil
1 teaspoon Dijon mustard
½ teaspoon oregano
⅛ teaspoon salt
⅛ teaspoon freshly ground pepper
1 naval orange, cut into half slices
Cranberry Plum Sauce (recipe follows)

Cut each chicken thigh into 12 small pieces. On a bamboo skewer, lace 3 pieces of chicken alternately with 1 piece green bell pepper and 1 piece red bell pepper. Set aside.

In large shallow baking dish, combine all remaining ingredients except the orange to make marinade. Dip chicken skewers in mixture to coat; arrange skewers in baking dish, cover and marinate for at least 2 hours or overnight.

At cooking time, prepare Cranberry Plum Sauce; keep warm until needed. Drain chicken. Place skewers over hot charcoals, grilling for 3 to 5 minutes; turn once or until chicken is done, about 2 minutes on each side. (Or, broil skewers for 4 minutes, turning skewers once to cook about 2 minutes on each side.)

Arrange on serving platter around bowl of Cranberry Plum Sauce. Garnish with orange slices. *Makes 24 appetizers*

Cranberry Plum Sauce

1 cup jellied cranberry sauce
¼ cup plum preserves
1 tablespoon rice vinegar
1 teaspoon prepared horseradish
⅛ teaspoon cinnamon
⅛ teaspoon salt

In medium saucepan, mix all ingredients. Whisk mixture over medium heat until well-blended and hot. Pour into small serving bowl. Serve warm with chicken.

Favorite recipe from **National Chicken Council**

Buffalo-Style Shrimp

⅓ cup *Frank's® RedHot®* **Cayenne Pepper Sauce**

⅓ cup **butter or margarine, melted**

1 pound **raw large shrimp, shelled and deveined**

2 ribs **celery, cut into large pieces**

1. Combine *Frank's RedHot* Sauce and butter in small bowl. Alternately thread shrimp and celery onto metal skewers. Place in shallow bowl. Pour ⅓ cup *Frank's RedHot* Sauce mixture over kabobs. Cover; refrigerate 30 minutes. Prepare grill.

2. Grill,* over medium coals, 3 to 5 minutes or until shrimp are opaque. Heat remaining *Frank's RedHot* Sauce mixture; pour over shrimp and celery.   *Makes 4 servings*

Or, broil 6-inches from heat.

Prep Time: 10 minutes
Marinate Time: 30 minutes
Cook Time: 5 minutes

Sticky Wings

24 **chicken wings (about 4 pounds)**

¾ cup **WISH-BONE® Italian Dressing***

1 cup **apricot or peach preserves**

1 tablespoon **hot pepper sauce (optional)****

Also terrific with WISH-BONE® Robusto Italian or Just 2 Good Dressing.

**Use more or less to taste.*

Cut tips off chicken wings (save tips for soup). Cut chicken wings in half at joint.

For marinade, blend Italian dressing, preserves and hot pepper sauce. In large, shallow nonaluminum baking dish or plastic bag, pour ½ of the marinade over chicken wings; toss to coat. Cover, or close bag, and marinate in refrigerator, turning occasionally, 3 to 24 hours. Refrigerate remaining marinade.

Remove wings, discarding marinade. Grill or broil wings, turning once and brushing frequently with refrigerated marinade, until wings are thoroughly cooked.   *Makes 48 appetizers*

Chicken Satay

1 pound boneless skinless
    chicken breast halves
1 recipe Peanut Dip (recipe
    follows), divided
Cucumber slices
Chopped fresh cilantro

1. Soak 8 (6-inch) bamboo skewers in hot water 20 minutes. Cut chicken lengthwise into 1-inch-wide strips; thread onto skewers.

2. Place skewers in large shallow glass dish. Pour ½ cup Peanut Dip over chicken, turning to coat evenly. Cover and marinate in refrigerator 30 minutes.

3. Place skewers on oiled grid and discard any remaining marinade. Grill over high heat 5 to 8 minutes or until chicken is no longer pink, turning once. Place on serving platter. Serve with cucumber, cilantro and remaining Peanut Dip.

Makes 8 appetizer or 4 main-dish servings

Prep Time: 15 minutes
Marinate Time: 30 minutes
Cook Time: 5 minutes

Peanut Dip

⅓ cup peanut butter
⅓ cup *French's*® Napa Valley Style Dijon Mustard
⅓ cup orange juice
1 tablespoon chopped peeled fresh ginger
1 tablespoon honey
1 tablespoon *Frank's*® *RedHot*® Cayenne Pepper Sauce
1 tablespoon teriyaki baste and glaze sauce
2 cloves garlic, minced

Combine peanut butter, mustard, juice, ginger, honey, *Frank's RedHot* Sauce, teriyaki sauce and garlic in large bowl. Refrigerate until ready to serve. *Makes 1 cup dip*

Prep Time: 10 minutes

Chicken Satay and Peanut Dip

Grilled Baby Artichokes with Pepper Dip

18 baby artichokes* (about
    1½ pounds)
½ teaspoon salt
¼ cup *Frank's® RedHot®*
    Cayenne Pepper Sauce
¼ cup butter or margarine,
    melted
Roasted Pepper Dip (recipe
    follows)

*You may substitute 2 packages (9 ounces each) frozen artichoke halves, thawed and drained. Do not microwave. Brush with Frank's® RedHot® butter mixture and grill as directed.

1. Wash and trim tough outer leaves from artichokes. Cut ½-inch off top of artichokes, then cut in half lengthwise. Place artichoke halves, 1 cup water and salt in 3-quart microwavable bowl. Cover; microwave on HIGH 8 minutes or until just tender. Thread artichoke halves onto metal skewers.

2. Prepare grill. Combine *Frank's RedHot* Sauce and butter in small bowl. Brush mixture over artichokes. Place artichokes on grid. Grill, over hot coals, 5 minutes or until tender, turning and basting often with sauce mixture. Serve artichokes with Roasted Pepper Dip. *Makes 6 servings*

Prep Time: 20 minutes
Cook Time: 13 minutes

Roasted Pepper Dip

1 jar (7 ounces) roasted red peppers, drained
1 clove garlic, chopped
¼ cup reduced-fat mayonnaise
2 tablespoons *French's®* Napa Valley Style Dijon
    Mustard
2 tablespoons *Frank's® RedHot®* Cayenne Pepper
    Sauce
¼ teaspoon salt

1. Place roasted peppers and garlic in food processor or blender. Cover; process on high until very smooth.

2. Add mayonnaise, mustard, *Frank's RedHot* Sauce and salt. Process until well blended. Cover; refrigerate 30 minutes. *Makes about 1 cup*

Prep Time: 10 minutes
Chill Time: 30 minutes

Grilled Baby Artichokes with
Pepper Dip

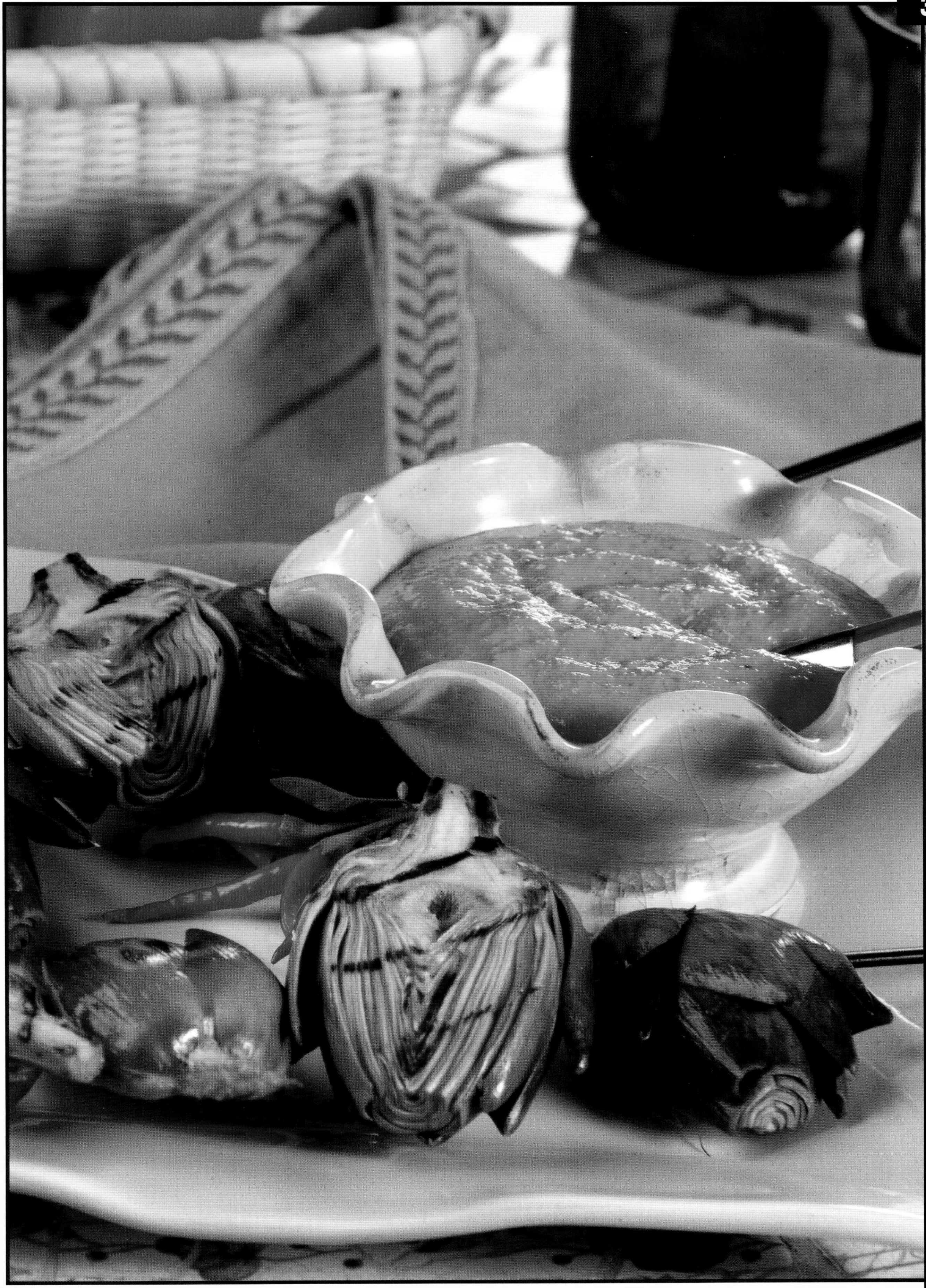

COOKOUT
FLAVORINGS

The right combinations of spices and herbs in sauces, rubs and marinades will help make your grill foods taste even better. Your family will be asking for more.

Smucker's® Orange Chili Barbecue Sauce

1 cup SMUCKER'S® Orange
    Marmalade
1 cup tomato sauce or
    crushed tomatoes packed
    in tomato purée
2 tablespoons chili powder
2 tablespoons red wine
    vinegar
1 teaspoon ground cumin
1 teaspoon chopped garlic
½ teaspoon salt
¼ teaspoon ground red
    pepper or hot pepper
    sauce (for spicier sauce)

Combine all ingredients in a small saucepan; mix well. Heat until sauce comes to a boil, stirring constantly. Simmer 1 minute. Use immediately or cool and store in refrigerator for future use.

Use sauce as a marinade and baste for baked or grilled chicken, ribs, beef or pork.

Makes 6 servings

Microwave Directions: Combine all ingredients in a microwave-safe bowl; mix well. Cover with plastic wrap and heat on HIGH (100% power) for 2 minutes. Stir; cover and heat for 1 minute.

Prep Time: 5 minutes
Cook Time: 1 to 2 minutes

Smucker's® Orange Chili
Barbecue Sauce

Rosemary Garlic Rub

2 tablespoons chopped fresh
    rosemary
1½ teaspoons LAWRY'S®
    Seasoned Salt
1 teaspoon LAWRY'S® Garlic
    Pepper
½ teaspoon LAWRY'S® Garlic
    Powder with Parsley
1 pound beef top sirloin steak
1 tablespoon olive oil

In small bowl, combine rosemary, Seasoned Salt, Garlic Pepper and Garlic Powder with Parsley; mix well. Brush both sides of steak with oil. Sprinkle with herb mixture, pressing onto steak. Grill or broil steak 15 to 20 minutes or until desired doneness, turning halfway through grilling time. *Makes 4 servings*

Serving Suggestion: Serve with oven-roasted or french-fried potatoes and honey-coated carrots.

Hint: This rub is also great on lamb or pork.

Zesty Apple Butter Barbecue Sauce

1 cup (11-ounce jar)
    SMUCKER'S® Cider
    Apple Butter
1 cup finely chopped onions
½ cup ketchup
1 tablespoon prepared
    mustard
3 teaspoons liquid smoke
1 teaspoon Worcestershire
    sauce
1 teaspoon apple cider
    vinegar
½ teaspoon coarse kosher salt
½ teaspoon red pepper
½ teaspoon freshly ground
    pepper
½ teaspoon minced garlic
½ cup firmly packed brown
    sugar
½ teaspoon paprika

In large bowl, combine all ingredients. Mix well.

Add desired meat portions, making sure all pieces are well coated. Cover and marinate in refrigerator 3 to 4 hours or overnight. Bake or barbecue according to your favorite technique. Use remaining sauce to baste. *Makes 3 cups sauce*

Rosemary Garlic Rub

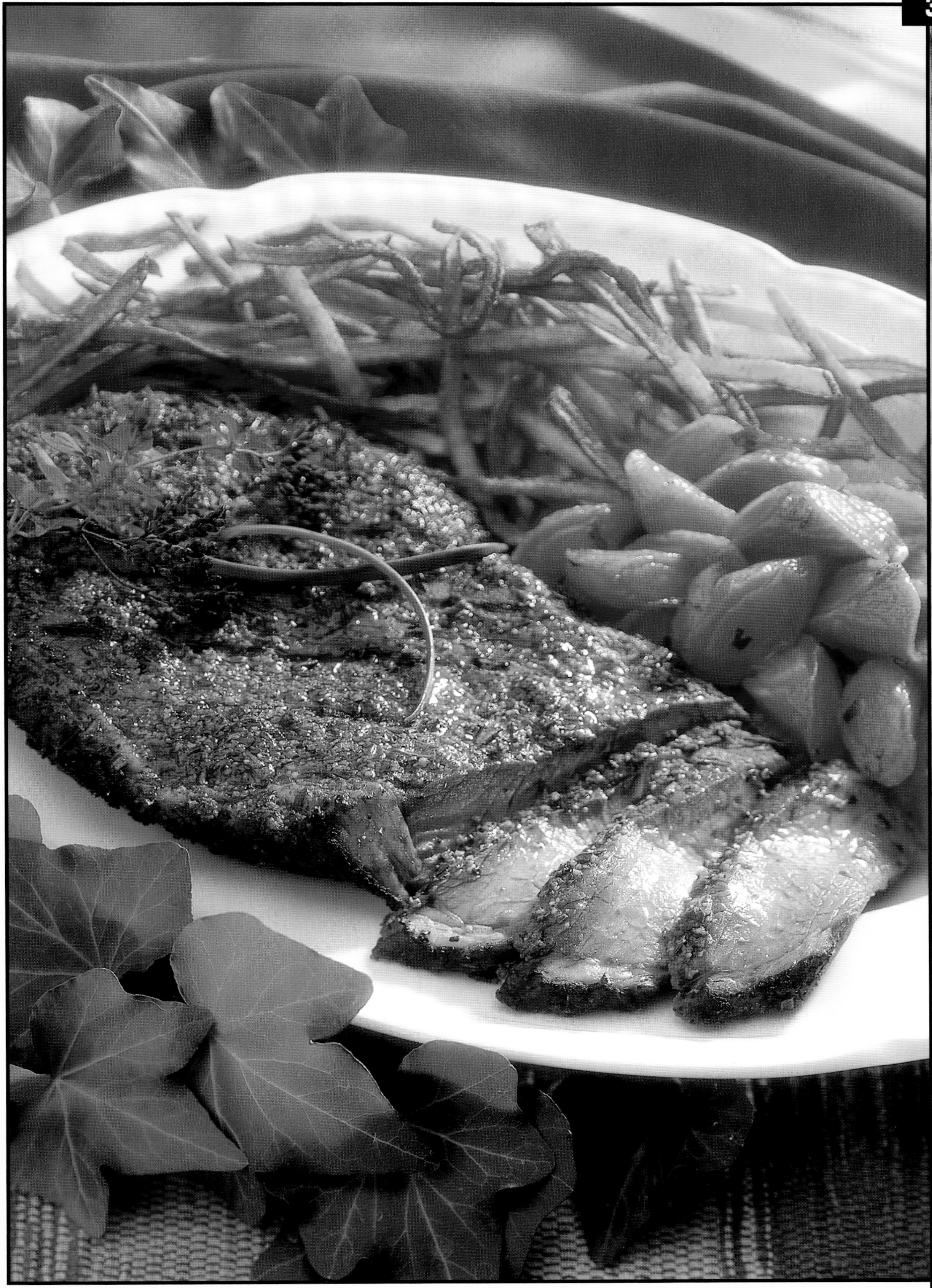

Barbecue Dipping Sauce

1 can (15-ounces)
    CONTADINA® Pizza
    Sauce
¼ cup firmly packed brown
    sugar
2 tablespoons vinegar
1 tablespoon prepared
    mustard
½ teaspoon liquid smoke

1. Combine pizza sauce, brown sugar, vinegar, mustard and liquid smoke in medium saucepan.

2. Bring to a boil. Reduce heat to low; simmer, uncovered, for 5 minutes, stirring occasionally. Serve with chicken nuggets, meatballs, shrimp or cocktail franks, if desired.   *Makes about 2 cups*

Prep Time: 3 minutes
Cook Time: 5 minutes

Lemon Pepper & Thyme Rub

¼ cup minced fresh thyme
    leaves
1 tablespoon LAWRY'S®
    Lemon Pepper
2 teaspoons LAWRY'S®
    Seasoned Salt
1 pound lamb chops
2 tablespoons olive oil

In small bowl, combine thyme, Lemon Pepper and Seasoned Salt; mix well. Brush both sides of chops with oil. Sprinkle with thyme mixture, pressing onto chops. Grill or broil chops until desired doneness, about 10 to 12 minutes, turning halfway through grilling time.   *Makes 4 servings*

Serving Suggestion: Serve with garlic mashed potatoes and steamed asparagus.

Hint: Also excellent on beef, pork or chicken.

Barbecue Sauce

1 (8-ounce) can tomato sauce
1 teaspoon red wine vinegar
1 teaspoon granulated sugar
½ teaspoon Worcestershire
    sauce
½ teaspoon chili powder
¼ teaspoon garlic powder

In medium saucepan, combine all ingredients; simmer 15 minutes, stirring occasionally. Use as dipping sauce for chicken nuggets.

Makes 1 cup

Favorite recipe from **The Sugar Association, Inc.**

Maple Cider Basted Turkey

1 PERDUE® Fresh Whole
   Turkey Breast
   (4-7 pounds)
1 to 2 tablespoons canola oil
1 tablespoon grainy,
   "country-style" mustard
   Salt and ground pepper to
   taste
1 apple, cored but unpeeled,
   sliced thinly
¼ cup maple syrup
2 tablespoons cider vinegar
   Dash Worcestershire sauce

Preheat oven to 350°F. Pat breast dry with paper towel. In small bowl, mix oil and mustard, rub over breast and under skin from neck end. Do not detach skin at base. Season with salt and pepper. Slide apple slices between skin and meat. If necessary, reinsert BIRD-WATCHER Thermometer to original location. Place breast in roasting pan and roast, uncovered, 1½ to 1¾ hours, until BIRD-WATCHER Thermometer pops up and meat thermometer inserted in thickest part of breast registers 170°F.

Meanwhile, combine syrup, vinegar and Worcestershire sauce. During last 20 minutes of roasting, baste breast with mixture. If skin is browning too quickly, tent with foil. Remove breast to serving platter and let rest 10 to 15 minutes before carving.

Makes 6 to 8 servings

Honey Barbecue Baste

1 tablespoon vegetable oil
¼ cup minced onion
1 clove garlic, minced
1 can (8 ounces) tomato
   sauce
⅓ cup honey
3 tablespoons vinegar
2 tablespoons dry sherry
1 teaspoon dry mustard
½ teaspoon salt
¼ teaspoon coarsely ground
   black pepper

Heat oil in medium saucepan over medium heat until hot. Add onion and garlic; cook and stir until onion is tender. Add remaining ingredients. Bring to a boil; reduce heat to low and simmer 20 minutes. Serve over grilled chicken, pork, spareribs, salmon or hamburgers. *Makes 1 cup*

*Favorite recipe from **National Honey Board***

Honey Mustard Magic

1 cup honey
1 cup Dijon or brown
    mustard

Combine honey and mustard in small bowl until smooth.
Makes 2 cups

Favorite recipe from **National Honey Board**

Honey Plum Sauce

1 cup pitted, chopped plums
⅓ cup honey
2 tablespoons lemon juice
1 tablespoon minced onion
½ teaspoon grated lemon peel
¼ teaspoon grated fresh
    gingerroot
⅛ teaspoon salt
⅛ teaspoon ground cloves
⅛ teaspoon ground allspice
    Pepper to taste

Combine all ingredients in medium saucepan; mix well. Bring mixture to a boil over medium heat; reduce heat to low and simmer 15 minutes or until plums are completely cooked. Transfer mixture to blender or food processor; process until smooth. Press plum mixture through sieve. Adjust sweetness with additional honey, if desired. Return plum mixture to saucepan and simmer 5 minutes. Serve with duck, chicken or lamb.
Makes about ¾ cup

Favorite recipe from **National Honey Board**

Herbed Honey Lime Sauce

½ cup minced onion
1 tablespoon olive oil
1 cup dry white wine or
    chicken broth
¼ cup honey
¼ cup lime juice
2 teaspoons dry mustard
1 teaspoon minced fresh
    rosemary
½ teaspoon salt
    Dash pepper
1 teaspoon cornstarch
1 teaspoon water

Cook and stir onion in olive oil in medium saucepan over medium heat until onion is softened. Stir in wine, honey, lime juice, mustard, rosemary, salt and pepper; mix well and bring to a boil. Combine cornstarch and water in small bowl or cup, mixing well. Add to sauce. Cook over low heat, stirring until sauce comes to a boil and thickens. Serve over cooked turkey, chicken, fish or pork.

Clockwise from top left: Honey Mustard Magic, Honey Plum Sauce, Honey Barbecue Baste (page 39), Honey-Dijon Fresh Fruit Chutney (page 346)

Ivory, Rubies and Jade

¾ pound lean pork, cut into
   thin 2-inch strips
2 tablespoons LA CHOY® Soy
   Sauce
1 teaspoon minced fresh
   garlic
4 tablespoons WESSON® Oil,
   divided
1½ cups diagonally sliced celery
1 cup chopped red bell
   pepper
1 jar (10 ounces) LA CHOY®
   Sweet & Sour Sauce
1 can (8 ounces) LA CHOY®
   Sliced Water Chestnuts,
   drained
1 package (6 ounces) frozen
   pea pods, thawed and
   drained
3 green onions, diagonally cut
   into 1-inch pieces
⅛ teaspoon cayenne pepper
1 can (5 ounces) LA CHOY®
   Chow Mein Noodles

In medium bowl, combine pork, soy sauce and garlic; cover and marinate 30 minutes in refrigerator. Drain. In large nonstick skillet or wok, heat 3 tablespoons oil. Add pork mixture; stir-fry until pork is no longer pink in center. Remove pork from skillet; set aside. Heat remaining 1 tablespoon oil in same skillet. Add celery and bell pepper; stir-fry until crisp-tender. Return pork to skillet with all remaining ingredients except noodles; heat thoroughly, stirring occasionally. Serve over noodles.

Makes 4 servings

Smoky Honey Barbecue Sauce

1 cup honey
1 cup chili sauce
½ cup cider vinegar
1 teaspoon prepared mustard
1 teaspoon Worcestershire
   sauce
½ teaspoon pepper
½ teaspoon minced garlic
2 to 3 drops liquid smoke

Combine all ingredients except liquid smoke in medium saucepan over medium heat. Cook, stirring frequently, 20 to 30 minutes. Remove from heat; add liquid smoke to taste. Serve over grilled chicken, turkey, pork, spareribs, salmon or hamburgers. *Makes about 2 cups*

*Favorite recipe from **National Honey Board***

Wyoming Wild Barbecue Sauce

1 cup chili sauce
1 cup ketchup
¼ cup steak sauce
3 tablespoons dry mustard
2 tablespoons horseradish
2 tablespoons TABASCO®
    brand Pepper Sauce
1 tablespoon Worcestershire
    sauce
1 tablespoon garlic, finely
    chopped
1 tablespoon dark molasses
1 tablespoon red wine vinegar

Combine ingredients in medium bowl. Whisk until sauce is well blended. Store in 1-quart covered jar in refrigerator up to 7 days. Use as a baste while grilling beef, chicken, pork or game.

Makes 3 cups

Texas Spice Rub

1 tablespoon paprika
1 teaspoon seasoned salt
½ teaspoon brown sugar
¼ teaspoon granulated garlic
⅛ teaspoon cayenne pepper
2 teaspoons water
4 skinned and boned chicken
    breast halves

Combine paprika, salt, sugar, garlic and cayenne. Add water to make paste. Rub on chicken to coat evenly. Grill chicken on covered grill over medium-hot KINGSFORD® Briquets 8 to 10 minutes, turning once, until just cooked through.

Makes 4 servings

Sage-Garlic Baste

Grated peel and juice of
    1 lemon
3 tablespoons olive oil
2 tablespoons minced fresh
    sage *or* 1½ teaspoons
    rubbed sage
2 cloves garlic, minced
½ teaspoon salt
¼ teaspoon black pepper

Combine all ingredients in small saucepan; cook and stir over medium heat 4 minutes. Use as baste for turkey or chicken.

Makes about ½ cup

Beef with Dry Spice Rub

3 tablespoons firmly packed
   brown sugar
1 tablespoon black
   peppercorns
1 tablespoon yellow mustard
   seeds
1 tablespoon whole coriander
   seeds
4 cloves garlic
1½ to 2 pounds beef top round
   (London Broil) steak,
   about 1½ inches thick
   Vegetable or olive oil
   Salt

Place sugar, peppercorns, mustard seeds, coriander seeds and garlic in blender or food processor; process until seeds and garlic are crushed. Rub beef with oil; pat on spice mixture. Season generously with salt.

Lightly oil hot grid to prevent sticking. Grill beef on covered grill over medium-low KINGSFORD® Briquets 16 to 20 minutes for medium rare or until desired doneness, turning once. Let stand 5 minutes before cutting across the grain into thin diagonal slices.   *Makes 6 servings*

Cowpoke Barbecue Sauce

1 teaspoon vegetable oil
¾ cup chopped green onions
3 cloves garlic, finely chopped
1 can (14½ ounces) crushed
   tomatoes
½ cup ketchup
¼ cup water
¼ cup orange juice
2 tablespoons cider vinegar
2 teaspoons chili sauce
   Dash Worcestershire sauce

Heat oil in large nonstick saucepan over medium heat until hot. Add onions and garlic. Cook and stir 5 minutes or until onions are tender. Stir in remaining ingredients. Reduce heat to medium-low. Cook 15 minutes, stirring occasionally.
          Makes 2 cups

Barbecue-Cranberry Dip

½ cup cranberry sauce
½ cup barbecue sauce

In medium bowl stir together cranberry sauce and barbecue sauce; cover loosely and heat in microwave at MEDIUM (50%) for 2 minutes.
          Makes 1 cup dip

Favorite recipe from **National Pork Board**

Beef with Dry Spice Rub

Easy Honey Mustard Barbecue Sauce

1 bottle (10.5 ounces)
   PLOCHMAN'S® Mild
   Yellow Mustard (about
   1 cup)
½ cup barbecue sauce
¼ cup honey
2 tablespoons finely minced
   onion

Mix all ingredients in medium bowl. Use as a condiment, or brush on chicken, pork chops or seafood.   *Makes 2 cups*

Preparation Time: 5 minutes

Chinese 5-Spice Butter Baste

⅓ cup melted butter
1 tablespoon soy sauce
2 teaspoons Chinese 5-spice
   powder

Combine all ingredients in small bowl. Use as baste for turkey or chicken.

Makes about 6 tablespoons

Spicy Orange Baste

3 tablespoons orange juice
3 tablespoons lemon juice
2 tablespoons vegetable oil
1 tablespoon grated orange
   peel
½ teaspoon ground ginger
½ teaspoon salt
⅛ teaspoon freshly ground
   pepper

Combine all ingredients in small bowl.

Makes about ½ cup

Easy Honey Mustard Barbecue Sauce

Wine and Herb Baste

¼ cup butter
¼ cup dry red wine
1 tablespoon chopped fresh
  parsley
1 teaspoon dried thyme leaves
1 clove garlic, minced
½ teaspoon dried rosemary
  leaves, crumbled

Combine all ingredients in small saucepan over low heat, stirring until butter is melted.

Sweet 'n Zesty Barbecue Sauce

¾ cup HOLLAND HOUSE®
  White Cooking Wine
½ cup GRANDMA'S®
  Molasses
½ cup chili sauce
¼ cup prepared mustard
1 small onion, chopped
1 tablespoon Worcestershire
  sauce

In medium saucepan, combine all ingredients; mix well. Bring to a boil, reduce heat. Simmer uncovered 10 minutes.   *Makes 2 cups*

Oriental Mustard Barbecue Sauce

1 bottle (10.5 ounces)
  PLOCHMAN'S® Mild
  Yellow Mustard (about
  1 cup)
½ cup barbecue sauce
¼ cup packed brown sugar
¼ cup hoisin sauce
¼ cup soy sauce
2 tablespoons sesame oil
2 tablespoons Chinese rice
  wine
1 tablespoon minced fresh
  ginger
1 clove garlic, minced

Mix together all ingredients. Use as a condiment, or brush on chicken, seafood or steak during the last 15 minutes of cooking.   *Makes 2 cups*

Preparation Time: 5 minutes

Texas BBQ Sauce

1½ cups ketchup
¾ cup honey
½ cup cider or white vinegar
1 small onion, finely chopped
2 tablespoons Worcestershire
    sauce
1 jalapeño pepper,* seeded
    and minced
1 tablespoon mustard
1 teaspoon olive oil

Jalapeño peppers can sting and irritate the skin; wear rubber gloves when handling peppers and do not touch eyes. Wash hands after handling.

Combine all ingredients; mix well.

Makes about 3 cups

Sour Cream Sauce

¾ cup sour cream
2 tablespoons prepared
    horseradish
1 tablespoon balsamic vinegar
½ teaspoon sugar

Combine all ingredients in small bowl; mix well.

Makes about 1 cup

Lemon Baste

½ cup olive oil
¼ cup lemon juice
½ teaspoon salt
¼ teaspoon black pepper

Whisk together all ingredients in small bowl until well blended.

Makes about ¾ cup

Honey Barbecue Sauce

1 can (10¾ ounces)
    condensed tomato soup
½ cup honey
2 to 3 tablespoons vegetable
    oil
2 tablespoons Worcestershire
    sauce
1 tablespoon lemon juice
1 teaspoon prepared mustard
    Dash ground red pepper or
    bottled hot pepper sauce
    (optional)

Combine ingredients in medium saucepan. Bring to a boil over medium heat. Reduce heat to low and simmer, uncovered, 5 minutes. Use as a baste while grilling beef, ribs or poultry.

Makes about 2 cups

*Favorite recipe from **National Honey Board***

Chef's Signature Steak Sauce

½ cup ketchup
¼ cup *French's®*
    Worcestershire Sauce
1 to 2 tablespoons *Frank's®*
    RedHot® Cayenne Pepper
    Sauce or to taste
2 cloves garlic, minced

Combine ingredients in small bowl; stir until smooth.   *Makes ¾ cup*

Prep Time: 30 minutes
Freeze Time: 2 hours
Cook Time: 25 minutes

Southern Barbecue Sauce

3 cups ketchup
½ cup molasses or dark brown
    sugar
⅓ cup prepared mustard
6 tablespoons cider vinegar
2 tablespoons Worcestershire
    sauce
2½ to 4½ teaspoons hot
    pepper sauce
2 teaspoons LAWRY'S®
    Seasoned Salt

In small saucepan, combine all ingredients; mix well. Bring to a boil over medium-high heat. Reduce heat to low and simmer, uncovered, 5 to 10 minutes, stirring occasionally.   *Makes 4 cups*

Serving Suggestion: Use to baste meats or poultry while barbecuing or baking in the oven.

**Top to bottom: Honey Barbecue Sauce,
Honey Strawberry Salsa (page 336),
Herbed Honey Lime Sauce (page 40)**

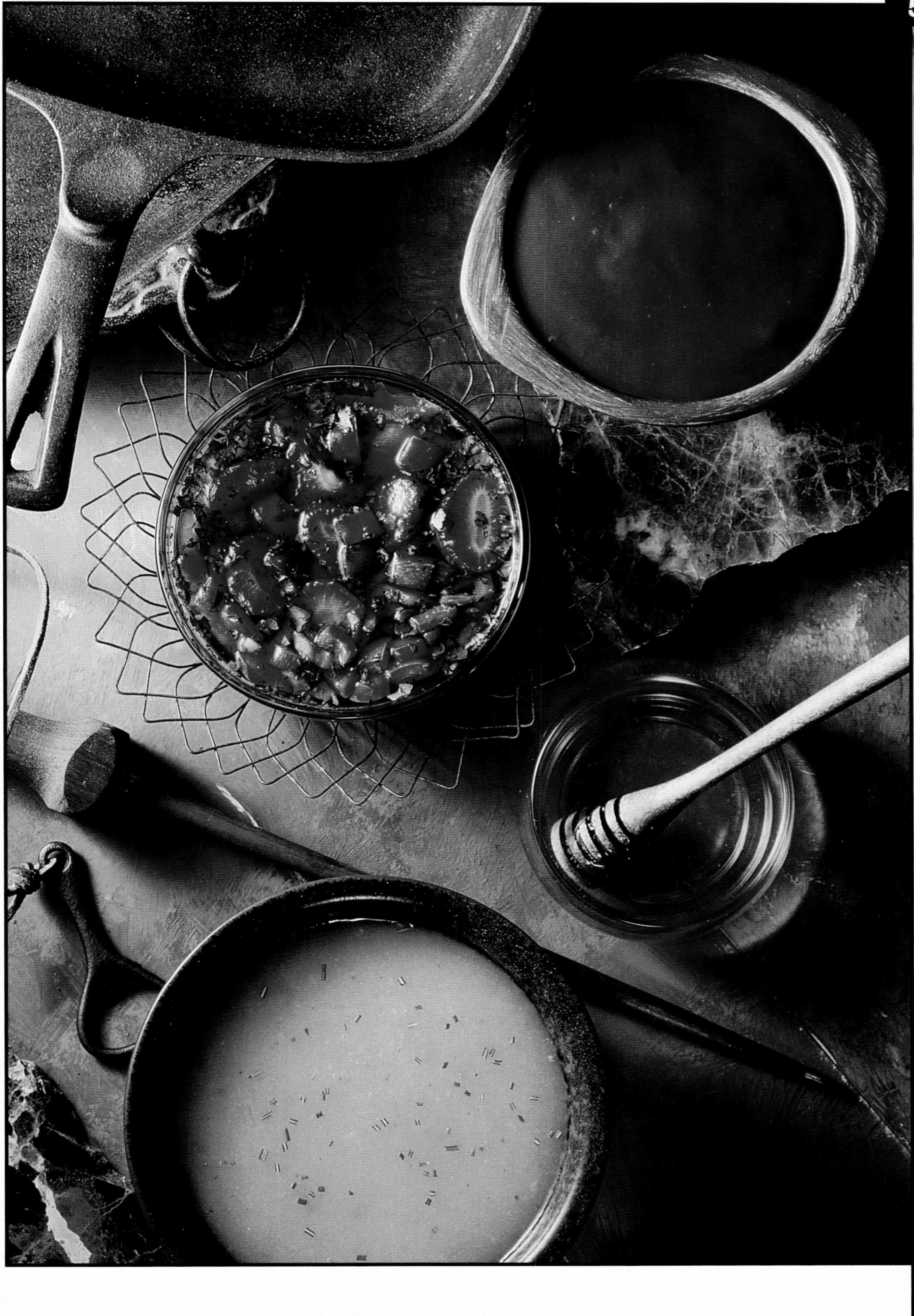

BARBECUE
BEEF

Beef takes center stage here and does not disappoint. Find out how to make The Definitive Steak (page 68) and Bold and Zesty Baby Back Ribs (page 60).

Southwest Steak

¾ cup Italian dressing
½ cup minced fresh parsley
⅓ cup *Frank's® RedHot®* Cayenne Pepper Sauce
3 tablespoons lime juice
1 tablespoon *French's®* Worcestershire Sauce
2 pounds boneless sirloin or top round steak (1½ inches thick)

1. Place dressing, parsley, *Frank's RedHot* Sauce, lime juice and Worcestershire in blender or food processor. Cover; process until smooth. Reserve ⅔ cup sauce. Pour remaining sauce over steak in deep dish. Cover; refrigerate 30 minutes.

2. Grill or broil steak 8 minutes per side for medium-rare or to desired doneness. Let stand 5 minutes. Slice steak and serve with reserved sauce. *Makes 6 to 8 servings*

Prep Time: 10 minutes
Marinate Time: 30 minutes
Cook Time: 20 minutes

Southwest Steak

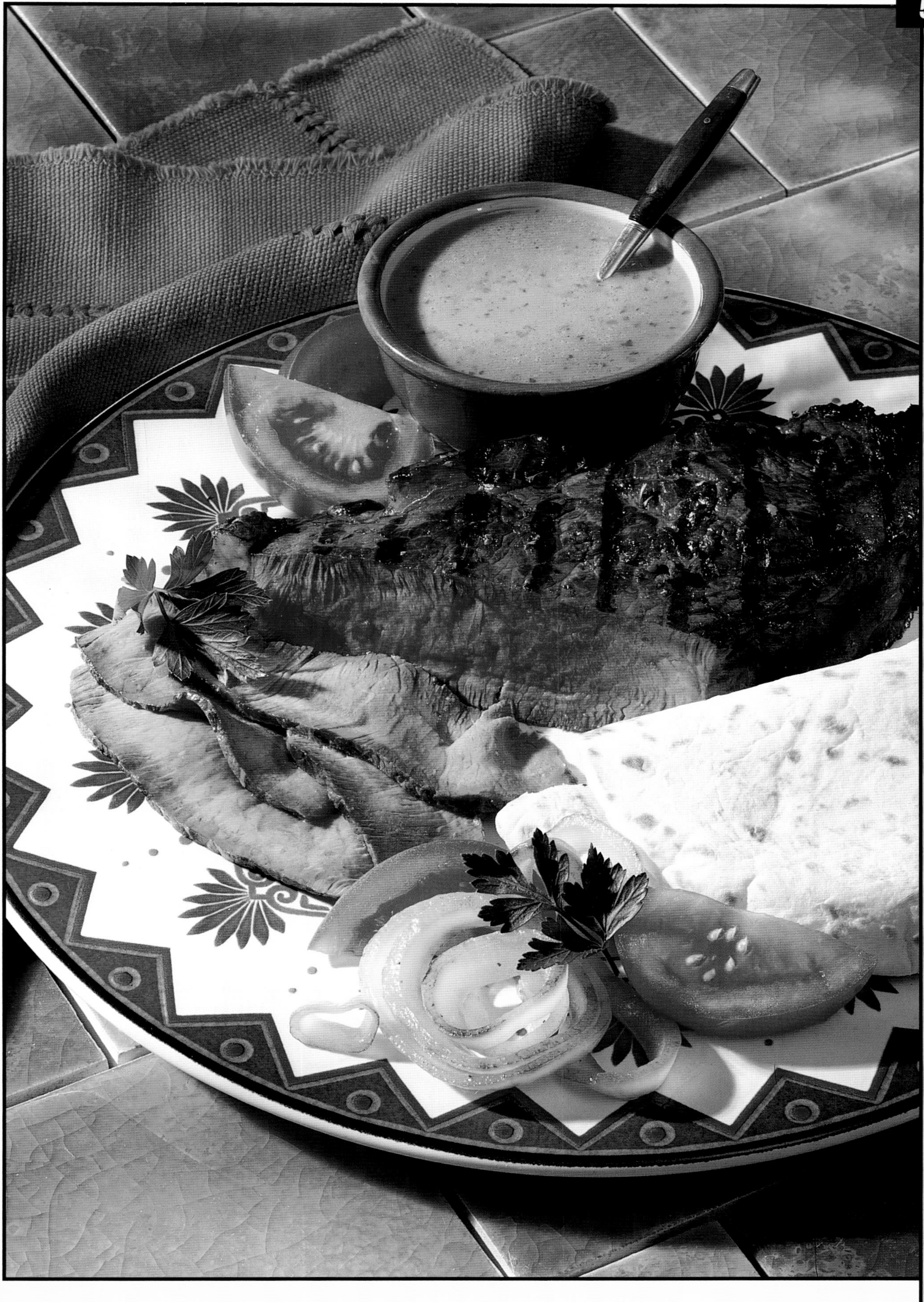

Grilled Beef with Creamy Jalapeño Sauce

2 egg yolks
1 to 1½ teaspoons chopped
    fresh or canned jalapeño
    peppers*
1 tablespoon coarsely
    chopped fresh cilantro
2 tablespoons lemon juice
¾ cup butter, melted and
    warm
2 to 3 drops hot pepper sauce
6 ground beef patties, about
    1 inch thick, *or* 6 small
    New York or club steaks,
    1 inch thick
    Salt
    Black pepper
3 tomatoes, sliced, for
    garnish
    Cilantro sprigs for garnish

Jalapeño peppers can sting and irritate the skin; wear rubber gloves when handling peppers and do not touch eyes. Wash hands after handling peppers.

To prepare sauce ahead, process egg yolks, jalapeño peppers and chopped cilantro in blender container until seasonings are finely chopped. Heat lemon juice in small pan to simmering. Add to egg yolk mixture; blend 45 seconds. With motor on medium speed, add butter, a few drops at a time in the beginning but increase to a thin, regular stream as mixture begins to thicken. (Sauce will be consistency of a creamy salad dressing.) Stir in hot pepper sauce. Pour into jar; cover. Let stand at room temperature up to 1 hour. While meat is cooking, place jar in hot water; stir until sauce is warm, not hot.

Preheat charcoal grill and grease grill rack. Place meat on grill 4 to 6 inches above solid bed of coals (coals should be evenly covered with gray ashes). Cook, turning once, 3 to 5 minutes on each side for rare or to desired doneness. Season with salt and black pepper to taste. Spoon sauce over meat; garnish with tomato slices and cilantro sprigs.

Makes 6 servings

GRILLING TIP

Cleanup is easier if the grill rack is coated with vegetable oil or nonstick cooking spray before grilling.

Pepper-Spiced Beef Skewers and Beans

1½ pounds tender, lean beef
   such as tenderloin
1 large red bell pepper
1 large green bell pepper
1 large onion, halved
   Pepper-Spice Seasoning
   (recipe follows)
2 tablespoons lemon juice
2 teaspoons olive oil
3 cups cooked and drained
   Great Northern, navy or
   pinto beans *or* 2 cans
   (16 ounces each) beans,
   rinsed and drained
1 can (28 ounces)
   no-salt-added stewed
   tomatoes, drained
2 tablespoons packed brown
   sugar
2 tablespoons chopped fresh
   parsley

Cut beef into ¾- to 1-inch cubes. Cut bell peppers and half of onion into ¾- to 1-inch squares (you will need 24 to 30 squares of each). Thread peppers and vegetables alternately onto 6 (10- to 12-inch) metal skewers beginning with 1 piece of each vegetable followed by 1 cube meat. Prepare Pepper-Spice Seasoning; combine 2 tablespoons seasoning with lemon juice in small bowl. Brush mixture over beef cubes.

Spray cold grid with nonstick cooking spray. Prepare grill for direct cooking. Place skewers on grid, 4 to 6 inches from medium-hot coals. Grill 8 to 10 minutes, turning every 2 to 3 minutes, or until meat is grilled to desired doneness.

Meanwhile, finely chop remaining onion half. Heat oil in medium saucepan over medium-high heat. Add onion and remaining 2 tablespoons spice mixture. Cook and stir 3 minutes or until onion is tender (do not let spices burn). Stir in beans, tomatoes and brown sugar. Cover; cook and stir until heated through. Stir in parsley.
Makes 6 servings

Pepper-Spice Seasoning: Combine 2 tablespoons lemon juice, 2 tablespoons minced garlic, 2 teaspoons dried oregano leaves, 2 teaspoons pepper, 1 teaspoon ground cumin and 1 teaspoon ground allspice in small bowl; mix well. Makes ¼ cup.

Beef Kabobs over Lemon Rice

½ **pound boneless beef sirloin steak, cut into 1-inch cubes**
1 **small zucchini, sliced**
1 **small yellow squash, sliced**
1 **small red bell pepper, cut into squares**
1 **small onion, cut into chunks**
¼ **cup Italian dressing**
1 **cup hot cooked rice**
2 **teaspoons fresh lemon juice**
1 **tablespoon snipped fresh parsley**
¼ **teaspoon seasoned salt**

Combine beef and vegetables in large resealable plastic food storage bag; add dressing. Seal bag and marinate 4 to 6 hours in refrigerator, turning bag occasionally. Thread beef and vegetables alternately onto 4 metal skewers. Grill over medium coals, or broil, 5 to 7 minutes or to desired doneness, turning occasionally. Combine rice and remaining ingredients. Serve kabobs over rice mixture. *Makes 2 servings*

Favorite recipe from **USA Rice Federation**

Garlic-Pepper Steak

1¼ **teaspoons LAWRY'S® Garlic Powder with Parsley**
1¼ **teaspoons LAWRY'S® Seasoned Pepper**
½ **teaspoon LAWRY'S® Seasoned Salt**
1 **pound sirloin steak**

In small bowl, combine Garlic Powder with Parsley, Seasoned Pepper and Seasoned Salt; mix well. Press seasoning mixture into both sides of steak with back of spoon. Let stand 30 minutes. Grill or broil as desired. *Makes 4 servings*

Serving Suggestion: Serve with rice pilaf and a crisp green salad.

Beef Kabobs over Lemon Rice

Grilled Beef Salad

½ cup mayonnaise

2 tablespoons cider vinegar or white wine vinegar

1 tablespoon spicy brown mustard

2 cloves garlic, minced

½ teaspoon sugar

6 cups torn assorted lettuces such as romaine, red leaf and Bibb

1 large tomato, seeded and chopped

⅓ cup chopped fresh basil

2 slices red onion, separated into rings

1 pound boneless beef top sirloin steak, cut 1 inch thick

½ teaspoon salt

½ teaspoon black pepper

½ cup herb or garlic croutons

Additional black pepper (optional)

Prepare grill for direct cooking. Combine mayonnaise, vinegar, mustard, garlic and sugar in small bowl; mix well. Cover and refrigerate until serving.

Toss together lettuce, tomato, basil and onion in large bowl; cover and refrigerate until serving.

Sprinkle both sides of steak with salt and ½ teaspoon pepper. Place steak on grid. Grill, covered, over medium-high heat 10 minutes for medium-rare or until desired doneness is reached, turning halfway through grilling time.

Transfer steak to carving board. Slice in half lengthwise; carve crosswise into thin slices.

Add steak and croutons to bowl with lettuce mixture; toss well. Add mayonnaise mixture; toss until well coated. Serve with additional pepper, if desired. *Makes 4 servings*

Grilled Beef Salad

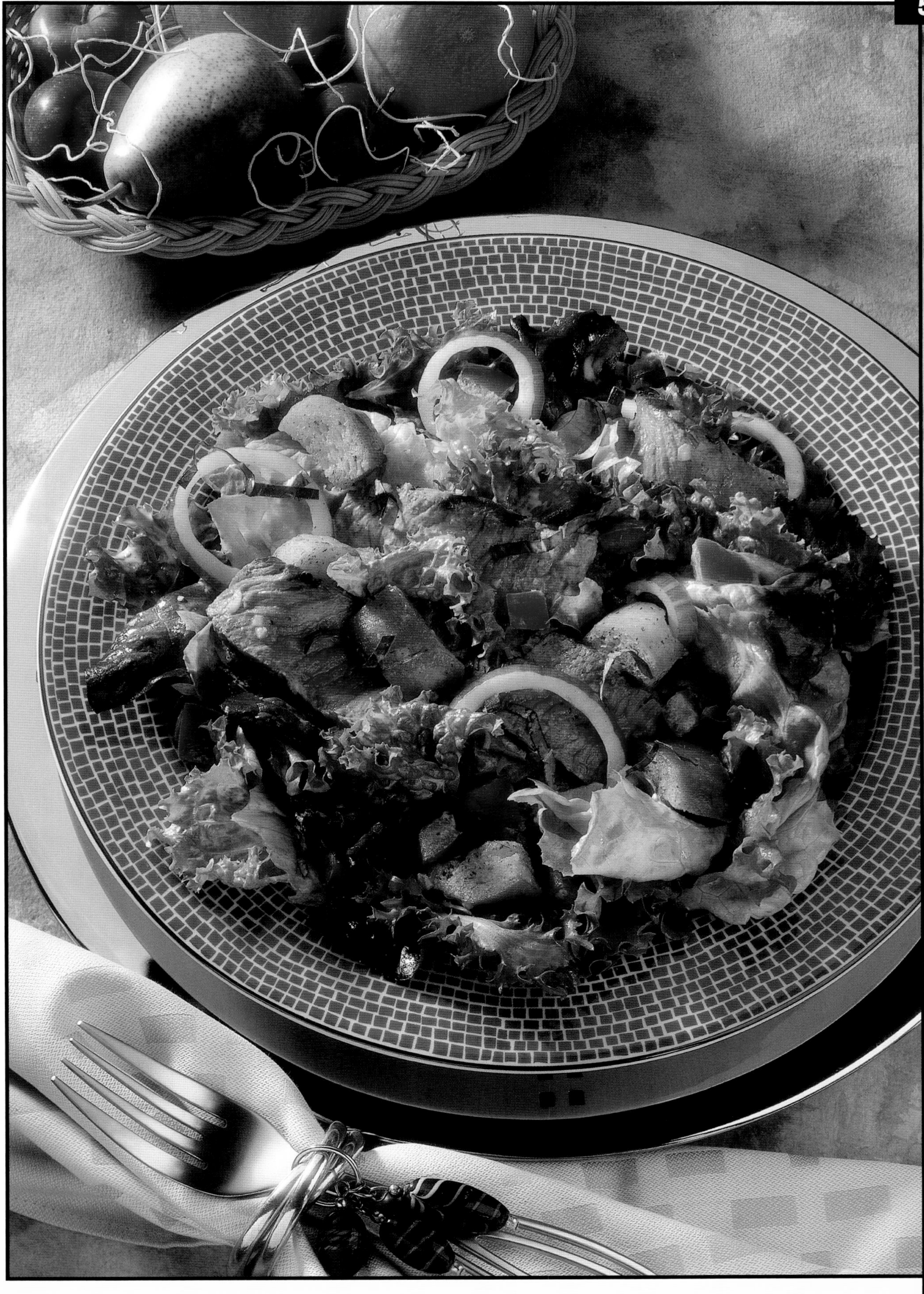

Bold and Zesty Beef Back Ribs

5 pounds beef back ribs, cut
    into 3 or 4 rib sections
Salt and black pepper
1 teaspoon vegetable oil
1 small onion, minced
2 cloves garlic, minced
1 cup ketchup
½ cup chili sauce
2 tablespoons lemon juice
1 tablespoon packed brown
    sugar
1 teaspoon hot pepper sauce

Place ribs in shallow pan; season to taste with salt and pepper. Keep in refrigerated until ready to grill.

Prepare grill for indirect cooking. While coals are heating, prepare barbecue sauce.

Heat oil in large nonstick saucepan over medium heat until hot. Add onion and garlic. Cook and stir 5 minutes or until onion are tender. Stir in remaining ingredients. Reduce heat to medium-low. Cook 15 minutes, stirring occasionally.

Baste ribs generously with sauce; grill 45 to 60 minutes or until ribs are tender and browned, turning occasionally.

Bring remaining sauce to a boil over medium-high heat; boil 1 minute. Serve ribs with remaining sauce. *Makes 5 to 6 servings*

Prep Time: 15 minutes
Cook Time: 55 minutes to 1 hour 15 minutes

GRILLING TIP

For indirect cooking, arrange coals to one side of the grill. Place a drip pan under the food at the other side. For more heat, divide the coals on either side of the drip pan. Use this method for slow-cooking foods, such as roasts and whole chicken.

Bold and Zesty Beef Back Ribs

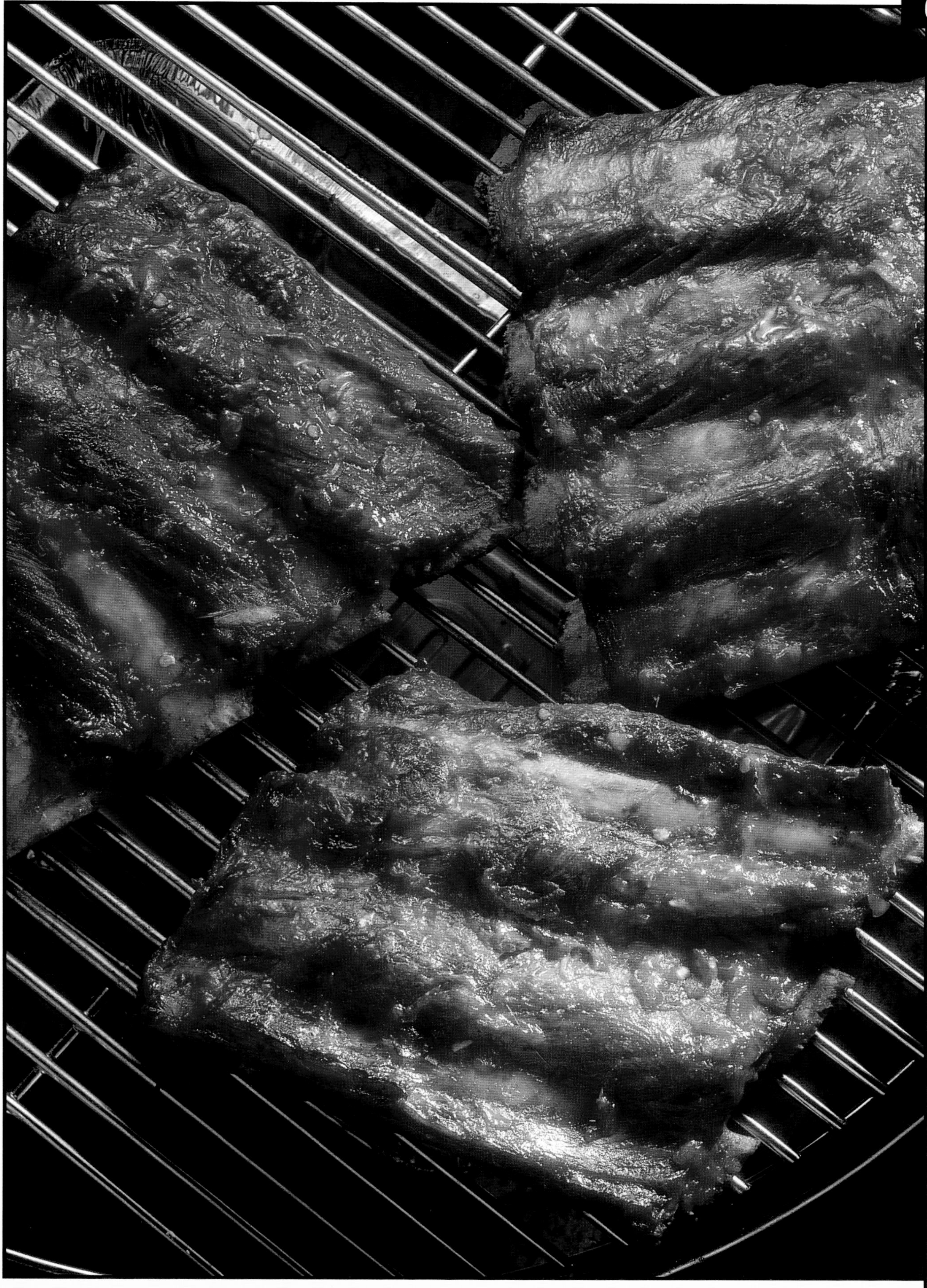

Beef Kabobs with Zucchini and Cherry Tomatoes

Marinade
- ¼ cup **FILIPPO BERIO®** Olive Oil
- 2 tablespoons chopped fresh parsley
- 2 tablespoons red wine vinegar
- 1 clove garlic, minced
- ½ teaspoon salt
- ⅛ teaspoon freshly ground black pepper

Kabobs
- 1 pound lean beef top sirloin or top round steak, well trimmed and cut into 1-inch cubes
- 1 small zucchini, cut into ½-inch-thick slices
- 12 cherry tomatoes
- 6 metal skewers

In medium glass bowl or dish, whisk together olive oil, parsley, vinegar, garlic, salt and pepper. Add steak, zucchini and tomatoes; toss until lightly coated. Cover; marinate in refrigerator 2 hours or overnight. Drain meat and vegetables, reserving marinade. Alternately thread beef and vegetables onto skewers, ending with cube of beef. Brush barbecue grid with olive oil. Grill kabobs, on covered grill, over hot coals 6 to 8 minutes for medium-rare or until desired doneness is reached, turning and brushing with reserved marinade halfway through grilling time. Or, broil kabobs, 4 to 5 inches from heat, 6 to 8 minutes for medium-rare or until desired doneness is reached, turning and brushing with reserved marinade halfway through broiling time.

Makes 6 servings

Chicken Kabobs With Pineapple, Corn And Red Peppers: For marinade, substitute 2 tablespoons pineapple juice for red wine vinegar. For kabobs, use 1 pound boneless skinless chicken breasts, cut into 1½-inch cubes, 2 cobs fresh or frozen corn, cut into 12 pieces, 12 cubes fresh or canned pineapple and 1 large red bell pepper, seeded and cut into 12 chunks. Alternately thread chicken, vegetables and pineapple onto skewers, ending with cube of chicken. Marinate kabobs as directed above. Grill or broil kabobs as directed above, 6 to 8 minutes or until chicken is no longer pink in center and juices run clear.

Stuffed Salisbury Steak with Mushroom & Onion Topping

2 pounds ground beef
¼ cup *French's®*
    Worcestershire Sauce
2⅔ cups *French's®* French Fried
    Onions, divided
1 teaspoon garlic salt
½ teaspoon ground black
    pepper
4 ounces Cheddar cheese, cut
    into 6 sticks (about
    2×½×½ inches)
Mushroom Topping (recipe
    follows)

Combine beef, Worcestershire, *1⅓ cups* French Fried Onions, garlic salt and pepper. Divide meat evenly into 6 portions. Place 1 stick cheese in center of each portion, firmly pressing and shaping meat into ovals around cheese.

Place steaks on grid. Grill over medium-high coals 15 minutes or until meat thermometer inserted into beef reaches 160°F, turning once. Serve with Mushroom Topping and sprinkle with remaining *1⅓ cups* onions.   *Makes 6 servings*

Mushroom Topping

2 tablespoons butter or margarine
1 package (12 ounces) mushrooms, wiped clean
    and quartered
2 tablespoons *French's®* Worcestershire Sauce

Melt butter in large skillet over medium-high heat. Add mushrooms; cook 5 minutes or until browned, stirring often. Add Worcestershire. Reduce heat to low. Cook 5 minutes, stirring occasionally.   *Makes 6 servings*

Prep Time: 25 minutes
Cook Time: 25 minutes

Pepper Stuffed Flank Steak with Chef's Signature Steak Sauce

1 flank steak (about
    1½ pounds)
    Salt
    Ground black pepper
2 cups thinly sliced bell
    peppers (green, red
    and/or yellow)
1 small onion, thinly sliced
    Chef's Signature Steak
    Sauce (recipe page 50)

Lay steak flat on baking sheet lined with plastic wrap. Cover and freeze about 2 hours or until nearly firm. Place steak on cutting board. Hold large sharp knife parallel to steak. Carefully cut steak in half lengthwise. Thaw in refrigerator until steak can be rolled up easily. Sprinkle inside of each piece of meat with salt and black pepper. Arrange bell peppers and onion on meat, leaving ½-inch edge around meat. Tightly roll up jelly-roll style; tie with kitchen string or secure with toothpicks.*

Prepare Chef's Signature Steak Sauce; set aside. Place steak on oiled grid. Grill over medium-hot coals 25 minutes for medium doneness, turning often. Baste with some of Chef's Signature Steak Sauce during last 10 minutes of cooking. Remove string or toothpicks. Let steak stand 5 minutes. Slice steak diagonally. Serve with remaining sauce.

Makes 6 servings

*Soak toothpicks in water 20 minutes to prevent burning.

Pepper Stuffed Flank Steak with Chef's
Signature Steak Sauce (page 50)

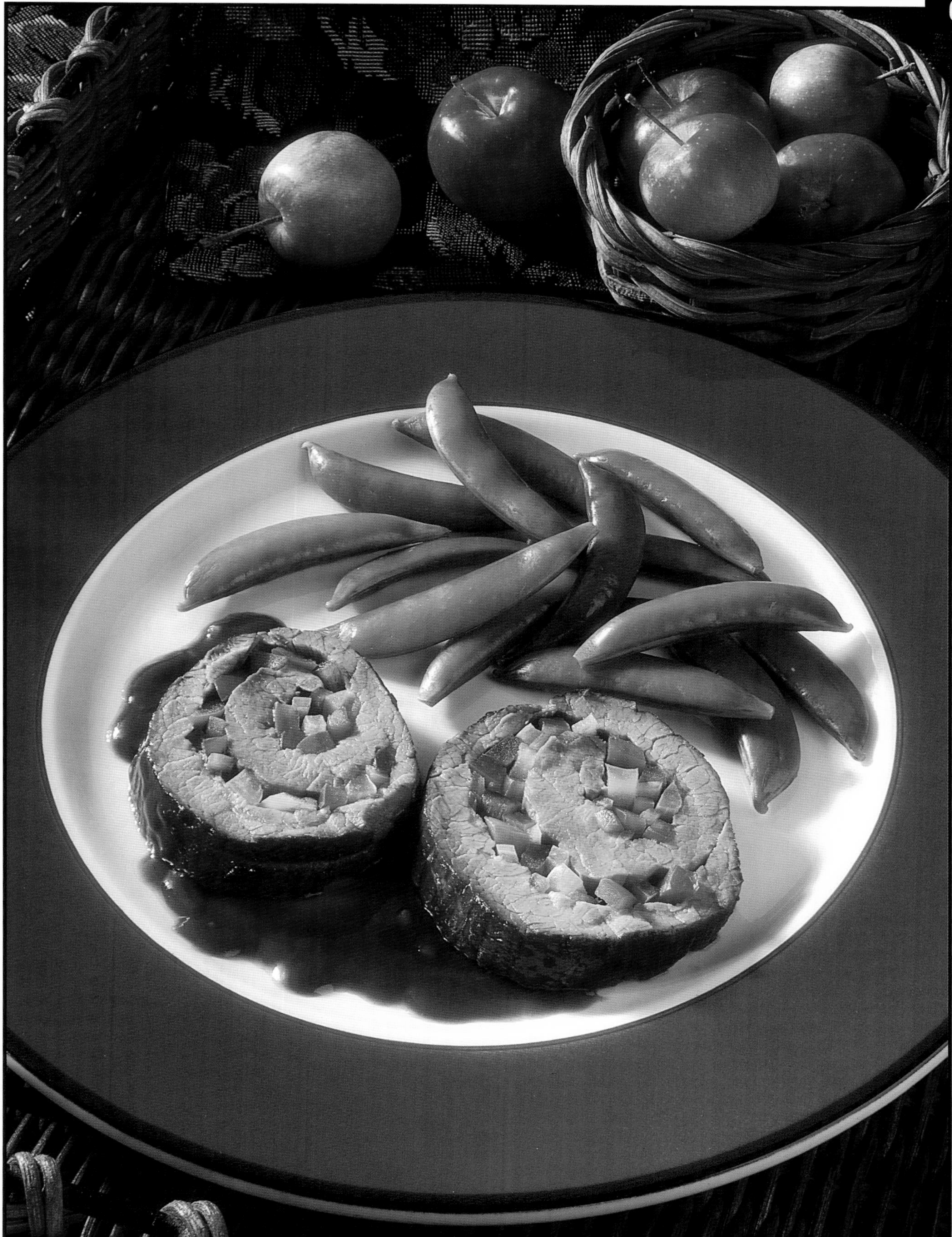

Beef and Pineapple Kabobs

1 pound boneless beef top
    sirloin steak or beef top
    round steak, cut 1 inch
    thick
1 small onion, finely chopped
½ cup bottled teriyaki sauce
16 pieces (1-inch cubes) fresh
    pineapple
1 can (8 ounces) water
    chestnuts, drained

Cut steak into ¼-inch-thick strips. For marinade, combine onion and teriyaki sauce in small bowl. Add beef strips, stirring to coat. Alternately thread beef strips (weaving back and forth), pineapple cubes and water chestnuts on bamboo or thin metal skewers. (If using bamboo skewers, soak in water for 20 to 30 minutes before using to prevent them from burning.) Place kabobs on grid over medium coals. Grill 4 minutes, turning once, or until meat is cooked through. Serve immediately.   *Makes 4 servings*

Note: Recipe may also be prepared with flank steak.

Serving Suggestion: Serve with hot cooked rice and stir-fried broccoli, mushrooms and red bell peppers.

GRILLING TIP

Skewers are threaded with small chunks or strips of meat, poultry, vegetables and sometimes fruit to make kabobs for grilling. Metal skewers are best for heavier foods like chunks of meat. Long, thin wooden skewers work well for individual servings consisting of small pieces of meat, vegetables and fruits. Soak wooden skewers in water for about 30 minutes before using to prevent burning.

The Definitive Steak

4 New York strip steaks
   (about 5 ounces each)
4 tablespoons olive oil
2 teaspoons minced garlic
1 teaspoon salt
½ teaspoon black pepper

Place steaks in shallow glass container. Combine oil, garlic, salt and pepper in small bowl; mix well. Pour oil mixture over steaks; turn to coat well. Cover; refrigerate 30 to 60 minutes.

Prepare grill for direct cooking.

Place steaks on grid. Grill, covered, over medium-high heat 14 minutes for medium, 20 minutes for well or according to desired doneness, turning halfway through grilling time.

Makes 4 servings

GRILLING TIP

To check the temperature of the coals, cautiously hold the palm of your hand at grid level--over the coals for direct heat and over the drip pan for indirect heat--and count the number of seconds you can hold your hand in that position before the heat forces you to pull it away.

2 Seconds: hot about 375°F or more
3 Seconds: medium-hot about 350°F to 375°F
4 Seconds: medium about 300°F to 350°F
5 Seconds: low about 200°F to 300°F

The Definitive Steak and
Chicken Tikka (page 138)

Barbecue Beef

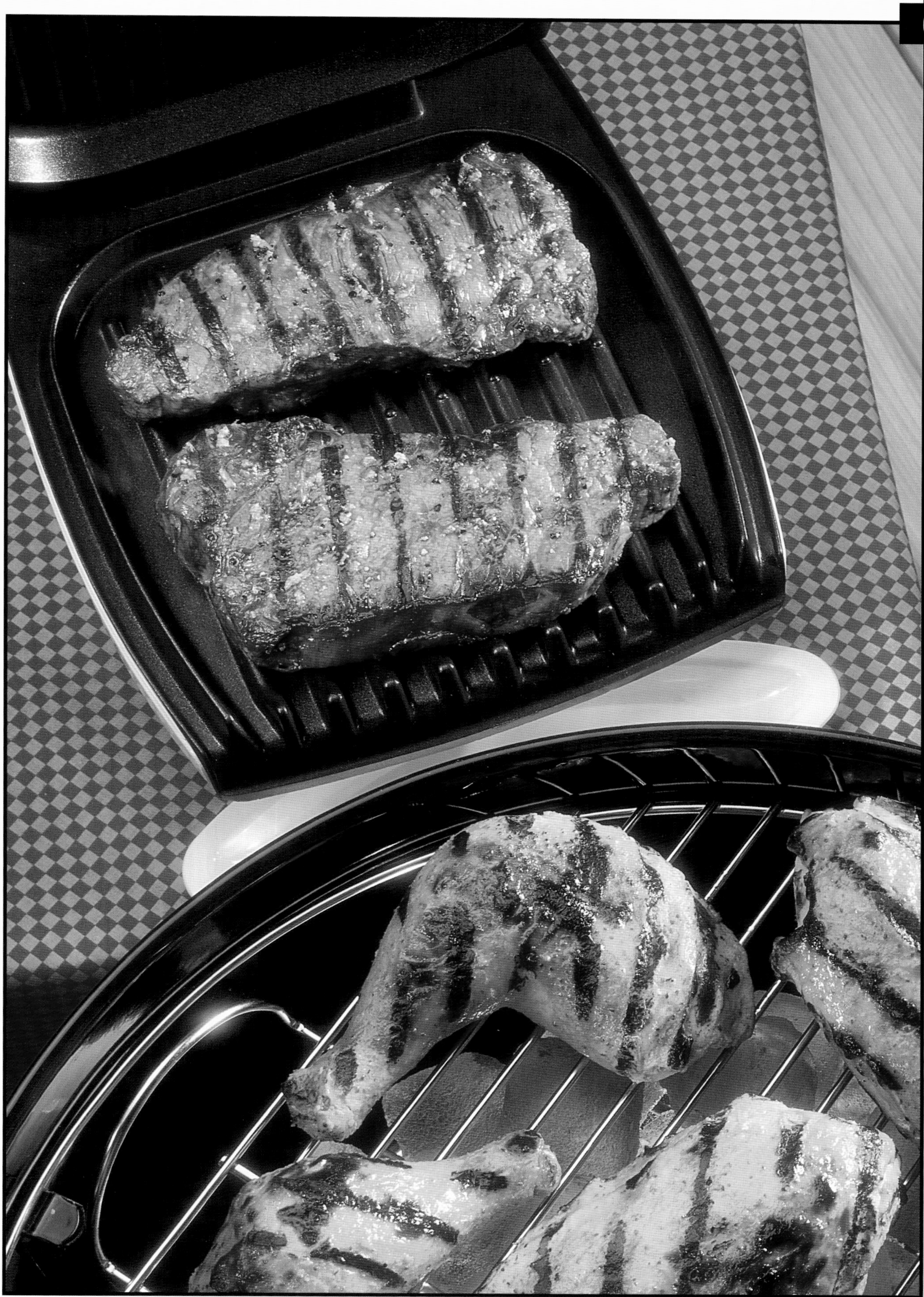

Steakhouse London Broil

1 package KNORR® Recipe
    Classics™ Roasted Garlic
    Herb or French Onion
    Soup, Dip and Recipe Mix
⅓ cup BERTOLLI® Olive Oil
2 tablespoons red wine
    vinegar
1 (1½- to 2-pound) beef
    round steak (for London
    Broil) or flank steak

- In large plastic food bag or 13×9-inch glass baking dish, blend recipe mix, oil and vinegar.

- Add steak, turning to coat. Close bag, or cover, and marinate in refrigerator 30 minutes to 3 hours.

- Remove meat from marinade, discarding marinade. Grill or broil, turning occasionally, until desired doneness.

- Slice meat thinly across the grain.

Makes 6 to 8 servings

Garlic Chicken: Substitute 6 to 8 boneless chicken breasts or 3 to 4 pounds bone-in chicken pieces for steak. Marinate as directed. Grill boneless chicken breasts 6 minutes or bone-in chicken pieces 20 minutes or until chicken is thoroughly cooked.

Prep Time: 5 minutes
Marinate Time: 30 minutes to 3 hours
Grill Time: 20 minutes

Steakhouse London Broil

Hickory Beef Kabobs

1 pound boneless beef top
   sirloin or tenderloin
   steak, cut into 1¼-inch
   pieces
2 ears fresh corn,* shucked,
   cleaned and cut crosswise
   into 1-inch pieces
1 red or green bell pepper, cut
   into 1-inch squares
1 small red onion, cut into
   ½-inch wedges
½ cup beer
½ cup chili sauce
1 teaspoon dry mustard
2 cloves garlic, minced
3 cups hot cooked white rice
¼ cup chopped fresh parsley

*Four small ears frozen corn, thawed, can be
substituted for fresh corn.

1. Place beef, corn, bell pepper and onion in
large resealable plastic food storage bag. Combine
beer, chili sauce, mustard and garlic in small bowl;
pour over beef and vegetables. Seal bag tightly,
turning to coat. Marinate in refrigerator at least
1 hour or up to 8 hours, turning occasionally.

2. Prepare grill for direct cooking. Meanwhile,
cover 1½ cups hickory chips with cold water; soak
20 minutes.

3. Drain beef and vegetables; reserve marinade.
Alternately thread beef and vegetables onto
4 (12-inch) metal skewers. Brush with reserved
marinade.

4. Drain hickory chips; sprinkle over coals. Place
kabobs on grid. Grill kabobs, on covered grill,
over medium-hot coals 5 minutes. Brush with
reserved marinade; turn and brush again. Discard
remaining marinade. Continue to grill, covered,
5 to 7 minutes for medium or until desired
doneness is reached.

5. Combine rice and chopped parsley; serve
kabobs over rice mixture.   *Makes 4 servings*

GRILLING TIP

*For additional flavor, toss water-soaked wood chips, such as
hickory or mesquite, onto hot coals before adding food. Adding
wood chips to the coals will create smoke, so make sure the grill
is in a well-ventilated area away from any open windows.*

Hickory Beef Kabob

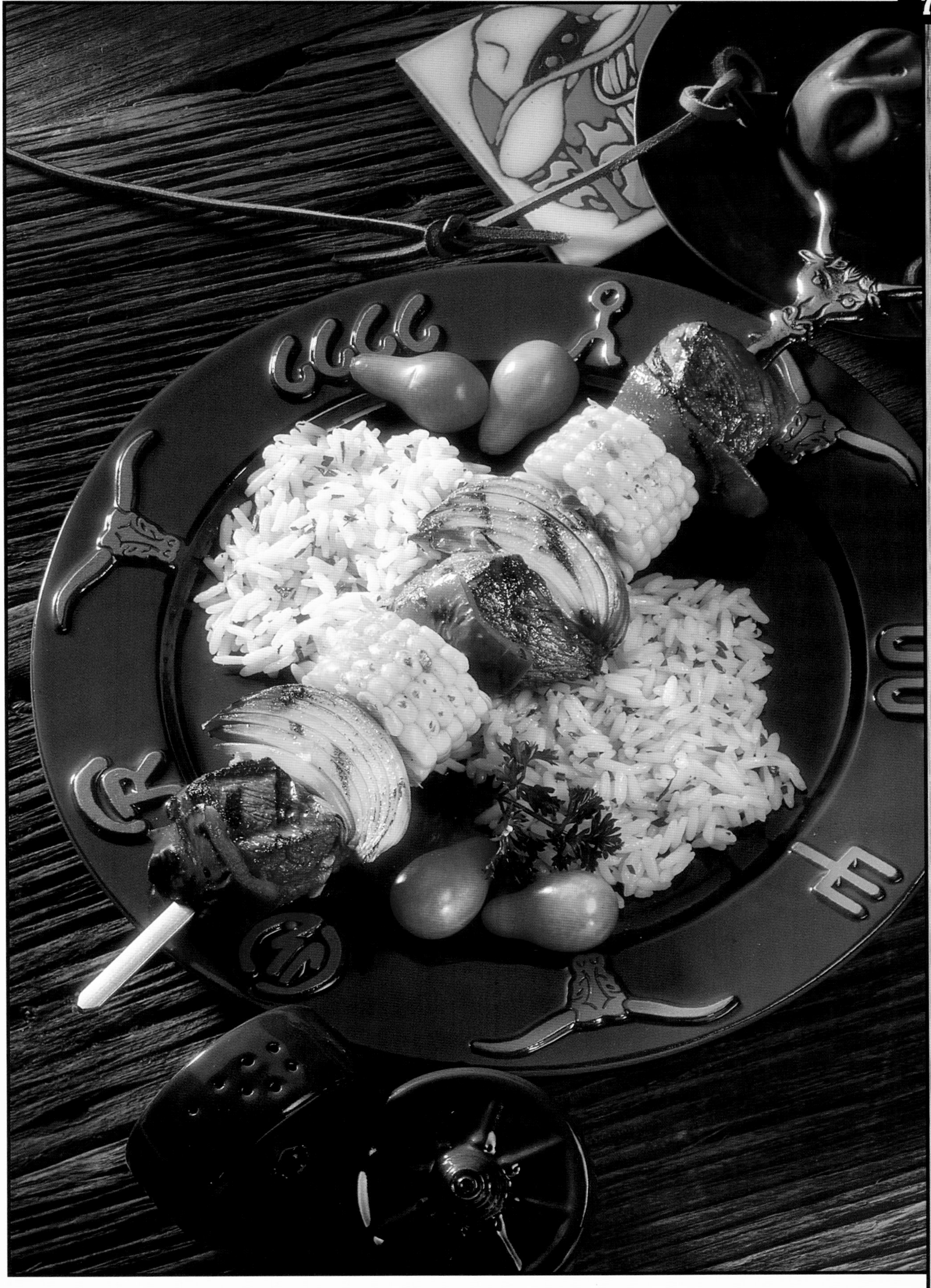

Grilled Peppered London Broil

1¼ cups canned crushed
    tomatoes
1 medium onion, quartered
1 tablespoon FILIPPO
    BERIO® Olive Oil
1 tablespoon cider vinegar
1 jalapeño pepper, seeded
    and chopped *or*
    1 tablespoon purchased
    chopped hot pepper
1 clove garlic
½ teaspoon salt
1 teaspoon freshly ground
    black pepper
1 (2-pound) beef London
    broil, 2 inches thick

Process tomatoes, onion, olive oil, vinegar, jalapeño pepper and garlic in blender container or food processor until smooth. Transfer mixture to small saucepan. Bring to a boil. Reduce heat to low; simmer 2 minutes. Pour marinade into shallow glass dish. Stir in salt and black pepper. Cool slightly. Add London broil to marinade; turn to coat both sides. Cover; marinate in refrigerator at least 4 hours or overnight, turning occasionally. Remove London broil, reserving marinade.

Brush barbecue grid with olive oil. Grill London broil, on covered grill, over hot coals 8 to 10 minutes, brushing frequently with reserved marinade. Turn with tongs. Grill an additional 18 to 20 minutes for medium-rare or until desired doneness is reached. *Makes 6 to 8 servings*

Sizzling Fajita Kabobs

1½ pounds beef sirloin, cut into 1-inch cubes
2 bell peppers (green, red and/or yellow), seeded and cut into 1-inch chunks
1 cup pearl onions, peeled
½ cup prepared olive oil vinaigrette salad dressing
¼ cup *French's*® Classic Yellow® Mustard
¼ cup *Frank's*® RedHot® Cayenne Pepper Sauce
2 teaspoons ground cumin
2 teaspoons garlic powder
Flour tortillas (optional)
Sour cream (optional)

Thread meat, peppers and onions alternately onto metal skewers. Place skewers in shallow glass dish. To prepare marinade, combine salad dressing, mustard, *Frank's RedHot* Sauce and seasonings in small bowl; mix well. Pour marinade over skewers, turning to coat evenly. Cover and marinate in refrigerator 15 minutes.

Place skewers on grid, reserving marinade. Grill over hot coals 15 minutes or until beef is medium-rare, turning and basting often with marinade. (Do not baste during last 5 minutes of cooking.) To serve, remove meat and vegetables from skewers. Place in tortillas and top with sour cream, if desired.

Makes 6 servings

Prep Time: 15 minutes
Marinate Time: 15 minutes
Cook Time: 15 minutes

FOOD FACT

Fajitas originated in Texas. The traditional dish is prepared by marinating beef skirt steak in oil, lime juice, garlic and ground red pepper before grilling it. The steak is cut into thin strips and rolled in flour tortillas. Fajitas now often include grilled bell peppers and onions. They are served with sour cream, guacamole and salsa. Sometimes the dish is prepared with beef flank steak, chicken strips or shrimp.

Mushroom-Sauced Steak

½ cup sliced onion
2 tablespoons margarine or
   butter
1½ cups sliced mushrooms
1 cup A.1.® BOLD & SPICY
   Steak Sauce
½ cup dairy sour cream
2 (8-ounce) beef club or strip
   steaks, about 1 inch thick

Sauté onion in margarine in medium skillet over medium heat until tender, about 5 minutes. Add mushrooms; sauté 5 minutes more. Stir in steak sauce; heat to a boil. Reduce heat and simmer 5 minutes; stir in sour cream. Cook and stir until heated through (do not boil); keep warm.

Grill steaks over medium heat 5 minutes on each side or until done. Serve steaks topped with mushroom sauce.   *Makes 4 servings*

FOOD FACT

The work steak comes from "steik" in the ancient Noorse language where it meant meat of any kind. America's beef steak is considered by most objective observers to be the best in the entire world.

Mushroom-Sauced Steak

Grilled Caribbean Steak with Tropical Fruit Rice

1 (1½-pound) flank steak
¼ cup soy sauce
1¼ cups orange juice, divided
1 teaspoon ground ginger
1 can (8 ounces) pineapple
    chunks in juice
¼ teaspoon ground allspice
1 cup UNCLE BEN'S®
    ORIGINAL
    CONVERTED® Brand
    Rice
1 can (11 ounces) mandarin
    orange segments, drained

1. Place steak in large resealable plastic food storage bag. In small bowl, combine soy sauce, ¼ cup orange juice and ginger; pour over steak. Seal bag, turning to coat steak with marinade. Refrigerate steak, turning bag occasionally, at least 8 or up to 24 hours.

2. Drain pineapple, reserving juice. Combine remaining 1 cup orange juice and pineapple juice in 1-quart glass measure; add enough water to make 2¼ cups liquid.

3. In medium saucepan, combine juice mixture, allspice and salt to taste. Bring to a boil; stir in rice. Cover; reduce heat to low and simmer 20 minutes. Remove from heat and let stand, covered, 5 minutes.

4. Meanwhile, remove steak from marinade; discard marinade. Grill steak 7 minutes on each side for medium or until desired doneness. Cut steak diagonally across the grain into thin slices.

5. Place rice in serving bowl. Stir in pineapple and oranges. Serve with steak.

Makes 6 servings

Serving Suggestion: For an authentic Caribbean touch, add 1 cup diced peeled mango to rice with pineapple chunks and oranges.

Grilled Caribbean Steak with Tropical Fruit Rice

Barbecue Beef

78

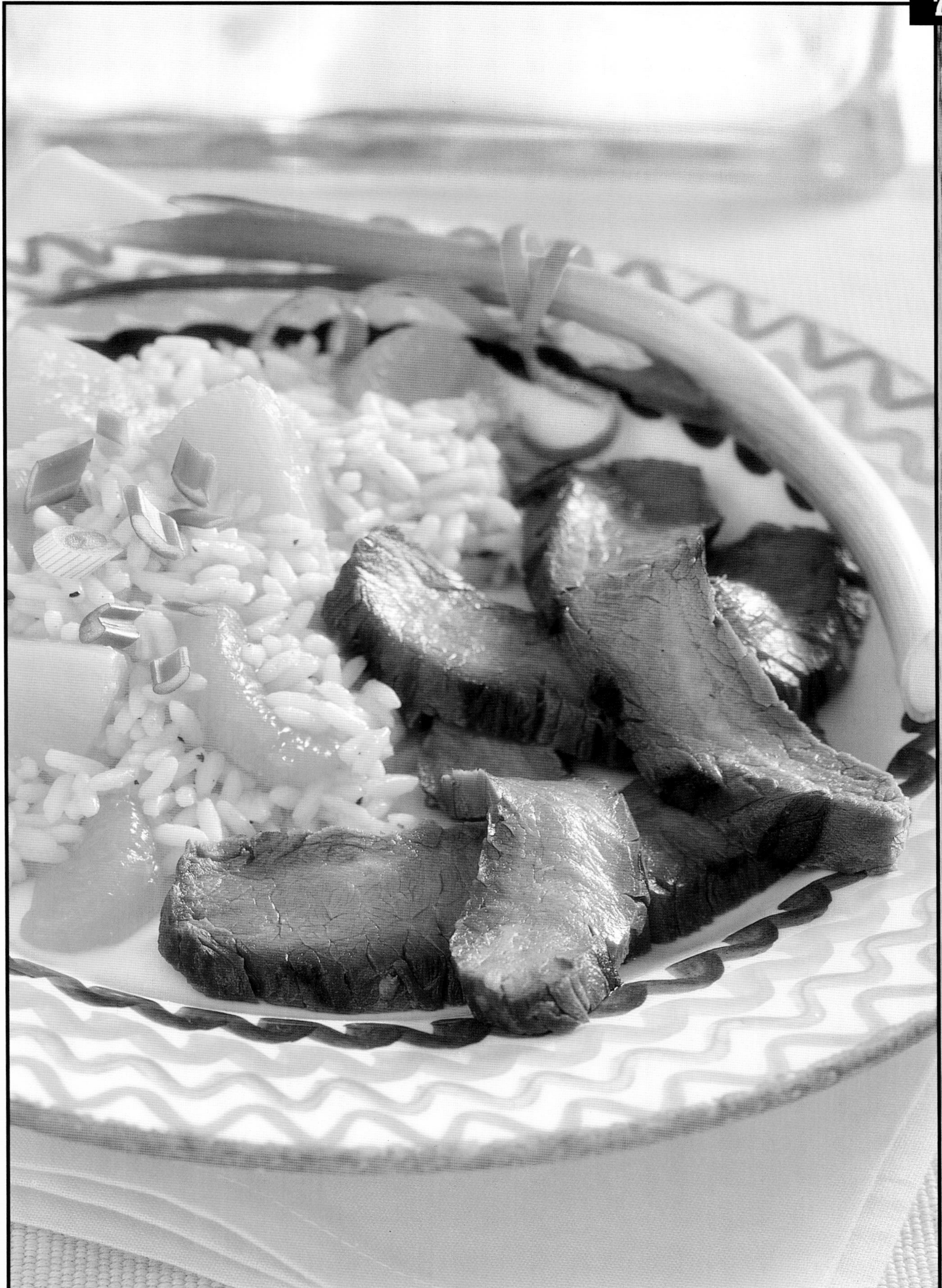

Grilled Meat Loaf

1½ pounds ground chuck or
  ground sirloin
½ cup seasoned dry bread
  crumbs
⅔ cup chili sauce, divided
⅓ cup grated onion
1 egg
½ teaspoon black pepper
¼ teaspoon salt
2 tablespoons packed light
  brown sugar
1 tablespoon spicy brown or
  Dijon mustard

Prepare barbecue grill for direct cooking. Combine beef, bread crumbs, ⅓ cup chili sauce, onion, egg, pepper and salt in large bowl; mix well. On cutting board or cookie sheet, shape mixture into 9×5-inch oval loaf, 1½ inches thick.

Combine remaining ⅓ cup chili sauce, sugar and mustard in small bowl; mix well. Set aside. Place meat loaf on grid. Grill meat loaf, on covered grill, over medium-hot coals 10 minutes. Carefully turn meat loaf over using 2 large spatulas.

Brush chili sauce mixture over top of meat loaf. Continue to grill, covered, 10 to 12 minutes until no longer pink in center. (If desired, insert instant-read thermometer* into center of thickest part of meat loaf. Thermometer should register 160°F. Let stand 10 minutes before slicing. Serve with mashed potatoes and peas and carrots, if desired.

Makes 4 to 6 servings

Do not leave instant-read thermometer in meat loaf during grilling since thermometer is not heatproof.

Grilled Meat Loaf

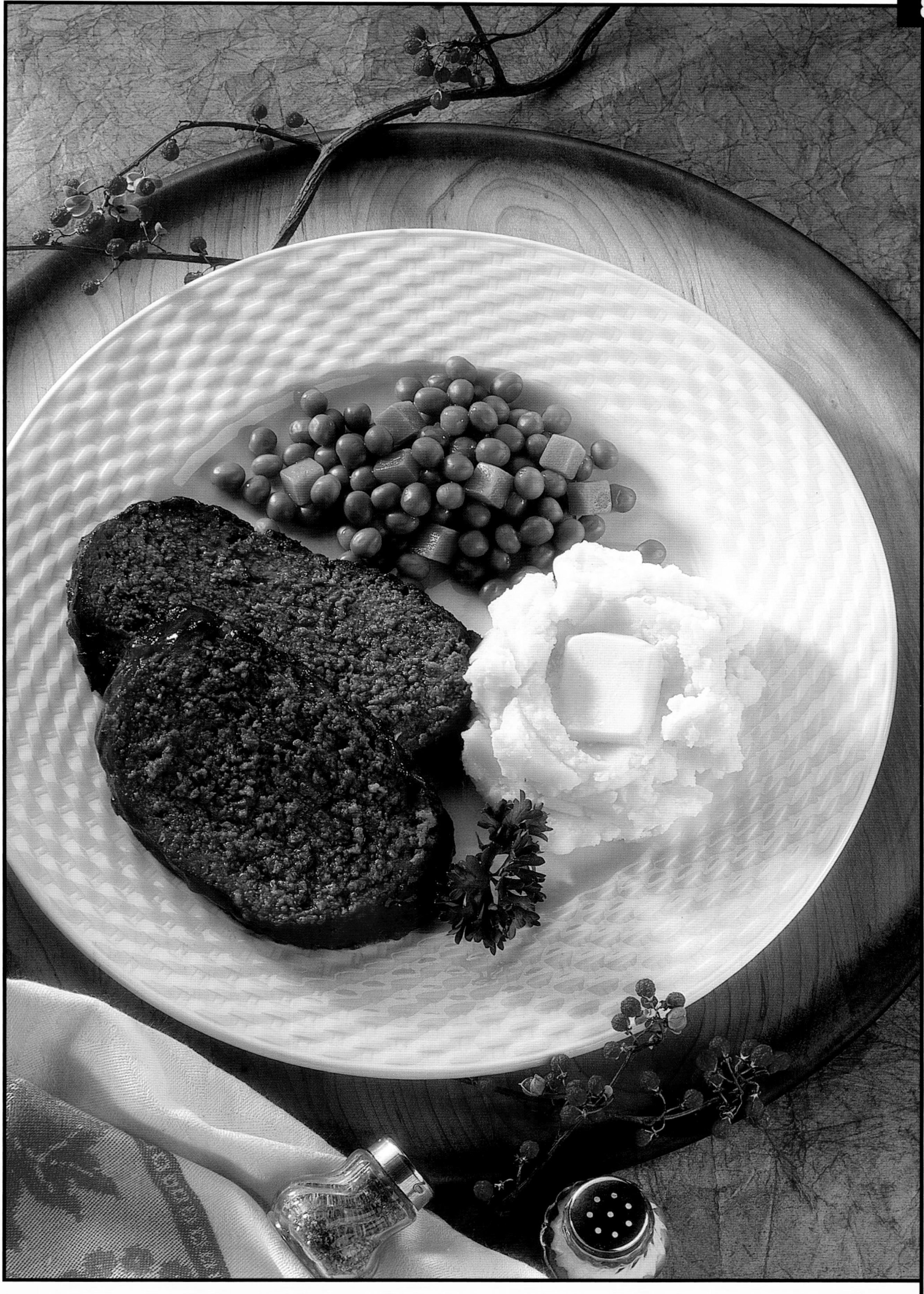

Fajitas with Avocado Salsa

1 beef flank steak (1¼ to
    1½ pounds)
¼ cup tequila or nonalcoholic
    beer
3 tablespoons fresh lime juice
1 tablespoon seeded and
    minced jalapeño pepper*
2 large cloves garlic, minced
    Avocado Salsa (recipe
      page 335)
8 (6- or 7-inch) flour tortillas
1 large red bell pepper, cut
    into 4 vertical strips
1 large green bell pepper, cut
    into 4 vertical strips
4 slices red onion, cut ¼ inch
    thick

*Jalapeño peppers can sting and irritate the skin; wear rubber gloves when handling peppers and do not touch eyes.

1. Place steak in large resealable plastic food storage bag. Combine tequila, lime juice, jalapeño and garlic in small bowl; pour over steak. Seal bag tightly, turning to coat. Marinate in refrigerator 1 to 4 hours, turning once.

2. Prepare barbecue grill for direct cooking.

3. Meanwhile, prepare Avocado Salsa. Wrap tortillas in heavy-duty foil.

4. Drain steak; discard marinade. Place steak, bell peppers and onion slices on grid. Grill, on covered grill, over medium-hot coals 14 to 18 minutes for medium or until desired doneness is reached, turning steak, bell peppers and onion slices halfway through grilling time. Place tortilla packet on grid during last 5 to 7 minutes of grilling; turn halfway through grilling time to heat through.

5. Transfer steak to carving board. Carve steak across the grain into thin slices. Slice bell peppers into thin strips. Separate onion slices into rings. Divide among tortillas; roll up and top with Avocado Salsa. *Makes 4 servings*

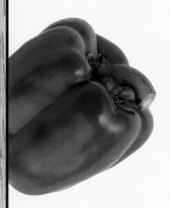

Fajitas with Avocado Salsa

Barbeque Beef

Szechuan Grilled Flank Steak

1 beef flank steak (1¼ to
   1½ pounds)
¼ cup soy sauce
¼ cup seasoned rice vinegar
2 tablespoons dark sesame oil
4 cloves garlic, minced
2 teaspoons minced fresh
   ginger
½ teaspoon red pepper flakes
¼ cup water
½ cup thinly sliced green
   onions
2 to 3 teaspoons sesame
   seeds, toasted
   Hot cooked rice (optional)

Place steak in large resealable plastic food storage bag. To prepare marinade, combine soy sauce, vinegar, oil, garlic, ginger and red pepper in small bowl; pour over steak. Press air from bag and seal; turn to coat. Marinate in refrigerator 3 hours, turning once.

To prevent sticking, spray grid with nonstick cooking spray. Prepare coals for grilling. Drain steak, reserving marinade in small saucepan. Place steak on grid; grill, covered, over medium-hot coals 14 to 18 minutes for medium or to desired doneness, turning steak halfway through grilling time.

Add water to reserved marinade. Bring to a boil over high heat. Reduce heat to low; simmer 5 minutes. Transfer steak to carving board. Slice steak across grain into thin slices. Drizzle steak with boiled marinade. Sprinkle with green onions and sesame seeds. Serve with rice.

Makes 4 to 6 servings

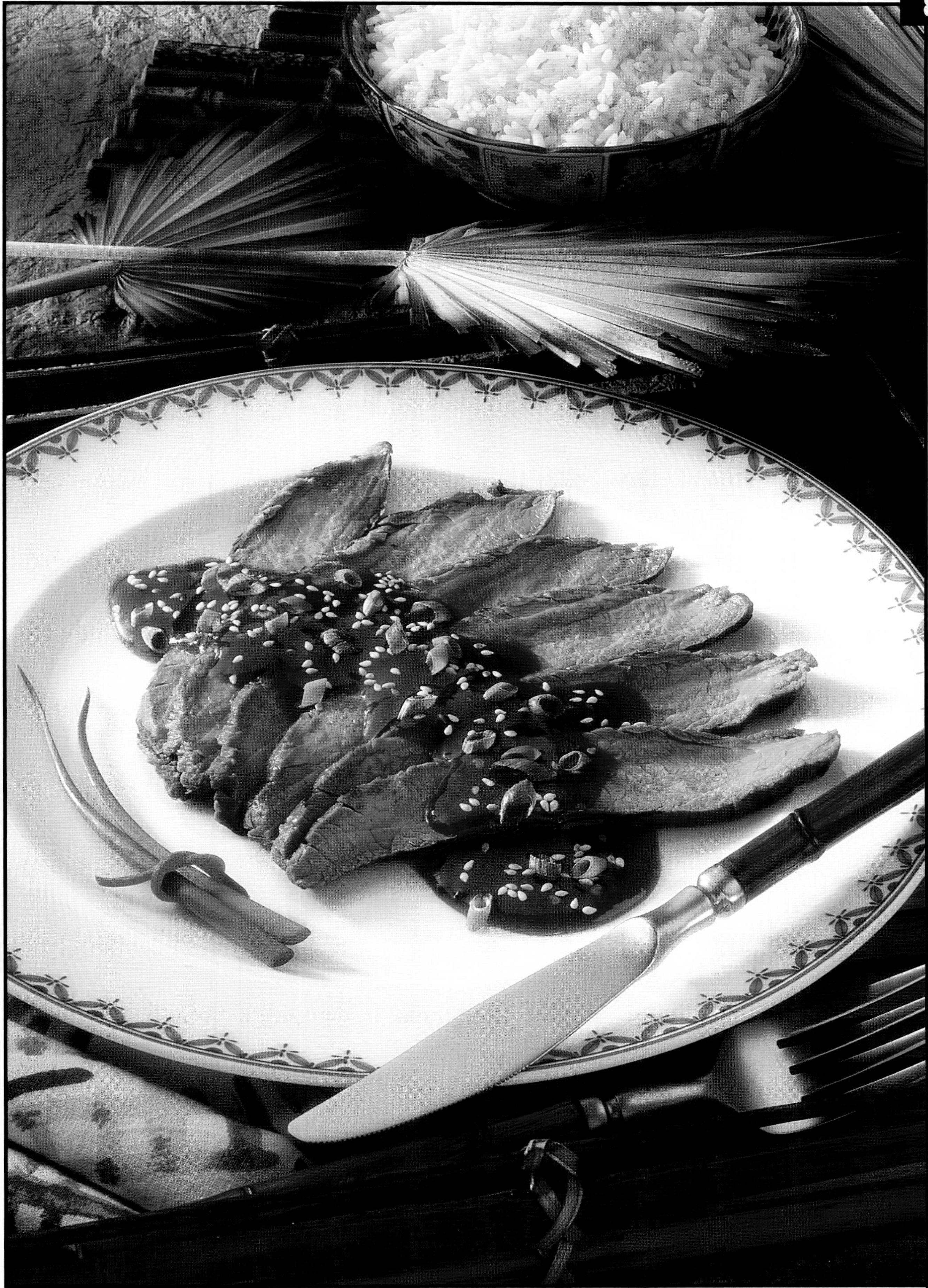

Peppered Steaks with Blackberry Sauce

Steaks
- ⅓ cup lemon juice
- ⅓ cup oil
- ¼ cup chopped onion
- 2 cloves garlic, crushed
- 4 (4 to 6-ounce) beef tenderloin or eye of round steaks, trimmed of fat
- 1 tablespoon coarsely ground pepper

Blackberry Sauce
- ½ cup SMUCKER'S® Seedless Blackberry Jam
- ¼ cup red wine vinegar
- ¼ teaspoon onion powder
- ¼ cup fresh or frozen blackberries, thawed

Combine lemon juice, oil, onion and garlic in large resealable plastic bag; mix well. Place steaks in bag, seal and refrigerate 6 to 24 hours, turning bag occasionally. When ready to cook, rub pepper around edges of each steak.

Heat grill. In small saucepan, combine jam, vinegar and onion powder. Cook over medium heat until jam is melted, stirring constantly. Remove from heat.

Oil grill rack. Place steaks on gas grill over medium heat or on charcoal grill 4 to 6 inches from medium-hot coals. Cook 8 to 12 minutes or until desired doneness, turning once halfway through cooking. To serve, spread steaks with blackberry sauce; top with fresh berries.

Makes 4 servings

Note: Steaks can be cooked in the broiler. Place on oiled broiler pan. Broil 4 to 6 inches from heat for 7 to 10 minutes or until desired doneness, turning once halfway through cooking.

Mexican Steak with Chimichurri Sauce

⅔ cup olive oil

½ cup minced fresh parsley

⅓ cup *Frank's® RedHot®*
   Cayenne Pepper Sauce

3 tablespoons lime juice

1 tablespoon *French's®*
   Worcestershire Sauce

2 teaspoons dried oregano
   leaves

2 cloves garlic, minced

2 pounds boneless beef sirloin
   (1½ inches thick)

Place oil, parsley, *Frank's RedHot* Sauce, lime juice, Worcestershire, oregano and garlic in blender or food processor. Cover and process until well blended. Reserve ⅔ cup sauce mixture. Place steak in large resealable plastic food storage bag. Pour remaining sauce mixture over steak. Seal bag and marinate in refrigerator 30 minutes.

Place steak on grid, discarding marinade. Grill over hot coals 10 minutes per side for medium-rare or to desired doneness. Let steak stand 5 minutes. Slice steak diagonally. Serve with reserved sauce mixture.   *Makes 6 to 8 servings*

Prep Time: 10 minutes
Marinate Time: 30 minutes
Cook Time: 20 minutes

GRILLING TIP

Do not crowd pieces of food on the grill. Food will cook more evenly with a ¾-inch space between pieces.

Peppered Beef Rib Roast

1½ tablespoons black
    peppercorns
1 boneless beef rib roast
    (2½ to 3 pounds), well
    trimmed
¼ cup Dijon mustard
2 cloves garlic, minced
    Sour Cream Sauce (recipe
    page 49)

Prepare grill for indirect cooking.

Place peppercorns in small resealable plastic food storage bag. Squeeze out excess air; close bag securely. Pound peppercorns using flat side of meat mallet or rolling pin until cracked. Set aside.

Pat roast dry with paper towels. Combine mustard and garlic in small bowl; spread over top and sides of roast. Sprinkle pepper over mustard mixture.

Place roast, pepper-side up, on grid directly over drip pan. Grill, covered, over medium heat 1 hour to 1 hour 10 minutes for medium or until internal temperature reaches 145°F when tested with meat thermometer inserted into the thickest part of roast, adding 4 to 9 briquets to both sides of the fire after 45 minutes to maintain medium heat.

Meanwhile, prepare Sour Cream Sauce. Cover; refrigerate until serving.

Transfer roast to cutting board; cover with foil. Let stand 10 to 15 minutes before carving. Internal temperature will continue to rise 5°F to 10°F during stand time. Serve with Sour Cream Sauce.

Makes 6 to 8 servings

Peppered Beef Rib Roast

Mini Beef & Colorado Potato Kabobs

2 COLORADO Sangre red
potatoes, baked
1 green bell pepper, cut into
¾-inch cubes
1 small onion, cut into
wedges
½ pound beef tenderloin, cut
into ¾-inch cubes
Bamboo skewers

Marinade
¼ cup olive oil
¼ cup balsamic vinegar
1 tablespoon snipped fresh
thyme
1 tablespoon snipped fresh
basil
1 tablespoon snipped fresh
parsley
1 clove garlic, minced
½ teaspoon sugar
½ teaspoon salt
½ teaspoon black pepper

Quarter baked potatoes lengthwise. Cut crosswise into ¾-inch chunks; set aside. Blanch bell pepper and onion in boiling water 1 to 2 minutes; drain. For marinade, combine olive oil, vinegar, herbs, garlic, sugar, salt and black pepper in medium bowl. Place beef, bell pepper and onion in marinade. Toss to coat well. Cover and chill several hours or overnight. Soak bamboo skewers in hot water 5 minutes. Thread beef, potatoes, bell pepper and onion on skewers. Grill over medium high heat 5 to 7 minutes, turning once. If desired, broil 5 to 6 inches from heat source 5 to 7 minutes or to desired doneness. *Makes 4 servings*

Favorite recipe from **Colorado Potato Administrative Committee**

Mini Beef & Colorado Potato Kabobs

Smoked Brisket of Beef with Barbecue Sauce

1 beef brisket, 4 to 5 pounds
1 tablespoon LAWRY'S®
    Seasoned Salt
1 teaspoon LAWRY'S® Garlic
    Powder with Parsley
1 teaspoon ground thyme
½ teaspoon white pepper
    Barbecue Sauce

In shallow glass dish, place beef brisket. In small bowl, combine Seasoned Salt, Garlic Powder with Parsley, thyme and pepper; rub on both sides of meat. Let stand 1 hour at room temperature. Cook slowly in smoker 45 to 60 minutes or until meat thermometer registers 175°F. for medium.

Makes 8 to 10 servings

Serving Suggestion: Slice thinly on a diagonal. Dip slices in Barbecue Sauce for sandwiches or ladle sauce over slices for an entrée.

Steak Au Poivre with Dijon Sauce

4 beef tenderloin steaks, cut
    1½ inches thick (about
    1½ pounds)
1 tablespoon *French's®*
    Worcestershire Sauce
    Crushed black peppercorns
⅓ cup *French's®* Napa Valley
    Style Dijon Mustard
⅓ cup mayonnaise
3 tablespoons dry red wine
2 tablespoons finely chopped
    red or green onion
2 tablespoons minced fresh
    parsley
1 clove garlic, minced

Brush steaks with Worcestershire and sprinkle with pepper to taste; set aside. To prepare Dijon Sauce, combine mustard, mayonnaise, wine, onion, parsley and garlic; mix well.

Place steaks on grid. Grill over hot coals 15 minutes for medium-rare or to desired doneness, turning often. Serve with Dijon Sauce.

Makes 4 servings

Note: Dijon Sauce is also great with grilled salmon and swordfish. To serve with fish, substitute white wine for the red wine and minced fresh dill for the parsley.

Prep Time: 10 minutes
Cook Time: 15 minutes

Grilled Beef with Two Sauces

1 (1-pound) boneless beef
    sirloin steak

Roasted Garlic Sauce
  ¾ cup mayonnaise*
  ¼ cup Roasted Garlic Purée
    (recipe follows)
  ¼ cup GREY POUPON® Dijon
    Mustard
  2 tablespoons chopped
    parsley
  1 tablespoon lemon juice

Sundried Tomato Sauce
  ¾ cup chopped roasted red
    peppers
  ½ cup sundried tomatoes,**
    chopped
  3 tablespoons GREY
    POUPON® Dijon
    Mustard
  2 tablespoons chopped
    parsley
  2 to 3 tablespoons olive oil
  ¼ teaspoon crushed red
    pepper flakes

Low-fat mayonnaise may be substituted for regular mayonnaise.

**If sundried tomatoes are very dry, soften in warm water for 5 minutes. Drain before using.*

1. Grill beef over medium heat to desired doneness and refrigerate.

2. For Roasted Garlic Sauce, blend all ingredients in medium bowl. Refrigerate at least 1 hour to blend flavors.

3. For Sundried Tomato Sauce, combine roasted red peppers, sundried tomatoes, mustard and parsley in medium bowl. Slowly add oil as needed to bind. Add red pepper flakes. Refrigerate at least 1 hour to blend flavors. Bring to room temperature before serving.

4. Slice beef and arrange on 4 serving plates. Spoon about 2 tablespoons of each sauce onto each plate. Serve with sliced tomatoes and cooled steamed asparagus; garnish as desired.

Makes 4 servings

Roasted Garlic Purée: Remove excess papery skin of 1 head garlic and separate into cloves. Place in 8×8×2-inch baking pan. Add 2 to 3 tablespoons olive oil and 1 cup chicken broth. Bake at 350°F for 25 to 30 minutes or until garlic is soft. Cool and squeeze garlic pulp from skins; discard liquid in pan.

Firehouse Marinated Steak

¼ cup WESSON® Best Blend
  or Vegetable Oil
6 dried pasilla or ancho
  chilies, seeded and cut
  into strips
1 cup coarsely chopped onion
1½ teaspoons chopped fresh
  garlic
½ cup beef broth
2 tablespoons fresh lime juice
2 teaspoons cumin seed
1½ teaspoons salt
1 teaspoon brown sugar
4 New York steaks *or*
  1 (2-pound) flank steak,
  tenderized lightly with
  meat mallet
2 limes

In a medium skillet, heat Wesson® Oil over medium-low heat. Add chilies, onion and garlic; sauté until onion is tender. *Do not drain.* Pour onion mixture into blender. Add *remaining* ingredients *except* steaks and limes; blend until smooth. If marinade is too thick, add additional beef broth. Place steaks in large resealable plastic food storage bag. Pour half the marinade over steaks; set aside *remaining* marinade. Seal bag and turn to coat. Marinate in refrigerator for 30 minutes. Bring steaks to room temperature. Over hot coals, grill steaks while basting with ¾ of reserved marinade. Grill to desired doneness. Before serving, brush beef with *remaining* ¼ marinade and generously squeeze fresh lime juice over steaks.   *Makes 4 servings*

Tip: This spicy marinade can be made up to 3 days ahead of time; the flavors improve with age.

Firehouse Marinated Steak

Spice-Rubbed Beef Brisket

2 cups hickory chips
1 teaspoon salt
1 teaspoon paprika
1 teaspoon chili powder
1 teaspoon garlic pepper
1 beef brisket (3 to
    3½ pounds)
¼ cup beer or beef broth
1 tablespoon Worcestershire
    sauce
1 tablespoon balsamic vinegar
1 teaspoon olive oil
¼ teaspoon dry mustard
6 ears corn, cut into 2-inch
    pieces
12 small new potatoes
6 carrots, cut into 2-inch
    pieces
2 green bell peppers, cut into
    2-inch squares
6 tablespoons lemon juice
1½ teaspoons salt-free dried
    Italian seasoning

1. Cover hickory chips with water; soak 30 minutes. Prepare grill for indirect grilling. Bank briquets on either side of water-filled drip pan.

2. Combine salt, paprika, chili powder and garlic pepper. Rub spice mixture on both sides of brisket; loosely cover with foil and set aside. Combine beer, Worcestershire sauce, vinegar, oil and dry mustard.

3. Drain hickory chips and sprinkle ½ cup over coals. Place brisket directly over drip pan; grill on covered grill over medium coals 30 minutes. Baste and turn over every 30 minutes for 3 hours or until meat thermometer reaches 160°F when inserted in thickest part of brisket. Add 4 to 9 briquets and ¼ cup hickory chips to each side of fire every hour.

4. Alternately thread vegetables onto metal skewers. Combine lemon juice with 6 tablespoons water and Italian seasoning; brush on vegetables. Grill vegetables with brisket 20 to 25 minutes or until tender, turning once.

5. Remove brisket to cutting board; tent loosely with foil and let stand 10 minutes before carving. Remove excess fat. Serve with vegetable kabobs. Garnish as desired. *Makes 12 servings*

Spice-Rubbed Beef Brisket

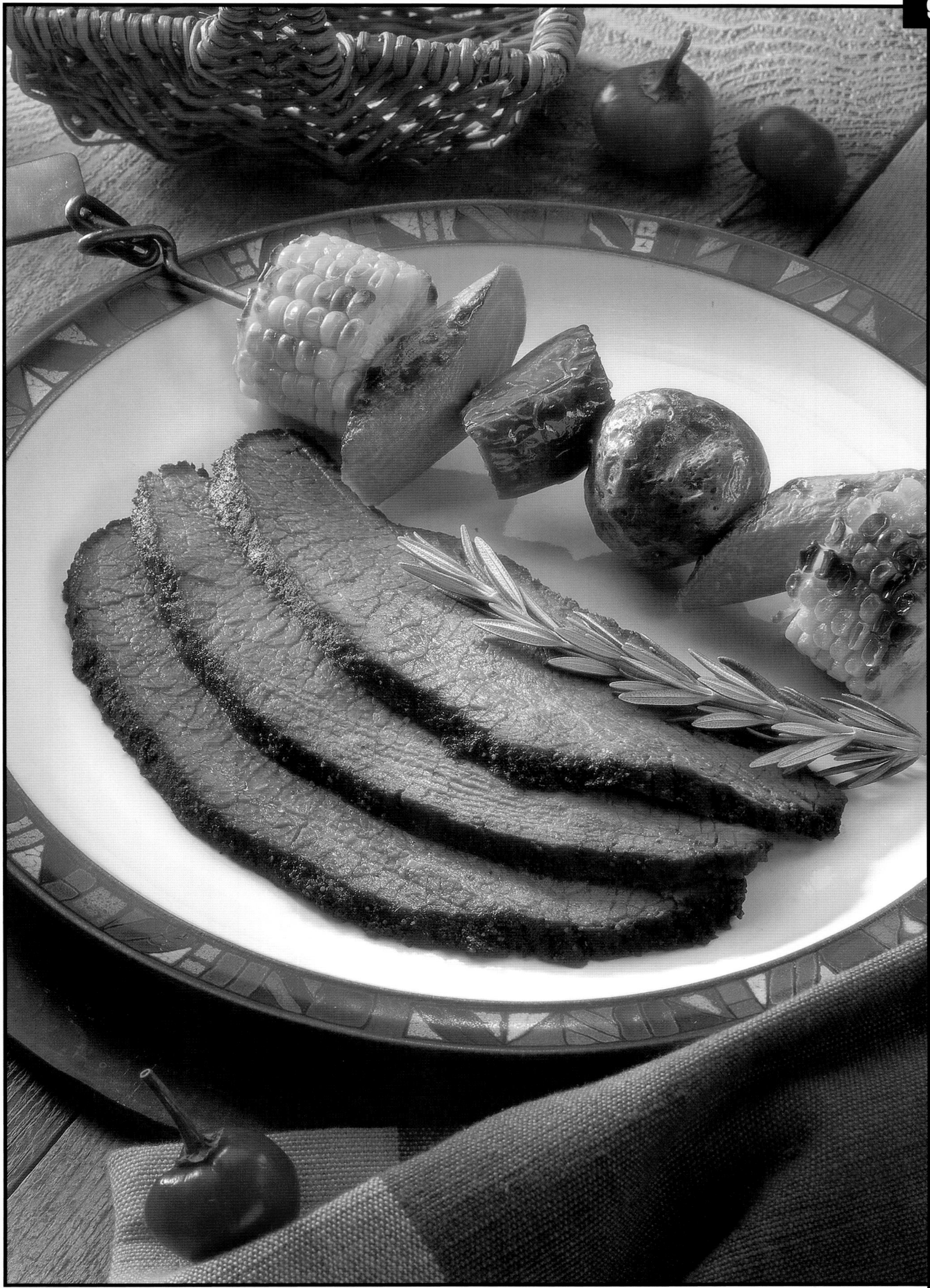

Fajitas

Fajita Marinade (recipe
   page 100)
1 pound flank steak
6 (10-inch) flour tortillas *or*
   12 (7-inch) flour tortillas
4 bell peppers, any color,
   halved
1 large bunch green onions
   salsa
1 cup coarsely chopped fresh
   cilantro
1 ripe avocado, thinly sliced
   (optional)
6 tablespoons reduced-fat
   sour cream (optional)

1. Combine Fajita Marinade and flank steak in resealable plastic food storage bag. Press air from bag and seal. Refrigerate 30 minutes or up to 24 hours.

2. Wrap tortillas in foil in stacks of 3; set aside.

3. Drain marinade from meat into small saucepan. Bring to a boil over high heat. Remove from heat.

4. Spray cold grid of grill with nonstick cooking spray. Adjust grid 4 to 6 inches above heat. Preheat grill to medium-high heat. Place meat in center of grid. Place bell peppers, skin side down, around meat; cover. Grill bell peppers 6 minutes or until skin is spotted brown. Turn over and continue grilling 6 to 8 minutes or until tender. Move to sides of grill to keep warm while meat finishes grilling.

5. Continue to grill meat, basting frequently with marinade, 8 minutes or until browned on bottom. Turn over; grill 8 to 10 minutes or until slightly pink in center.

6. During the last 4 minutes of grilling, brush green onions with remaining marinade and place on grid; grill 1 to 2 minutes or until browned in spots. Turn over; grill 1 to 2 minutes or until tender.

7. Place packets of tortillas on grid; heat about 5 minutes. Slice bell peppers and onions into thin 2-inch-long pieces. Thinly slice meat across the grain.

Continued on page 100

Fajitas

8. Place each tortilla on plate. Place meat, bell peppers, onions, salsa and cilantro in center of each tortilla. Fold bottom 3 inches of each tortilla up over filling; fold sides completely over filling to enclose. Serve with avocado and sour cream, if desired. *Makes 6 servings*

Cook's Tip: Bell peppers are naturally delicious and grilling them at medium-high heat gives them a wonderful new flavor without adding any fat.

Fajita Marinade

½ cup lime juice *or* ¼ cup lime juice and ¼ cup tequilla or beer
1 tablespoon dried oregano leaves
1 tablespoon minced garlic
2 teaspoons ground cumin
2 teaspoons black pepper

Combine lime juice, oregano, garlic, cumin and black pepper in 1-cup glass measure.

Mexican Flank Steak

½ cup A.1.® Steak Sauce

1 (4-ounce) can diced green
chiles

2 tablespoons lime juice*

1 (1½-pound) beef flank
steak, lightly scored

Lemon juice may be substituted.

Blend steak sauce, chiles and lime juice in blender or food processor until smooth. Place steak in glass dish; coat with ½ cup chile mixture and reserve remaining marinade. Cover; refrigerate 1 hour, turning occasionally.

Remove steak from marinade; discard marinade. Grill steak over medium heat for 6 minutes on each side or until done, brushing often with reserved marinade. Thinly slice steak to serve.

Makes 6 servings

Sizzle Marinated Steak

2 pounds boneless sirloin or
top round steak

½ cup *French's®*
Worcestershire Sauce

½ cup red wine vinegar

¼ cup *French's®* Napa Valley
Style Dijon Mustard

¼ cup olive oil

1 teaspoon minced garlic

1. Place steak into deep dish or resealable plastic food storage bag.

2. Combine remaining ingredients in small bowl. Pour over steak. Marinate in refrigerator 30 minutes. Broil or grill about 5 minutes per side or until desired doneness. Serve with Signature Steak Sauce. *Makes 8 servings*

Signature Steak Sauce: Combine ½ cup ketchup, ¼ cup *French's®* Worcestershire Sauce, 1 tablespoon *Frank's® RedHot®* Sauce and 1 teaspoon minced garlic in small bowl until well blended.

Marinate Time: 30 minutes
Prep Time: 5 minutes
Cook Time: 10 minutes

Honey Mustard Steaks with Grilled Onions

4 boneless beef top loin
    steaks, cut 1 inch thick
⅓ cup coarse-grain Dijon-style
    mustard
1 tablespoon plus
    1½ teaspoons honey
1 tablespoon chopped parsley
1 tablespoon cider vinegar
1 tablespoon water
¼ teaspoon hot pepper sauce
⅛ teaspoon coarse grind black
    pepper
1 large red onion, sliced
    ½ inch thick

Combine mustard, honey, parsley, vinegar, water, hot pepper sauce and pepper. Place beef steaks and onion on grid over medium coals; brush both with mustard mixture. Grill 9 to 12 minutes for rare (140°F) to medium (160°F), turning once and brushing with mustard mixture.

Makes 4 servings

Prep Time: 30 minutes

*Favorite recipe from **North Dakota Beef Commission***

GRILLING TIP

A spray bottle filled with water is useful to control wild sparks and very small flare-ups on a charcoal grill. Care should be taken not to overuse the water spray and inadvertently extinguish the coals. Do not use water to quench flare-ups on a gas grill. Simply close the hood and turn down the heat until the flames subside.

**Honey Mustard Steaks with
Grilled Onions**

Texas-Style Short Ribs

2 tablespoons chili powder

1 tablespoon LAWRY'S®
  Seasoned Salt

2 teaspoons LAWRY'S® Garlic
  Powder with Parsley

2 teaspoons ground cumin

1 teaspoon ground coriander

¼ teaspoon hot pepper sauce
  (optional)

5 pounds trimmed beef short
  ribs

1 bottle (12 ounces) chili
  sauce

1 cup finely chopped onion

1 cup dry red wine

½ cup water

½ cup beef broth

½ cup olive oil

In small bowl, combine chili powder, Seasoned Salt, Garlic Powder with Parsley, cumin, coriander and hot pepper sauce, if desired; mix well. Rub both sides of ribs with spice mixture. Place in large resealable plastic food storage bag; refrigerate 1 hour. In medium bowl, combine remaining ingredients. Remove ½ cup marinade for basting. Add additional marinade to ribs; seal bag. Marinate in refrigerator at least 1 hour. Remove ribs; discard used marinade. Grill ribs over low heat 45 to 60 minutes or until tender, turning once and basting often with additional ½ cup marinade. *Do not baste during last 5 minutes of cooking.* Discard any remaining marinade.

Makes 8 to 10 servings

Serving Suggestion: Serve with coleslaw and potato wedges.

Hint: Ribs may be baked in 375°F. oven 45 to 60 minutes or until tender, turning once and basting often with additional ½ cup marinade.

London City Broil with Onion Marmalade

2 pounds top round steak

½ cup balsamic vinegar or red wine vinegar

¼ cup olive oil

¼ cup *French's*® Bold n' Spicy Brown Mustard

2 cloves garlic, pressed

½ teaspoon salt

½ teaspoon black pepper

Onion Marmalade

¼ cup butter or margarine

4 medium red onions, thinly sliced

⅓ cup *French's*® Bold n' Spicy Brown Mustard

¼ cup balsamic vinegar or red wine vinegar

¾ teaspoon salt

1. Place steak in large resealable plastic food storage bag. Combine ½ cup vinegar, oil, ¼ cup mustard, garlic, ½ teaspoon salt and pepper in small bowl. Pour over steak; turn steak to coat evenly. Seal bag and marinate in refrigerator 1 hour.

2. To prepare Onion Marmalade, melt butter in large skillet over medium-high heat. Add onions; cook until very tender, stirring constantly. Add ⅓ cup mustard, ¼ cup vinegar and ¾ teaspoon salt. Cook over medium-low heat until mixture thickens, stirring often.

3. Place steak on grid, reserving marinade. Grill over high heat 15 minutes for medium rare or to desired doneness, turning and basting often with marinade. *Do not baste during last 5 minutes of cooking.* Slice steak diagonally into thin pieces and serve with Onion Marmalade.

Makes 8 servings

Prep Time: 20 minutes
Marinate Time: 1 hour
Cook Time: 30 minutes

Mexican Pepper Steak

1 cup WISH-BONE® Italian
   Dressing*
1 cup salsa
3 medium red, green and
   yellow bell peppers,
   quartered
1 small red onion, cut into
   thick rings
1½ pounds boneless sirloin or
   top loin steak, about
   2 inches thick

*Also terrific with WISH-BONE® Robusto
Italian or Just2Good! Italian Dressing.*

In large, shallow nonaluminum baking dish or plastic bag, combine all ingredients except steak. Add steak; turn to coat. Cover, or close bag, and marinate in refrigerator, turning occasionally, 3 to 24 hours.

Remove steak and vegetables, reserving marinade. Grill or broil steak and vegetables, turning steak and vegetables once, until steak is done. Meanwhile, in small saucepan, bring reserved marinade to a boil and continue boiling 1 minute. Serve with steak and vegetables.

Makes 6 servings

GRILLING TIP

Never use an outdoor grill indoors, even in a tent, cabin or garage. Indoor use can create a fire hazard as well as introduce the danger of carbon monoxide fumes.

Flank Steak Salad with Wine-Mustard Dressing

1 flank steak (about
    1½ pounds) *or* 3½ cups
    thinly sliced cooked roast
    beef
2 tablespoons white wine
    vinegar
1 tablespoon Dijon mustard
½ teaspoon LAWRY'S®
    Seasoned Pepper
6 tablespoons vegetable oil
1 pound small red potatoes,
    cooked and sliced
½ pound fresh green beans,
    steamed until tender-
    crisp
1 jar (6 ounces) marinated
    artichoke hearts, drained
¼ pound mushrooms, sliced
5 green onions including tops,
    sliced

Grill or broil steak 10 to 12 minutes or until desired doneness, turning halfway through grilling time. In small bowl, combine vinegar, mustard and Seasoned Pepper; mix well with wire whisk. Slowly add oil, beating constantly. Thinly slice steak on the diagonal across the grain. Cut each slice into 2-inch strips. Place in large salad bowl; add dressing and toss gently. Add remaining ingredients and toss. Serve at room temperature. *Makes 6 to 8 servings*

Serving Suggestion: Arrange bed of lettuce on individual plates and serve steak and vegetable mixture on top.

Hint: For extra flavor, marinate steak in Lawry's® Seasoned Marinade or Dijon & Honey Marinade with Lemon Juice.

Flank Steak Salad with
Wine-Mustard Dressing

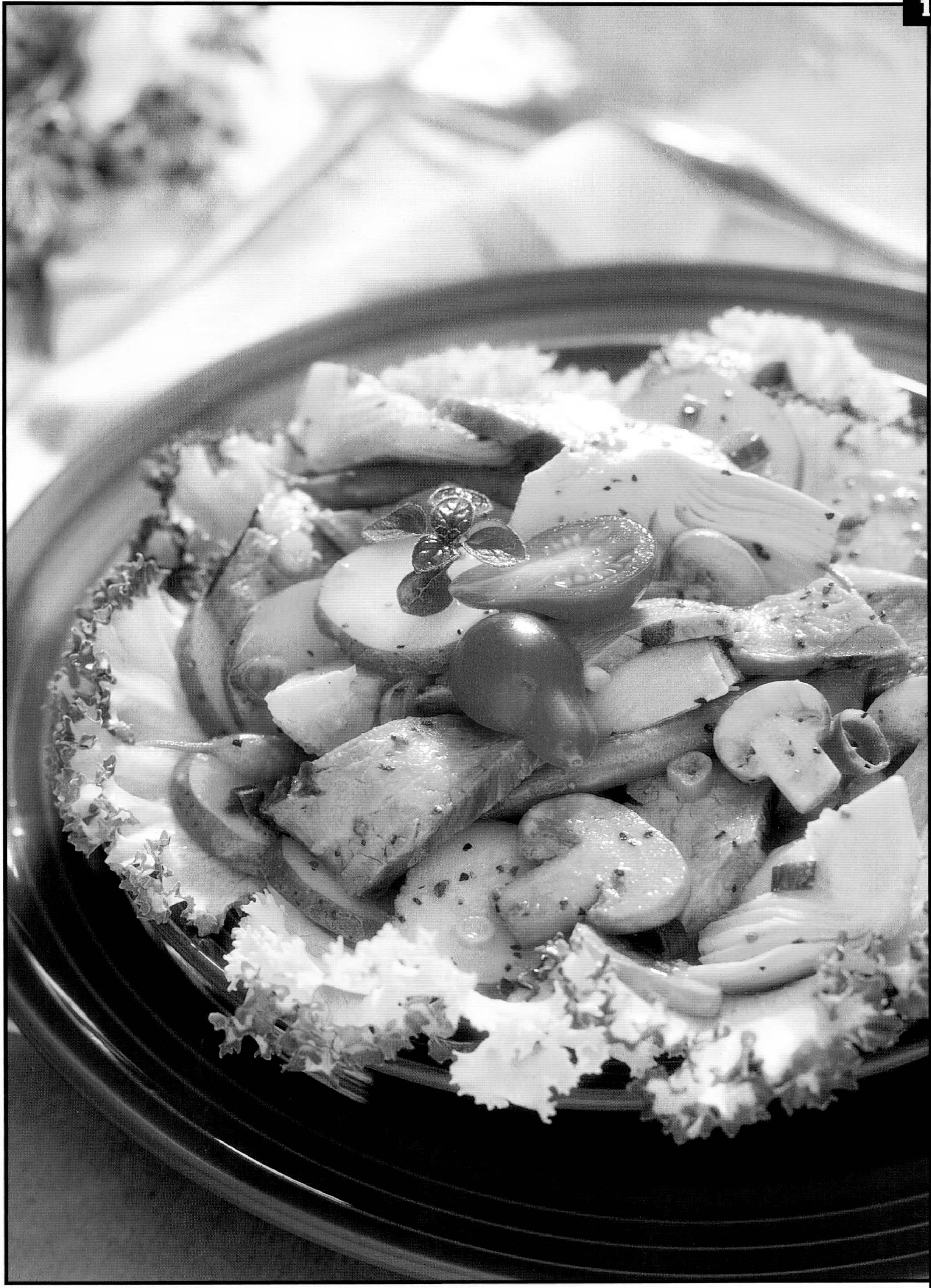

Thai Grilled Beef Salad

3 tablespoons Thai seasoning, divided
1 pound beef flank steak
2 red Thai chilies *or* 1 red jalapeño pepper,* seeded and sliced into thin slivers
2 tablespoons chopped fresh cilantro
2 tablespoons chopped fresh basil
1 tablespoon minced red onion
1 tablespoon fish sauce
1 tablespoon finely chopped lemon grass
Juice of 1 lime
1 clove garlic, minced
1 large carrot, grated
1 cucumber, chopped
4 cups assorted salad greens

Thai chilies and jalapeño peppers can sting and irritate the skin; wear rubber gloves when handling peppers and do not touch eyes. Wash hands after handling peppers.

1. Prepare grill for direct grilling.

2. Sprinkle 1 tablespoon Thai seasoning over beef; turn to coat. Cover and marinate 15 minutes. Grill beef 5 to 6 minutes per side or until desired doneness is reached. Cool 10 minutes.

3. Meanwhile, combine remaining 2 tablespoons Thai seasoning, chilies, cilantro, basil, onion, fish sauce, lemon grass, lime juice and garlic in medium bowl; mix well.

4. Thinly slice beef across grain. Add beef, carrot and cucumber to dressing; toss to coat. Arrange on bed of greens. *Makes 4 servings*

Thai Grilled Beef Salad

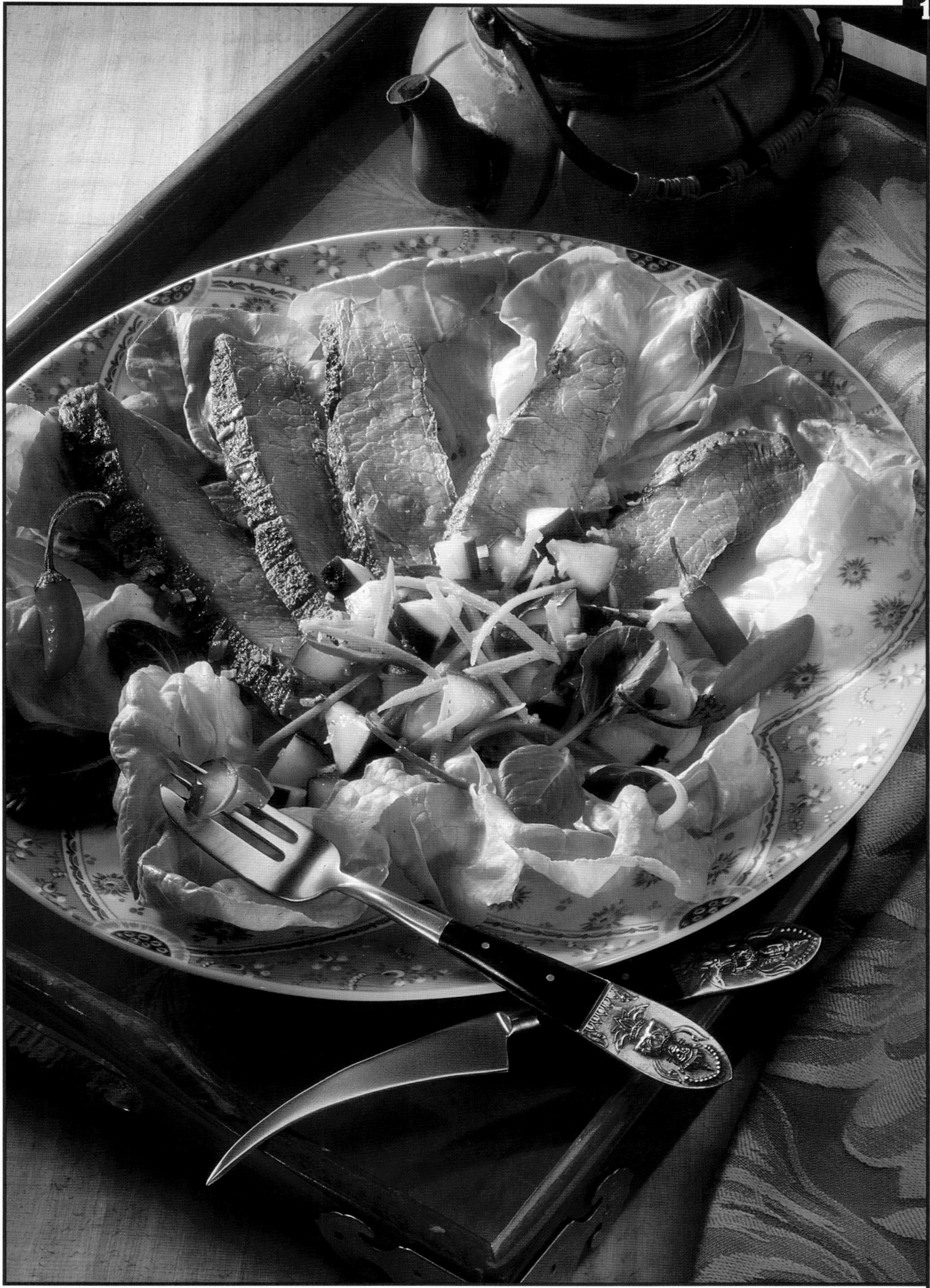

Vietnamese Loin Steaks with Black Bean Relish

1 stalk lemon grass, outer leaves removed and upper stalk trimmed

1 tablespoon sugar

1 tablespoon fish sauce

1 teaspoon minced garlic

½ to 1 teaspoon hot chili oil

2 boneless beef top loin steaks (8 ounces each), about 1 inch thick

1 can (about 8¾ ounces) whole baby corn (about 8 cobs), rinsed and drained

1 can (about 15 ounces) black beans, rinsed and drained

1 cup diced mango

½ green bell pepper, cut into strips

2 tablespoons chopped red onion

1 jalapeño pepper,* seeded and sliced (optional)

Juice of ½ lemon

½ teaspoon vegetable oil

½ teaspoon honey

⅛ teaspoon salt

*Jalapeños can sting and irritate the skin; wear rubber gloves when handling and do not touch eyes. Wash hands after handling.

1. Flatten lemon grass with meat mallet and mince. Combine with sugar, fish sauce, garlic and chili oil in baking dish. Cut each steak lengthwise into 2 strips. Place in dish with marinade, coating both sides. Cover; refrigerate 1 hour, turning once.

2. Halve corn cobs diagonally; combine with beans, mango, bell pepper, onion and jalapeño, if desired, in large bowl. Combine lemon juice, oil, honey and salt in small bowl; stir into bean mixture.

3. Grill steaks on covered grill over medium-hot coals 10 minutes for medium-rare or until desired doneness is reached, turning once. Serve with black bean relish. *Makes 4 servings*

Vietnamese Loin Steak with Black Bean Relish

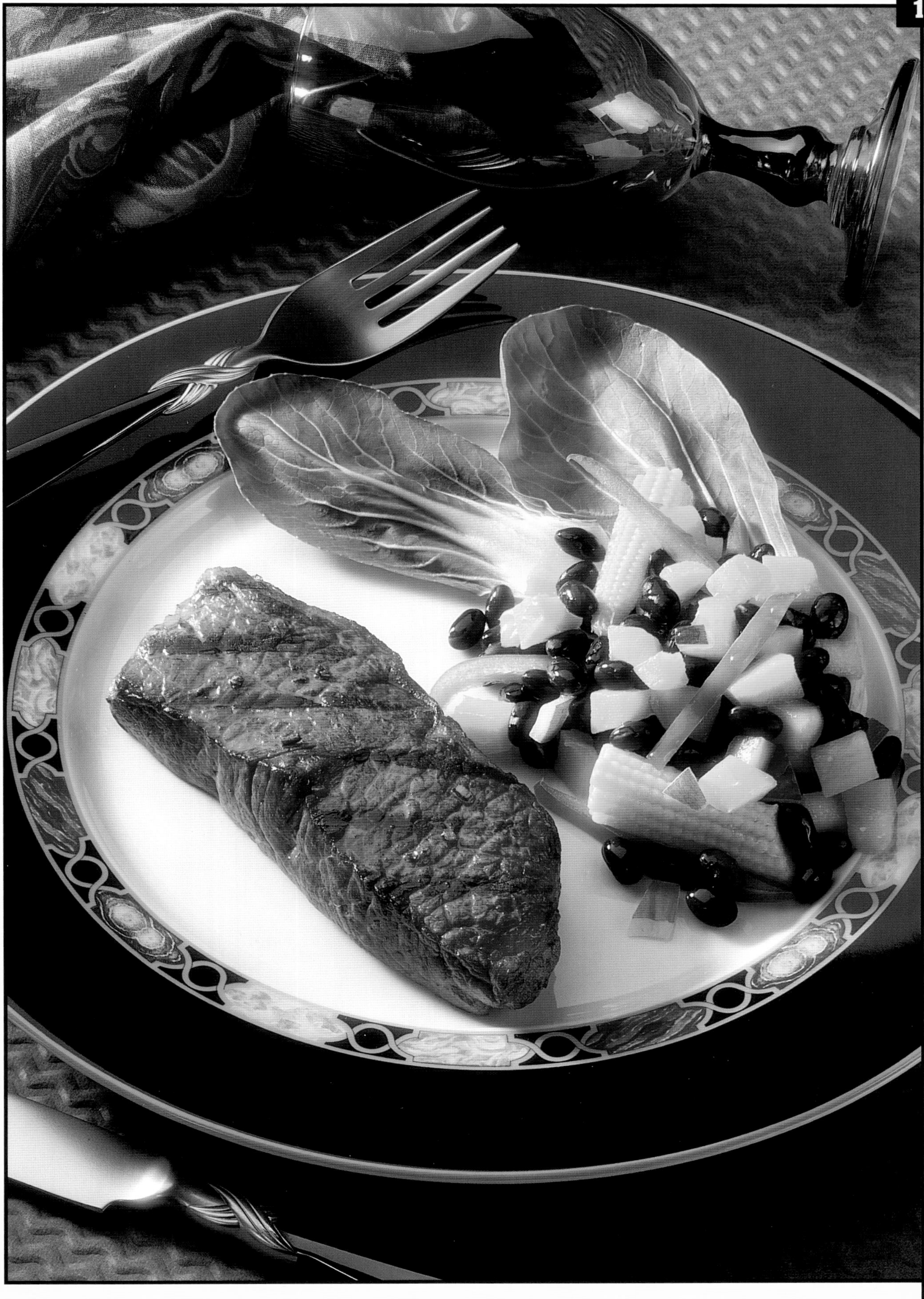

Hot and Spicy Flank Steak

¼ cup vegetable oil

2 tablespoons red wine vinegar

2 tablespoons sherry

2 tablespoons soy sauce

2 tablespoons brown sugar

2 teaspoons LAWRY'S® Seasoned Salt

1½ to 2 teaspoons red pepper flakes

1 teaspoon paprika

1 teaspoon chili powder

1 teaspoon Worcestershire sauce

½ teaspoon LAWRY'S® Garlic Powder with Parsley

1½ pounds flank steak, scored across grain on both sides

In large resealable plastic food storage bag, combine all ingredients except steak; mix well. Remove ¼ cup marinade for basting. Add steak; seal bag. Marinate in refrigerator at least 1 hour. Remove steak from marinade; discard used marinade. Grill or broil steak until desired doneness, about 10 to 12 minutes, turning once and basting often with additional ¼ cup marinade. *Do not baste during last 5 minutes of cooking.* Discard any remaining marinade. Thinly slice steak on the diagonal across the grain.

Makes 4 to 6 servings

Serving Suggestion: Serve with grilled halved potatoes brushed with oil and sprinkled with Lawry's® Garlic Salt.

GRILLING TIP

If you want to start cooking and the coals are too hot, use tongs to spread them apart. Or, remove a few of the coals and partially close the vents to slow the fire. Or, adjust the grilling rack so the food will be farther from the heat.

Grilled Italian Steak

¾ cup WISH-BONE® Italian
    Dressing*
2 tablespoons grated
    Parmesan cheese
2 teaspoons dried basil
    leaves, crushed
¼ teaspoon cracked black
    pepper
2 to 3-pound boneless sirloin
    or top round steak

*Also terrific with WISH-BONE® Robusto
Italian or Just2Good Italian Dressing.

In large, shallow nonaluminum baking dish or
plastic bag, combine all ingredients except steak.
Add steak; turn to coat. Cover or close bag and
marinate in refrigerator, turning occasionally, 3 to
24 hours.

Remove steak from marinade, reserving
marinade. Grill or broil steak, turning once, until
steak is done.

Meanwhile, in small saucepan, bring reserved
marinade to a boil and continue boiling 1 minute.
Pour over steak. *Makes 8 servings*

GRILLING TIP

*To start a charcoal fire, pile the briquettes in a loose pyramid,
soak with charcoal lighting fluid and allow the fluid to soak in
for a minute or two before lighting. Or, use an electric charcoal
starter by following the manufacturer's instructions.*

Skewered Beef Strips with Spicy Honey Glaze

1 pound beef top sirloin steak
⅓ cup soy sauce
2 tablespoons white vinegar
1 teaspoon ground ginger
⅛ teaspoon ground red
   pepper
⅓ cup honey

1. Slice beef across grain into ¼-inch-thick strips. Thread beef strips onto 12 wooden skewers and place in large glass baking dish. (Soak skewers in cold water 20 minutes before using to prevent them from burning.)

2. Heat broiler or prepare grill. Combine soy sauce, vinegar, ginger and ground red pepper; pour over skewers and marinate 10 minutes, turning once.

3. Drain marinade into small saucepan; stir in honey and brush mixture over beef. Bring remaining mixture to a boil; boil 2 minutes.

4. Broil or grill skewered beef 3 to 4 minutes. Serve remaining honey glaze as dipping sauce.

Makes 4 servings

Prep and Cook Time: 30 minutes

Skewered Beef Strips with
Spicy Honey Glaze

Texas Beef Brisket

1 tablespoon paprika
2 teaspoons salt
1 teaspoon black pepper
¼ teaspoon ground red pepper
20 ounces beef brisket, trimmed
Texas BBQ Sauce (recipe page 49)

Combine paprika, salt, black and red pepper in small bowl; mix well. Rub spice mixture onto brisket. Cover; marinate in refrigerator overnight.

Prepare Texas BBQ Sauce; set aside. Prepare grill for direct cooking.

Place brisket on grid. Grill, covered, over medium heat 2½ hours or until brisket offers a slight resistance when pierced; check occasionally and baste with sauce as needed. Boil any remaining sauce and serve on the side for dipping.

Makes 4 servings

Roscoe's Ribs

1 to 2 tablespoons LAWRY'S® Seasoned Salt
5 pounds beef or pork ribs
1 cup Worcestershire sauce
¾ cup apple cider vinegar
1 tablespoon olive oil
½ teaspoon minced garlic

Sprinkle Seasoned Salt over ribs. In large resealable plastic food storage bag, combine Worcestershire, vinegar, oil and garlic; mix well. Remove at least ½ cup marinade for basting. Add ribs; seal bag. Marinate in refrigerator at least 1 hour. Remove ribs; discard used marinade. Grill over low heat or bake ribs in 350°F oven 1 to 1¼ hours or until no longer pink, turning and basting often with additional ½ cup marinade.

Makes 4 to 6 servings

Hint: For extra flavor, marinate ribs overnight.

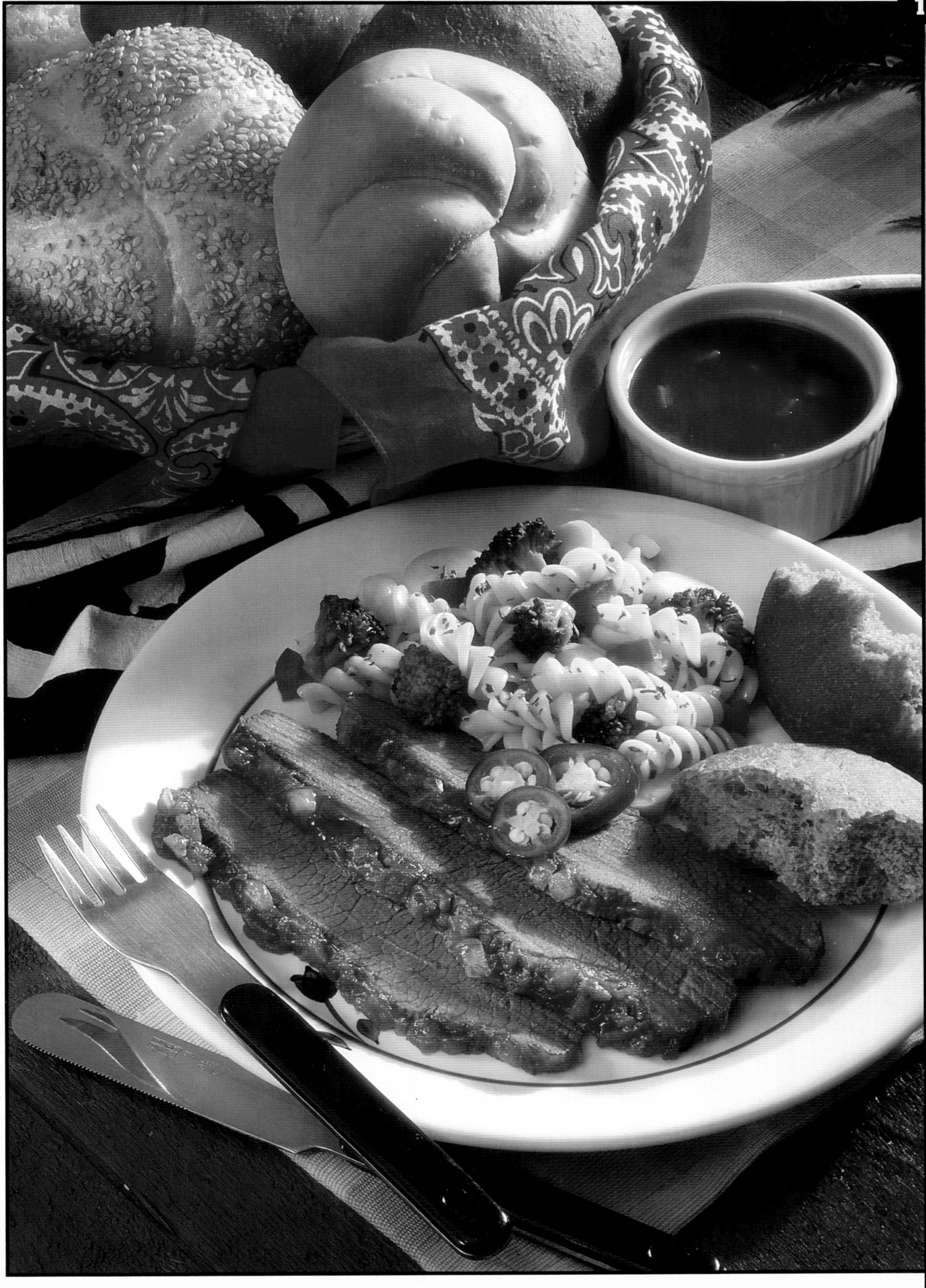

Guadalajara Beef

1 bottle (12 ounces) dark
    beer
¼ cup reduced-sodium soy
    sauce
3 cloves garlic, minced
1 teaspoon ground cumin
1 teaspoon ground chili
    powder
½ teaspoon ground red
    pepper
1 pound beef flank steak
6 medium red, yellow or
    green bell peppers,
    seeded and cut
    lengthwise into quarters
8 (6- to 8-inch) flour tortillas
   Sour cream
   Salsa

1. Combine beer, soy sauce, garlic, cumin, chili powder and red pepper in resealable plastic food storage bag; knead bag to combine. Add beef and seal. Refrigerate up to 24 hours, turning occasionally.

2. Remove beef from marinade; discard remaining marinade. Grill beef over hot coals 7 minutes per side or until desired doneness. Grill bell peppers 7 to 10 minutes or until tender, turning once.

3. Slice beef and serve with bell peppers, tortillas, sour cream and salsa.

Makes 4 servings

Make-Ahead Time: up to 1 day before serving
Final Prep Time: 20 minutes

Barbecue Beef

Guadalajara Beef

Pineapple Teriyaki Marinated Steak

1 (8-ounce) can sliced
    pineapple in its own juice,
    drained (reserve juice)
½ cup A.1.® THICK & HEARTY
    Steak Sauce
3 tablespoons teriyaki sauce
1 teaspoon ground ginger
1 (1½-pound) beef flank or
    top round steak, lightly
    scored

Combine reserved juice, steak sauce, teriyaki sauce and ginger in small bowl. Place steak in nonmetal dish; coat with steak sauce mixture. Cover; refrigerate 1 hour, turning occasionally.

Remove steak from marinade; reserve marinade. Grill steak over medium-high heat or broil 4 inches from heat source 15 to 20 minutes or to desired doneness, turning and basting with marinade occasionally. Grill or broil pineapple slices 1 minute, turning once.

Heat reserved marinade to a boil in small saucepan over high heat; simmer 5 minutes or until thickened. Slice steak across grain; serve with pineapple slices and warm sauce. Garnish as desired. *Makes 6 servings*

FOOD FACT

Teriyaki is the term for a Japanese preparation of grilled meat or poultry that has first been marinated in a mixture of soy sauce, sake (Japanese rice wine), sugar and seasonings. The soy sauce and sugar combine to give the cooked food an appealing brown glaze. Teriyaki also can refer to a sauce made with these ingredients. It is sold bottled in most supermarkets and can be used for marinating or for adding flavor to simple stir-fry preparations.

Pineapple Teriyaki Marinated Steak

PLAYING
CHICKEN

Try some of the best chicken recipes ever with this selection of new and delicious grilling ideas.

Carolina-Style Barbecue Chicken

2 pounds boneless skinless chicken breast halves or thighs

¾ cup packed light brown sugar, divided

¾ cup *French's® Classic Yellow®* Mustard

½ cup cider vinegar

¼ cup *Frank's® RedHot®* Cayenne Pepper Sauce

2 tablespoons vegetable oil

2 tablespoons *French's®* Worcestershire Sauce

½ teaspoon salt

¼ teaspoon black pepper

1. Place chicken in large resealable plastic food storage bag. Combine ½ cup brown sugar, mustard, vinegar, *Frank's RedHot* Sauce, oil, Worcestershire, salt and pepper in 4-cup measure; mix well. Pour 1 cup mustard mixture over chicken. Seal bag; marinate in refrigerator 1 hour or overnight.

2. Pour remaining mustard mixture into small saucepan. Stir in remaining ¼ cup sugar. Bring to a boil. Reduce heat; simmer 5 minutes or until sugar dissolves and mixture thickens slightly, stirring often. Reserve for serving sauce.

3. Place chicken on well-oiled grid, reserving marinade. Grill over high heat 10 to 15 minutes or until chicken is no longer pink in center, turning and basting once with marinade. *Do not baste during last 5 minutes of cooking.* Discard any remaining marinade. Serve chicken with reserved sauce. *Makes 8 servings*

Prep Time: 15 minutes
Marinate Time: 1 hour
Cook Time: 10 minutes

Carolina-Style Barbecue Chicken and Herbed Corn on the Cob (page 343)

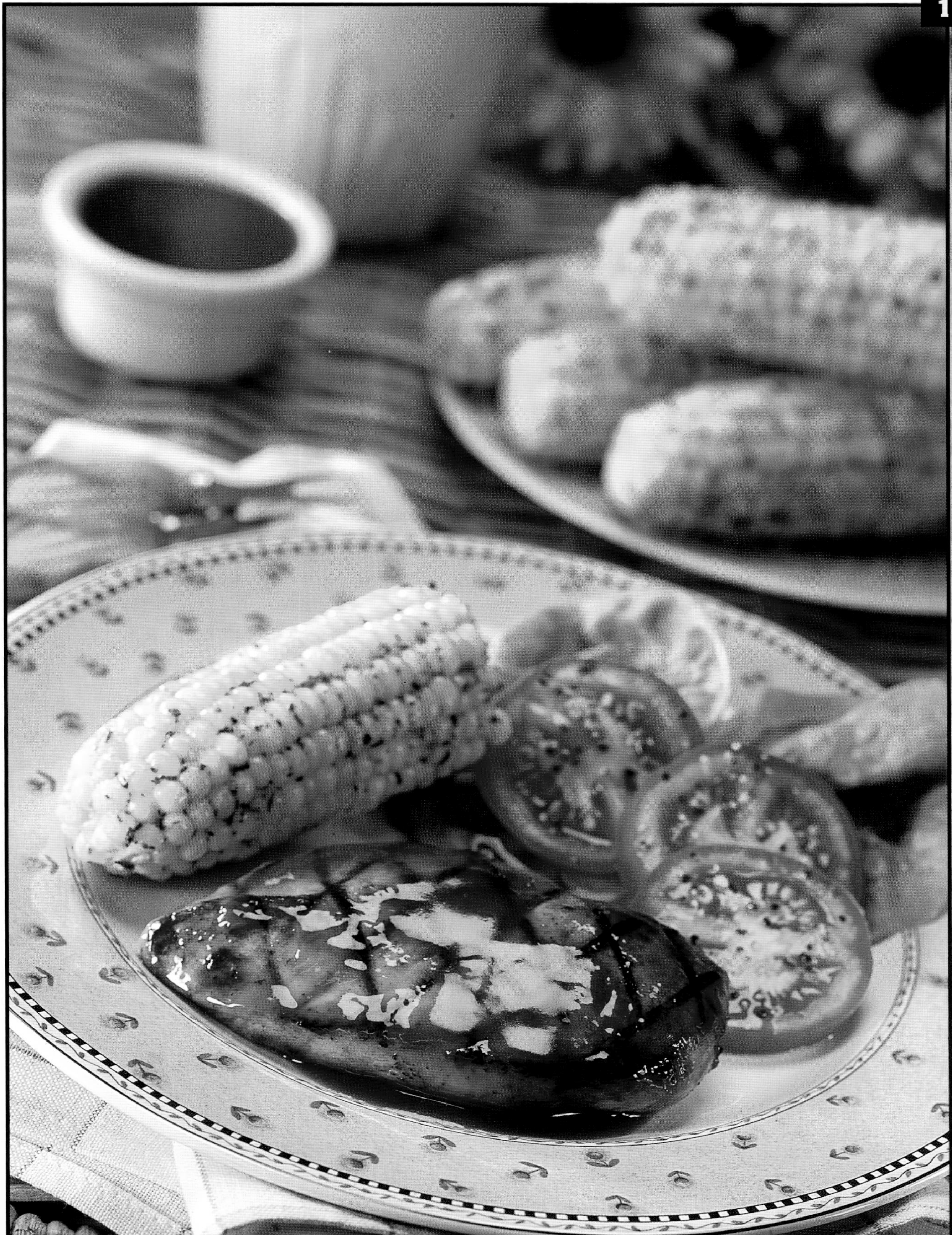

Summer Raspberry Chicken

4 boneless, skinless chicken
  breast halves (about
  1 pound), pounded to
  ¼-inch thickness
¾ cup LAWRY'S® Dijon &
  Honey Marinade with
  Lemon Juice, divided
1 cup fresh or frozen
  raspberries
½ cup walnut pieces
  Fresh raspberries (optional
  garnish)

Grill or broil chicken 10 to 15 minutes or until no longer pink in center and juices run clear when cut, turning once and basting often with ½ cup Dijon & Honey Marinade. *Do not baste during last 5 minutes of cooking.* Discard any remaining marinade. Cut chicken into strips. In food processor or blender, process raspberries and additional ¼ cup Dijon & Honey Marinade 10 seconds. Drizzle raspberry sauce over chicken; sprinkle with walnuts.   *Makes 4 servings*

Serving Suggestion: Serve chicken on field greens or angel hair pasta. Garnish with fresh raspberries, if desired.

Grilled Lime Chicken

4 boneless skinless chicken
  breast halves
  CRISCO® No-Stick Cooking
  Spray
1 teaspoon grated lime peel
2 tablespoons fresh lime juice
1 tablespoon finely minced
  fresh gingerroot
1 tablespoon chopped fresh
  cilantro
1 teaspoon honey
⅛ teaspoon cayenne pepper
¼ teaspoon salt

1. Wash and trim chicken breasts. Place between 2 sheets of waxed paper and flatten. Spray both sides of chicken with cooking spray and place in shallow pan.

2. Mix together lime peel and juice, gingerroot, cilantro, honey, pepper and salt. Coat both sides of chicken breasts with lime mixture. Cover with plastic wrap and chill 2 to 6 hours.

3. Remove chicken from pan. Spray both sides again with cooking spray.

4. Grill over hot grill, turning just once, 10 to 12 minutes, or until browned and done through. (Or broil under a preheated broiler, close to the heat source, turning just once.)

Makes 4 servings

Summer Raspberry Chicken

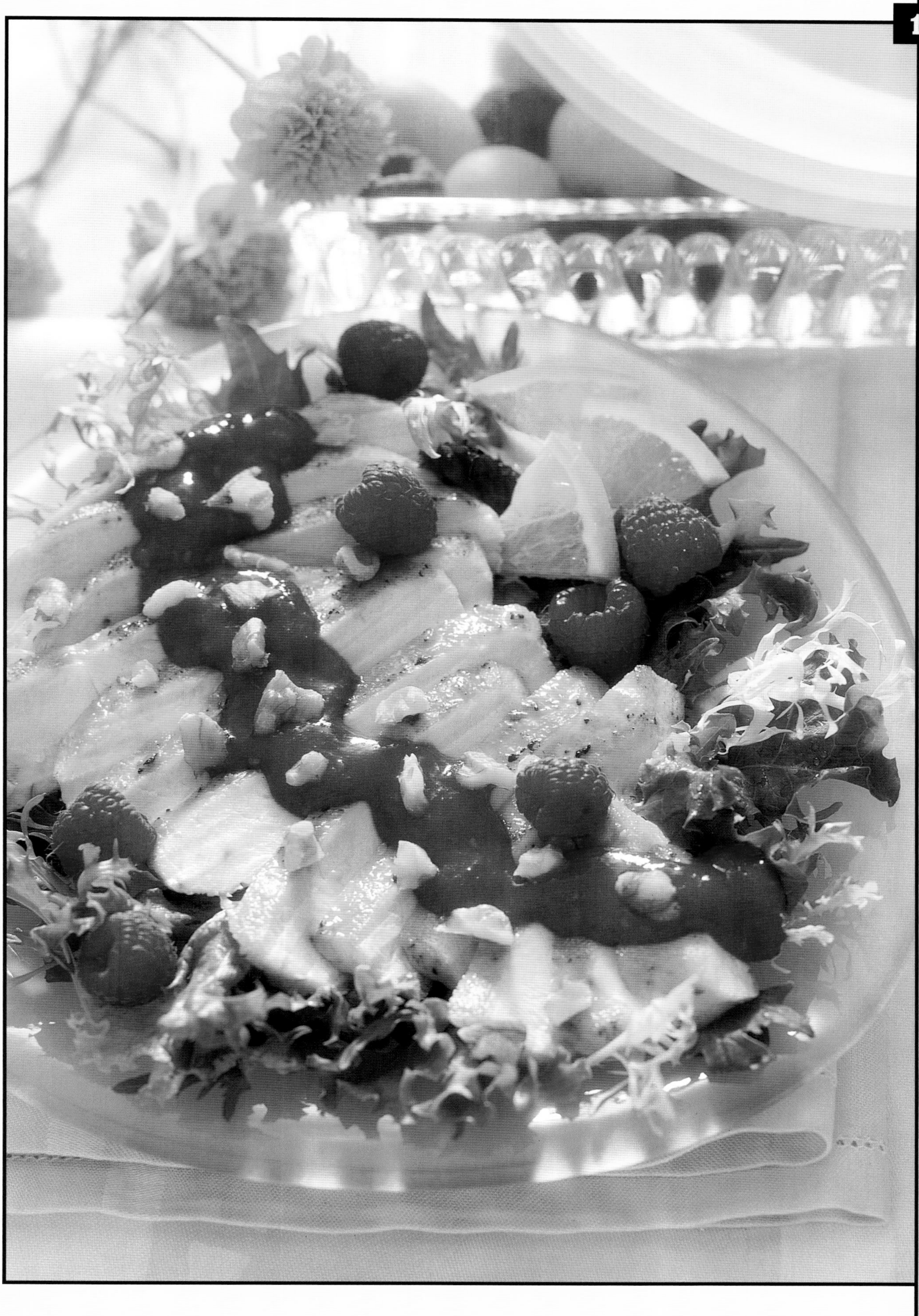

Honey 'n' Spice Chicken Kabobs

1 medium green bell pepper,
   cut into 1-inch squares
2 boneless skinless chicken
   breasts, halved (about
   1¼ pounds)
1 can (8 ounces) pineapple
   chunks, drained
½ cup HEINZ® 57 Sauce®
¼ cup honey

In small saucepan, blanch green pepper in boiling water 1 minute; drain. Cut each chicken breast half into 4 pieces. Alternately thread chicken, green pepper and pineapple onto skewers. In small bowl, combine 57 Sauce and honey. Brush kabobs with 57 Sauce mixture. Grill or broil kabobs, about 6 inches from heat, 12 to 14 minutes or until chicken is tender and no longer pink in center, turning and brushing with 57 Sauce mixture once. *Makes 4 servings*

Jamaican Grilled Chicken

1 whole chicken (4 pounds),
   cut into pieces *or* 6 whole
   chicken legs
1 cup coarsely chopped fresh
   cilantro leaves and stems
½ cup *Frank's® RedHot®*
   Cayenne Pepper Sauce
⅓ cup vegetable oil
6 cloves garlic, coarsely
   chopped
¼ cup fresh lime juice (juice of
   2 limes)
1 teaspoon grated lime peel
1 teaspoon ground turmeric
1 teaspoon ground allspice

1. Loosen and pull back skin from chicken pieces. Do not remove skin. Place chicken pieces in large resealable plastic food storage bag or large glass bowl.

2. Place remaining ingredients in blender or food processor. Cover; process until smooth. Reserve ⅓ cup marinade. Pour remaining marinade over chicken pieces, turning to coat evenly. Seal bag or cover bowl; refrigerate 1 hour.

3. Prepare grill. Reposition skin on chicken pieces. Place chicken on oiled grid. Grill, over medium to medium-low coals, 45 minutes or until chicken is no longer pink near bone and juices run clear, turning and basting often with reserved marinade. *Makes 6 servings*

Prep Time: 15 minutes
Marinate Time: 1 hour
Cook Time: 45 minutes

Lemon Pepper Chicken

⅓ cup lemon juice

¼ cup finely chopped onion

¼ cup olive oil

1 tablespoon brown sugar

1 tablespoon cracked black pepper

3 cloves garlic, minced

2 teaspoons grated lemon peel

¾ teaspoon salt

4 chicken quarters (about 2½ pounds)

Combine lemon juice, onion, oil, sugar, pepper, garlic, lemon peel and salt in small bowl; reserve 2 tablespoons marinade. Combine remaining marinade and chicken in large resealable plastic food storage bag. Seal bag; knead to coat. Refrigerate at least 4 hours or overnight.

Remove chicken from marinade; discard marinade. Arrange chicken on microwavable plate; cover with waxed paper. Microwave at HIGH (100%) 5 minutes. Turn and rearrange chicken. Cover and microwave at HIGH (100%) 5 minutes.

Transfer chicken to grill. Grill covered over medium-hot coals 15 to 20 minutes or until juices run clear, turning several times and basting often with reserved marinade. *Makes 4 servings*

Crunchy Apple Salsa with Grilled Chicken

2 cups Washington Gala apples, halved, cored and chopped

¾ cup (1 large) Anaheim chili pepper, seeded and chopped

½ cup chopped onion

¼ cup lime juice

Salt and black pepper to taste

Grilled Chicken (recipe follows)

Combine all ingredients except chicken and mix well; set aside to allow flavors to blend about 45 minutes. Prepare Grilled Chicken. Serve salsa over or alongside Grilled Chicken.

Makes 3 cups salsa

Grilled Chicken: Marinate 2 whole boneless, skinless chicken breasts in a mixture of ¼ cup dry white wine, ¼ cup apple juice, ½ teaspoon grated lime peel, ½ teaspoon salt and dash pepper for 20 to 30 minutes. Drain and grill over medium-hot coals, turning once, until chicken is no longer pink in center.

*Favorite recipe from **Washington Apple Commission***

Asian Grilled Chicken Salad

1 pound boneless skinless chicken breast halves, cut in half lengthwise

⅓ cup *French's®* Napa Valley Style Dijon Mustard

3 tablespoons soy sauce

2 tablespoons Oriental sesame oil

½ cup orange juice or apricot nectar

2 tablespoons rice wine vinegar

2 teaspoons grated peeled fresh ginger

¾ pound asparagus, washed and trimmed

4 green onions, trimmed

1 yellow or red bell pepper, cut into thin strips

2 plums, cut into thin wedges

1 bunch washed and torn watercress *or* 3 cups mixed torn greens

½ cup chopped cashews

1. Place chicken in large resealable plastic food storage bag. Combine mustard, soy sauce and sesame oil in 1-cup measure. Pour ⅓ cup mustard mixture over chicken. Seal bag; marinate in refrigerator 20 minutes. Combine remaining mustard mixture with orange juice, vinegar and ginger; mix well. Reserve for dressing.

2. Place chicken, asparagus and onions on oiled grid. Grill 8 minutes over medium-high heat or until chicken is no longer pink in center and asparagus and onions are tender, turning often. Cool slightly. Cut chicken and vegetables into bite-sized pieces.

3. Place chicken and grilled vegetables in large bowl. Add yellow bell pepper and plums. Pour reserved dressing over all; toss well to coat evenly. Arrange watercress on serving platter; mound salad over watercress. Sprinkle with cashews.

Makes 4 servings

Prep Time: 30 minutes
Marinate Time: 20 minutes
Cook Time: 8 minutes

Jamaican Rum Chicken

½ cup dark rum
2 tablespoons lime juice or
    lemon juice
2 tablespoons soy sauce
2 tablespoons brown sugar
4 large cloves garlic, minced
1 to 2 jalapeño peppers,*
    seeded and minced
1 tablespoon minced fresh
    ginger
1 teaspoon dried thyme
    leaves, crushed
½ teaspoon black pepper
6 boneless skinless chicken
    breast halves

*Jalapeño peppers can sting and irritate the
skin; wear rubber gloves when handling peppers
and do not touch eyes. Wash hands after
handling.

1. To prepare marinade, combine rum, lime juice, soy sauce, sugar, garlic, peppers, ginger, thyme and black pepper in 2-quart glass measuring cup.

2. Rinse chicken and pat dry with paper towels. Place chicken in resealable plastic food storage bag. Pour marinade over chicken. Press air out of bag and seal tightly. Turn bag over to completely coat chicken with marinade. Refrigerate 4 hours or overnight, turning bag once or twice.

3. Prepare barbecue grill for direct grilling by spreading hot coals in single layer that extends 1 to 2 inches beyond area of food.

4. Drain chicken; reserve marinade. Place chicken on grid. Grill chicken, on uncovered grill, over medium-hot coals 6 minutes per side or until chicken is no longer pink in center.

5. Meanwhile, bring remaining marinade to a boil in small saucepan over medium-high heat. Boil 5 minutes or until marinade is reduced by about half.

6. To serve, drizzle marinade over chicken. Garnish as desired. *Makes 6 servings*

Oriental Grilled Chicken

½ cup soy sauce
¼ cup prepared mustard
2 tablespoons honey
2 tablespoons lemon juice
½ teaspoon ground ginger
4 chicken quarters
    Hot cooked rice pilaf
    (optional)

Combine soy sauce, mustard, honey, lemon juice and ginger in large glass bowl. Add chicken, turning to coat. Cover; marinate in refrigerator 1 hour. Remove chicken. Place marinade in small saucepan. Bring to a boil over medium-high heat; keep warm. Place chicken on prepared grill, skin sides up, about 8 inches from heat. Grill, turning occasionally, 45 minutes. Grill, basting occasionally with marinade, 15 minutes more or until fork can be inserted into chicken with ease and juices run clear, not pink. Serve with hot rice.

Makes 4 servings

Favorite recipe from **National Chicken Council**

Grilled Rosemary Chicken

2 tablespoons lemon juice
2 tablespoons olive oil
2 cloves garlic, minced
2 tablespoons minced fresh
    rosemary
¼ teaspoon salt
4 boneless skinless chicken
    breasts

1. Whisk together lemon juice, oil, garlic, rosemary and salt in small bowl. Pour into shallow glass dish. Add chicken, turning to coat both sides with lemon juice mixture. Cover and marinate in refrigerator 15 minutes, turning chicken once.

2. Grill chicken over medium-hot coals 5 to 6 minutes per side or until chicken is no longer pink in center. *Makes 4 servings*

Cook's Notes: For added flavor, moisten a few sprigs of fresh rosemary and toss on the hot coals just before grilling. Store rosemary in the refrigerator for up to five days. Wrap sprigs in a barely damp paper towel and place in a sealed plastic bag.

Prep and Cook Time: 30 minutes

Italian Marinated Chicken

1 bottle (8 ounces)
    LAWRY'S® Herb & Garlic
    Marinade with Lemon
    Juice
2 tablespoons finely chopped
    onion
2 tablespoons lemon juice
¾ teaspoon LAWRY'S®
    Seasoned Pepper
6 boneless, skinless chicken
    breast halves (about
    1½ pounds)

In large resealable plastic food storage bag, combine all ingredients except chicken; mix well. Add chicken to marinade; seal bag. Marinate in refrigerator at least 1 hour, turning occasionally. Remove chicken; discard used marinade. Grill or broil chicken 10 to 15 minutes or until no longer pink in center and juices run clear when cut. *Makes 6 to 8 servings*

Serving Suggestion: Perfect served with any pasta or crisp green salad.

Hint: Chill leftover chicken and slice for use in salads or sandwiches.

Grilled Rosemary Chicken

Playing Chicken

134

Cajun Chicken Nuggets & Grilled Fruit

½ cup beer or non-alcoholic
    malt beverage
¼ cup *French's®* Bold n' Spicy
    Brown Mustard
2 tablespoons oil
1 pound boneless skinless
    chicken breasts, cut into
    1½-inch pieces
¾ cup plain dry bread crumbs
1 tablespoon plus 1 teaspoon
    prepared Cajun seasoning
    blend
1 pineapple, peeled, cored
    and cut into ½-inch-thick
    rings
2 peaches, cut into
    1-inch-thick wedges

1. Combine beer, mustard and oil in large bowl. Add chicken pieces; toss to coat evenly. Cover and marinate in refrigerator 20 minutes.

2. Preheat oven to 350°F. Coat baking sheet with nonstick cooking spray. Combine bread crumbs and Cajun seasoning in pie plate. Remove chicken from marinade; roll in bread crumb mixture to coat. Discard any remaining marinade. Place on prepared baking sheet. Bake 20 minutes or until chicken is lightly golden brown and no longer pink in center, turning once. Remove to serving plate.

3. Coat fruit with nonstick cooking spray. Place fruit on oiled grid. Grill 5 to 8 minutes over medium heat until just tender. Serve with chicken nuggets and Peachy Mustard Glaze (recipe follows). *Makes 4 servings*

Prep Time: 20 minutes
Marinate Time: 20 minutes
Cook Time: 20 minutes

Peachy Mustard Glaze

¾ cup peach preserves
¼ cup *French's®* Classic Yellow® Mustard
2 tablespoons orange juice

Microwave preserves in small bowl on HIGH (100%) 2 minutes or until melted, stirring once. Stir in mustard and juice. *Makes 1 cup glaze*

Prep Time: 5 minutes

Cajun Chicken Nuggets & Grilled Fruit

Chicken Tikka (Tandoori-Style Grilled Chicken)

2 chickens (3 pounds each),
    cut up
1 pint nonfat yogurt
½ cup *Frank's® RedHot®*
    Cayenne Pepper Sauce
1 tablespoon grated peeled
    fresh ginger
3 cloves garlic, minced
1 tablespoon paprika
1 tablespoon cumin seeds,
    crushed *or* 1½ teaspoons
    ground cumin
2 teaspoons salt
1 teaspoon ground coriander

Remove skin and visible fat from chicken pieces. Rinse with cold water and pat dry. Randomly poke chicken all over with tip of sharp knife. Place chicken in resealable plastic food storage bags or large glass bowl. Combine yogurt, *Frank's RedHot* Sauce, ginger, garlic, paprika, cumin, salt and coriander in small bowl; mix well. Pour over chicken pieces, turning pieces to coat evenly. Seal bags or cover bowl and marinate in refrigerator 1 hour or overnight.

Place chicken on oiled grid, reserving marinade. Grill over medium coals 45 minutes or until chicken is no longer pink near bone and juices run clear, turning and basting often with marinade. (Do not baste during last 10 minutes of cooking.) Discard any remaining marinade. Serve warm.

Makes 6 to 8 servings

Prep Time: 15 minutes
Marinate Time: 1 hour
Cook Time: 45 minutes

Chicken Tikka
(Tandoori-Style Grilled Chicken)

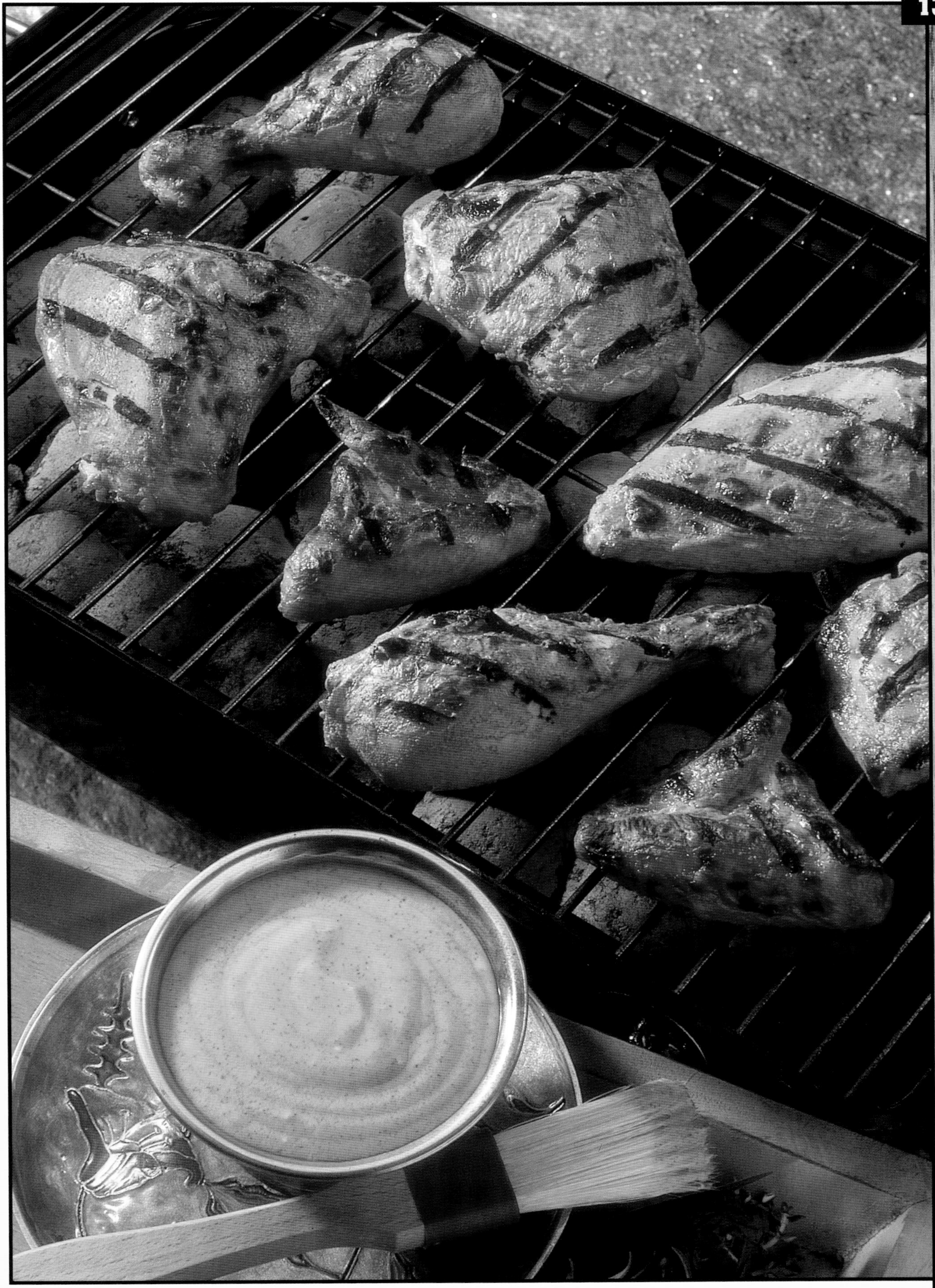

Lime Salsa Chicken

4 boneless, skinless chicken
    breast halves
¼ cup lime juice
2 tablespoons sherry
2 tablespoons light olive oil
½ teaspoon dried oregano
    leaves
½ teaspoon garlic salt
    Salsa (recipe follows)
    Avocado slices
    Tortilla chips

In a large non-metallic bowl or resealable plastic bag, make marinade by mixing lime juice, sherry, oil, oregano and garlic salt. Remove 3 tablespoons marinade; set aside. Add chicken to remaining marinade, turn to coat. Marinate in refrigerator 1 hour.

Remove chicken from marinade; reserve marinade. In small saucepan, place reserved marinade; heat to boling and boil 1 minute. Place chicken on grill with rack positioned about 8 inches from heat source. Brush marinade over chicken. Grill turning and basting frequently with marinade, about 16 to 20 minutes or until chicken is fork tender. Arrange chicken on platter. Serve with Salsa. Garnish with avocado slices and tortilla chips. *Makes 4 servings*

Favorite recipe from **Delmarva Poultry Industry, Inc.**

Salsa

1 tomato, peeled, seeded and chopped
1 green onion, sliced
¼ cup sliced black olives
3 tablespoons reserved marinade
1 tablespoon seeded, chopped jalapeño pepper
1 tablespoon chopped fresh cilantro
1 tablespoon chopped fresh mint
1 tablespoon slivered almonds
¼ teaspoon salt
¼ teaspoon black pepper

In a bowl, make salsa by mixing together tomato, green onion, olives, reserved marinade, jalapeño pepper, cilantro, mint, almonds, salt and pepper. Chill salsa. *Makes 1 cup*

Mesquite Grilled Chicken in Cornbread Bundles

¾ cup LAWRY'S® Mesquite
　　Marinade with Lime Juice
4 boneless, skinless chicken
　　breast halves (about
　　1 pound)
½ cup chopped red bell
　　pepper
½ cup toasted pine nuts, finely
　　chopped
¼ cup toasted walnuts, finely
　　chopped (optional)
1 can (7 ounces) diced green
　　chiles
1 tablespoon lime juice
½ teaspoon LAWRY'S®
　　Seasoned Salt
½ teaspoon LAWRY'S® Garlic
　　Powder with Parsley
1 package (11 ounces)
　　refrigerated cornstick
　　dough or refrigerated
　　breadstick dough
1 egg white, beaten

In large resealable plastic food storage bag, combine Mesquite Marinade and chicken; seal bag. Marinate in refrigerator at least 30 minutes. Remove chicken; discard used marinade. Grill or broil chicken 10 to 15 minutes until no longer pink in center and juices run clear when cut, turning halfway through grilling time. In small bowl, combine bell pepper, nuts, chiles, lime juice, Seasoned Salt and Garlic Powder with Parsley; mix well. Roll dough out into four equal squares. On each square, place 1 chicken breast and ¼ nut mixture. Fold dough to enclose; pinch edges to seal. Brush tops with egg white. Bake in 350°F oven about 3 to 5 minutes until golden and puffy.

Makes 4 servings

Serving Suggestion: Serve with cucumber slices and french-fried potaotes.

Zesty Caribbean Chicken Breasts

¼ cup CRISCO® Oil*
1 teaspoon grated lemon peel
¼ cup lemon juice
1 tablespoon paprika
1 tablespoon honey
1 teaspoon garlic salt
1 teaspoon ginger
1 teaspoon dried oregano
　　leaves
¼ teaspoon hot pepper sauce
6 boneless, skinless chicken
　　breast halves (about
　　1½ pounds)

Use your favorite Crisco Oil product.

1. Combine oil, lemon peel, lemon juice, paprika, honey, garlic salt, ginger, oregano and hot pepper sauce in shallow baking dish. Stir well. Add chicken. Turn to coat. Refrigerate 30 minutes or up to 4 hours, turning occasionally.

2. Heat broiler or prepare grill.

3. Remove chicken from lemon juice mixture. Broil or grill 3 to 5 minutes per side or until chicken is no longer pink in center.

Makes 6 servings

Black Bean Garnachas

1 can (14½ ounces) DEL
    MONTE® Diced
    Tomatoes with Garlic &
    Onion
1 can (15 ounces) black or
    pinto beans, drained
2 cloves garlic, minced
1 to 2 teaspoons minced
    jalapeño peppers
    (optional)
½ teaspoon ground cumin
1 cup cubed grilled chicken
4 flour tortillas
½ cup (2 ounces) shredded
    sharp Cheddar cheese

1. Combine undrained tomatoes, beans, garlic, jalapeño peppers and cumin in large skillet. Cook over medium-high heat 5 to 7 minutes or until thickened, stirring occasionally. Stir in chicken. Season with salt and pepper, if desired.

2. Arrange tortillas in single layer on grill over medium coals. Spread about ¾ cup chicken mixture over each tortilla. Top with cheese.

3. Cook about 3 minutes or until bottoms of tortillas are browned and cheese is melted. Top with shredded lettuce, diced avocado and sliced jalapeño peppers, if desired.   *Makes 4 servings*

Variation: Prepare chicken mixture as directed above. Place a tortilla in a dry skillet over medium heat. Spread with about ¾ cup chicken mixture; top with 2 tablespoons cheese. Cover and cook about 3 minutes or until bottom of tortilla is browned and cheese is melted. Repeat with remaining tortillas.

Prep Time: 5 minutes
Cook Time: 10 minutes

Black Bean Garnachas

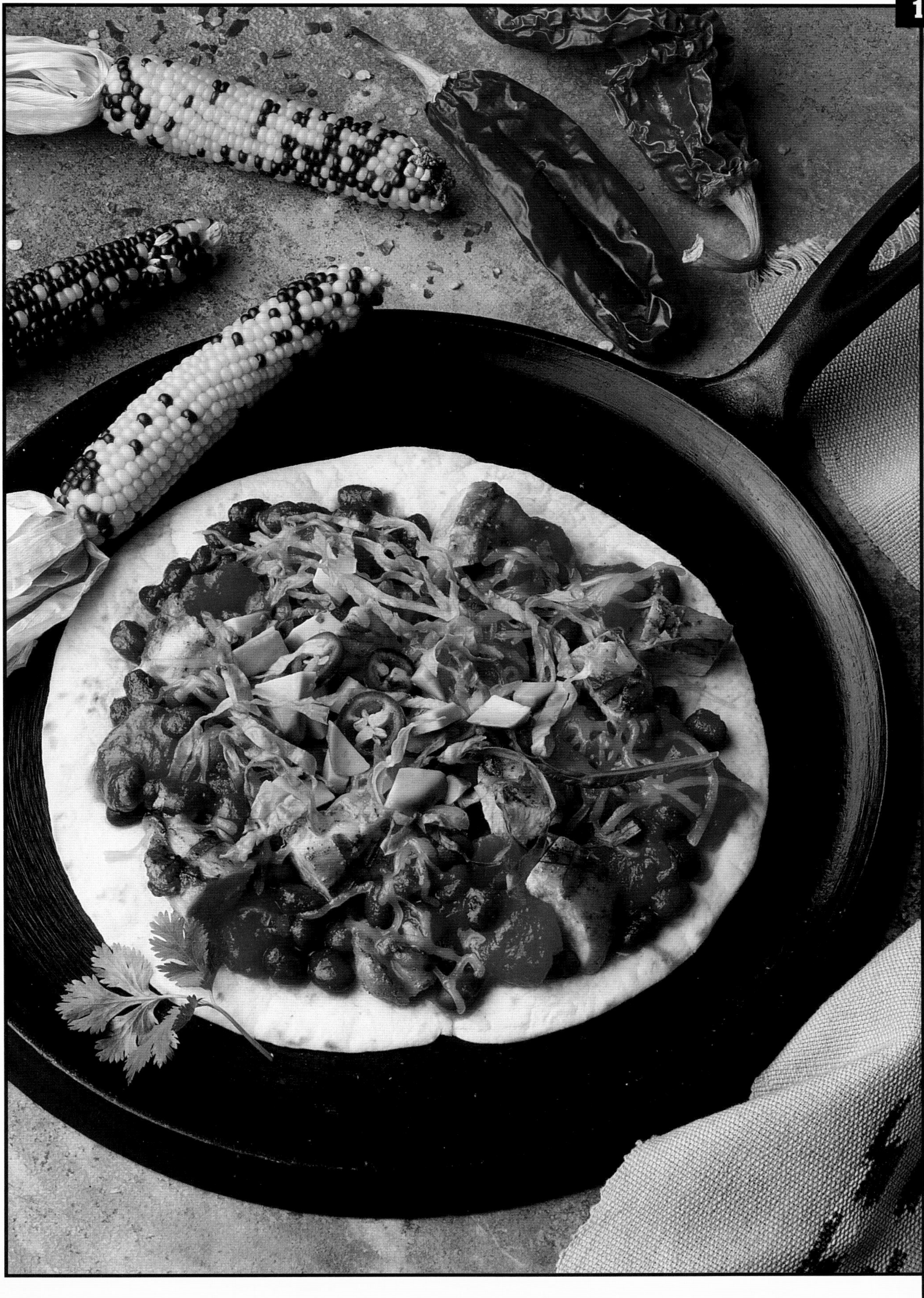

Grilled Garlic Chicken

1 envelope LIPTON® RECIPE
SECRETS® Savory Herb
with Garlic Soup Mix
3 tablespoons BERTOLLI®
Olive Oil
4 boneless, skinless chicken
breast halves (about
1¼ pounds)

1. In medium bowl, combine soup mix with oil.

2. Add chicken; toss to coat.

3. Grill or broil until chicken is thoroughly cooked.　　*Makes 4 servings*

Chicken Teriyaki

8 large chicken drumsticks
(about 2 pounds)
⅓ cup teriyaki sauce
2 tablespoons brandy or
apple juice
1 green onion, minced
1 tablespoon vegetable oil
1 teaspoon ground ginger
½ teaspoon sugar
¼ teaspoon garlic powder
Prepared sweet and sour
sauce (optional)

Remove skin from drumsticks, if desired, by pulling skin toward end of leg with paper towel; discard skin.

Place chicken in large resealable plastic food storage bag. Combine teriyaki sauce, brandy, onion, oil, ginger, sugar and garlic powder in small bowl; pour over chicken. Close bag securely, turning to coat. Marinate in refrigerator at least 1 hour or overnight, turning occasionally.

Prepare grill for indirect cooking.

Drain chicken; reserve marinade. Place chicken on grid directly over drip pan. Grill, covered, over medium-high heat 60 minutes or until chicken is no longer pink in center and juices run clear, turning and brushing with reserved marinade every 20 minutes. Discard remaining marinade. Serve with sweet and sour sauce, if desired.

Makes 4 servings

Grilled Garlic Chicken

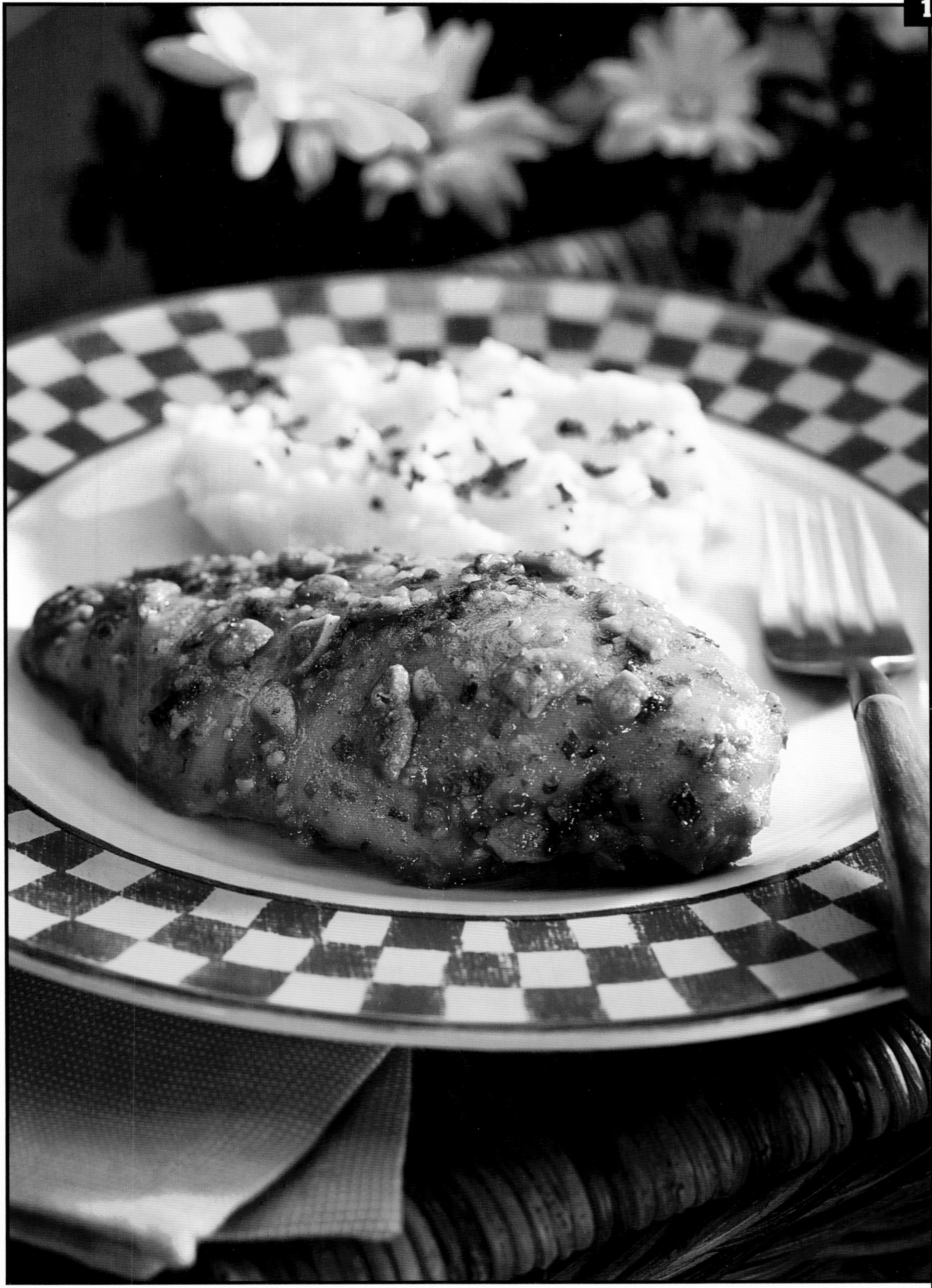

Chicken Fajitas

¾ cup WISH-BONE® Italian
    Dressing*
1 tablespoon lime juice
1½ teaspoon ground cumin
    (optional)
¾ teaspoon grated lime peel
    (optional)
1 pound boneless, skinless
    chicken breast
8 (8-inch) flour tortillas,
    warmed

*Also terrific with WISH-BONE® Robusto
Italian or Just2Good! Italian Dressing.*

For marinade, combine Italian dressing, lime juice, cumin and lime peel. In large, shallow nonaluminum baking dish or plastic bag, add chicken and ½ cup of marinade; turn to coat. Cover, or close bag, and marinate in refrigerator, turning occasionally, up to 3 hours. Refrigerate remaining ⅓ cup marinade.

Remove chicken, discarding marinade. Grill or broil chicken, turning once and brushing occasionally with refrigerated marinade, until chicken is thoroughly cooked.

To serve, thinly slice chicken. Serve in tortillas and, if desired, with shredded lettuce, chopped tomatoes, sliced green onions and sour cream.

Makes 4 servings

Barbecued Chicken

2½ to 3-pound broiler-fryer
    chicken, cut up

Barbecue Sauce
    1 cup catsup
    ¼ cup GRANDMA'S®
        Molasses Unsulphured
    ¼ cup cider vinegar
    ¼ cup Dijon mustard
    2 tablespoons Worcestershire
        sauce
    1 teaspoon garlic powder
    1 teaspoon hickory flavor
        liquid smoke
    ¼ teaspoon cayenne pepper
    ¼ teaspoon hot pepper sauce

In 12×8-inch (2-quart) microwave-safe baking dish, arrange chicken pieces with thickest portions to outside. In small bowl, combine all sauce ingredients, set aside.

Prepare barbecue grill. Cover chicken with waxed paper. Microwave on HIGH (100%) for 10 minutes. Immediately place chicken on grill over medium heat. Brush with sauce. Cook 20 to 25 minutes or until no longer pink, turning once and brushing frequently with sauce. *Makes 4 to 6 servings*

Note: This Barbecue Sauce is equally delicious on ribs.

Deviled Chicken

3 tablespoons butter or margarine

1 package (about 2¾ pounds) PERDUE® Fresh Split Chicken Breasts

Salt and ground pepper to taste

2 tablespoons chili sauce or ketchup

2 tablespoons Worcestershire sauce

2 teaspoons grainy, "country-style" mustard

⅛ teaspoon ground red pepper

Prepare outdoor grill for cooking or preheat broiler. In small saucepan over low heat, melt butter. Brush chicken breasts with butter and season with salt and pepper. To butter remaining in pan, add chili sauce, Worcestershire sauce, mustard and ground red pepper; stir to combine. Over medium heat, bring to a boil; set aside. Grill or broil chicken 6 to 8 inches from heat source 10 to 15 minutes per side, until nicely browned, cooked through and a meat thermometer inserted in thickest part of breast registers 170°F. During last 10 minutes of cooking time, baste 2 to 3 times with butter mixture. *Makes 4 servings*

Honey-Mustard Glazed Chicken

2 tablespoons Dijon-style mustard

2 tablespoons honey

1 tablespoon butter or margarine, melted

1 teaspoon McCORMICK® Basil Leaves

½ teaspoon McCORMICK® California Style Garlic Powder

1 pound boneless, skinless chicken breasts (4 half breasts)

1. Preheat broiler or grill.

2. Combine mustard, honey, butter, basil and garlic powder in small bowl and beat until well mixed.

3. Arrange chicken on lightly greased broiler pan or grill and broil 3 to 4 minutes. Brush half of mustard mixture on chicken and broil 2 minutes.

4. Turn chicken over and broil 3 to 4 minutes. Brush with remaining mustard mixture. Broil 2 minutes or until chicken is no longer pink in center. *Makes 4 servings*

Spicy Mango Chicken

¼ cup mango nectar

¼ cup chopped fresh cilantro

2 jalapeño chile peppers, seeded and finely chopped

2 teaspoons vegetable oil

2 teaspoons LAWRY'S® Seasoned Salt

½ teaspoon LAWRY'S® Garlic Powder with Parsley

½ teaspoon ground cumin

4 boneless, skinless chicken breast halves (about 1 pound)

Mango & Black Bean Salsa (recipe follows)

In small bowl, combine all ingredients except chicken and salsa; mix well. Brush marinade on both sides of chicken. Grill or broil chicken 10 to 15 minutes or until no longer pink in center and juices run clear when cut, turning once and basting often with additional marinade. *Do not baste during last 5 minutes of cooking.* Discard any remaining marinade. Top chicken with Mango & Black Bean Salsa.   *Makes 4 servings*

Hint: Jalapeño peppers can sting and irritate the skin; wear rubber gloves when handling peppers and do not touch eyes.

Mango & Black Bean Salsa

1 ripe mango, peeled, seeded and chopped

1 cup canned black beans, rinsed and drained

½ cup chopped tomato

2 thinly sliced green onions

1 tablespoon chopped fresh cilantro

1½ teaspoons lime juice

1½ teaspoons red wine vinegar

½ teaspoon LAWRY'S® Seasoned Salt

In medium bowl, combine all ingredients; mix well. Let stand 30 minutes to allow flavors to blend.   *Makes about 2¾ cups*

Serving Suggestion: Serve with chicken or fish.

Spicy Mango Chicken

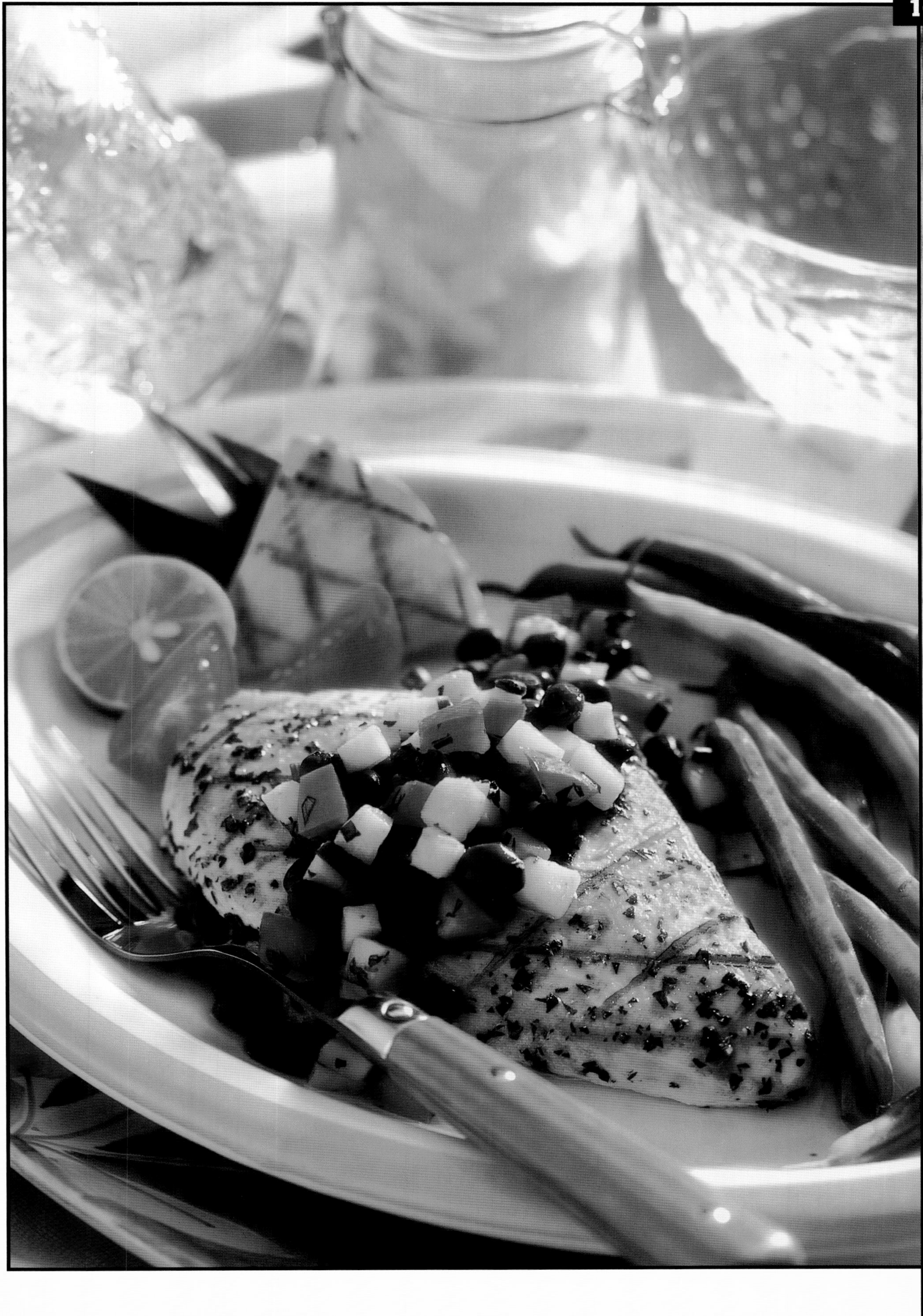

Grilled Chicken Skewers

⅓ cup lemon juice
⅓ cup honey
1½ teaspoons LAWRY'S®
　　Lemon Pepper
½ teaspoon LAWRY'S®
　　Seasoned Salt
2 boneless, skinless chicken
　　breast halves (about
　　½ pound), cut into thin
　　strips
½ pound bacon slices
　　Skewers

In large resealable plastic food storage bag, combine lemon juice, honey, Lemon Pepper and Seasoned Salt; mix well. Add chicken; seal bag. Marinate in refrigerator at least 30 minutes. Remove chicken; discard used marinade. Alternately thread chicken and bacon onto skewers. Grill or broil skewers 10 to 15 minutes or until chicken is no longer pink in center and juices run clear when cut, and bacon is crisp.

Makes 2 servings

Serving Suggestion: Garnish with lemon wedges. Serve as a light entree or divide and serve as appetizers.

Hint: If using wooden skewers, soak in water overnight before using to prevent scorching.

Santa Fe Grilled Chicken

Juice of 2 to 3 fresh limes
　　(½ cup), divided
2 tablespoons vegetable oil,
　　divided
1 package (about 3 pounds)
　　PERDUE® Fresh Skinless
　　Pick of the Chicken
Salt and black pepper to
　　taste
1 cup fresh or frozen diced
　　peaches
¼ cup finely chopped red
　　onion
1 jalapeño pepper, seeded
　　and minced
2 cloves garlic, minced
1 teaspoon ground cumin
　　Chili powder

In medium-sized bowl, combine 7 tablespoons lime juice and 1 tablespoon plus 1½ teaspoons oil. Add chicken, salt and pepper; cover and marinate in the refrigerator 2 to 4 hours. Meanwhile to prepare salsa, in small bowl, combine remaining 1 tablespoon lime juice and 1½ teaspoons oil, peaches, onion, jalapeño pepper, garlic and cumin.

Prepare outdoor grill or preheat broiler. Remove chicken from marinade. Sprinkle with chili powder and place on cooking surface of grill over medium-hot coals or on broiler pan. Grill or broil 6 to 8 inches from heat source, allowing 20 to 30 minutes for breasts and 30 to 40 minutes for thighs and drumsticks, turning occasionally or until juices run clear. Serve grilled chicken with salsa.

Makes 4 to 5 servings

Grilled Chicken Skewers

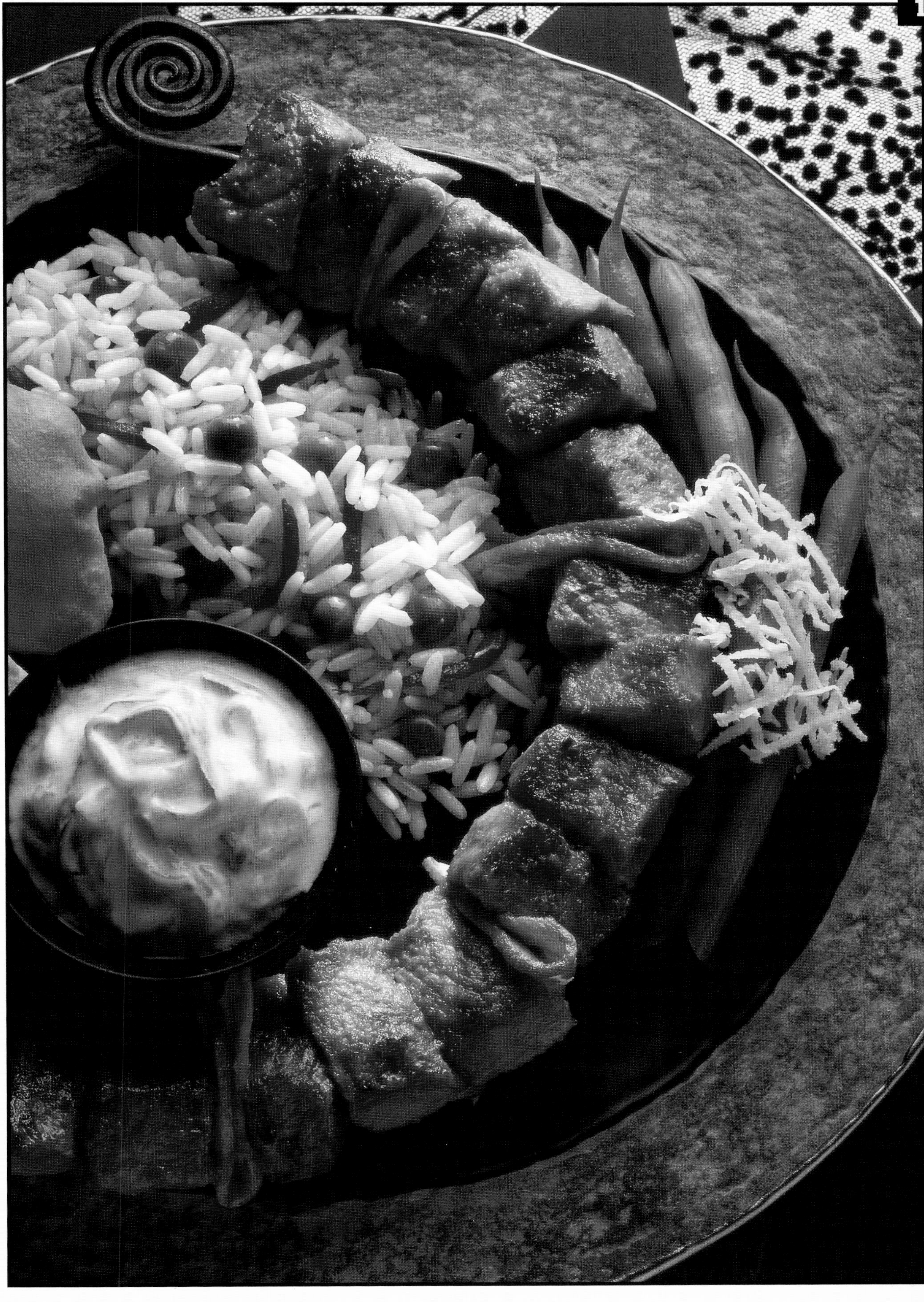

Lime-Mustard Marinated Chicken

2 boneless skinless chicken
    breast halves (about
    4 ounces each)
¼ cup fresh lime juice
3 tablespoons honey
    mustard, divided
2 teaspoons olive oil
¼ teaspoon ground cumin
⅛ teaspoon garlic powder
⅛ teaspoon ground red
    pepper
¾ cup plus 2 tablespoons
    fat-free reduced-sodium
    chicken broth, divided
¼ cup uncooked rice
1 cup broccoli florets
⅓ cup matchstick carrots

1. Rinse chicken. Pat dry with paper towels. Place in resealable plastic food storage bag. Whisk together lime juice, 2 tablespoons mustard, olive oil, cumin, garlic powder and red pepper. Pour over chicken. Seal bag. Marinate in refrigerator 2 hours.

2. Combine ¾ cup chicken broth, rice and remaining 1 tablespoon mustard in small saucepan. Bring to a boil. Reduce heat and simmer, covered, 12 minutes or until rice is almost tender. Stir in broccoli, carrots and remaining 2 tablespoons chicken broth. Cook, covered, 2 to 3 minutes more or until vegetables are crisp-tender and rice is tender.

3. Meanwhile, drain chicken; discard marinade. Prepare grill for direct grilling. Grill chicken over medium coals 10 to 13 minutes or until no longer pink in center. Serve chicken with rice mixture.

Makes 2 servings

Easy Grilled Chicken

⅔ cup white wine vinegar
⅔ cup water
3 tablespoons butter or
    margarine
2 tablespoons Worcestershire
    sauce
2 tablespoons garlic salt
1 tablespoon ground black
    pepper
4 chicken quarters

Combine vinegar, water, butter, Worcestershire, garlic salt and pepper in small saucepan. Bring to a boil over high heat. Brush sauce on chicken. Place chicken on prepared grill, skin sides up, about 8 inches from heat. Grill, turning and basting liberally with sauce every 5 to 10 minutes, about 60 to 70 minutes or until fork can be inserted into chicken with ease and juices run clear, not pink. Serve immediately.

Makes 4 servings

Favorite recipe from **USA Rice Federation**

Lime-Mustard Marinated Chicken

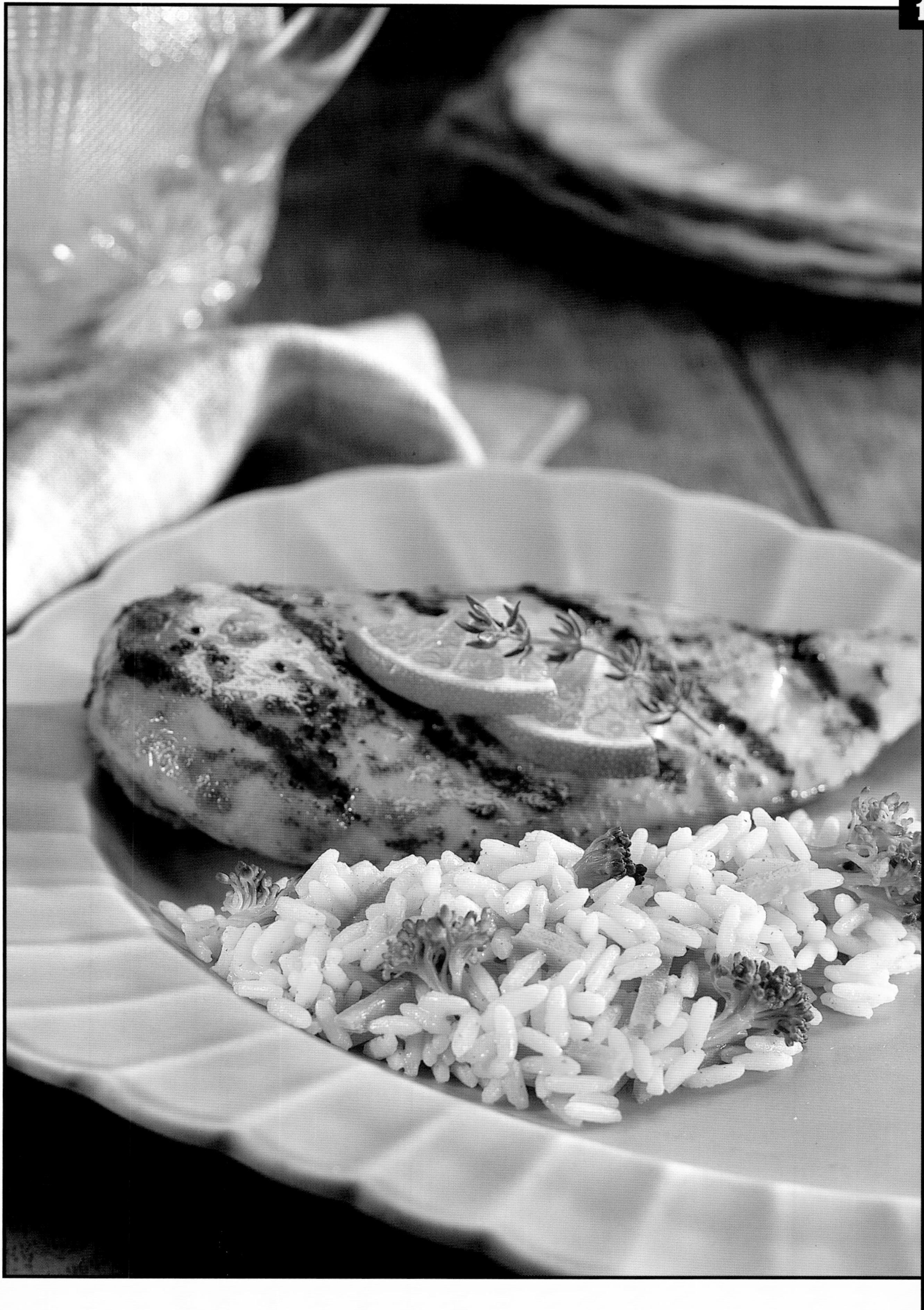

Hot, Spicy, Tangy, Sticky Chicken

1 chicken (3½ to 4 pounds),
    cut up
1 cup cider vinegar
1 tablespoon Worcestershire
    sauce
1 tablespoon chili powder
1 teaspoon salt
1 teaspoon black pepper
1 teaspoon hot pepper sauce
¾ cup KC MASTERPIECE™
    Original Barbecue Sauce

Place chicken in a shallow glass dish or large heavy plastic bag. Combine vinegar, Worcestershire sauce, chili powder, salt, black pepper and hot pepper sauce in small bowl; pour over chicken pieces. Cover dish or seal bag. Marinate in refrigerator at least 4 hours, turning several times.

Oil hot grid to help prevent sticking. Place dark meat pieces on grill 10 minutes before white meat pieces (dark meat takes longer to cook). Grill chicken on a covered grill, over medium KINGSFORD® Briquets, 30 to 45 minutes, turning once or twice. Turn and baste with KC MASTERPIECE™ Original Barbecue Sauce the last 10 minutes of cooking. Remove chicken from grill; baste with barbecue sauce. Chicken is done when meat is no longer pink near bone.

Makes 4 servings

Grilled Chicken and Apple with Fresh Rosemary

½ cup apple juice
¼ cup white wine vinegar
¼ cup vegetable oil or light
    olive oil
1 tablespoon chopped fresh
    rosemary *or* 1 teaspoon
    dried rosemary leaves,
    crushed
¼ teaspoon salt
¼ teaspoon ground black
    pepper
3 boneless skinless chicken
    breasts, halved
2 Washington Golden
    Delicious apples,
    cored and sliced into
    ½-inch-thick rings

1. Combine juice, vinegar, oil, rosemary, salt and pepper in shallow baking dish or bowl. Add chicken and apples; marinate in refrigerator at least 30 minutes.

2. Heat grill. Remove chicken and apples from marinade; arrange on hot grill. Discard marinade. Cook chicken 20 minutes or until cooked through, turning to grill both sides. Cook and turn apples about 6 minutes or until crisp-tender.

Makes 6 servings

Favorite recipe from **Washington Apple Commission**

Hot, Spicy, Tangy, Sticky Chicken

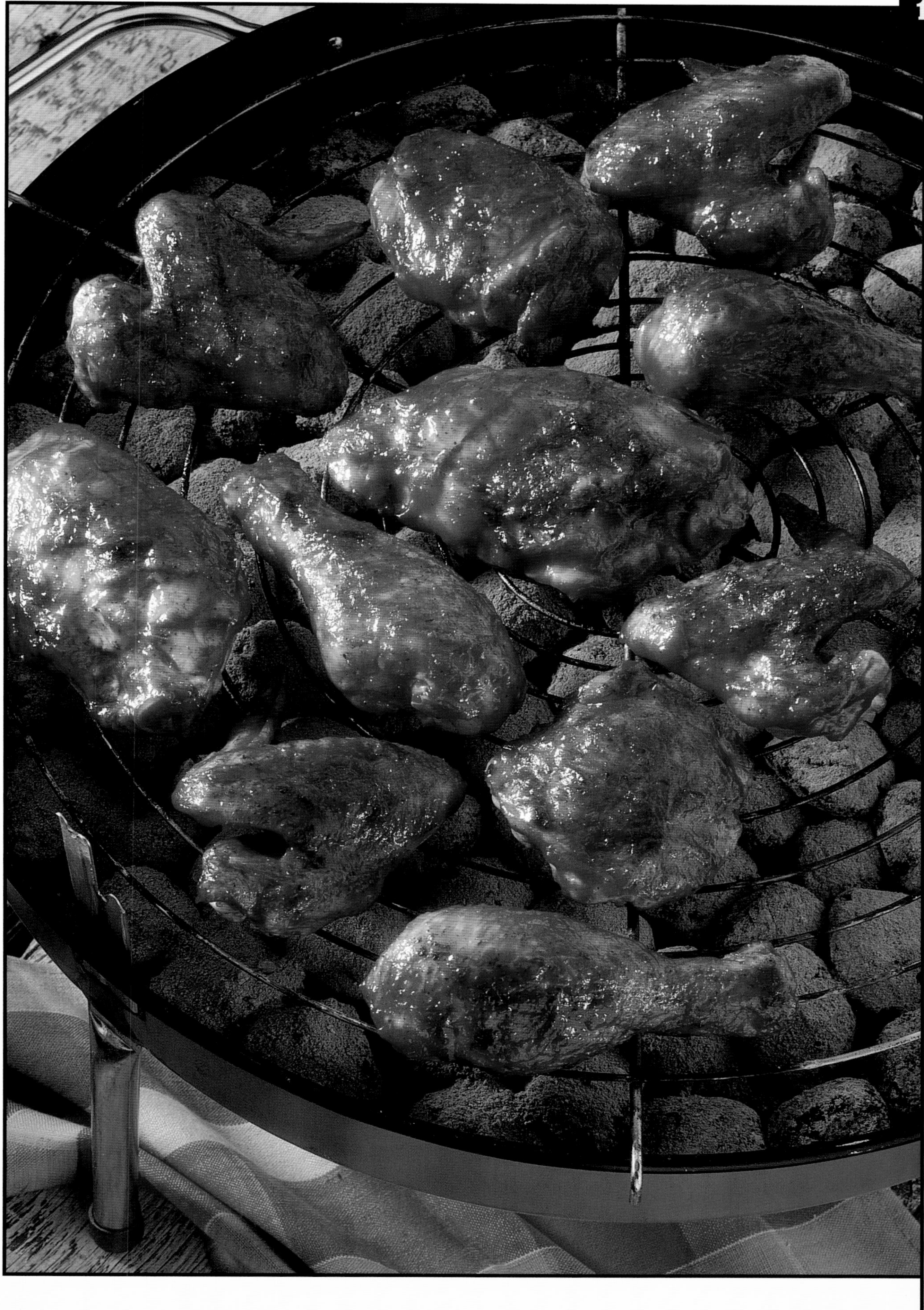

French Country Tidbits

4 pounds boneless, skinless
   chicken breast halves
   (about 1 pound), cut into
   chunks
1 bottle (12 ounces)
   LAWRY'S® Dijon & Honey
   Marinade with Lemon
   Juice
   Skewers
1 pound kielbasa (smoked
   sausage), sliced into
   ½-inch pieces
1 pound baby red potatoes,
   cooked and halved

In large resealable plastic food storage bag, combine chicken pieces with ⅔ cup Dijon & Honey Marinade; seal bag and shake to coat. Marinate in refrigerator for at least 30 minutes. Remove chicken; discard used marinade. Thread chicken onto skewers alternately with kielbasa and potatoes. Grill or broil skewers 10 to 15 minutes until chicken is no longer pink in center and juices run clear when cut, turning once and basting often with additional Marinade. Do not baste during last 5 minutes of cooking

Makes appetizers for about 24

Serving Suggestion: Serve on skewers or with toothpicks on large platter.

Hint: If using wooden skewers, soak in water overnight before using to prevent scorching.

Chicken Thighs with Ginger-Lime Marinade

¾ cup WISH-BONE® Italian
   Dressing*
2½ tablespoons honey
4 teaspoons lime juice
1 teaspoon ground ginger
¼ teaspoon crushed red
   pepper flakes (optional)
6 medium chicken thighs
   (about 2 pounds)

Also terrific with WISH-BONE® Robusto Italian Dressing.

For marinade, combine all ingredients except chicken. In large, shallow nonaluminum baking dish or plastic bag, add chicken and ¾ cup of the marinade; turn to coat. Cover, or close bag, and marinate in refrigerator, turning occasionally, 3 to 24 hours. Refrigerate remaining marinade.

Remove chicken, discarding marinade. Grill or broil chicken, turning once and brushing frequently with refrigerated marinade, until chicken is thoroughly cooked.

Makes 4 servings

Grilled Chicken Tortillas

6 boneless, skinless chicken
    breast halves
  Juice of 2 limes
3 tablespoons olive oil
1 clove garlic, crushed
½ teaspoon salt
¼ teaspoon bottled hot
    pepper sauce
12 flour tortillas
3 cups shredded lettuce
2 cups diced tomatoes
1½ cups shredded Monterey
    Jack cheese
1 jar (10 ounces) chunky
    salsa

In large non-metallic container or self-sealing plastic bag, mix lime juice, olive oil, garlic, salt, and hot pepper sauce. Add chicken, turning to coat with marinade. Marinate in refrigerator at least 1 hour. Stack tortillas and wrap in foil; set aside. Remove chicken from marinade; discard marinade. Place chicken on prepared grill about 8 inches from heat. Grill, turning frequently, about 16 to 20 minutes or until chicken is fork tender. While chicken is cooking, heat tortillas by placing foil-wrapped package on side of grill; turn package once or twice. Remove chicken to platter; cut into ¼-inch strips. To assemble, place equal portions of lettuce over each tortilla. Top with equal portions of chicken. Layer tomatoes and cheese over chicken; drizzle salsa over all. Roll up.

Makes 6 servings (2 tortillas per serving)

Favorite recipe from **Delmarva Poultry Industry, Inc.**

Lemon Herbed Chicken

½ cup butter or margarine
½ cup vegetable oil
⅓ cup lemon juice
2 tablespoons finely chopped
    parsley
2 tablespoons garlic salt
1 teaspoon dried rosemary,
    crushed
1 teaspoon dried summer
    savory, crushed
½ teaspoon dried thyme,
    crushed
¼ teaspoon coarsely cracked
    black pepper
6 chicken quarters (breast-
    wing or thigh-drumstick
    combinations)

Combine butter, oil, lemon juice, parsley, garlic salt, rosemary, summer savory, thyme and pepper in small saucepan. Heat until butter melts. Place chicken in shallow glass dish. Brush with some of sauce. Let stand 10 to 15 minutes.

Oil hot grid to help prevent sticking. Place dark meat pieces on grill 10 minutes before white meat pieces (dark meat takes longer to cook). Grill chicken, on uncovered grill, over medium-hot KINGSFORD® Briquets, 30 to 45 minutes for breast quarters or 50 to 60 minutes for leg quarters. Chicken is done when meat is no longer pink by bone. Turn quarters over and baste with sauce every 10 minutes. *Makes 6 servings*

Chicken Roll-Ups

¼ cup fresh lemon juice
1 tablespoon olive oil
¼ teaspoon salt
¼ teaspoon black pepper
4 boneless skinless chicken breast halves
¼ cup finely chopped fresh Italian parsley
2 tablespoons grated Parmesan cheese
2 tablespoons chopped fresh chives
1 teaspoon finely grated lemon peel
2 large cloves garlic, pressed in garlic press
16 toothpicks soaked in hot water 15 minutes

1. Combine lemon juice, oil, salt and pepper in 11×7-inch casserole. Pound chicken to ⅜-inch thickness. Place chicken in lemon mixture; turn to coat. Cover; marinate in refrigerator at least 30 minutes.

2. Prepare grill for direct cooking.

3. Combine parsley, cheese, chives, lemon peel and garlic in small bowl. Discard chicken marinade. Spread ¼ of parsley mixture over each chicken breast, leaving an inch around edges free. Starting at narrow end, roll chicken to enclose filling; secure with toothpicks.

4. Grill chicken, covered, over medium-hot coals about 2 minutes on each side or until golden brown. Transfer chicken to low or indirect heat; grill, covered, about 5 minutes or until chicken is no longer pink in center.

5. Remove toothpicks; slice each chicken breast into 3 or 4 pieces. *Makes 4 servings*

Barbecued Chicken with Chili-Orange Glaze

1 to 2 dried de arbol chilies*

1½ teaspoons grated orange peel

½ cup fresh orange juice

2 tablespoons tequila

2 cloves garlic, minced

¼ teaspoon salt

¼ cup vegetable oil

1 broiler-fryer chicken (about 3 pounds), cut into quarters

Orange slices (optional)

Cilantro sprigs (optional)

For milder flavor, discard seeds from chili peppers. Since chili peppers can sting and irritate the skin, wear rubber gloves when handling peppers and do not touch eyes. Wash hands after handling chili peppers.

Crush chilies into coarse flakes in mortar with pestle. Combine chilies, orange peel, orange juice, tequila, garlic and salt in small bowl. Gradually add oil, whisking continuously, until marinade is thoroughly blended.

Arrange chicken in single layer in shallow glass baking dish. Pour marinade over chicken; turn pieces to coat. Marinate, covered, in refrigerator 2 to 3 hours, turning chicken over and basting with marinade several times.

Prepare charcoal grill for direct cooking or preheat broiler. Drain chicken, reserving marinade. Bring marinade to a boil in small saucepan over high heat. Grill chicken on covered grill or broil, 6 to 8 inches from heat, 15 minutes, brushing frequently with marinade. Turn chicken over. Grill or broil 15 minutes more or until chicken is no longer pink in center and juices run clear, brushing frequently with marinade. *Do not baste during last 5 minutes of grilling.* Garnish with orange slices and cilantro, if desired.

Makes 4 servings

Barbecued Chicken with Chili-Orange Glaze

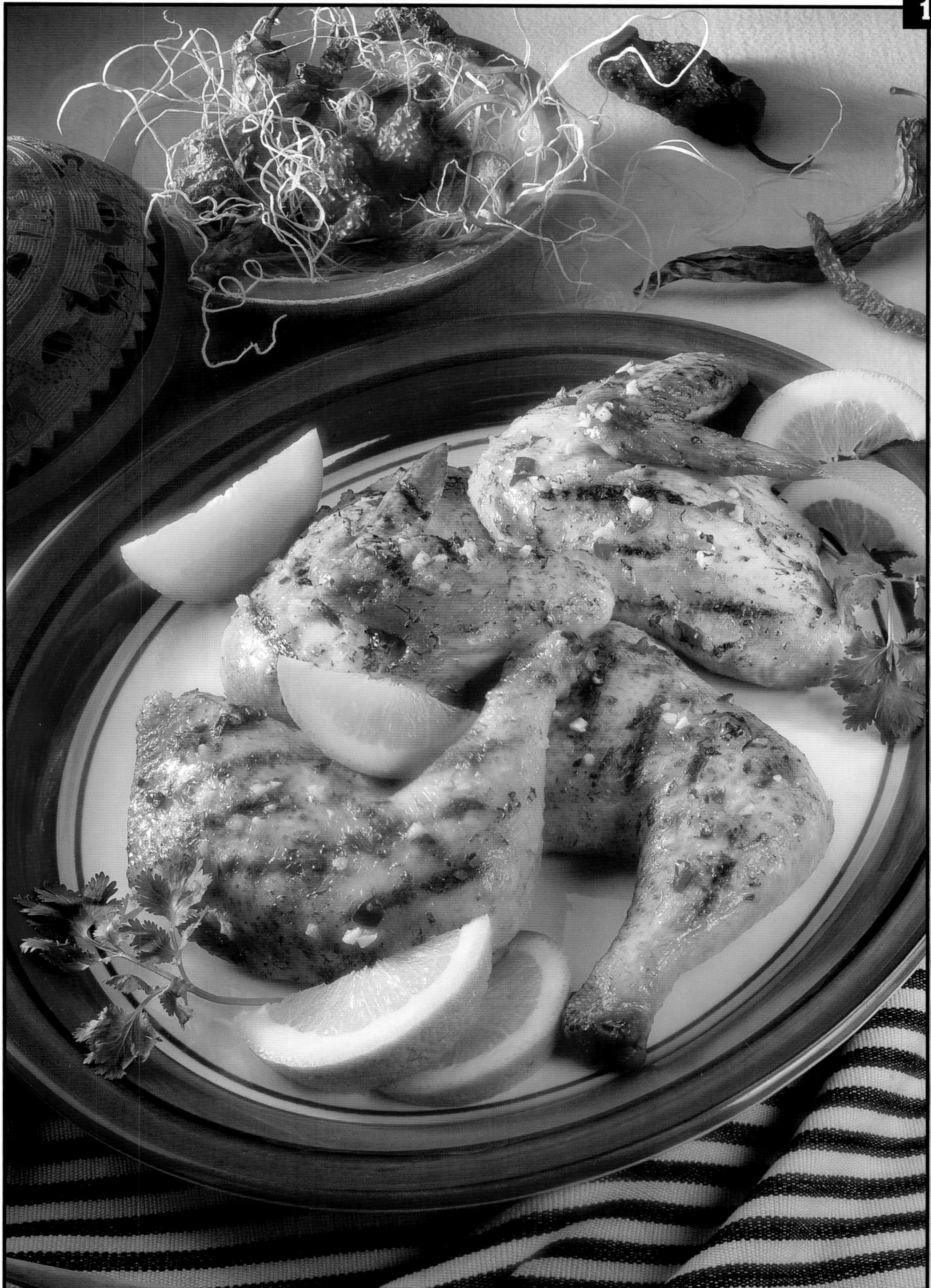

Japanese Yakitori

1 pound boneless skinless chicken breast halves, cut into ¾-inch-wide strips
2 tablespoons sherry or pineapple juice
2 tablespoons reduced-sodium soy sauce
1 tablespoon sugar
1 tablespoon peanut oil
½ teaspoon minced garlic
½ teaspoon minced ginger
5 ounces red pearl onions
½ fresh pineapple, cut into 1-inch wedges

1. Place chicken in large heavy-duty resealable plastic food storage bag. Combine sherry, soy sauce, sugar, oil, garlic and ginger in small bowl; mix thoroughly to dissolve sugar. Pour into plastic bag with chicken; seal bag and turn to coat thoroughly. Refrigerate 30 minutes or up to 2 hours, turning occasionally. (If using wooden or bamboo skewers, prepare by soaking skewers in water 20 to 30 minutes to keep from burning.)

2. Meanwhile, place onions in boiling water for 4 minutes; drain and cool in ice water to stop cooking. Cut off root ends and slip off outer skins; set aside.

3. Drain chicken, reserving marinade. Weave chicken accordion-style onto skewers, alternating onions and pineapple with chicken. Brush with reserved marinade; discard remaining marinade.

4. Grill on uncovered grill over medium-hot coals 6 to 8 minutes or until chicken is no longer pink in center, turning once. *Makes 6 servings*

Grilled Chicken au Brie

1 (5-ounce) package Crème de Brie® Original flavor
½ cup chopped walnuts, divided
4 strips bacon, cooked crisp and crumbled
2 tablespoons brown sugar
4 boneless, skinless chicken breasts

Blend Crème de Brie, ¼ cup of walnuts, crumbled bacon and brown sugar over low heat, stirring just until mixture thins. Grill chicken until no longer pink in center. Place chicken on individual serving dishes, ladle cheese sauce over chicken and sprinkle with remaining ¼ cup walnuts.

Makes 4 servings

Citrus Chicken

1 large orange
1 large lime*
¾ cup WISH-BONE® Italian
  Dressing
2½ to 3 pounds chicken pieces

*Substitution: Omit lime peel. Use
3 tablespoons lime juice.

From the orange, grate enough peel to measure 1½ teaspoons and squeeze enough juice to measure ⅓ cup; set aside.

From the lime, grate enough peel to measure 1 teaspoon and squeeze enough juice to measure 3 tablespoons; set aside.

For marinade, combine Italian dressing, orange and lime juices and orange and lime peels. In large, shallow nonaluminum baking dish or plastic bag, pour ¾ cup marinade over chicken; turn to coat. Cover, or close bag, and marinate in refrigerator, turning occasionally, 3 to 24 hours. Refrigerate remaining ½ cup marinade.

Remove chicken from marinade, discarding marinade. Grill or broil chicken, turning once and brushing frequently with refrigerated marinade, until chicken is thoroughly cooked.

Makes 4 servings

Thai Grilled Chicken

4 boneless chicken breast
  halves, skinned if desired
  (about 1¼ pounds)
¼ cup soy sauce
2 teaspoons bottled minced
  garlic
½ teaspoon red pepper flakes
2 tablespoons honey
1 tablespoon fresh lime juice

1. Prepare grill for grilling. Place chicken in shallow dish or plate. Combine soy sauce, garlic and pepper flakes in measuring cup. Pour over chicken, turning to coat. Let stand 10 minutes.

2. Meanwhile, combine honey and lime juice in small bowl until blended; set aside.

3. Place chicken on grid over medium coals; brush with some of marinade remaining in dish. Discard remaining marinade. Grill over covered grill 5 minutes. Brush chicken with half of honey mixture; turn and brush with remaining honey mixture. Grill 5 minutes more or until chicken is cooked through. *Makes 4 servings*

Serving suggestion: Serve with steamed white rice, Oriental vegetables and fresh fruit salad.

Prep/Cook Time: 25 minutes

Persian Chicken Breasts

1 medium lemon
2 teaspoons olive oil
1 teaspoon ground cinnamon
½ teaspoon salt
¼ teaspoon black pepper
¼ teaspoon turmeric
4 boneless skinless chicken
    breast halves
4 flour tortillas or soft lavosh
    (optional)
  Grilled vegetables
    (optional)

1. Remove lemon peel in long strips with paring knife; reserve for garnish. Juice lemon; combine juice with oil, cinnamon, salt, pepper and turmeric in large heavy-duty resealable plastic food storage bag. Gently knead ingredients in bag to mix thoroughly; add chicken. Seal bag and turn to coat thoroughly. Refrigerate 4 hours or overnight.

2. Remove chicken from marinade and gently shake to remove excess. Discard remaining marinade. Grill chicken 5 to 7 minutes per side or until chicken is no longer pink in center. Serve chicken with lightly grilled tortillas or lavosh and grilled vegetables, if desired. *Makes 4 servings*

Grilled Chicken with Pesto Sauce

⅓ cup olive oil
⅓ cup loosely packed parsley
    sprigs
⅓ cup GREY POUPON® Dijon
    or COUNTRY DIJON®
    Mustard
⅓ cup pine nuts or pignoli
    nuts
2 tablespoons grated
    Parmesan cheese
2 cloves garlic
1 teaspoon dried basil leaves
6 boneless, skinless chicken
    thighs (1 pound)

1. Blend oil, parsley, mustard, nuts, cheese, garlic and basil in blender or food processor until combined. Reserve ½ cup for serving.

2. Grill or broil chicken 6 inches from heat source for 15 to 20 minutes or until chicken is tender and no longer pink in center, turning once. Brush frequently with remaining pesto sauce during last 10 minutes of grilling. Serve with reserved pesto sauce. *Makes 6 servings*

Prep Time: 10 minutes
Cooking Time: 20 minutes

Persian Chicken Breast

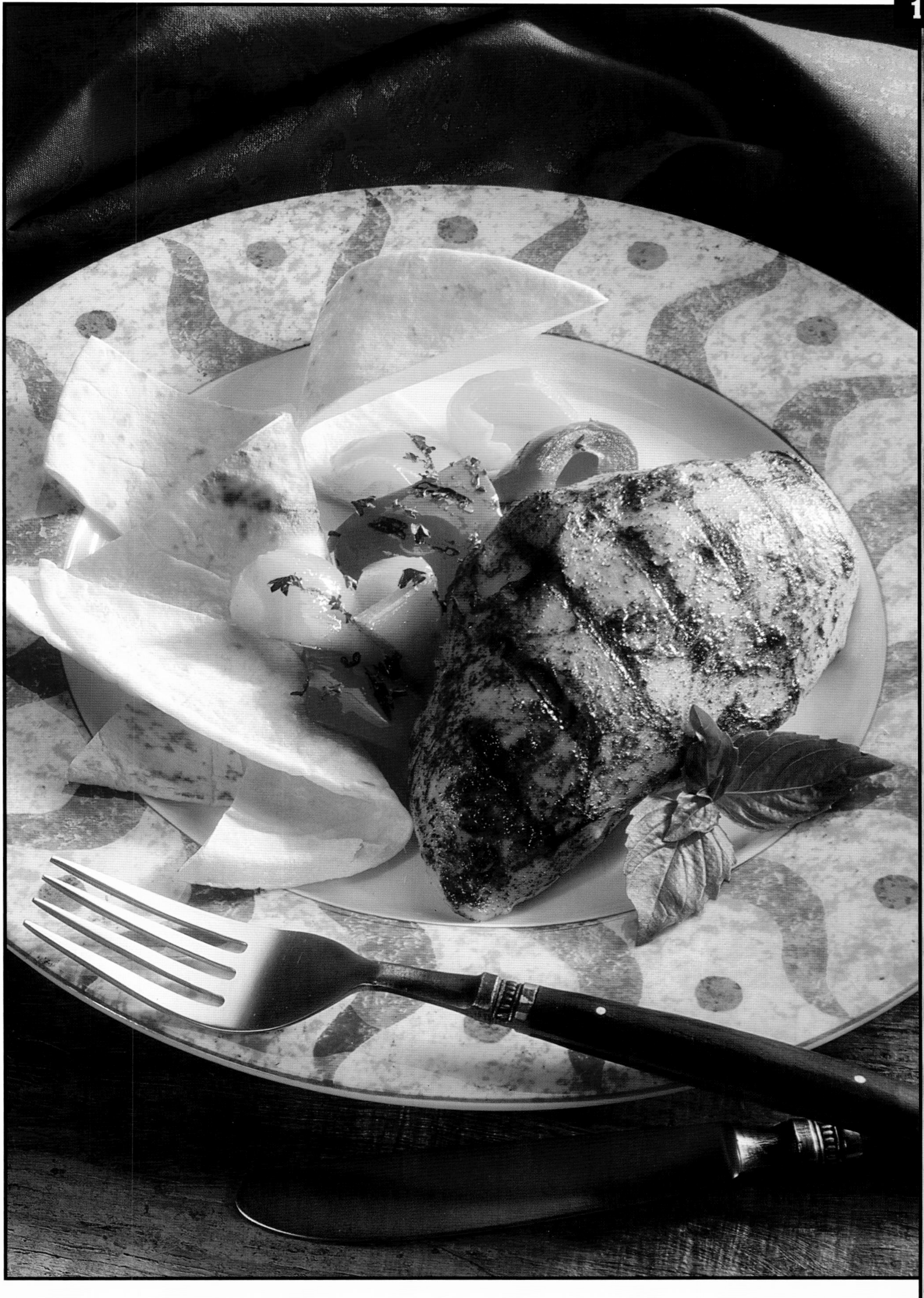

Rotisserie Chicken with Pesto Brush

2 BUTTERBALL® Fresh Young
   Roasters
¼ cup chopped fresh oregano
¼ cup chopped fresh parsley
2 tablespoons chopped fresh
   rosemary
2 tablespoons chopped fresh
   thyme
½ cup olive oil
½ cup balsamic vinegar

Combine oregano, parsley, rosemary, thyme, oil and vinegar in small bowl. Roast chicken according to rotisserie directions. Dip brush into herb mixture; brush chicken with herb mixture every 30 minutes for first 2 hours of roasting. Brush every 15 minutes during last hour of roasting. Roast chicken until internal temperature reaches 180°F in thigh and meat is no longer pink.

Makes 16 servings

Tip: To make an aromatic herb brush, bundle sprigs of rosemary, thyme, oregano and parsley together. Tie bundle with kitchen string. Use as brush for pesto.

Prep Time: 15 minutes plus roasting time

Grilled Summer Chicken & Vegetables

1¼ cups WISH-BONE® Italian
   Dressing, divided*
4 chicken breast halves
   (about 2 pounds)
4 ears fresh or frozen corn
   (about 2 pounds)
2 large tomatoes, halved
   crosswise

*Also terrific with WISH-BONE® Robusto
Italian or Just2Good! Italian Dressing.*

In large, shallow nonaluminum baking dish, pour 1 cup Italian dressing over chicken, corn and tomatoes. Cover and marinate chicken and vegetables in refrigerator, turning occasionally, 3 to 24 hours.

Remove chicken and vegetables from marinade, discarding marinade. Grill or broil chicken and corn 20 minutes, turning and brushing frequently with remaining dressing. Arrange tomato halves, cut sides up, on grill or broiler pan and continue cooking chicken and vegetables, turning and brushing occasionally with dressing, 10 minutes or until chicken is thoroughly cooked in center and corn is tender.

Makes 4 servings

Rotisserie Chicken with Pesto Brush

Blue Cheese Stuffed Chicken Breasts

2 tablespoons margarine or
  butter, softened, divided
½ cup (2 ounces) crumbled
  blue cheese
¾ teaspoon dried thyme leaves
2 whole boneless chicken
  breasts with skin (not
  split)
1 tablespoon bottled or fresh
  lemon juice
½ teaspoon paprika

1. Prepare grill for grilling. Combine 1 tablespoon margarine, blue cheese and thyme in small bowl until blended. Season with salt and pepper.

2. Loosen skin over breast of chicken by pushing fingers between skin and meat, taking care not to tear skin. Spread blue cheese mixture under skin with rubber spatula or small spoon; massage skin to evenly spread cheese mixture.

3. Place chicken, skin side down, on grid over medium coals. Grill over covered grill 5 minutes. Meanwhile, melt remaining 1 tablespoon margarine; stir in lemon juice and paprika. Turn chicken; brush with lemon juice mixture. Grill 5 to 7 minutes more or until chicken is cooked through. Transfer chicken to carving board; cut each breast in half.   *Makes 4 servings*

Serving Suggestion: Serve with steamed new potatoes and broccoli.

Prep and Cook Time: 22 minutes

Blue Cheese Stuffed Chicken Breast

Buffalo Chicken Drumsticks

8 large chicken drumsticks
   (about 2 pounds)
3 tablespoons hot pepper
   sauce
1 tablespoon vegetable oil
1 clove garlic, minced
¼ cup mayonnaise
3 tablespoons sour cream
1½ tablespoons white wine
   vinegar
¼ teaspoon sugar
⅓ cup (1½ ounces) crumbled
   Roquefort or blue cheese
2 cups hickory chips
   Celery sticks

Place chicken in large resealable plastic food storage bag. Combine pepper sauce, oil and garlic in small bowl; pour over chicken. Seal bag tightly; turn to coat. Marinate in refrigerator at least 1 hour or, for hotter flavor, up to 24 hours, turning occasionally.

For blue cheese dressing, combine mayonnaise, sour cream, vinegar and sugar in another small bowl. Stir in cheese; cover and refrigerate until serving.

Prepare grill. Meanwhile, cover hickory chips with cold water; soak 20 minutes. Drain chicken, discarding marinade. Drain hickory chips; sprinkle over coals. Place chicken on grid. Grill, on covered grill, over medium-hot coals 25 to 30 minutes or until chicken is tender when pierced with fork and no longer pink near bone, turning 3 to 4 times. Serve with blue cheese dressing and celery sticks.   *Makes 4 servings*

Grilled Chicken Adobo

½ cup chopped onion
⅓ cup lime juice
6 cloves garlic, coarsely
   chopped
1 teaspoon dried oregano
   leaves
1 teaspoon ground cumin
½ teaspoon dried thyme leaves
¼ teaspoon ground red
   pepper
6 boneless skinless chicken
   breast halves
3 tablespoons chopped fresh
   cilantro

1. Combine onion, lime juice and garlic in food processor. Process until onion is finely minced. Transfer to resealable plastic food storage bag. Add oregano, cumin, thyme and red pepper; knead bag until blended. Place chicken in bag; press out air and seal. Turn to coat chicken with marinade. Refrigerate 30 minutes or up to 4 hours.

2. Spray grid with nonstick cooking spray. Prepare grill for direct cooking. Remove chicken from marinade; discard marinade. Place chicken on grid, 3 to 4 inches from medium-hot coals. Grill 5 to 7 minutes on each side or until no longer pink in center. Transfer to serving platter and sprinkle with cilantro.   *Makes 6 servings*

Buffalo Chicken Drumsticks

PORK
APLENTY

Pork is more than just another white meat, it's also some of the best grilling meat around. So, give it a whirl and you just might be surprised.

Barbecued Pork Kabobs

 1 onion, finely chopped
½ cup ketchup or chili sauce
¼ cup apple cider vinegar
¼ cup vegetable oil
 1 teaspoon LAWRY'S®
   Seasoned Salt
½ teaspoon Worcestershire
   sauce
¼ teaspoon hot pepper sauce
   (optional)
¼ teaspoon liquid smoke
   (optional)
 4 boneless pork chops, cut
   into 1½-inch cubes
 2 green bell peppers, cut into
   chunks
 2 onions, cut into chunks
   Skewers

In large resealable plastic food storage bag, combine chopped onion, ketchup, vinegar, oil, Seasoned Salt, Worcestershire, hot pepper sauce and liquid smoke, if desired; mix well. Remove ¼ cup marinade for basting. Add pork; seal bag. Marinate in refrigerator at least 1 hour. Remove pork from marinade; discard used marinade. Alternately thread pork, bell peppers and onions onto skewers. Grill or broil skewers 15 to 20 minutes or until no longer pink in center, turning once and basting often with additional ¼ cup marinade. *Do not baste during last 5 minutes of cooking.* Discard any remaining marinade.

Makes 4 servings

Serving Suggestion: Serve over red beans and rice.

Hint: If using wooden skewers, soak in water overnight before using to prevent scorching.

Barbecued Pork Kabobs

Fiery Grilled Buffalo-Style Chops and Vegetables

Zesty Blue Cheese Butter
  (recipe page 176)
4 medium baking potatoes,
  unpeeled
Vegetable oil
4 (¾-inch-thick) boneless
  pork loin chops (about
  4 ounces each)
2 medium red bell peppers,
  cut into halves and
  seeded
⅓ cup butter or margarine
⅓ cup hot pepper sauce
Prepared coleslaw
  (optional)

1. Prepare Zesty Blue Cheese Butter up to 2 days in advance; refrigerate.

2. Preheat oven to 375°F. Pierce each potato several times with fork. Pat potatoes dry with paper towels; rub skins with oil. Bake 1 hour or until just fork-tender. While hot, cut potatoes lengthwise in half. Cool to room temperature.

3. Prepare grill for direct cooking.

4. Place pork chops, bell peppers and potatoes in large resealable plastic food storage bag. Melt butter in small saucepan over low heat. Stir in pepper sauce; pour over chops, bell peppers and potatoes. Seal bag tightly; turn to coat. Marinate at room temperature no more than 15 minutes, turning once.

5. Place chops and vegetables on grid, reserving marinade in small saucepan. Grill, uncovered, over medium coals 5 minutes. Turn chops and vegetables and baste once with reserved marinade; discard any remaining marinade. Cook 5 minutes more or until pork is barely pink in center. (Do not overcook.)

6. Serve chops and vegetables with slices of Zesty Blue Cheese Butter. *Makes 4 servings*

continued on page 176

Fiery Grilled Buffalo-Style Chops and Vegetables

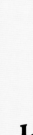

Zesty Blue Cheese Butter

4 ounces blue cheese, such as Gorgonzola or
    Roquefort
½ cup butter or margarine, softened
1 package (3 ounces) cream cheese, softened
2 tablespoons finely chopped green onion
2 slices bacon, cooked, drained and crumbled

1. Crumble blue cheese with fingers to measure
1 cup; place in small bowl.

2. Add butter and cream cheese; beat with
electric mixer at medium speed until smooth. Stir
in onion and bacon.

3. Place butter mixture on sheet of waxed paper.
Using waxed paper, roll mixture back and forth
into 8-inch log.

4. Wrap waxed paper around butter log to seal.
Refrigerate at least 1 hour or up to 2 days.

Makes about 1 cup

Spicy Grilled Pork Chops

¼ cup minced onion
¼ cup soy sauce
2 tablespoons fresh lime juice
2 cloves garlic, minced
½ teaspoon red pepper flakes
4 center cut well-trimmed
    pork loin or rib chops,
    cut ¾ inch thick

1. Combine onion, soy sauce, lime juice, garlic
and crushed red pepper in large plastic bag; add
chops. Close bag securely; turn to coat. Marinate
in refrigerator at least 4 hours or up to 24 hours,
turning once.

2. Drain chops; reserve marinade. Brush with
some of the reserved marinade. Grill or broil
chops 5 to 6 inches from heat 7 minutes. Turn
chops over; brush with marinade, discarding
remaining marinade. Grill or broil 8 to 13 minutes
until no longer pink in center.

Makes 4 servings

Apricot-Glazed Spareribs

6 pounds pork spareribs, cut
  into 2-rib portions
4 cloves garlic, crushed
  Water
1 cup (12-ounce jar)
  SMUCKER'S® Apricot
  Preserves
¼ cup chopped onion
¼ cup ketchup
2 tablespoons firmly packed
  brown sugar
1 tablespoon oil
1 teaspoon ground ginger
1 teaspoon soy sauce
½ teaspoon salt

In very large saucepot or Dutch oven, combine pork spareribs and garlic; cover with water. Over high heat, heat to boiling. Reduce heat to low; cover and simmer 1 hour or until spareribs are fork-tender. Remove ribs to platter; cover and refrigerate.

Meanwhile, prepare apricot glaze. Combine preserves, onion, ketchup, brown sugar, oil, ginger, soy sauce and salt in small saucepan; mix well. Heat to boiling; boil 1 minute. Cover and refrigerate apricot glaze.

About 1 hour before serving, heat grill. When ready to barbecue, place cooked spareribs on grill over medium heat. Cook 12 to 15 minutes or until heated through, turning spareribs often. Brush occasionally with apricot glaze during last 10 minutes of cooking.   *Makes 6 servings*

Note: The precooked spareribs can be broiled in the oven. Place spareribs on broiler pan; brush with some apricot glaze. Broil about 7 to 9 inches from heat for 7 to 8 minutes, brushing with apricot glaze halfway through cooking time. Turn ribs, brush with apricot glaze and broil for 5 to 6 minutes, brushing with apricot glaze halfway through cooking time.

Grilled Apple-Stuffed Pork Chops

5 tablespoons *French's®*
   Bold n' Spicy Brown
   Mustard, divided
3 tablespoons honey, divided
1 cup corn bread stuffing mix
1 small McIntosh apple,
   peeled, cored and
   chopped
¼ cup minced onion
¼ cup chopped fresh parsley
4 rib pork chops, cut
   1¼ inches thick (about
   2 pounds)

1. Combine ¼ cup water, 2 tablespoons mustard and 1 tablespoon honey in medium bowl. Add stuffing mix, apple, onion and parsley; toss until crumbs are moistened. Combine remaining 3 tablespoons mustard and 2 tablespoons honey in small bowl; set aside for glaze.

2. Cut horizontal slits in pork chops, using sharp knife, to make pockets for stuffing. Spoon stuffing evenly into pockets. Secure openings with toothpicks.

3. Place pork chops on oiled grid. Grill over medium heat 40 to 45 minutes until no longer pink near bone, turning often. Baste chops with reserved glaze during last 10 minutes of cooking.

Makes 4 servings

Prep Time: 20 minutes
Cook Time: 40 minutes

Grilled Apple-Stuffed Pork Chop

Memphis Pork Ribs

1 tablespoon chili powder
1 tablespoon dried parsley
2 teaspoons onion powder
2 teaspoons garlic powder
2 teaspoons dried oregano
    leaves
2 teaspoons paprika
2 teaspoons black pepper
1½ teaspoons salt
4 pounds pork spareribs, cut
    into 4 racks
  Tennessee BBQ Sauce
    (recipe follows)

Combine chili powder, parsley, onion powder, garlic powder, oregano, paprika, pepper and salt in small bowl; mix well.

Rub spice mixture onto ribs. Cover; marinate in refrigerator at least 2 hours or overnight.

Preheat oven to 350°F. Place ribs in foil-lined shallow roasting pan. Bake 30 minutes.

Meanwhile, prepare grill for direct cooking. Prepare Tennessee BBQ sauce.

Place ribs on grid. Grill, covered, over medium heat 10 minutes. Brush with sauce. Continue grilling 10 minutes or until ribs are tender, brushing with sauce occasionally. Serve any remaining sauce on the side for dipping.

Makes 4 servings

Tennessee BBQ Sauce

3 cups prepared barbecue sauce
¼ cup cider vinegar
¼ cup honey
2 teaspoons onion powder
2 teaspoons garlic powder
  Dash hot pepper sauce

Combine all ingredients in medium bowl; mix well.

Makes about 3½ cups

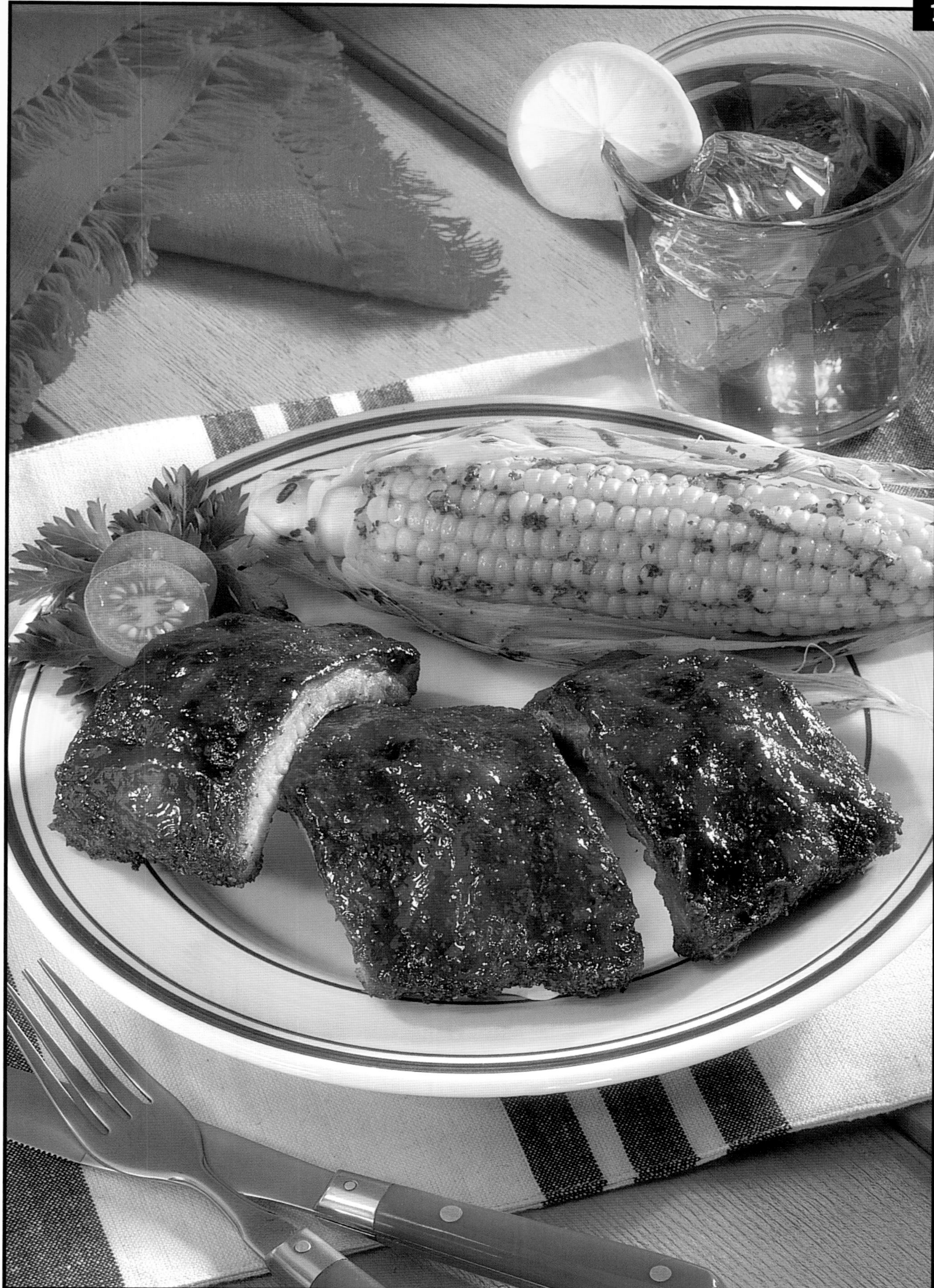

Hickory Pork Tenderloin with Apple Topping

1¼ cups plus 2 tablespoons LAWRY'S® Hickory Marinade with Apple Cider, divided
1 pork tenderloin (2½ to 3 pounds)
1 can (21 ounces) apple pie filling or topping

In large resealable plastic food storage bag, combine 1 cup Hickory Marinade and tenderloin; seal bag. Marinate in refrigerator at least 30 minutes. Remove tenderloin from marinade; discard used marinade. Grill tenderloin, using indirect heat method, until no longer pink, about 35 minutes, turning once and basting often with additional ¼ cup Hickory Marinade. Let stand 10 minutes before slicing. In medium saucepan, combine additional 2 tablespoons Hickory Marinade and apple pie filling. Cook over low heat until heated throughout. Spoon over tenderloin slices. *Makes 6 to 8 servings*

Serving Suggestion: Serve with brussels sprouts and cornbread. Garnish with cranberries, if desired.

Hint: Various flavored applesauces can be substituted for the apple pie filling. Try chunky applesauce with brown sugar and cinnamon.

Hickory Pork Tenderloin with Apple Topping

Honey-Garlic Pork Chops

4 boneless center pork loin
  chops, 1¼- to
  1½-inches-thick
¼ cup lemon juice
¼ cup honey
2 tablespoons soy sauce
1 tablespoon dry sherry
2 cloves garlic, minced

Combine all ingredients except chops. Pour over chops in resealable plastic food storage bag; seal. Refrigerate 4 to 24 hours. Prepare covered grill with drip pan in center banked by medium-hot coals. Remove chops from marinade, reserve marinade. Grill chops 12 to 15 minutes, turning once, and basting occasionally with reserved marinade. To broil, place chops 5 inches from heat source, turning once, 12 to 15 minutes or until barely pink in center. *Makes 4 servings*

Favorite recipe from **National Pork Board**

August Moon Korean Ribs

⅓ cup water
⅓ cup soy sauce
¼ cup thinly sliced green
  onions
3 tablespoons dark sesame oil
3 tablespoons honey
2 tablespoons minced garlic
2 tablespoons sesame seeds
1 tablespoon grated fresh
  ginger
1 teaspoon black pepper
3½ pounds pork back ribs

To prepare marinade, combine all ingredients except ribs in small bowl. Place ribs in large resealable plastic food storage bag. Pour marinade over ribs, turning to coat. Seal bag. Marinate in refrigerator overnight. Arrange medium KINGSFORD® Briquets on each side of rectangular metal or foil drip pan. Grill ribs in center of grid on covered grill 35 to 45 minutes or until ribs are browned and cooked through, turning once. *Makes 8 servings*

Honey-Garlic Pork Chops

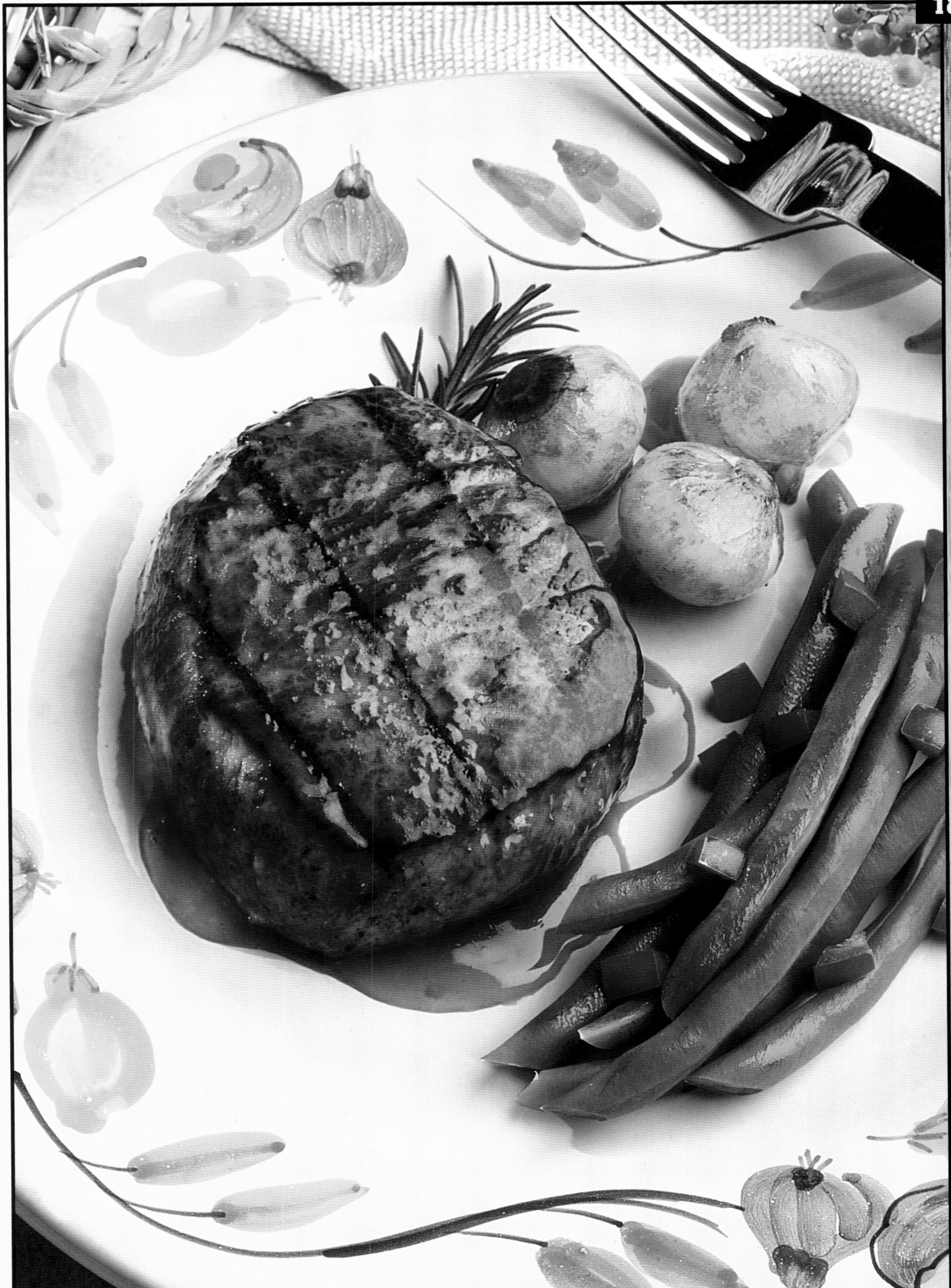

Seasoned Baby Back Ribs

1 tablespoon paprika
1½ teaspoons garlic salt
1 teaspoon celery salt
½ teaspoon black pepper
¼ teaspoon ground red
    pepper
4 pounds pork baby back
    ribs, cut into 3- to 4-rib
    portions, well trimmed
Barbecue Sauce (recipe
    follows)
Rib rack (optional)
Orange peel for garnish

1. Preheat oven to 350°F.

2. Combine paprika, garlic salt, celery salt, black pepper and ground red pepper in small bowl. Rub over all surfaces of ribs with fingers.

3. Place ribs in foil-lined shallow roasting pan. Bake 30 minutes.

4. Meanwhile, prepare grill for direct cooking. Prepare Barbecue Sauce; set aside.

5. Transfer ribs to rib rack set on grid. Or, place ribs directly on grid. Grill ribs, on covered grill, over medium coals 10 minutes.

6. Remove ribs from rib rack with tongs; brush with half the Barbecue Sauce evenly over both sides of ribs. Return ribs to rib rack. Continue to grill, covered, 10 minutes or until ribs are tender and browned. Serve with reserved sauce. Garnish, if desired. *Makes 6 servings*

Barbecue Sauce

½ cup ketchup
⅓ cup packed light brown sugar
1 tablespoon cider vinegar
2 teaspoons Worcestershire sauce
2 teaspoons soy sauce

Combine ketchup, sugar, vinegar, Worcestershire and soy sauce in glass measuring cup or small bowl. Reserve half of sauce for serving.

Makes about ⅔ cup

Bacon-Wrapped Pork and Apple Patties

1 pound lean ground pork
¾ cup quick-cooking rolled
    oats
  Salt
½ teaspoon ground sage
¼ teaspoon pepper
¼ teaspoon dried thyme
    leaves, crushed
⅓ cup applesauce
1 egg, slightly beaten
2 tablespoons chopped green
    onion
4 slices bacon
1 large tart green apple, cut
    into thin wedges
½ medium onion, cut into
    small wedges
1 tablespoon olive oil

In large bowl combine oats, ½ teaspoon salt, sage, pepper and thyme. Stir in applesauce, egg and green onion; mix well. Stir in ground pork until well blended. Form into 4 patties about ¾ to 1-inch thick. Wrap 1 bacon strip around each patty; secure with toothpick. Grill or broil patties 4 to 5 minutes on each side until no longer pink in center.

Meanwhile in small skillet, cook and stir apple and onion in hot oil until tender. Sprinkle lightly with salt. Serve with patties.   *Makes 4 servings*

Favorite recipe from **National Pork Board**

Tex-Mex Pork Kabobs with Chili Sour Cream Sauce

2¼ teaspoons chili powder, divided

1¾ teaspoons cumin, divided

¾ teaspoon garlic powder, divided

¾ teaspoon onion powder, divided

¾ teaspoon oregano, divided

1 pork tenderloin (1½ pounds), trimmed and cut into 1-inch pieces

1 cup reduced-fat sour cream

¾ teaspoon salt

¼ teaspoon black pepper

1 large red bell pepper, cored, seeded and cut into small chunks

1 large green bell pepper, cored, seeded and cut into small chunks

1 large yellow bell pepper, cored, seeded and cut into small chunks

Blend 1½ teaspoons chili powder, 1 teaspoon cumin, ½ teaspoon garlic powder, ½ teaspoon onion powder and ½ teaspoon oregano in medium bowl. Add pork. Toss well to coat. Cover tightly and refrigerate 2 to 3 hours.

Combine sour cream, remaining spices, ¼ teaspoon salt and black pepper in small bowl. Mix well. Cover tightly and refrigerate 2 to 3 hours.

If using wooden skewers, soak in water 20 minutes before using. Preheat grill or broiler.

Toss pork with remaining ½ teaspoon salt. Thread meat and peppers onto skewers. Grill over medium-hot coals 10 minutes until meat is no longer pink in center, turning several times. If broiling, place skewers on foil-lined baking sheet. Broil 8 inches from heat 5 minutes per side until no longer pink in center, turning once. Serve immediately with sour cream sauce.

Makes 4 to 6 servings

Tex-Mex Pork Kabobs with Chili Sour Cream Sauce

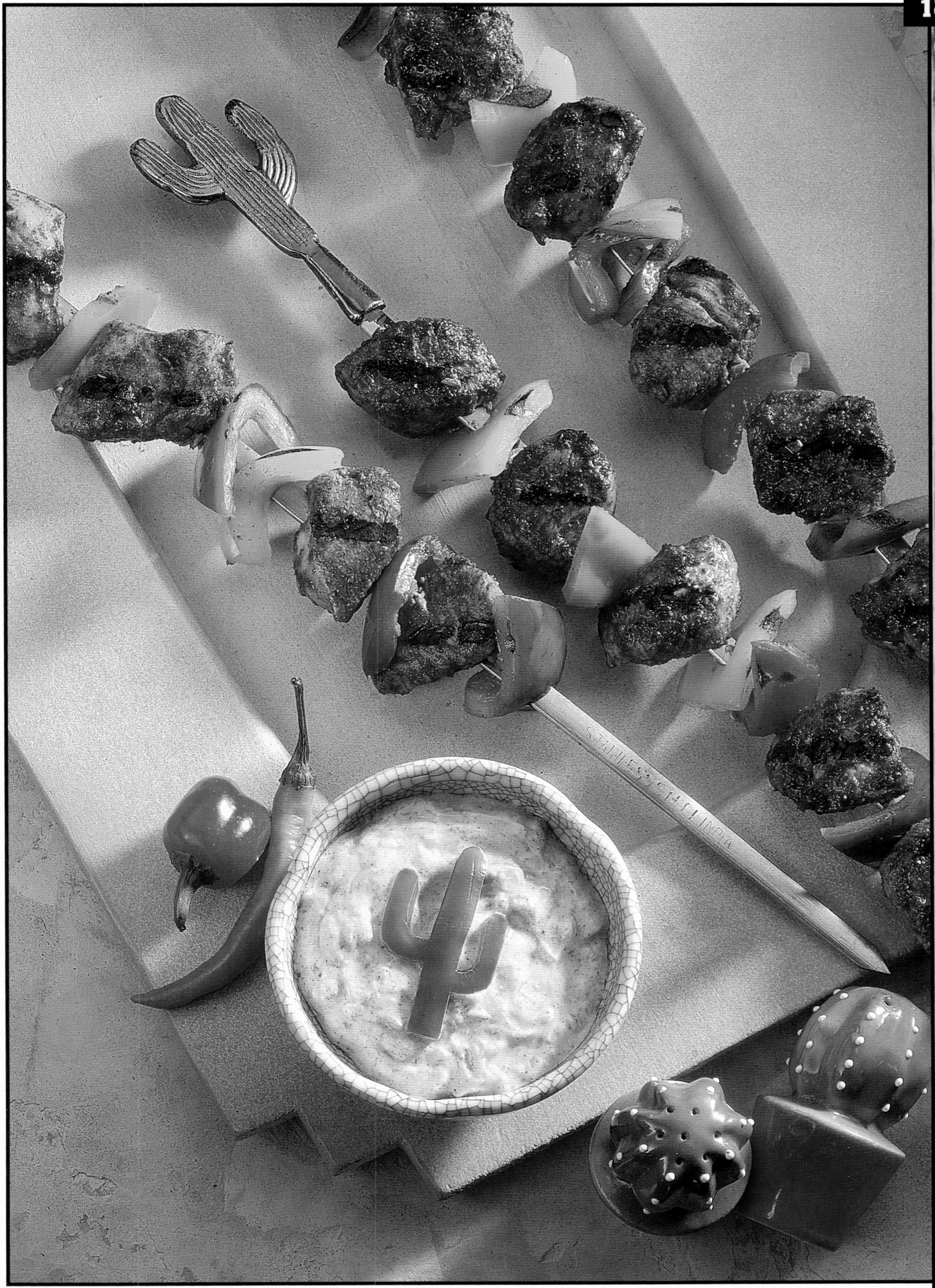

Herb and Orange Pork Chops

2 cups orange juice

3 tablespoons vegetable oil, divided

1½ teaspoons LAWRY'S® Seasoned Salt

1½ teaspoons LAWRY'S® Lemon Pepper

1½ teaspoons LAWRY'S® Garlic Powder with Parsley

1 teaspoon dried basil, crushed

½ teaspoon dried rosemary, crushed

4 pork loin chops, cut ½ inch thick

½ cup thinly sliced green onions

1 teaspoon grated fresh orange peel

In large resealable plastic food storage bag combine orange juice, 2 tablespoons oil and next 5 ingredients; mix well. Remove 1 cup marinade for basting. Add chops; seal bag. Marinate in refrigerator at least 1 hour. Remove chops from marinade; discard used marinade. Grill or broil chops until no longer pink about 8 to 10 minutes, turning halfway through grilling time. In large skillet, heat 1 tablespoon oil. Add onions and orange peel and cook over medium heat 1 minute. Add additional marinade; reduce heat to low and cook until reduced by half. Serve over chops.

Makes 4 servings

Serving Suggestion: Serve with fresh fruit.

Maple-Mustard-Glazed Spareribs

4 pounds pork spareribs
½ teaspoon salt
½ teaspoon pickling spices*
2 teaspoons vegetable oil
1 small onion, coarsely
    chopped
½ cup maple-flavored syrup
¼ cup cider vinegar
2 tablespoons water
1 tablespoon Dijon mustard
    Dash salt
¼ teaspoon black pepper

*Pickling spices is a blend of seasonings used for pickling foods. It can include allspice, bay leaves, cardamom, coriander, cinnamon, cloves, ginger, mustard seeds and/or pepper. Most supermarkets carry prepackaged pickling spices in the spice aisle.

Sprinkle spareribs with ½ teaspoon salt. Place pickling spices in several thicknesses of cheesecloth; tie up to make a bouquet garni. Set aside. For glaze, heat oil in small saucepan; add onion. Cook and stir until tender. Add bouquet garni. Stir in syrup, vinegar, water, mustard, dash salt and pepper. Bring to a boil over medium-high heat; reduce heat to low and simmer 20 minutes. Discard bouquet garni.

Prepare grill with rectangular foil drip pan. Bank briquets on either side of drip pan for indirect cooking. Place ribs on grid over drip pan. Grill, on covered grill, over low coals 1½ hours or until ribs are tender, turning and basting occasionally with glaze. (Do not baste during last 5 minutes of grilling.) *Makes 4 servings*

Prep time: 20 minutes
Cook time: 90 minutes

*Favorite recipe from **National Pork Board***

Maple-Mustard-Glazed Spareribs

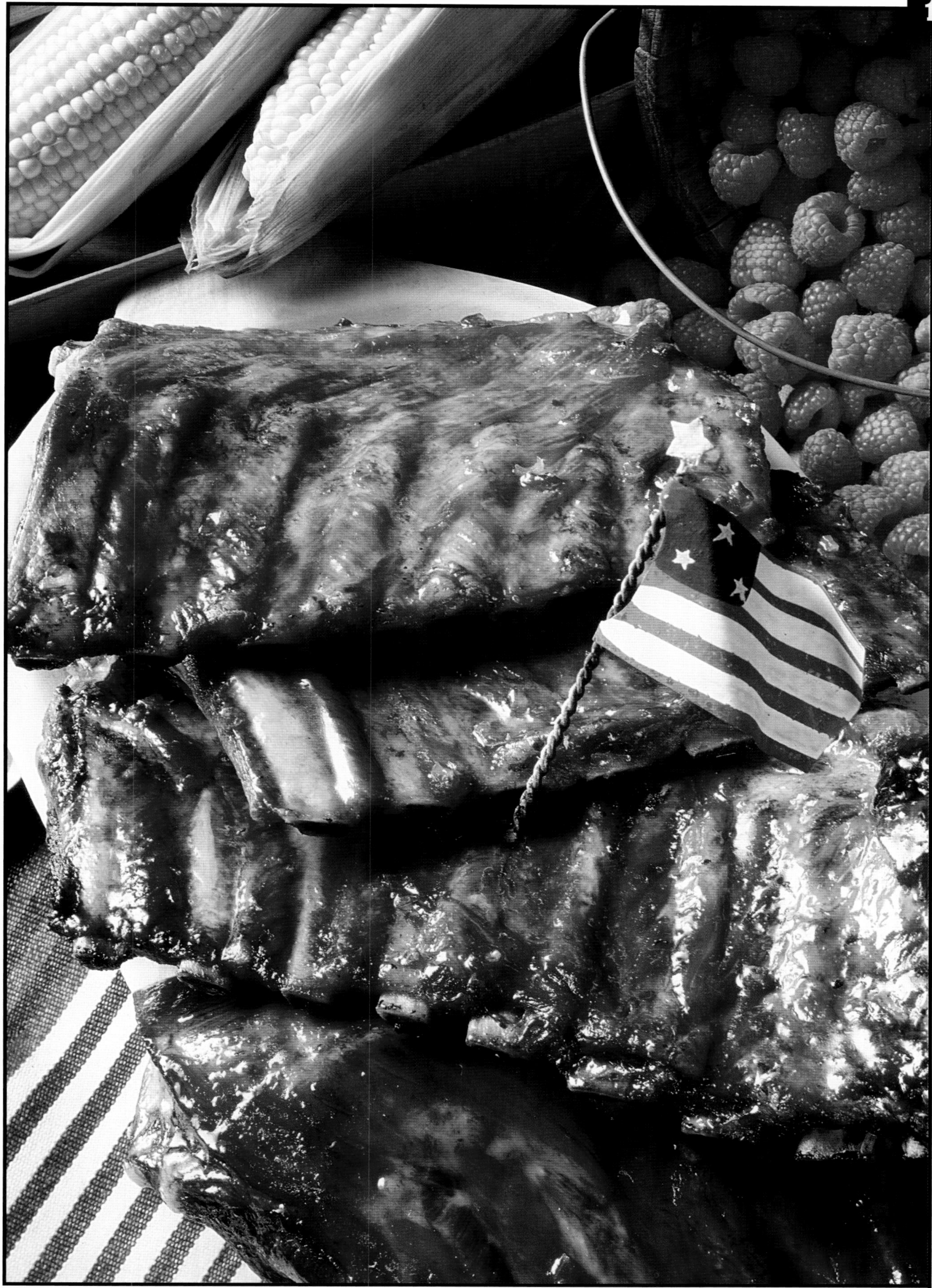

Cuban Garlic & Lime Pork Chops

6 boneless pork chops, ¾ inch thick (about 1½ pounds)

2 tablespoons olive oil

2 tablespoons lime juice

2 tablespoons orange juice

2 teaspoons bottled minced garlic

½ teaspoon salt, divided

½ teaspoon red pepper flakes

2 small seedless oranges, peeled and chopped

1 medium cucumber, peeled, seeded and chopped

2 tablespoons chopped onion

2 tablespoons chopped fresh cilantro

1. Place pork in large resealable plastic food storage bag. Add oil, juices, garlic, ¼ teaspoon salt and pepper. Seal bag and shake to evenly distribute marinade; refrigerate up to 24 hours.

2. To make salsa, combine oranges, cucumber, onion and cilantro in small bowl; toss lightly. Cover and refrigerate 1 hour or overnight. Add remaining ¼ teaspoon salt just before serving.

3. To complete recipe, remove pork from marinade; discard marinade. Grill or broil pork 6 to 8 minutes on each side or until pork is no longer pink in center. Serve with salsa.

Makes 4 to 6 servings

Make-Ahead Time: 1 day before cooking
Final Prep and Cook Time: 16 minutes

Cuban Garlic & Lime Pork Chop

Grilled Chili-Marinated Pork

3 tablespoons ground seeded
   dried pasilla chilies
1 teaspoon coarse or kosher
   salt
½ teaspoon ground cumin
2 tablespoons vegetable oil
1 tablespoon fresh lime juice
3 cloves garlic, minced
2 pounds pork tenderloin or
   thick boneless pork loin
   chops, trimmed of fat
Shredded romaine lettuce
   (optional)
Radishes for garnish
   (optional)

1. Mix chilies, salt and cumin in small bowl. Stir in oil and lime juice to make smooth paste. Stir in garlic.

2. Butterfly pork by cutting lengthwise about ⅔ of the way through, leaving meat in one piece; spread meat flat. Cut tenderloin crosswise into 8 equal pieces. Do not cut chops into pieces.

3. Place pork between pieces of plastic wrap. Pound with flat side of meat mallet to ¼-inch thickness.

4. Spread chili paste on both sides of pork pieces to coat evenly. Place in shallow glass baking dish. Marinate, covered, in refrigerator 2 to 3 hours.

5. Prepare coals for grill or preheat broiler. Grill or broil pork 6 inches from heat 8 to 10 minutes for grilling or 6 to 7 minutes for broiling, turning once. Serve on lettuce-lined plate and garnish, if desired. *Makes 6 to 8 servings*

Grilled Chili-Marinated Pork

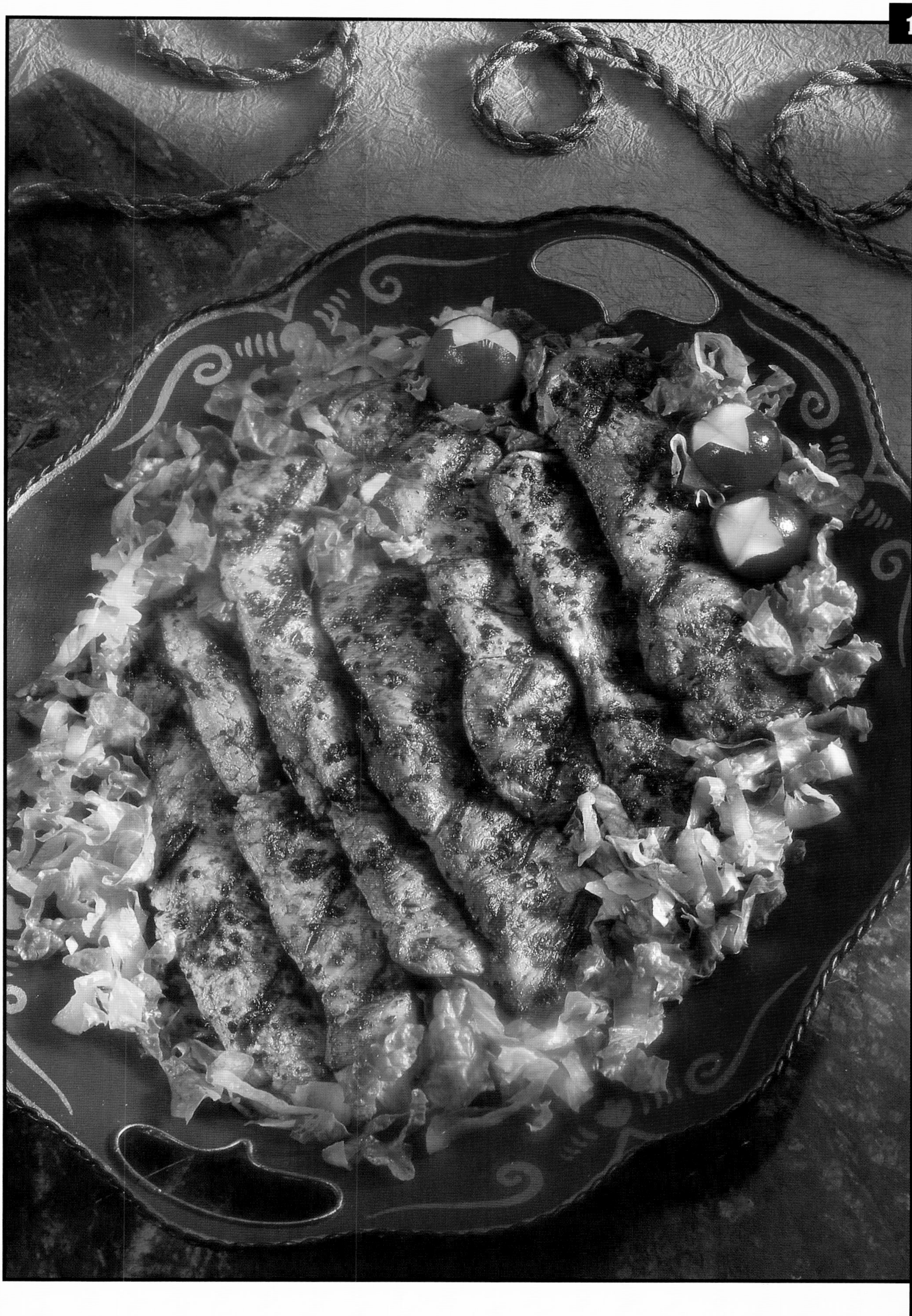

Jerk Ribs

2 pounds pork back ribs
2 tablespoons dried minced onion
1 tablespoon onion powder
4 teaspoons ground thyme
2 teaspoons salt
2 teaspoons ground allspice
½ teaspoon ground nutmeg
½ teaspoon ground cinnamon
1 tablespoon sugar
2 teaspoons black pepper
1 teaspoon ground red pepper

Place all ingredients except ribs in small jar with tight-fitting lid; cover and shake until well blended. Rub dry mixture onto all surfaces of ribs.

Prepare grill with rectangular foil drip pan. Bank briquets on either side of drip pan for indirect cooking. Place ribs on grid over drip pan. Grill, on covered grill, over low coals 1½ hours or until ribs are tender, turning occasionally. To serve, cut into 1- or 2-rib portions. *Makes 10 servings*

Conventional Directions: Prepare rub as directed. Roast ribs on rack in shallow pan in 350°F oven for 1½ hours or until ribs are tender.

Prep time: 10 minutes
Cooking time: 90 minutes

*Favorite recipe from **National Pork Board***

Peanut Pork Tenderloin

⅓ cup chunky unsweetened peanut butter
⅓ cup regular or light canned coconut milk
¼ cup lemon juice or dry white wine
3 tablespoons soy sauce
3 cloves garlic, minced
2 tablespoons sugar
1 piece (1-inch cube) fresh ginger, minced
½ teaspoon salt
¼ to ½ teaspoon cayenne pepper
¼ teaspoon ground cinnamon
1½ pounds pork tenderloin

Combine peanut butter, coconut milk, lemon juice, soy sauce, garlic, sugar, ginger, salt, cayenne pepper and cinnamon in 2-quart glass dish until blended. Add pork; turn to coat. Cover and refrigerate at least 30 minutes or overnight. Remove pork from marinade; discard marinade. Grill pork on covered grill over medium KINGSFORD® Briquets about 20 minutes until just barely pink in center, turning 4 times. Cut crosswise into ½-inch slices. Serve immediately. *Makes 4 to 6 servings*

Garlic-Pepper Skewered Pork

1 boneless pork loin roast
(about 2½ pounds)
6 to 15 cloves garlic, minced
⅓ cup lime juice
3 tablespoons firmly packed
brown sugar
3 tablespoons soy sauce
2 tablespoons vegetable oil
2 teaspoons black pepper
¼ teaspoon cayenne pepper
8 green onions, cut into
2-inch pieces (optional)

Cut pork crosswise into six ½-inch-thick chops, reserving remaining roast. (Each chop may separate into 2 pieces.) Set chops aside in 13×9×2-inch glass dish. Cut remaining pork roast lengthwise into 2 pieces. Cut each piece into ⅛-inch-thick strips; place in dish with chops. To prepare marinade, combine all remaining ingredients except green onions in small bowl. Pour marinade over pork chops and slices; cover and refrigerate at least 1 hour or overnight. Thread pork slices ribbon style onto metal skewers, alternating pork with green onions. Grill skewered pork slices and chops over medium-hot KINGSFORD® Briquets about 3 minutes per side until no longer pink in center. (Chops may require 1 to 2 minutes longer.) *Do not overcook.* Serve skewered pork immediately.

Makes 4 to 6 servings

Greek-Style Loin Roast

1 boneless pork loin roast
   (3 pounds)
¼ cup olive oil
¼ cup lemon juice
1 teaspoon dried oregano
   leaves, crushed
1 teaspoon salt
1 teaspoon black pepper
6 cloves garlic, minced
   Spicy Yogurt Sauce (recipe
   follows)

Place pork loin in large resealable plastic food storage bag. Combine all remaining ingredients except Spicy Yogurt Sauce in small bowl; pour over pork. Seal bag and marinate in refrigerator overnight, turning bag occasionally. Meanwhile, prepare Spicy Yogurt Sauce.

Prepare grill with rectangular foil drip pan. Bank briquets on either side of drip pan for indirect cooking. Remove pork, discarding marinade. Place pork on grill over drip pan. Grill, on covered grill, over low coals 1½ hours or to an internal temperature of 155°F. Let rest 10 minutes. (Internal temperature will rise slightly upon standing.) To serve, thinly slice roast and serve with Spicy Yogurt Sauce.   *Makes 8 servings*

Spicy Yogurt Sauce: Combine 1 cup plain yogurt, 1 peeled and chopped cucumber, ¼ cup minced red onion, ½ teaspoon crushed garlic, ½ teaspoon crushed coriander seeds and ¼ teaspoon crushed red pepper in small bowl; blend well. Cover and refrigerate until ready to serve.

Favorite recipe from **National Pork Board**

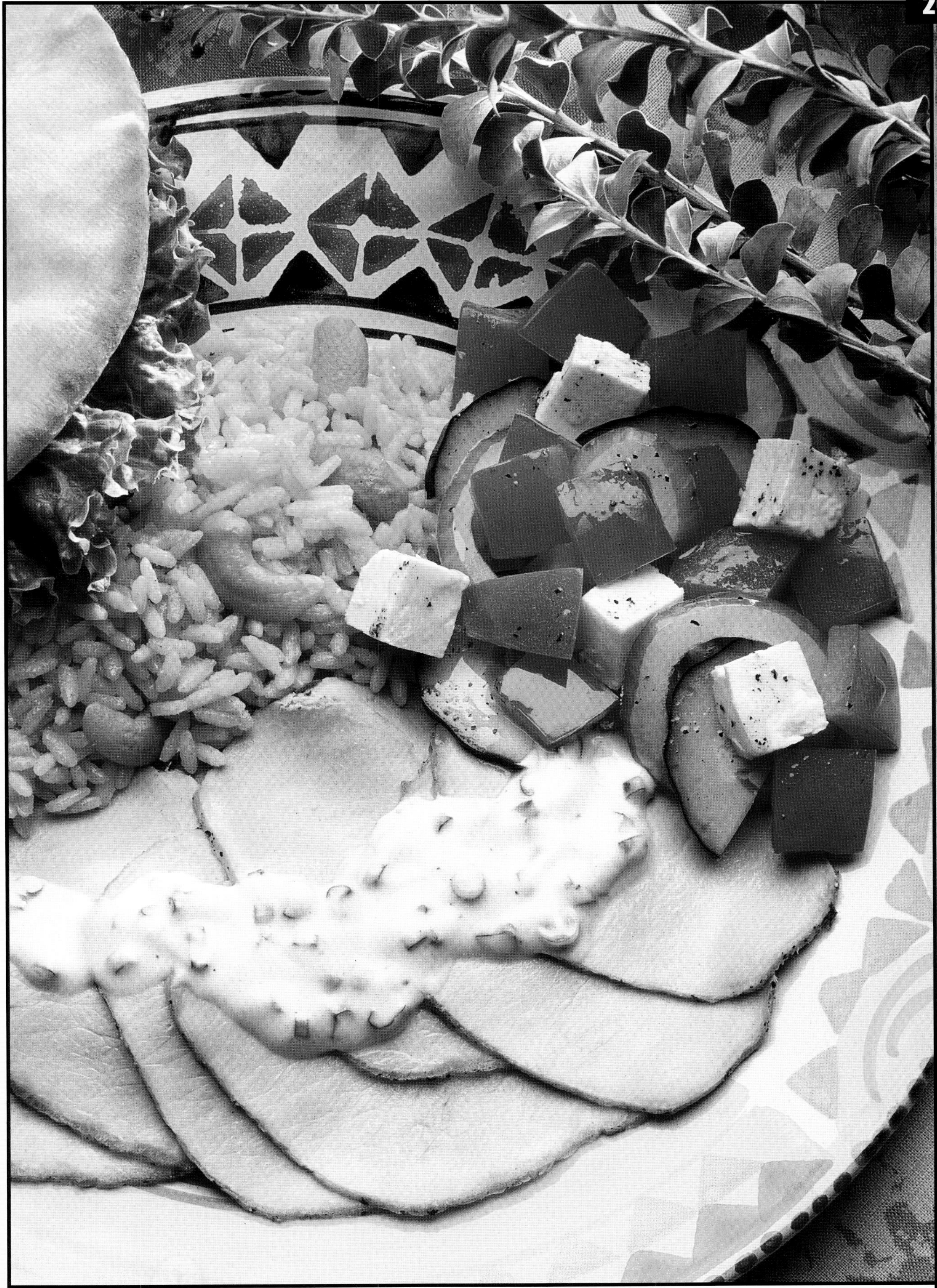

Grilled Pork Tenderloin Medallions

Pepper & Herb Rub

    1 tablespoon dried basil
        leaves

    1 tablespoon garlic salt

    1 tablespoon dried thyme
        leaves

  1½ teaspoons cracked black
        pepper

  1½ teaspoons dried rosemary

    1 teaspoon paprika

Pork

    2 tablespoons Pepper & Herb
        Rub

  12 pork tenderloin medallions
        (about 1 pound)

1. For rub, combine basil, salt, thyme, pepper, rosemary and paprika in small jar or resealable plastic food storage bag. Store in cool dry place up to 3 months.

2. Prepare barbecue for direct cooking. Sprinkle rub evenly over both sides of pork; pressing lightly. Spray pork with olive-oil-flavored nonstick cooking spray.

3. Place pork on grid over medium-hot coals. Grill, uncovered, 4 to 5 minutes per side or until pork is no longer pink in center.

Makes 4 servings

Serving Suggestion: Serve with steamed red potatoes and broccoli.

Grilled Pork Tenderloin Medallions

Smoked Pork Chops with Spinach, Polenta and Cranberry Chutney

6 pork chops, cured and
    smoked (12 ounces *each*)
Sautéed Spinach (recipe
    follows)
Polenta (recipe follows)
Cranberry Chutney (recipe
    follows)

Prepare grill. Grill chops over medium-high heat about 10 minutes or until heated through. Serve with Sautéed Spinach, Polenta and Cranberry Chutney. *Makes 6 servings*

Sautéed Spinach: Melt 1 tablespoon butter in medium skillet over medium heat. Add 12 ounces cleaned fresh spinach; cook and stir 3 to 4 minutes or until softened.

Polenta: Bring 6 cups water to a boil in large saucepan; slowly pour in 1 pound coarse cornmeal and 2 teaspoons salt. Cook and stir 5 to 8 minutes. Stir in 1 cup grated Parmesan cheese and 4 tablespoons butter.

Cranberry Chutney: Heat 1 tablespoon vegetable oil in medium skillet over medium-high heat. Add 1 chopped onion; cook and stir until tender. Stir in 2 cups fresh cranberries, 1 cup water and ¾ cup sugar. Bring to a boil; boil 1 minute. Stir in 2 tablespoons dry mustard and ⅛ teaspoon each ground cloves, cinnamon and mace.

Prep time: 30 minutes
Cooking time: 10 minutes

Favorite recipe from **National Pork Board**

Grilled Pork Loin with Honey and Port

1½ pounds boneless pork loin
2 tablespoons olive oil
1 tablespoon kosher salt
1½ cups tawny port
1 cup orange juice
¼ cup honey
2 tablespoons cider vinegar
¼ cup minced green onions
1 cup dried apricots
1 teaspoon dried rosemary
    leaves, crushed

Rub pork loin with olive oil and kosher salt. Place in shallow glass baking dish. Combine remaining ingredients in saucepan. Bring to a boil over medium-high heat; reduce heat to low and simmer 5 minutes. Pour hot marinade over pork; cover and marinate in refrigerator 2 to 3 hours.

Prepare grill. Remove pork, reserving marinade. Sear all sides of pork roast on grill. Place on roasting rack. Grill, on covered grill, over medium coals about 35 minutes or to an internal temperature of 150°F, basting frequently with marinade. Remove from grill. Cover and keep warm 15 minutes. Reserve all juices.

Bring reserved marinade to a boil over medium-high heat; reduce heat to low and simmer 5 minutes. Add pork juices and simmer 2 to 3 minutes more. To serve, slice pork loin; arrange on plates. Pour warm sauce over slices.

Makes 6 servings

Prep time: 10 minutes
Cooking time: 40 minutes

*Favorite recipe from **National Pork Board***

Hot and Spicy Spareribs

1 rack pork spareribs
   (3 pounds)
2 tablespoons butter or
   margarine
1 medium onion, finely
   chopped
2 cloves garlic, minced
1 can (15 ounces) tomato
   sauce
⅔ cup packed brown sugar
⅔ cup cider vinegar
2 tablespoons chili powder
1 tablespoon prepared
   mustard
½ teaspoon black pepper

Melt butter in large skillet over low heat. Add onion and garlic; cook and stir until tender. Add remaining ingredients, except ribs, and bring to a boil. Reduce heat and simmer 20 minutes, stirring occasionally.

Place large piece of aluminum foil over coals to catch drippings. Baste meaty side of ribs with sauce. Place ribs on grill, meaty side down, about 6 inches above low coals; baste top side. Cover. Cook about 20 minutes; turn ribs and baste. Cook 45 minutes more or until done, basting every 10 to 15 minutes with sauce. *Makes 3 servings*

Favorite recipe from **National Pork Board**

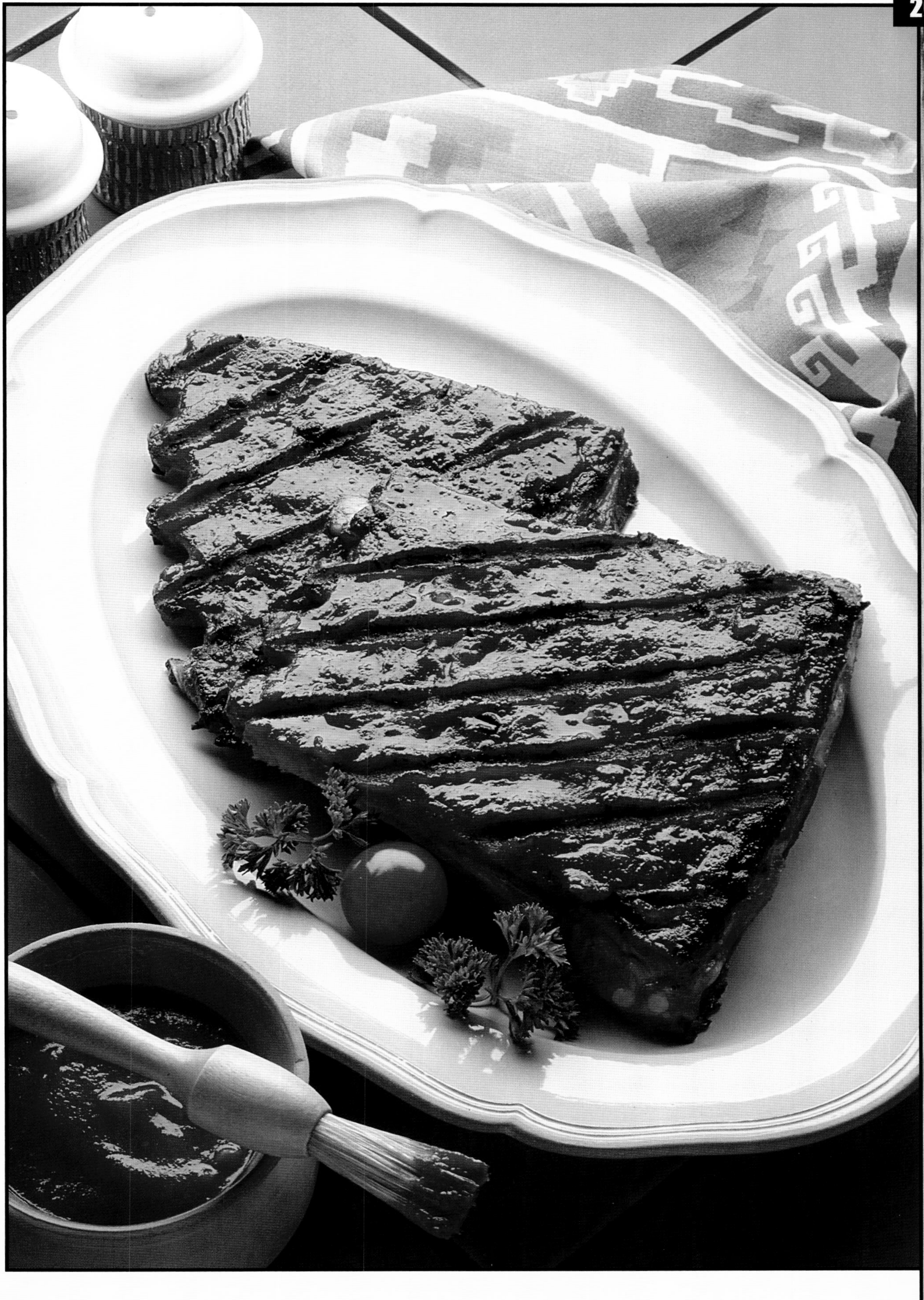

Grilled Pork Tenderloin with Tomato-Mango Salsa

2 (¾-pound) pork tenderloins
⅓ cup reduced-sodium teriyaki sauce
2 medium tomatoes, seeded and diced
1 cup diced mango
½ cup minced yellow or green bell pepper
¼ cup hot jalapeño jelly, melted
2 tablespoons white wine vinegar

1. Rub pork tenderloins all over with teriyaki sauce; let stand 5 minutes.

2. Combine tomatoes, mango, bell pepper, jelly and vinegar in medium bowl; mix well. Set aside.

3. Grill pork, covered, over medium-hot coals 20 to 25 minutes or until meat thermometer inserted in thickest part registers 160°F, turning once. Slice and serve with salsa.

Makes 6 servings

Prep and Cook Time: 30 minutes

Margarita Pork Kabobs

1 cup margarita drink mix *or*
    1 cup lime juice,
    4 teaspoons sugar and
    ½ teaspoon salt
1 teaspoon ground coriander
1 clove garlic, minced
1 pound pork tenderloin, cut into 1-inch cubes
2 tablespoons margarine, melted
1 tablespoon minced fresh parsley
2 teaspoons lime juice
⅛ teaspoon sugar
1 large green or red bell pepper, cut into 1-inch cubes
2 ears corn, cut into 8 pieces

For marinade, combine margarita mix, coriander and garlic in small bowl. Place pork cubes in large resealable plastic food storage bag; pour marinade over pork. Close bag securely; turn to coat. Marinate for at least 30 minutes. Combine margarine, parsley, lime juice and sugar in small bowl; set aside. Thread pork cubes onto four skewers, alternating with pieces of bell pepper and corn. (If using bamboo skewers, soak in water 20 to 30 minutes before using to prevent them from burning.) Grill over hot coals for 15 to 20 minutes or until barely pink in center, basting with margarine mixture and turning frequently.

Makes 4 servings

Favorite recipe from **National Pork Board**

Grilled Pork Tenderloin with
Tomato Mango Salsa

Grilled Pork and Potatoes Vesuvio

1 center-cut boneless pork
    loin roast (1½ pounds),
    well trimmed and cut into
    1-inch cubes
½ cup dry white wine
2 tablespoons olive oil
4 cloves garlic, minced and
    divided
1½ to 2 pounds small red
    potatoes (about
    1½ inches in diameter),
    scrubbed
6 lemon wedges
  Salt (optional)
  Pepper (optional)
¼ cup chopped fresh Italian or
    curly leaf parsley
1 teaspoon finely grated
    lemon peel

1. Place pork in large resealable plastic food storage bag. Combine wine, oil and 3 cloves garlic in small bowl; pour over pork.

2. Place potatoes in single layer in microwavable dish. Pierce each potato with tip of sharp knife. Microwave at HIGH (100% power) 6 to 7 minutes or until almost tender when pierced with fork. (Or, place potatoes in large saucepan. Cover with cold water. Bring to a boil over high heat. Simmer about 12 minutes or until almost tender when pierced with fork.) Immediately rinse with cold water; drain. Add to pork in bag. Seal bag tightly, turning to coat. Marinate in refrigerator at least 2 hours or up to 8 hours, turning occasionally.

3. Prepare barbecue grill for direct cooking.

4. Meanwhile, drain pork mixture; discard marinade. Alternately thread about 3 pork cubes and 2 potatoes onto each of 6 skewers. Place 1 lemon wedge on end of each skewer. Season pork and potatoes to taste with salt and pepper.

5. Place skewers on grid. Grill skewers, on covered grill, over medium coals 14 to 16 minutes or until pork is juicy and no longer pink in center and potatoes are tender, turning halfway through grilling time.

6. Remove skewers from grill. Combine parsley, lemon peel and remaining minced garlic clove in small bowl. Sprinkle over pork and potatoes. To serve, squeeze lemon wedges over pork and potatoes. *Makes 6 servings*

Grilled Pork and Potatoes Vesuvio

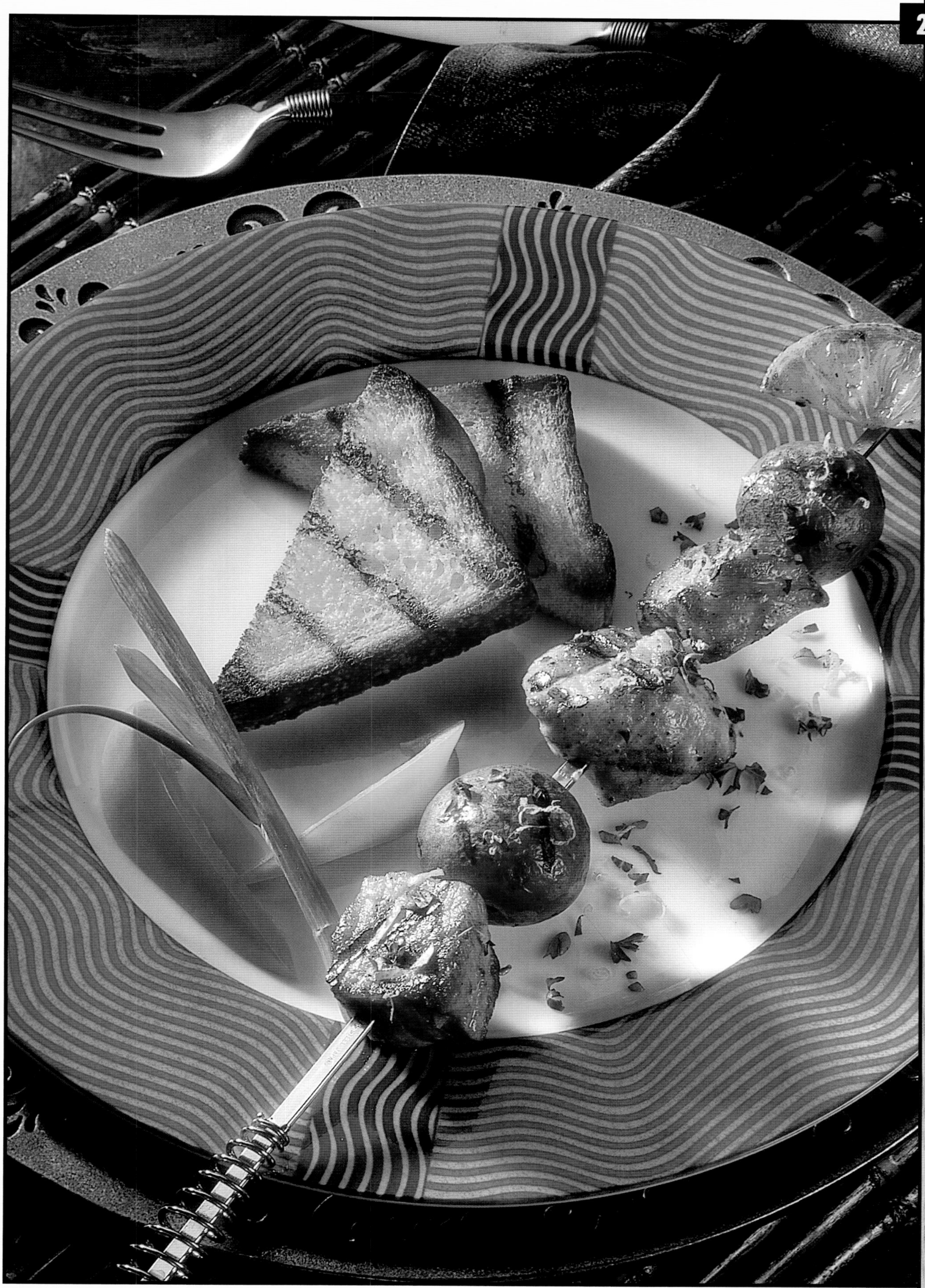

Grilled Honey Garlic Pork Chops

¼ cup lemon juice

¼ cup honey

2 tablespoons soy sauce

1 tablespoon dry sherry

2 cloves garlic, minced

4 boneless center-cut lean
   pork chops (about
   4 ounces each)

Combine all ingredients except pork chops in small bowl. Place pork in shallow baking dish; pour marinade over pork. Cover and refrigerate 4 hours or overnight. Remove pork from marinade. Heat remaining marinade in small saucepan over medium heat to a simmer. Grill pork over medium-hot coals 12 to 15 minutes, turning once during cooking and basting frequently with marinade, until meat thermometer registers 155° to 160°F.

Makes 4 servings

Favorite recipe from **National Honey Board**

Spicy Baby Back Ribs

2 tablespoons olive oil

2 racks pork baby back ribs
   (3½ to 4 pounds)

¼ cup packed brown sugar

2 teaspoons dry mustard

2 teaspoons seasoned salt

1 teaspoon garlic powder

1 teaspoon black pepper

⅓ to ½ cup barbecue sauce

½ teaspoon hot pepper sauce

1. Prepare grill for indirect cooking.

2. Pour 1 tablespoon olive oil over each rack of ribs; rub to coat. Combine brown sugar, mustard, salt, garlic powder and pepper in small bowl. Rub mixture evenly over ribs. Place ribs on grid directly over drip pan. Grill, covered, over medium coals 1 hour, turning occasionally.

3. Meanwhile, combine barbecue sauce and hot pepper sauce in small bowl. Baste ribs generously with sauce; grill 30 minutes more or until ribs are tender, turning and basting with sauce occasionally. Bring any remaining barbecue sauce to boil over medium-high heat; boil 1 minute. Serve ribs with remaining sauce.

Makes 4 servings

Grilled Honey Garlic Pork Chop

Citrus Barbecued Pork Loin

1 cup orange juice
¼ cup soy sauce
1 teaspoon LAWRY'S® Garlic
    Powder with Parsley
½ teaspoon LAWRY'S®
    Seasoned Pepper
2 teaspoons LAWRY'S®
    Seasoned Salt
1 boneless pork loin (3 to
    3½ pounds)

In large resealable plastic food storage bag, combine orange juice, soy sauce, Garlic Powder with Parsley and Seasoned Pepper; mix well. Remove ½ cup marinade for basting. Sprinkle additional Seasoned Salt on all sides of pork. Add pork to marinade; seal bag. Marinate in refrigerator 1 hour. Remove pork from marinade; discard used marinade. Grill pork 30 minutes or until internal temperature reaches 170°F. turning once and basting often with additional ½ cup marinade. *Do not baste during last 5 minutes of cooking.* Discard any remaining marinade. Let stand 10 minutes before slicing.

Makes 6 servings

Serving Suggestion: Serve with grilled potato slices or potato salad. Garnish with sprig of rosemary and thin orange slice, if desired.

Hint: Pork loin may be baked, uncovered, in 350°F. oven 1 hour or until internal temperature reaches 160°F.

Barbecued Ribs with Oriental Plum Sauce

3 pounds pork spareribs
½ cup water
   Oriental Plum Sauce (recipe
     follows)

Arrange ribs in single layer in 13×9-inch microwave-safe dish. Pour water over ribs. Cover loosely with plastic wrap. Microwave on MEDIUM-HIGH (70% power) 20 minutes, rearranging ribs once.

Place ribs on grid. Grill over medium coals 20 minutes or until barely pink near bone, basting with Oriental Plum Sauce during last 10 minutes of cooking. Serve with remaining sauce.

Makes 4 servings

Oriental Plum Sauce

1 jar (10 ounces) plum jam
2 tablespoons *Frank's® RedHot®* Cayenne Pepper
   Sauce
2 tablespoons prepared seafood cocktail sauce
   or chili sauce
1 teaspoon grated peeled fresh ginger

Combine ingredients in small saucepan. Cook over medium heat 3 minutes or until hot and bubbly, stirring occasionally. Cool completely.

Makes about 1½ cups

Prep Time: 20 minutes
Cook Time: 40 minutes

Honey Dijon Barbecue Ribettes

2½ **pounds baby back pork
      spareribs, split**
 2 **cloves garlic, minced**
 1 **tablespoon vegetable oil**
⅔ **cup chili sauce**
⅓ **cup GREY POUPON® Dijon
      Mustard**
¼ **cup honey**
 6 **thin lemon slices**
½ **teaspoon liquid hot pepper
      seasoning**

1. Place ribs in large heavy pot; fill pot with water to cover ribs. Bring to a boil over high heat; reduce heat. Cover; simmer for 30 to 40 minutes or until ribs are tender. Drain.

2. Meanwhile, cook garlic in oil in medium saucepan over low heat until tender. Stir in chili sauce, mustard, honey, lemon slices and hot pepper seasoning. Cook over medium heat until heated through, about 2 to 3 minutes.

3. Brush ribs with prepared sauce. Grill over medium heat for 15 to 20 minutes or until done, turning and brushing often with remaining sauce. Slice into individual pieces to serve; garnish as desired. Serve hot. *Makes 8 servings*

Honey Dijon Barbecue Ribettes

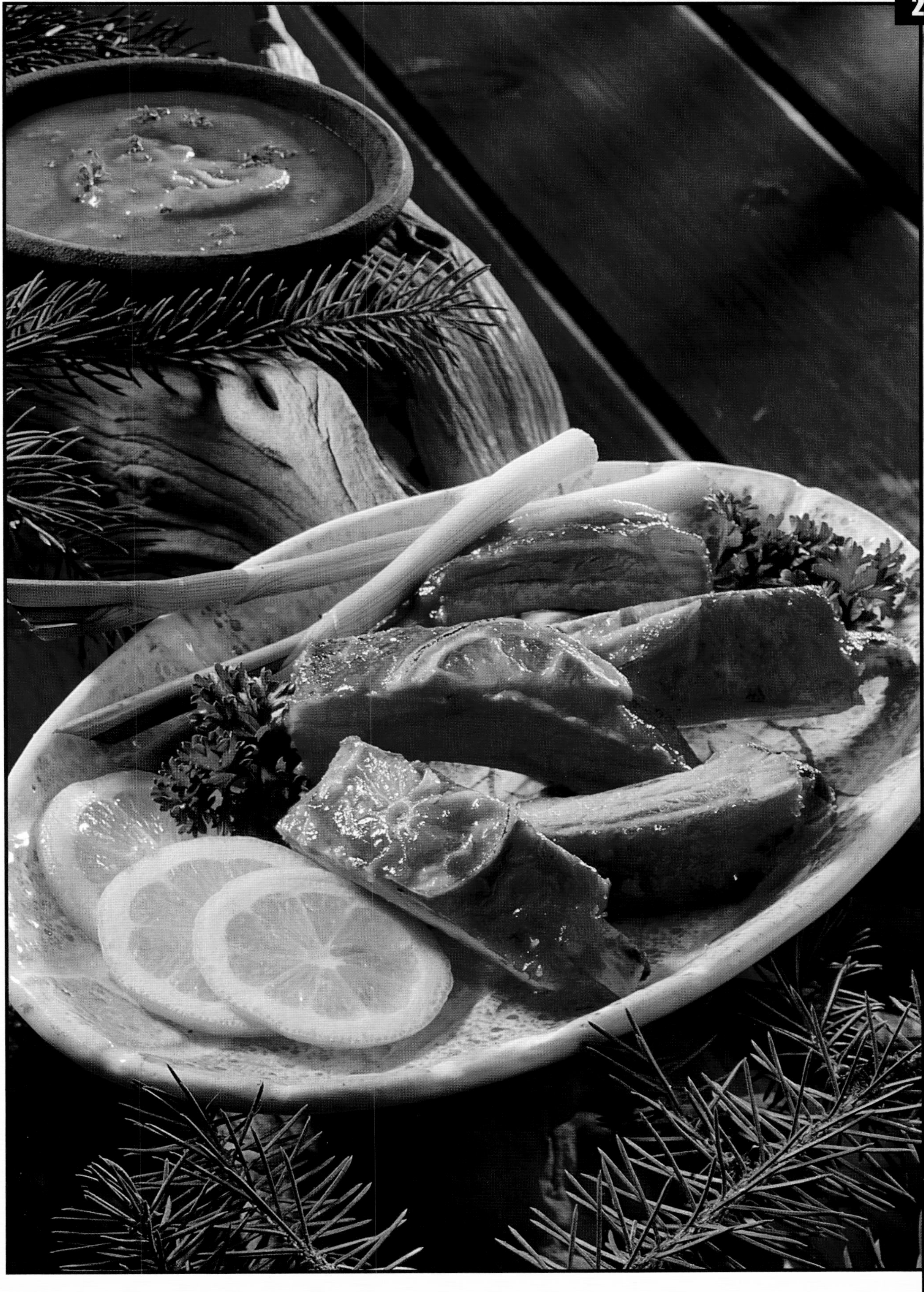

1 ripe medium papaya,
   peeled, halved lengthwise
   and seeded
1 teaspoon paprika
½ teaspoon dried thyme leaves
¼ teaspoon salt
¼ teaspoon ground allspice
4 center-cut pork loin chops
   (about 1½ pounds), cut
   ¾ inch thick
5 tablespoons fresh lime juice,
   divided
2 tablespoons plus
   1½ teaspoons seeded,
   chopped jalapeño
   peppers,* divided
1 tablespoon vegetable oil
1½ teaspoons grated fresh
   ginger, divided
1 teaspoon sugar
¼ cup finely diced red bell
   pepper
   Additional chopped
   jalapeño pepper for
   garnish

*Jalapeño peppers can sting and irritate the skin; wear rubber gloves when handling peppers and do not touch eyes. Wash hands after handling peppers.

1. Chop enough papaya into ¼-inch pieces to measure 1½ cups; set aside.

2. Combine paprika, thyme, salt and allspice in small bowl; rub over both sides of pork chops with fingers. Place chops in large resealable plastic food storage bag.

3. Combine 3 tablespoons lime juice, 2 tablespoons jalapeños, oil, 1 teaspoon ginger and sugar in small bowl; pour over chops. Seal bag tightly, turning to coat. Marinate in refrigerator 1 to 2 hours.

4. Combine papaya, bell pepper, remaining 2 tablespoons lime juice, remaining 1½ teaspoons jalapeños and remaining ½ teaspoon ginger in another small bowl; cover and refrigerate until serving.

5. Prepare barbecue grill for direct cooking.

6. Drain chops; discard marinade. Place chops on grid. Grill chops, on covered grill, over medium coals 10 to 12 minutes or until pork is juicy and barely pink in center, turning halfway through grilling time. Serve chops topped with papaya mixture. Garnish, if desired. *Makes 4 servings*

Calypso Pork Chop

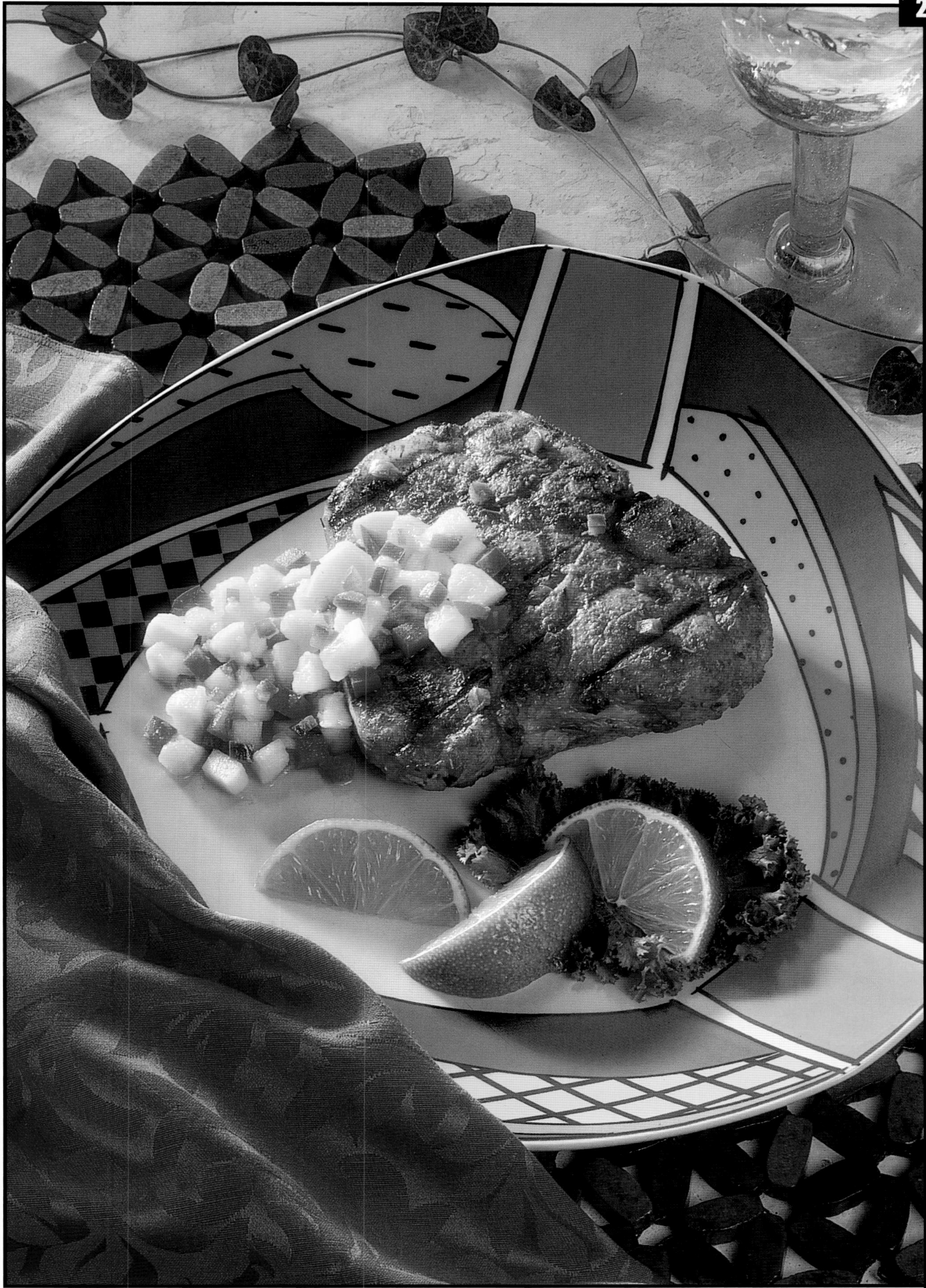

Jamaican Pork Chops with Tropical Fruit Salsa

⅔ cup prepared Italian salad
    dressing
⅓ cup *Frank's® RedHot®*
    Cayenne Pepper Sauce
⅓ cup lime juice
2 tablespoons brown sugar
2 teaspoons dried thyme
    leaves
1 teaspoon ground allspice
½ teaspoon ground nutmeg
½ teaspoon ground cinnamon
6 loin pork chops, cut 1 inch
    thick (about 2½ pounds)
Tropical Fruit Salsa (recipe
    follows)

Place salad dressing, *Frank's RedHot* Sauce, lime juice, sugar and seasonings in blender or food processor. Cover and process until smooth. Reserve ½ cup dressing mixture for Tropical Fruit Salsa. Place pork chops in large resealable plastic food storage bag. Pour remaining dressing mixture over chops. Seal bag and marinate in refrigerator 1 hour.

Place chops on grid, reserving dressing mixture. Grill over medium coals 30 minutes or until pork is juicy and barely pink in center, turning and basting frequently with dressing mixture. (Do not baste during last 5 minutes of cooking.) Serve chops with Tropical Fruit Salsa. Garnish as desired.
Makes 6 servings

Tropical Fruit Salsa

1 cup finely chopped fresh pineapple
1 ripe mango, peeled, seeded and finely chopped
2 tablespoons finely chopped red onion
1 tablespoon minced fresh cilantro leaves

Combine pineapple, mango, onion, cilantro and reserved ½ cup dressing mixture in small bowl. Refrigerate until chilled.
Makes about 2½ cups

Prep Time: 20 minutes
Marinate Time: 1 hour
Cook Time: 30 minutes

**Jamaican Pork Chop with
Tropical Fruit Salsa**

BURGER
BOUNTY

Think a burger is just a burger? Think again. Take a closer look and you'll find an abundance of burger options that will surprise everyone, including you.

Easy Salmon Burgers with Honey Barbecue Sauce

⅓ cup honey

⅓ cup ketchup

1½ teaspoons cider vinegar

1 teaspoon prepared horseradish

¼ teaspoon minced garlic

⅛ teaspoon crushed red pepper flakes (optional)

1 can (7½ ounces) salmon, drained

½ cup dried bread crumbs

¼ cup chopped onion

3 tablespoons chopped green bell pepper

1 egg white

2 hamburger buns, toasted

In small bowl, combine honey, ketchup, vinegar, horseradish, garlic and red pepper flakes until well blended. Set aside half of sauce. In separate bowl, mix together salmon, bread crumbs, onion, green pepper and egg white. Blend in 2 tablespoons remaining sauce. Divide salmon mixture into 2 patties, ½ to ¾ inch thick. Place patties on well-oiled grill, 4 to 6 inches from hot coals. Grill, turning 2 to 3 times and basting with sauce, until burgers are browned and cooked through. Or place patties on lightly greased baking sheet. Broil 4 to 6 inches from heat source, turning 2 to 3 times and basting with remaining sauce, until cooked through. Place on hamburger buns and serve with reserved sauce.

Makes 2 servings

Favorite recipe from **National Honey Board**

Easy Salmon Burgers with Honey Barbecue Sauce

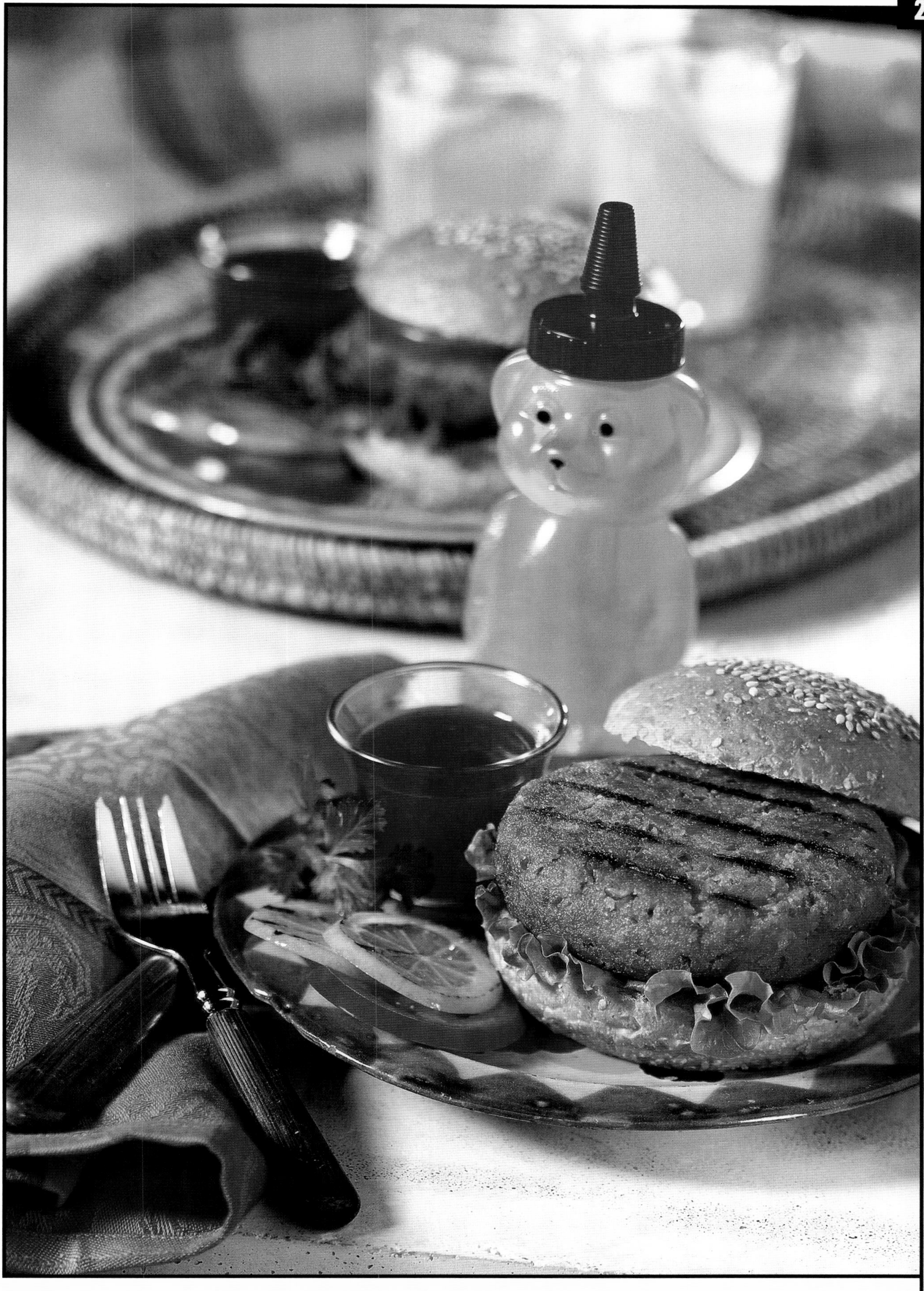

Blue Cheese Burgers with Red Onion

2 pounds ground beef chuck
2 cloves garlic, minced
1 teaspoon salt
½ teaspoon black pepper
4 ounces blue cheese
⅓ cup coarsely chopped walnuts, toasted
1 torpedo (long) red onion *or* 2 small red onions, sliced into ⅜-inch-thick rounds
2 baguettes (each 12 inches long)
Olive or vegetable oil

Combine beef, garlic, salt and pepper in medium bowl. Shape meat mixture into 12 oval patties. Mash cheese and blend with walnuts in small bowl. Divide cheese mixture equally; place onto centers of 6 meat patties. Top with remaining meat patties; tightly pinch edges together to seal in filling.

Oil hot grid to help prevent sticking. Grill patties and onion, if desired, on covered grill, over medium KINGSFORD® Briquets, 7 to 12 minutes for medium doneness, turning once. Cut baguettes into 4-inch lengths; split each piece and brush cut side with olive oil. Move cooked burgers to edge of grill to keep warm. Grill bread, oil side down, until lightly toasted. Serve burgers on toasted baguettes. *Makes 6 servings*

Blue Cheese Burger with Red Onions

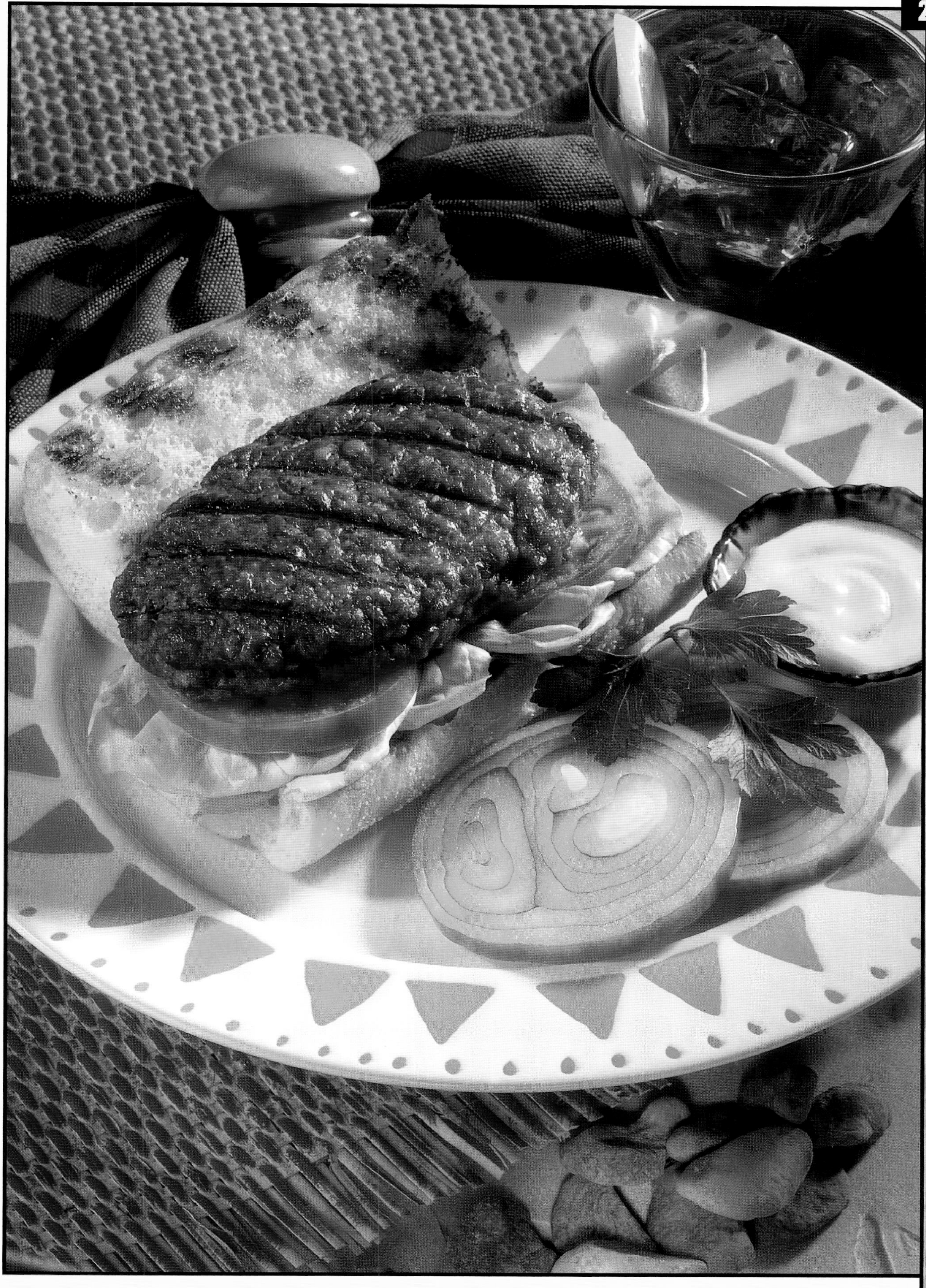

Santa Monica Burgers

1 package (about 1¼ pounds)
    PERDUE® Fresh Ground
    Turkey, Ground Turkey
    Breast Meat or Ground
    Chicken
4 strips crisp bacon, crumbled
¼ cup chopped tomato
¼ cup chopped onion
1 teaspoon salt
¼ teaspoon ground pepper
4 to 5 sourdough rolls

In mixing bowl, combine turkey, bacon, tomato, onion, salt and pepper. Form into 4 or 5 burgers and grill following package directions. Serve on split, lightly toasted rolls, garnished with Guaco-Mayo (recipe below), if desired.

Makes 4 servings

To make Guaco-Mayo: In food processor or blender, combine 1 small ripe avocado, ½ cup mayonnaise, 2 tablespoons chopped onion, 2 tablespoons lemon juice and 1 pickled jalapeño pepper. Purée; stir in 1 chopped mild chile and ¼ cup peeled, seeded and chopped tomato.

Velveeta® Stuffed Burgers

1½ pounds lean ground beef
½ pound (8 ounces)
    VELVEETA® Pasteurized
    Prepared Cheese Product
    or VELVEETA LIGHT®
    Reduced Fat Pasteurized
    Prepared Cheese Product,
    cut up
4 hamburger buns, split,
    toasted
Lettuce leaves, tomato
    slices, red onion slices

SHAPE meat into 8 thin patties. Top 4 patties each with ¼ of VELVEETA. Top with remaining 4 patties; pinch edges together to seal.

PLACE on grill over medium coals. Grill 7 to 9 minutes on each side or until cooked through (160°F). Serve patties in buns topped with lettuce, tomato and onion. *Makes 4 sandwiches*

Great Substitute: Substitute ½ pound (8 ounces) VELVEETA Mexican Pasteurized Prepared Cheese Product with Jalapeño Peppers for VELVEETA Pasteurized Prepared Cheese Product.

Prep: 15 minutes
Grill: 18 minutes

Taco Burgers

2 pounds ground beef
1 envelope LIPTON® RECIPE
SECRETS® Onion Soup
Mix*
½ cup finely chopped green
bell pepper
1 medium tomato, chopped
2 teaspoons chili powder

*Also terrific with Lipton® Recipe Secrets® Beefy
Onion or Beefy Mushroom Soup Mix.

In large bowl, combine all ingredients; shape into 12 oblong burgers. Grill or broil until meat is no longer pink. Serve, if desired, in taco shells or frankfurter rolls and top with shredded lettuce and shredded Cheddar cheese.

Makes 12 servings

Pita Burgers

1 package (about 1¼ pounds)
PERDUE® Fresh Ground
Chicken or Turkey
2 garlic cloves, minced
2 teaspoons paprika
1 teaspoon salt
1 teaspoon ground cumin
1 teaspoon ground allspice
¼ teaspoon ground red
pepper
6 pita breads, opened and
lightly grilled
Yogurt Sauce (recipe
follows)
3 plum tomatoes, thinly sliced
1 small cucumber, thinly
sliced

Prepare lightly greased grill for cooking. In medium bowl, combine ground turkey, garlic and seasonings. Form mixture into 6 burgers. Grill, uncovered, 5 to 6 inches over medium-hot coals 4 to 5 minutes on each side or until burgers are cooked through and spring back when touched.

Serve burgers in pita pockets topped with yogurt sauce, tomatoes and cucumbers.

Makes 4 to 6 servings

Yogurt Sauce: In small bowl, combine 1 cup plain yogurt, 1 tablespoon minced fresh parsley, 2 teaspoons minced fresh cilantro, and 1½ teaspoons minced fresh mint or ½ teaspoon dried mint. Season with salt and ground pepper to taste.

Greek Lamb Burgers

¼ cup pine nuts
1 pound lean ground lamb
¼ cup finely chopped onion
3 cloves garlic, minced and divided
¾ teaspoon salt
¼ teaspoon black pepper
¼ cup plain yogurt
¼ teaspoon sugar
4 slices red onion (¼ inch thick)
1 tablespoon olive oil
8 pumpernickel bread slices
12 thin cucumber slices
4 tomato slices

Prepare grill for direct cooking. Meanwhile, heat small skillet over medium heat until hot. Add pine nuts; cook 30 to 45 seconds until light brown, shaking pan occasionally.

Combine lamb, pine nuts, chopped onion, 2 cloves garlic, salt and pepper in large bowl; mix well. Shape mixture into 4 patties, about ½ inch thick and 4 inches in diameter. Combine yogurt, sugar and remaining 1 clove garlic in small bowl; set aside.

Brush 1 side of each patty and onion slice with oil; place on grid, oiled sides down. Brush tops with oil. Grill, on covered grill, over medium-hot coals 8 to 10 minutes for medium or to desired doneness, turning halfway through grilling time. Place bread on grid to toast during last few minutes of grilling time; grill 1 to 2 minutes per side.

Top 4 bread slices with patties and red onion slices; top each with 3 cucumber slices and 1 tomato slice. Dollop evenly with yogurt mixture. Top sandwiches with remaining 4 bread slices. Serve immediately. *Makes 4 servings*

Greek Lamb Burger

Mushroom-Stuffed Pork Burgers

¾ **cup thinly sliced fresh mushrooms**
¼ **cup thinly sliced green onion**
1 **clove garlic, minced**
2 **teaspoons butter or margarine**
1½ **pounds lean ground pork**
1 **teaspoon Dijon-style mustard**
1 **teaspoon Worcestershire sauce**
¼ **teaspoon salt**
⅛ **teaspoon freshly ground pepper**

In skillet, sauté mushrooms, onion and garlic in butter until tender, about 2 minutes; set aside.

Combine ground pork, mustard, Worcestershire sauce, salt and pepper; mix well. Shape into 12 patties, about 4 inches in diameter. Spoon mushroom mixture onto center of 6 patties. Spread to within ½ inch of edges. Top with remaining 6 patties; seal edges.

Place patties on grill about 6 inches over medium coals. Grill 10 to 15 minutes or until no longer pink in center, turning once. Serve on buns, if desired. *Makes 6 servings*

Prep Time: 15 minutes
Cook Time: 15 minutes

Favorite recipe from **National Pork Board**

Mushroom-Stuffed Pork Burger

Polynesian Burgers

¼ cup LAWRY'S® Teriyaki Marinade with Pineapple Juice
1 pound ground beef
½ cup chopped green bell pepper
4 onion-flavored hamburger buns
1 can (5¼ ounces) pineapple slices, drained
Lettuce leaves

In medium bowl, combine Teriyaki Marinade, ground beef and bell pepper; mix well. Let stand 10 to 15 minutes. Shape into 4 patties. Grill or broil burgers 8 to 10 minutes or until desired doneness, turning halfway through grilling time. Serve burgers on onion buns topped with pineapple slices and lettuce. *Makes 4 servings*

Serving Suggestion: Serve with assorted fresh fruits.

Hint: For extra teriyaki flavor, brush buns and pineapple slices with additional Teriyaki Marinade; grill or broil until buns are lightly toasted and pineapple is heated through.

Bistro Burgers with Blue Cheese

1 pound ground turkey or beef
¼ cup chopped fresh parsley
2 tablespoons minced chives
¼ teaspoon dried thyme leaves
2 tablespoons *French's®* Napa Valley Style Dijon Mustard
Lettuce and tomato slices
4 crusty rolls, split in half
2 ounces blue cheese, crumbled
1⅓ cups *French's®* French Fried Onions

1. In large bowl, gently mix meat, herbs and mustard. Shape into 4 patties.

2. Grill or broil patties 10 minutes or until no longer pink in center. Arrange lettuce and tomatoes on bottom half of rolls. Place burgers on top. Sprinkle with blue cheese and French Fried Onions. Cover with top half of rolls. Serve with additional mustard.

Toast onions in microwave 1 minute for extra crispness. *Makes 4 servings*

Prep Time: 10 minutes
Cook Time: 10 minutes

Polynesian Burger

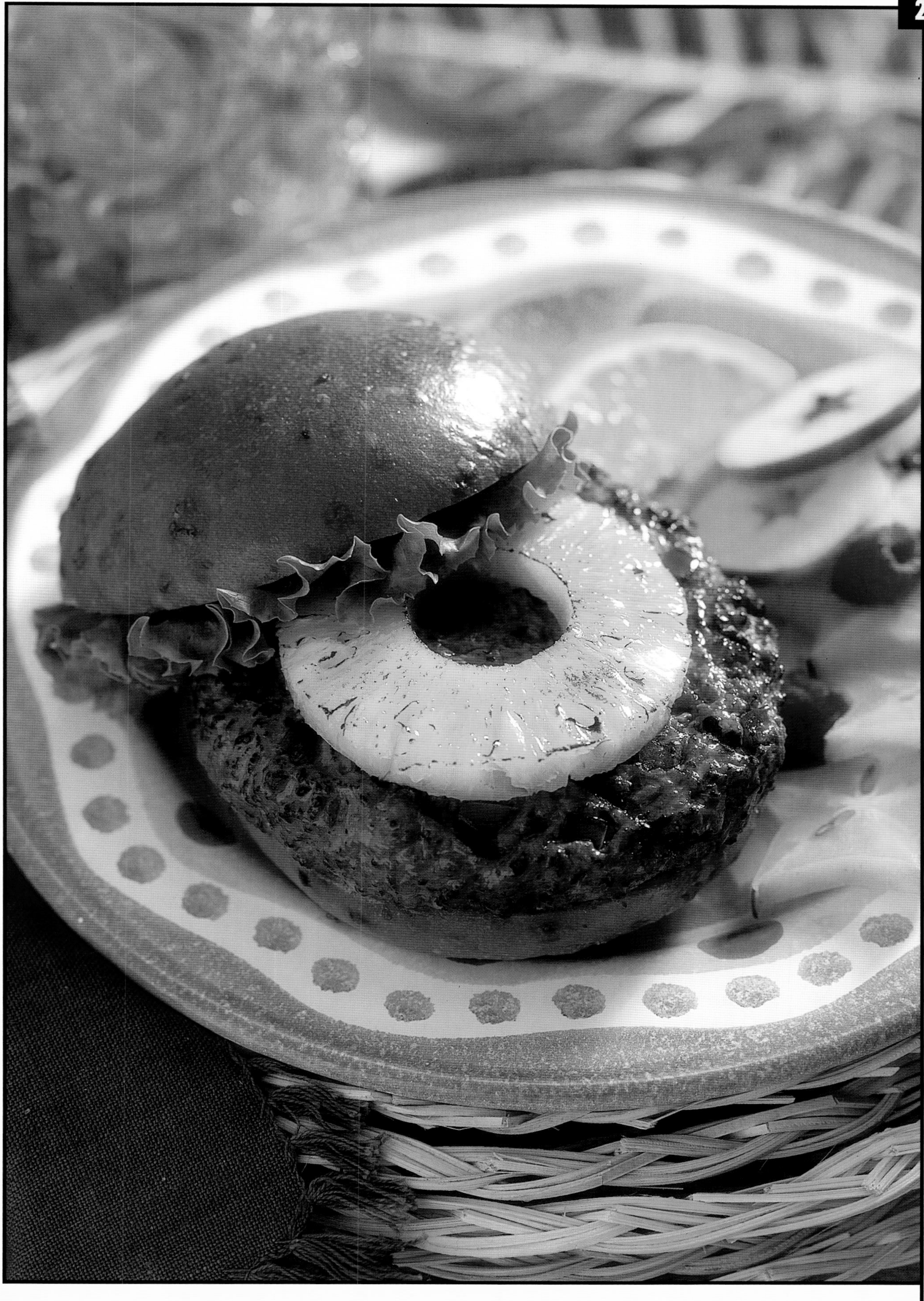

Zesty Italian Turkey Burgers

1 pound ground turkey
¼ cup fat-free Italian dressing
¼ cup seasoned dry bread
    crumbs
4 hamburger buns
4 lettuce leaves
4 slices tomato
4 slices onion

1. Preheat charcoal grill for direct-heat cooking.

2. In medium bowl combine turkey, dressing and bread crumbs. Shape turkey mixture into 4 patties, approximately ½ inch thick.

3. Grill turkey burgers 5 to 6 minutes per side until 160°F is reached on meat thermometer and meat is no longer pink in center.

4. To serve, place each burger on bottom half of bun and top with lettuce, tomato, onion and top half of bun. *Makes 4 servings*

Favorite recipe from **National Turkey Federation**

Wisconsin Cheese Burgers

3 pounds ground beef
½ cup dry bread crumbs
2 eggs, beaten
1¼ cups (5 ounces) your
    favorite shredded
    Wisconsin cheese or
    Pepper Havarti cheese,
    shredded
    Blue cheese, crumbled
    Basil & Tomato Feta cheese,
    crumbled

In large bowl, combine beef, bread crumbs and eggs; mix well, but lightly. Divide mixture into 24 balls; flatten each on waxed paper to 4 inches across. Place 1 heaping tablespoonful cheese on each of 12 patties. Top with remaining patties, carefully pressing edges to seal. Grill patties 4 inches from coals, turning only once, 6 to 9 minutes on each side or until no longer pink. To keep cheese between patties as it melts, do not flatten burgers with spatula while grilling.

Makes 12 servings

Caution: Cheese filling may be very hot if eaten immediately after cooking.

Favorite recipe from **Wisconsin Milk Marketing Board**

Swiss Onion Burgers

1 pound lean ground beef
¼ cup LA CHOY® Teriyaki
   Sauce
1 can (3 ounces) French fried
   onions
4 slices (¾ ounces) Swiss
   cheese
4 hamburger buns, toasted
4 teaspoons French salad
   dressing (optional)

In a large bowl, combine beef, Teriyaki sauce and onions; mix well. Divide mixture into 4 equal portions; shaping into ½-inch thick patties. Place patties on medium-hot grill 4 minutes on each side or until done. Top with cheese; cover and cook 1 minute or until cheese begins to melt. Place patties on bottom halves of buns; top with French dressing, if desired. *Makes 4 servings*

Grilled Salmon Burgers

1 pound fresh boneless,
   skinless salmon
2 tablespoons sliced green
   onions
1 teaspoon LAWRY'S® Garlic
   Pepper
½ teaspoon LAWRY'S®
   Seasoned Salt
2 tablespoons LAWRY'S®
   Citrus Grill Marinade
   with Orange Juice

In food processor, combine all ingredients; process on pulse setting until salmon is well minced and mixed. Form into 4 patties. Broil or grill, 4 to 5 inches from heat source, 3 to 4 minutes on each side, or until cooked through. *Makes 4 servings*

Serving Suggestion: Serve on warm toasted hamburger buns.

Mediterranean Burgers

1½ **pounds ground beef**
¼ **cup (1 ounce) shredded**
   mozzarella cheese
2 **tablespoons grated**
   Parmesan cheese
2 **tablespoons chopped**
   kalamata olives
1 **tablespoon chopped fresh**
   parsley
1 **tablespoon diced tomato**
2 **teaspoons dried oregano**
   leaves
1 **teaspoon black pepper**
4 **hamburger buns, split**

Prepare grill for direct cooking.

Shape beef into eight ¼-inch-thick burger patties.

Combine cheeses, olives, parsley, tomato, oregano and pepper in small bowl. Place ¼ of cheese mixture on top of 1 burger patty; spread to within ½ inch of edge. Top cheese mixture with another burger patty; seal edges to enclose filling. Repeat with remaining cheese mixture and burger patties.

Place burgers on grid. Grill, covered, over medium heat 8 to 10 minutes (or, uncovered, 13 to 15 minutes) to medium (160°F) or to desired doneness, turning halfway through grilling time.

Remove burgers from grill. Place burgers between buns. *Makes 4 servings*

Mediterranean Burger

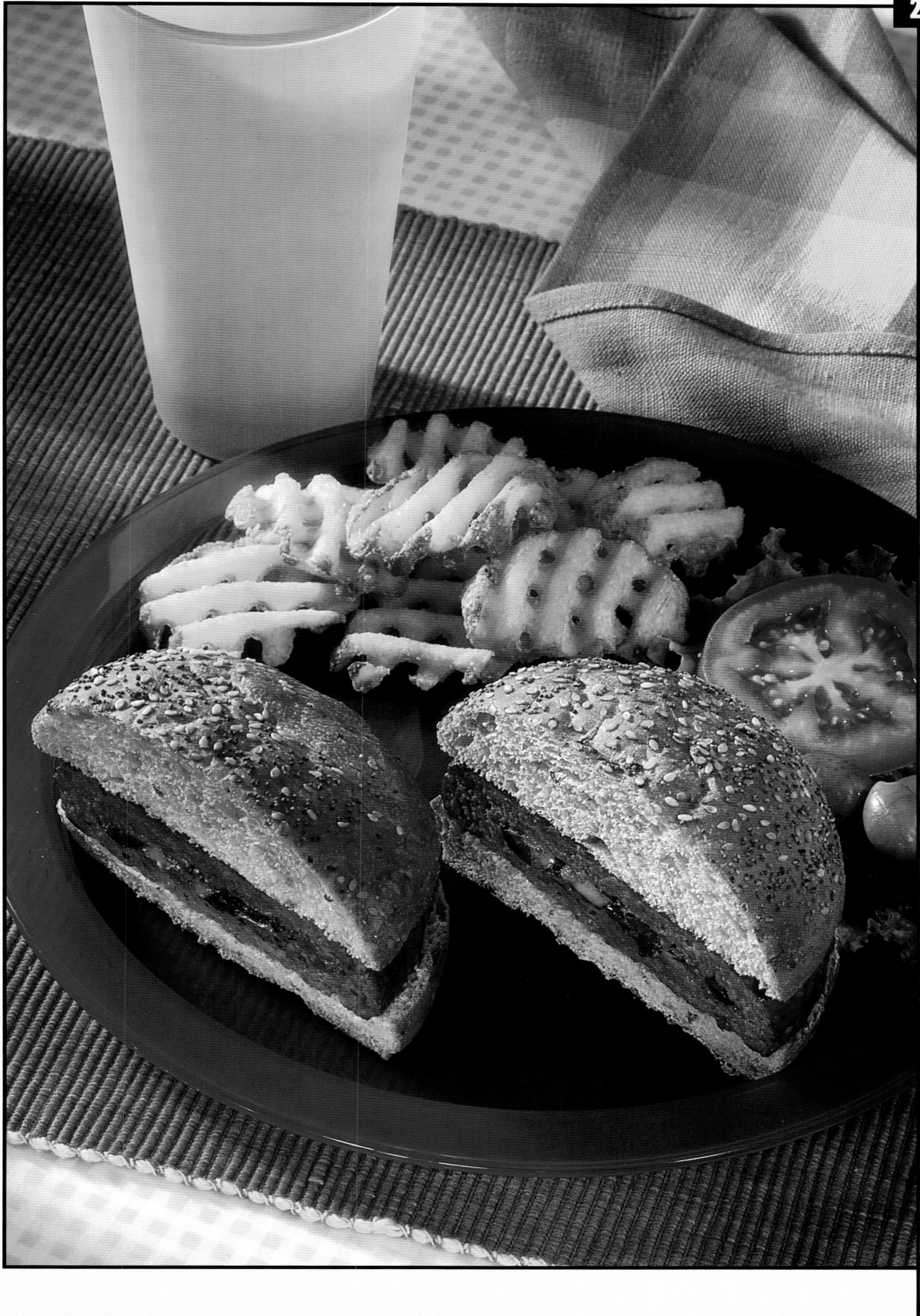

California Turkey Burgers

1 pound ground turkey
½ cup finely chopped cilantro
⅓ cup plain dry bread crumbs
3 tablespoons *French's*®
    Classic Yellow® Mustard
1 egg, beaten
½ teaspoon salt
¼ teaspoon black pepper
8 thin slices (3 ounces)
    Monterey Jack cheese
½ red or yellow bell pepper,
    seeded and cut into rings
4 hamburger buns

1. Combine turkey, cilantro, bread crumbs, mustard, egg, salt and pepper in large bowl. Shape into 4 patties, pressing firmly.

2. Place patties on oiled grid. Grill over high heat 15 minutes or until no longer pink in center. Top burgers with cheese during last few minutes of grilling. Grill pepper rings 2 minutes. To serve, place burgers on buns and top with pepper rings. Serve with additional mustard, if desired.

Makes 4 servings

Prep Time: 15 minutes
Cook Time: 15 minutes

California Turkey Burger

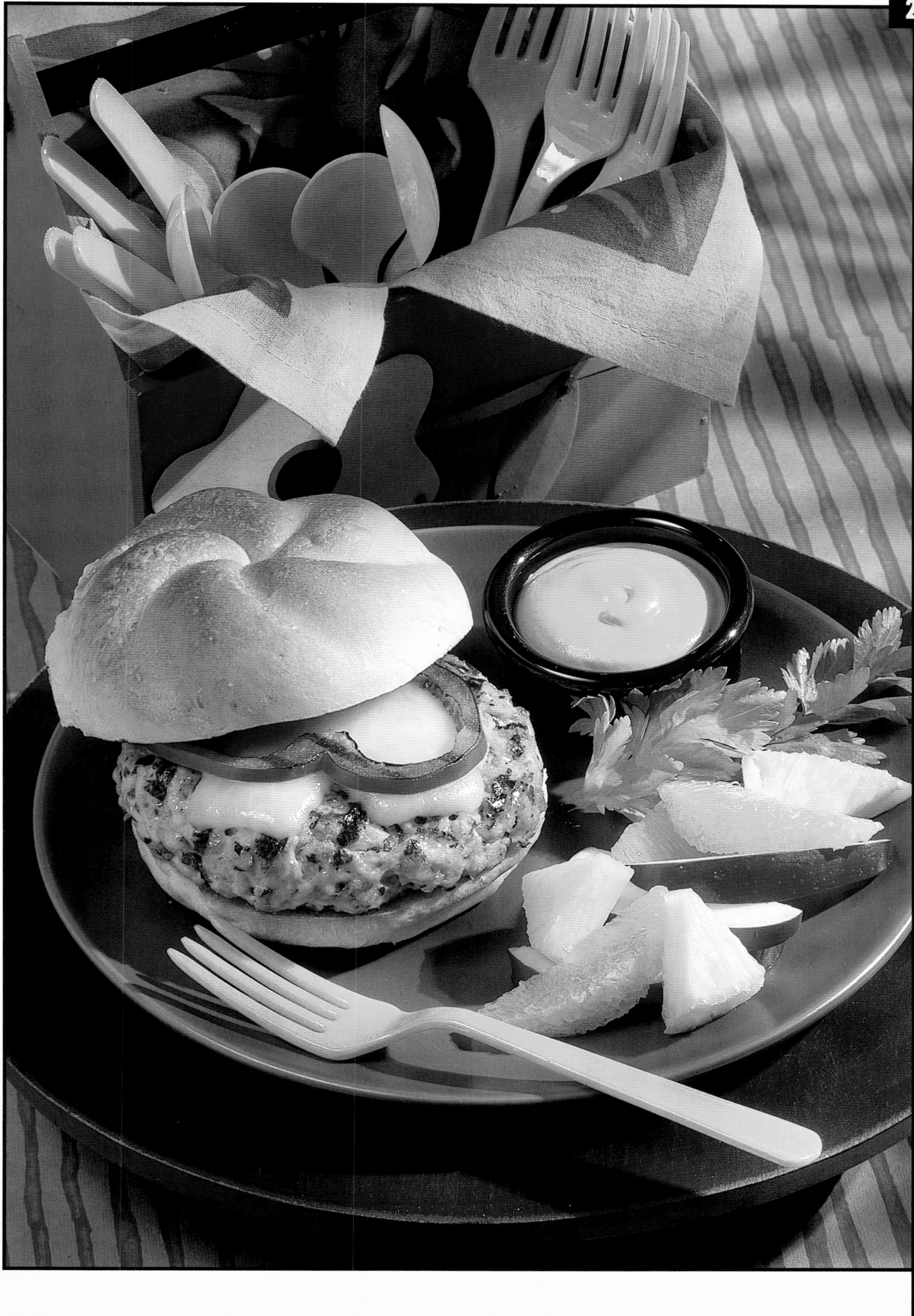

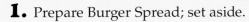

Burger Spread (recipe
   follows)
1½ pounds ground beef
  2 tablespoons chopped fresh
     parsley
  2 teaspoons onion powder
  2 teaspoons Worcestershire
     sauce
  1 teaspoon garlic powder
  1 teaspoon salt
  1 teaspoon black pepper
  4 hamburger buns, split

1. Prepare Burger Spread; set aside.

2. Prepare grill for direct cooking.

3. Combine beef with parsley, onion powder, Worcestershire sauce, garlic powder, salt and pepper in medium bowl; mix lightly, but thoroughly. Shape mixture into four ½-inch-thick burgers.

4. Place burgers on grid. Grill, covered, over medium heat 8 to 10 minutes (or, uncovered, 13 to 15 minutes) to medium (160°F) or to desired doneness, turning halfway through grilling time.

5. Remove burgers from grill. Place burgers between buns; top each burger with Burger Spread. *Makes 4 servings*

Burger Spread

½ cup ketchup
¼ cup prepared mustard
 2 tablespoons chopped onion
 1 tablespoon relish or chopped pickles
 1 tablespoon chopped fresh parsley

Combine all ingredients in small bowl; mix well.
Makes 1 cup

Cook's Nook: Accompany burger with fries, chips, garden salad, coleslaw or potato salad.

Cheddar-Stuffed Mesquite Burgers

½ cup LAWRY'S® Mesquite Marinade with Lime Juice
1 pound ground beef
½ cup chopped green bell pepper
½ cup finely chopped onion
¼ cup unseasoned bread crumbs
½ teaspoon LAWRY'S® Seasoned Pepper
½ cup (2 ounces) shredded cheddar cheese
4 hamburger buns, toasted
 Lettuce leaves
 Tomato slices

In large bowl, combine Mesquite Marinade, ground beef, bell pepper, onion, bread crumbs and Seasoned Pepper; mix well. Let stand 20 minutes. Shape meat into 8 thin patties. In center of 4 patties, place layer of cheese. Top with remaining patties. Press edges tightly together to seal. Grill or broil burgers 8 to 10 minutes or until no longer pink in center (160°F), turning halfway through grilling time. Serve burgers on toasted buns with lettuce and tomato.

Makes 4 servings

Hint: Ground turkey is an excellent substitute for ground beef.

Teriyaki Turkey Burgers

1 pound ground turkey
⅓ cup LAWRY'S® Teriyaki
    Marinade with Pineapple
    Juice
3 tablespoons thinly sliced
    green onions
¼ cup crushed pineapple,
    drained
½ teaspoon LAWRY'S® Garlic
    Powder with Parsley

In medium bowl, combine all ingredients; mix well. Form into 4 patties (mixture will be moist). Grill or broil 5 inches from heat source 3 to 5 minutes on each side or until no longer pink in center (160°F). *Makes 4 servings*

Serving Suggestion: Excellent on onion buns with lettuce, red onion and pineapple slices.

Zesty Burgers

2 pounds ground beef
½ cup WISH-BONE® Italian
    Dressing*
2 tablespoons horseradish
    (optional)
1 carrot, grated
1 medium onion, finely
    chopped
2 eggs
1 cup plain dry bread crumbs

Also terrific with Wish-Bone® Robusto Italian Dressing.

In large bowl, combine all ingredients; shape into 6 patties. Grill or broil until burgers are no longer pink in center (160°F). Serve, if desired, on hamburger rolls. *Makes 6 servings*

Curried Walnut Grain Burgers

2 eggs

⅓ cup plain yogurt

2 teaspoons Worcestershire sauce

2 teaspoons curry powder

½ teaspoon salt

¼ teaspoon ground red pepper

1⅓ cups cooked couscous or brown rice

½ cup finely chopped walnuts

½ cup grated carrot

½ cup minced green onions

⅓ cup fine, dry plain bread crumbs

4 sesame seed hamburger buns

Honey mustard

Thinly sliced cucumber or apple

Alfalfa sprouts

1. Combine eggs, yogurt, Worcestershire sauce, curry, salt and red pepper in large bowl; beat until blended. Stir in couscous, walnuts, carrot, green onions and bread crumbs. Shape into 4 (1-inch-thick) patties.

2. Coat grill rack with nonstick cooking spray; place rack on grill over medium-hot coals (350° to 400°F). Place burgers on rack and grill 5 to 6 minutes per side or until done. Serve on buns with mustard, cucumber and sprouts.

Makes 4 servings

Note: Burgers may be broiled 4 inches from heat source for 5 to 6 minutes per side or until done.

Prep and Cook Time: 25 minutes

Curried Walnut Grain Burger

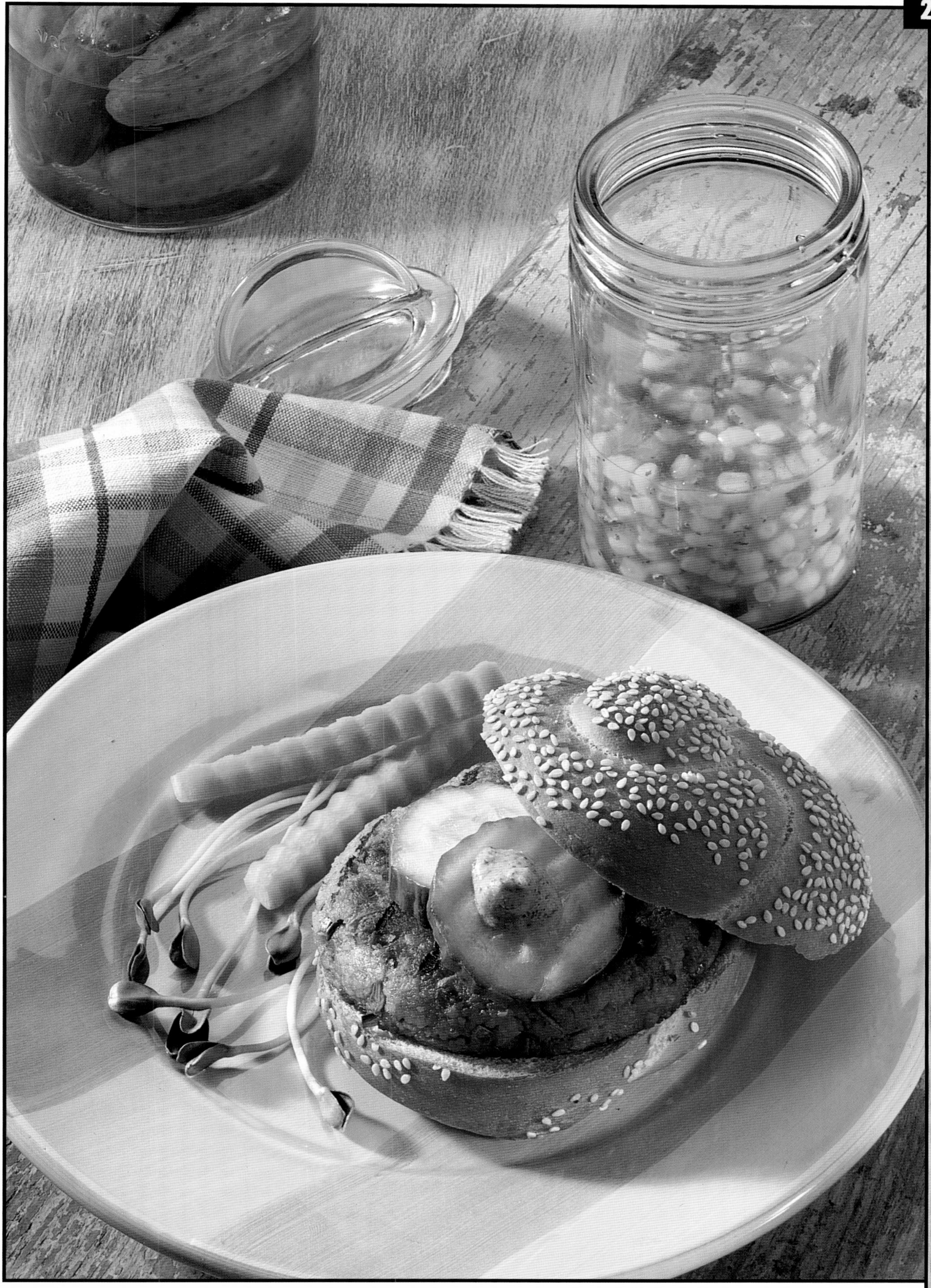

Mexicali Burgers

Guacamole (recipe follows)
1 pound ground beef
⅓ cup crushed tortilla chips
⅓ cup prepared salsa or
    picante sauce
3 tablespoons finely chopped
    fresh cilantro
2 tablespoons finely chopped
    onion
1 teaspoon ground cumin
4 slices Monterey Jack or
    Cheddar cheese
4 Kaiser rolls or hamburger
    buns, split
Lettuce leaves (optional)
Sliced tomatoes (optional)

To prevent sticking, spray grill with nonstick cooking spray. Prepare coals for grilling. Meanwhile, prepare Guacamole.

Combine beef, tortilla chips, salsa, cilantro, onion and cumin in medium bowl until well blended. Shape mixture into 4 burgers. Place burgers on grid over medium heat. Grill, covered, 8 to 10 minutes (or, uncovered, 13 to 15 minutes) to medium (160°F), turning once. Place 1 slice cheese on each burger during last 1 to 2 minutes of grilling. If desired, place rolls, cut side down, on grill to toast lightly during last 1 to 2 minutes of grilling. Place burgers between rolls; top burgers with Guacamole. Serve with lettuce and tomatoes. Garnish as desired. *Makes 4 servings*

Guacamole

1 ripe avocado, seeded
1 tablespoon salsa or picante sauce
1 teaspoon lime or lemon juice
¼ teaspoon garlic salt

Place avocado in medium bowl; mash with fork until avocado is slightly chunky. Add salsa, lime juice and garlic salt; blend well.

Makes about ½ cup

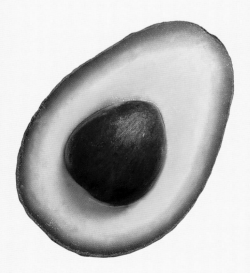

Mexicali Burger

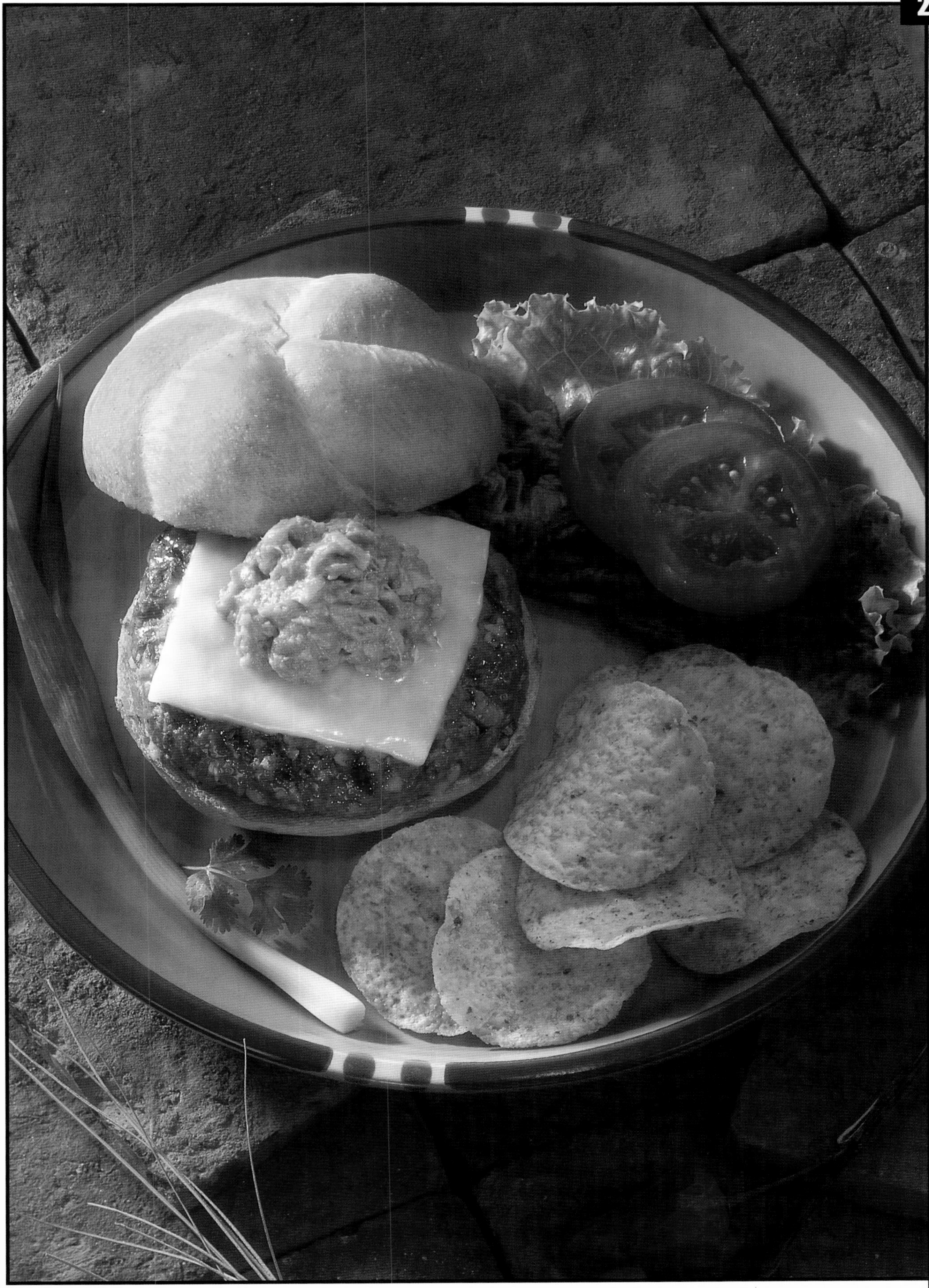

SHORELINE
CREATIONS

*Need some great ideas for your next seaside cookout? You'll find them here.
That's right, beach volleyball, sand castles and fresh seafood grilled to perfection.*

Teriyaki Salmon with Asian Slaw

4 tablespoons light teriyaki
   sauce, divided
2 (5 to 6 ounce) boneless
   salmon fillets with skin
   (1 inch thick)
2½ cups packaged cole slaw
   mix
1 cup fresh or frozen pea
   pods cut lengthwise into
   thin strips
½ cup thinly sliced radishes
2 tablespoons orange
   marmalade
1 teaspoon sesame oil

1. Preheat broiler or prepare grill. Spoon 2 tablespoons teriyaki sauce over meaty sides of salmon. Let stand while preparing vegetable mixture.

2. Combine cole slaw mix, pea pods and radishes in large bowl. Combine remaining 2 tablespoons teriyaki sauce, marmalade and sesame oil in small bowl. Add to cabbage mixture; toss well.

3. Broil salmon 4 to 5 inches from heat source or grill over medium coals without turning 6 to 10 minutes until center is opaque.

4. Transfer cabbage mixture to serving plates; top with salmon. *Makes 2 servings*

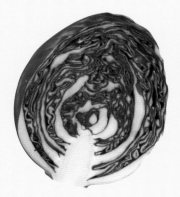
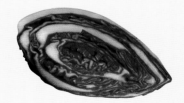

Teriyaki Salmon with Asian Slaw

Tuna Steaks with Shrimp Creole Sauce

4 tablespoons olive oil,
   divided
1 medium red onion, chopped
1 red or yellow bell pepper,
   seeded and chopped
2 stalks celery, sliced
2 cloves garlic, minced
1 can (14½ ounces) stewed
   tomatoes
¼ cup *Frank's® RedHot®*
   Cayenne Pepper Sauce
¼ cup tomato paste
½ teaspoon dried thyme leaves
1 bay leaf
½ pound medium-size raw
   shrimp, shelled and
   deveined
4 tuna, swordfish or codfish
   steaks, cut 1 inch thick
   (about 1½ pounds)
Hot cooked rice (optional)

Heat 2 tablespoons oil in medium skillet over medium-high heat. Add onion, pepper, celery and garlic; cook and stir 1 minute. Stir in tomatoes, *Frank's RedHot* Sauce, tomato paste, thyme and bay leaf. Bring to a boil. Reduce heat to medium-low. Cook 5 minutes, stirring often. Add shrimp; cook 3 minutes or until shrimp turn pink. Remove and discard bay leaf. Set aside shrimp sauce.

Brush both sides of fish steaks with remaining 2 tablespoons oil. Place steaks on grid. Grill over medium-high coals 10 minutes or until fish flakes easily with a fork, turning once. Transfer to serving platter. Spoon shrimp sauce over fish. Serve with rice, if desired. Garnish as desired.

Makes 4 servings

Prep Time: 15 minutes
Cook Time: 20 minutes

GRILLING TIP

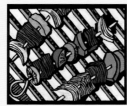

Tuna becomes dry and tough if overcooked. Cook tuna until it is opaque, but still feels somewhat soft in center. Watch carefully while grilling.

Tuna Steak with Shrimp Creole Sauce

Trout Stuffed with Fresh Mint and Oranges

2 pan-dressed* trout (1 to
    1¼ pounds each)
½ teaspoon coarse salt, such
    as Kosher salt
1 orange, sliced
1 cup fresh mint leaves
1 sweet onion, sliced

*A pan-dressed trout has been gutted and
scaled with head and tail removed.*

1. Rinse trout under cold running water; pat dry with paper towels.

2. Sprinkle cavities of trout with salt; fill each with orange slices and mint. Cover each fish with onion slices.

3. Spray 2 large sheets of foil with nonstick cooking spray. Place 1 fish on each sheet and seal using Drugstore Wrap technique.**

4. Place foil packets, seam side down, directly on medium-hot coals; grill on covered grill 20 to 25 minutes or until trout flakes easily when tested with fork, turning once.

5. Carefully open foil packets, avoiding hot steam; remove and discard orange-mint stuffing and trout skin. Serve immediately.

Makes 6 servings

**Place food in the center of an oblong piece of heavy-duty foil, leaving at least a two-inch border around the food. Bring the two long sides together above the food; fold down in a series of locked folds, allowing for heat circulation and expansion. Fold short ends up and over again. Press folds firmly to seal the foil packet.

**Trout Stuffed
with Fresh Mint and Oranges**

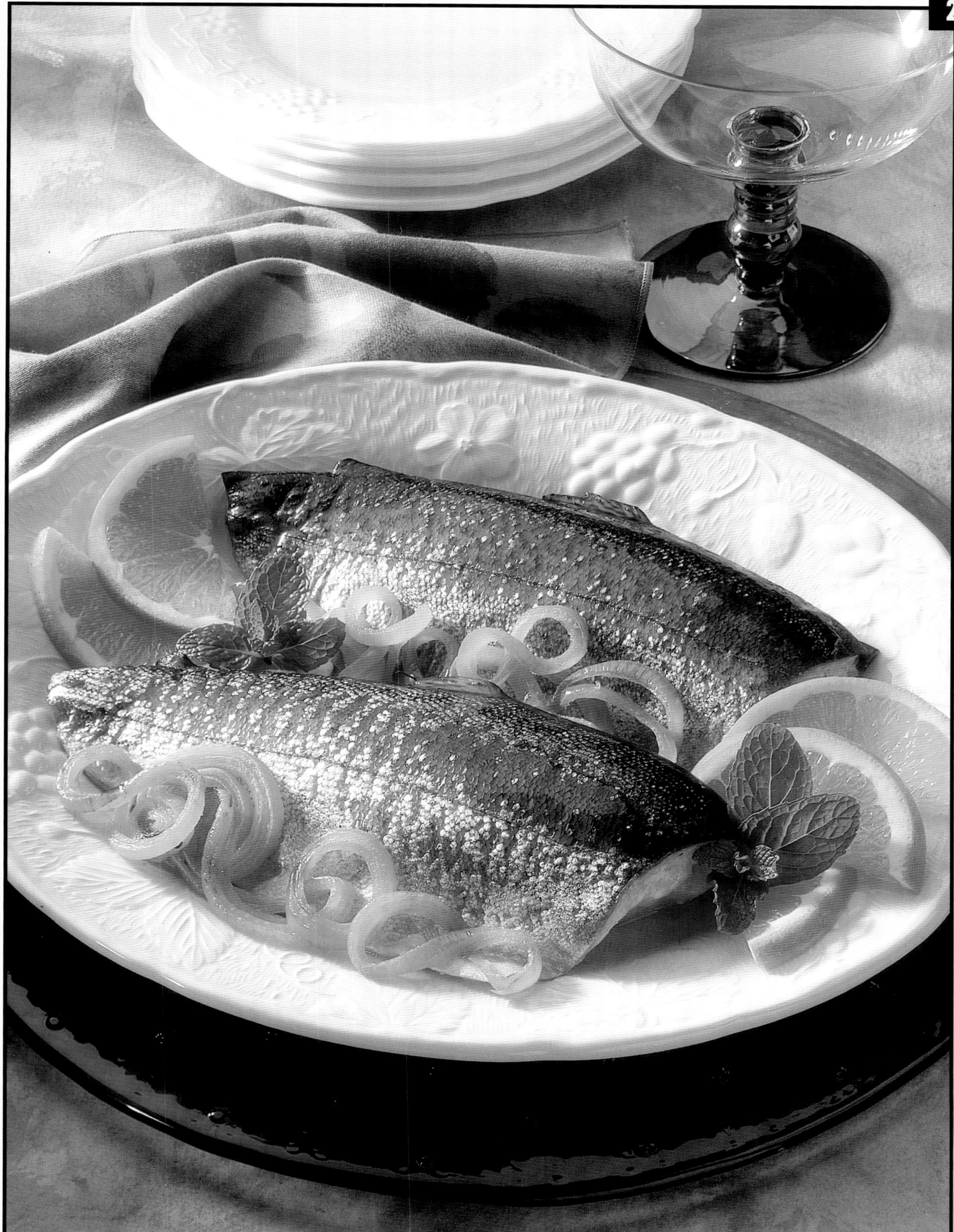

Blackened Fish Fillets

3 tablespoons Chef Paul
    Prudhomme's Blackened
    Redfish Magic® or
    Seafood Magic®
½ stick unsalted butter,
    melted
6 (8 to 10 ounces each)
    redfish (or other firm-
    fleshed fish fillets such as
    red snapper, wall-eyed
    pike, salmon or tuna)
    steaks, at room
    temperature cut about
    ½ inch thick

Heat large, cast-iron skillet over very high heat until it is extremely hot.

With a spoon, spread a little of the butter on one side of one of the fillets. Sprinkle with the Blackened Redfish Magic® or Seafood Magic® and place the fillet in the heated skillet seasoned side down. Spread a little of the butter on the side of the fillet that is facing up and sprinkle with the Blackened Redfish Magic® or Seafood Magic®. Cook, turning frequently until the fish starts to flake, about 4 minutes. Repeat with remaining fillets. Serve each fillet piping hot.

Makes 6 servings

Note: If you don't have a commercial hood vent over your stove, this dish will set off every smoke alarm in your neighborhood! It's better to cook it outdoors on a gas grill or a butane burner. Or you can use a charcoal grill, but you'll need to make the coals hotter by giving them extra air. (A normal charcoal fire doesn't get hot enough to "blacken" the fish properly.) Meanwhile, heat your cast-iron skillet as hot as possible on your kitchen stove, at least 10 minutes. When the coals are glowing, use very thick potholders to carefully transfer the hot skillet to the grill.

Note: Because this method is simple, any variation will make a dramatic difference. Be sure the skillet is hot enough and absolutely dry. Be sure not to overseason—the herbs and spices should highlight the taste rather than hide it. And you don't want to overcook the fillet—there's a big difference between blackened and burned. Avoid a burned, bitter taste by wiping out the skillet between batches.

Grilled Fish Steaks with Tomato Basil Butter Sauce

Tomato Basil Butter Sauce (recipe follows)
4 fish steaks, such as halibut, swordfish, tuna or salmon (at least ¾ inch thick)
Olive oil
Salt and black pepper
Fresh basil leaves and summer squash slices for garnish
Hot cooked seasoned noodles (optional)

Prepare Tomato Basil Butter Sauce; set aside. Rinse fish; pat dry with paper towels. Brush one side of fish lightly with oil; season with salt and pepper.

Oil hot grid to help prevent sticking. Grill fish, oil side down, on a covered grill, over medium KINGSFORD® Briquets, 6 to 10 minutes. Halfway through cooking time, brush top with oil and season with salt and pepper, then turn and continue grilling until fish turns from translucent to opaque throughout. (Grilling time depends on the thickness of fish; allow 3 to 5 minutes for each ½ inch of thickness.) Serve with Tomato Basil Butter Sauce. Garnish with basil leaves and squash slices. Serve with noodles, if desired.

Makes 4 servings

Tomato Basil Butter Sauce

4 tablespoons butter or margarine, softened, divided
1½ cups chopped seeded peeled tomatoes (about 1 pound)
½ teaspoon sugar
1 clove garlic, minced
Salt and black pepper
1½ tablespoons very finely chopped fresh basil

Melt 1 tablespoon butter in a small skillet. Add tomatoes, sugar and garlic. Cook over medium-low heat, stirring frequently, until liquid evaporates and mixture thickens. Remove pan from heat; stir in remaining butter until mixture has a saucelike consistency. Season to taste with salt and pepper, then stir in basil.

Makes about 1 cup

Mustard-Grilled Red Snapper

½ cup Dijon mustard
1 tablespoon red wine vinegar
1 teaspoon ground red
    pepper
4 red snapper fillets (about
    6 ounces each)
  Fresh parsley sprigs and red
    peppercorns (optional)

Spray grid with nonstick cooking spray. Prepare grill for direct cooking.

Combine mustard, vinegar and pepper in small bowl; mix well. Coat fish thoroughly with mustard mixture.

Place fish on grid. Grill, covered, over medium-high heat 8 minutes or until fish flakes easily when tested with fork, turning halfway through grilling time. Garnish with parsley sprigs and red peppercorns, if desired. *Makes 4 servings*

Barbecued Catfish in Red Pepper Butter

2 pounds catfish fillets
  LAWRY'S® Seasoned Salt
  White pepper
2 tablespoons butter
¼ cup minced green onion
    bottoms
1 large red bell pepper,
    minced
1½ tablespoons red wine
    vinegar
2 tablespoons fresh lemon
    juice
¼ cup dry white wine
½ cup unsalted butter
  Aluminum foil,
    16×11 inches
  Lime slices (garnish)

In shallow glass baking dish, place catfish fillets and sprinkle generously with Seasoned Salt and white pepper. In large skillet, heat butter. Add red bell pepper and green onion and cook over medium-high heat until tender. Add remaining ingredients except aluminum foil. Allow to cool. Pour over fish. Marinade, covered, 2 hours; turn once. Remove from marinade; reserve liquid. Place fillets in square of foil, crimp up edges of foil to form tray. Grill over wood or charcoal embers. Baste often with red bell pepper butter. Cook 3 to 5 minutes on each side. Discard used marinade.

Makes 4 servings

Serving Suggestion: Serve with lime slices.

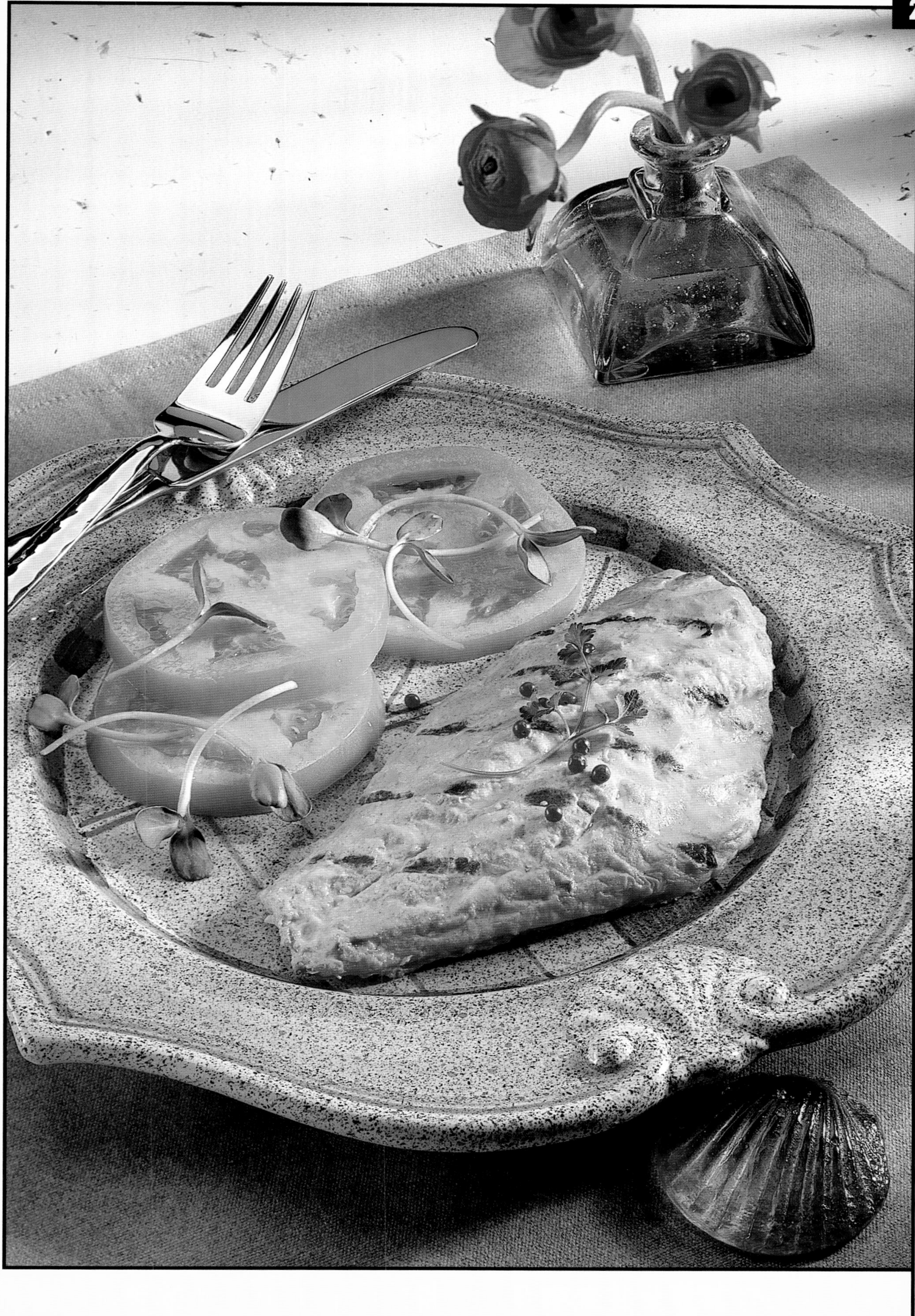

Barbecued Salmon

4 salmon steaks, ¾ to 1 inch
   thick
3 tablespoons lemon juice
2 tablespoons soy sauce
   Salt and black pepper
½ cup KC MASTERPIECE™
   Original Barbecue Sauce
   Fresh oregano sprigs
   Grilled mushrooms
   (optional)

Rinse salmon; pat dry with paper towels. Combine lemon juice and soy sauce in shallow glass dish. Add salmon; let stand at cool room temperature no more than 15 to 20 minutes, turning salmon several times. Remove salmon from marinade; discard marinade. Season lightly with salt and pepper.

Lightly oil hot grid to prevent sticking. Grill salmon on covered grill over medium KINGSFORD® Briquets 10 to 14 minutes. Halfway through cooking time brush salmon with barbecue sauce, then turn and continue grilling until fish flakes easily when tested with fork. Remove fish from grill; brush with barbecue sauce. Garnish with oregano sprigs and mushrooms. *Makes 4 servings*

Halibut Kabobs

1 cup LAWRY'S® Lemon
   Pepper Marinade with
   Lemon Juice, divided
1 pound halibut steaks, cut
   into 1-inch cubes
1 green bell pepper, cut into
   chunks
12 cherry tomatoes
12 mushrooms, stems removed
   Skewers

In large resealable plastic food storage bag, combine ¾ cup Lemon Pepper Marinade and halibut; seal bag. Marinate in refrigerator at least 30 minutes. Remove halibut; discard used marinade. Alternately thread halibut, bell pepper, tomatoes and mushrooms onto skewers. Grill or broil skewers 8 to 10 minutes or until fish flakes easily when tested with fork, turning once and basting often with additional ¼ cup Lemon Pepper Marinade. *Do not baste during last 5 minutes of cooking.* Discard remaining marinade.
Makes 4 servings

Serving Suggestion: Serve with hot cooked orzo pasta or rice pilaf.

Variation: Lawry's® Herb & Garlic Marinade with Lemon Juice can be substituted for Lemon Pepper Marinade with Lemon Juice.

Barbecued Salmon

Grilled Swordfish with Hot Red Sauce

2 to 3 green onions
4 swordfish or halibut steaks
    (about 1½ pounds total)
2 tablespoons hot bean
    paste*
2 tablespoons soy sauce
2 tablespoons Sesame Salt
    (recipe follows)
1 tablespoon dark sesame oil
4 teaspoons sugar
4 cloves garlic, minced
⅛ teaspoon black pepper

Available in specialty stores or Asian markets.

1. Spray grid of grill or broiler rack with nonstick cooking spray. Prepare coals for grill or preheat broiler.

2. Cut off and discard root ends of green onions. Finely chop enough green onions to measure ¼ cup; set aside. Prepare Sesame Salt; set aside.

3. Rinse swordfish and pat dry with paper towels. Place in shallow glass dish.

4. Combine green onions, hot bean paste, soy sauce, Sesame Salt, sesame oil, sugar, garlic and pepper in small bowl; mix well.

5. Spread half of marinade over fish; turn fish over and spread with remaining marinade. Cover with plastic wrap and refrigerate 30 minutes.

6. Remove fish from marinade; discard remaining marinade. Place fish on prepared grid. Grill fish over medium-hot coals or broil 4 to 5 minutes per side or until fish is opaque and flakes easily with fork. Garnish as desired.

Makes 4 servings

Sesame Salt

½ cup sesame seeds
¼ teaspoon salt

Heat small skillet over medium heat. Add sesame seeds; cook and stir about 5 minutes or until seeds are golden. Cool. Crush toasted sesame seeds and salt with mortar and pestle or process in clean coffee or spice grinder. Refrigerate in covered glass jar.

Seafood Tacos with Fruit Salsa

2 tablespoons lemon juice
1 teaspoon chili powder
1 teaspoon ground allspice
1 teaspoon olive oil
1 teaspoon minced garlic
1 to 2 teaspoons grated
    lemon peel
½ teaspoon ground cloves
1 pound halibut or snapper
    fillets
12 (6-inch) corn tortillas *or*
    6 (7- to 8-inch) flour
    tortillas
3 cups shredded romaine
    lettuce
1 small red onion, halved and
    thinly sliced
   Fruit Salsa (recipe follows)

1. Combine lemon juice, chili powder, allspice, oil, garlic, lemon peel and cloves in small bowl. Rub fish with spice mixture; cover and refrigerate while grill heats. (Fish may be cut into smaller pieces for easier handling.)

2. Prepare Fruit Salsa. Spray grid with nonstick cooking spray. Adjust grid 4 to 6 inches above heat. Preheat grill to medium-high heat. Grill fish, covered, 3 minutes or until fish is lightly browned on bottom. Carefully turn fish over; grill 2 minutes or until fish is opaque in center and flakes easily when tested with fork. Remove from heat and cut into 12 pieces, removing bones if necessary. Cover to keep warm.

3. Place tortillas on grill in single layer and heat 5 to 10 seconds; turn and cook 5 to 10 seconds or until hot and pliable. Stack; cover to keep warm.

4. Top each tortilla with ¼ cup lettuce and red onion. Add 1 piece of fish and about 2 tablespoons Fruit Salsa. *Makes 6 servings*

Fruit Salsa

1 small ripe papaya, peeled, seeded and diced
1 firm small banana, diced
2 green onions, minced
3 tablespoons chopped fresh cilantro or mint
3 tablespoons lime juice
2 jalapeño peppers,* seeded and minced

*Jalapeño peppers can sting and irritate the skin; wear rubber gloves when handling peppers and do not touch eyes. Wash hands after handling.

Combine all ingredients in small bowl. Serve at room temperature. *Makes 12 servings*

Grilled Salmon Quesadillas with Cucumber Salsa

1 medium cucumber, peeled, seeded and finely chopped

½ cup green or red salsa

1 (8-ounce) salmon fillet

3 tablespoons olive oil, divided

4 (10-inch) flour tortillas, warmed

6 ounces goat cheese, crumbled *or* 1½ cups (6 ounces) shredded Monterey Jack cheese

¼ cup drained sliced pickled jalapeño peppers*

*Jalapeño peppers can sting and irritate the skin; wear rubber gloves when handling peppers and do not touch eyes. Wash hands after handling.

1. Prepare grill for direct cooking. Combine cucumber and salsa in small bowl; set aside.

2. Brush salmon with 2 tablespoons oil. Grill, covered, over medium-hot coals 5 to 6 minutes per side or until fish flakes easily when tested with fork. Transfer to plate; flake with fork.

3. Spoon salmon evenly over half of each tortilla, leaving 1-inch border. Sprinkle with cheese and jalapeño pepper slices. Fold tortillas in half. Brush tortillas with remaining 1 tablespoon oil.

4. Grill quesadillas over medium-hot coals until browned on both sides and cheese is melted. Serve with cucumber salsa. *Makes 4 servings*

Prep and Cook Time: 20 minutes

Grilled Fish with Roasted Jalapeño Rub

3 tablespoons chopped cilantro

2 tablespoons lime juice

1 tablespoon minced garlic

1 tablespoon minced fresh ginger

1 tablespoon minced roasted jalapeño peppers*

1½ pounds firm white fish fillets, such as orange roughy or red snapper

Lime wedges

*To roast peppers, place them on uncovered grill over hot coals. Grill until skin is blistered, turning frequently. Remove from grill and place peppers in large resealable plastic food storage bag for 15 minutes. Remove skins. Seed peppers, if desired, and cut them into thin slices.

Combine cilantro, lime juice, garlic, ginger and peppers in small bowl. Lightly oil grid to prevent sticking. Grill fish on covered grill over hot KINGSFORD® Briquets 5 minutes. Turn; spread cilantro mixture on fish. Grill 3 to 5 minutes longer or until fish flakes easily when tested with fork. Serve with lime wedges. *Makes 4 servings*

Grilled Salmon Quesadilla with Cucumber Salsa

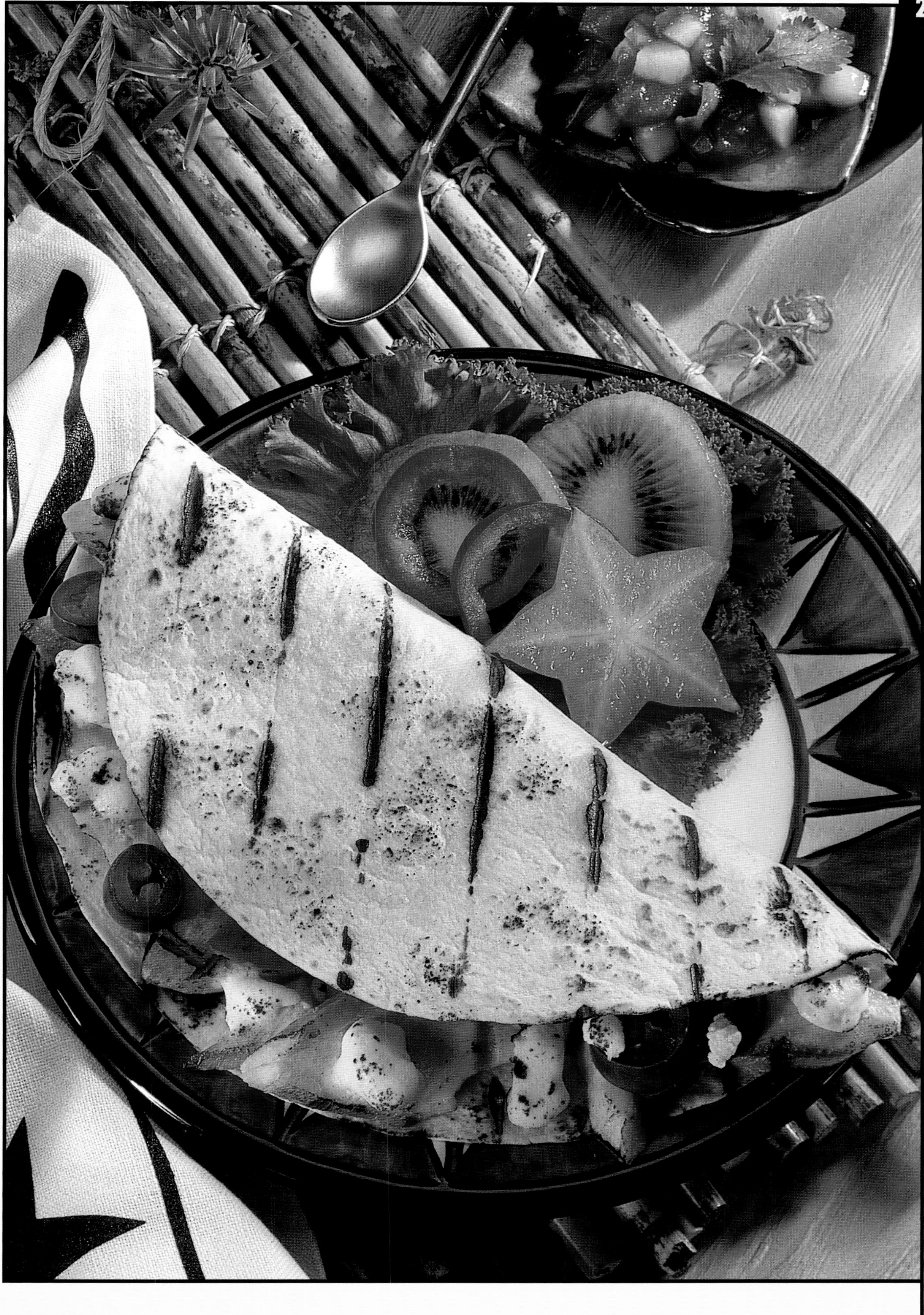

Blackened Sea Bass

Hardwood charcoal*
2 teaspoons paprika
1 teaspoon garlic salt
1 teaspoon dried thyme
  leaves, crushed
¼ teaspoon white pepper
¼ teaspoon ground red
  pepper
¼ teaspoon black pepper
3 tablespoons butter or
  margarine
4 skinless sea bass or catfish
  fillets (4 to 6 ounces
  each)
Lemon halves
Fresh dill sprigs for garnish

*Hardwood charcoal takes somewhat longer
than regular charcoal to become hot, but results
in a hotter fire than regular charcoal. A hot fire
is necessary to seal in juices and cook fish
quickly. If hardwood charcoal is not available,
scatter dry hardwood, mesquite or hickory
chunks over hot coals to create a hot fire.

1. Prepare barbecue grill for direct cooking using hardwood charcoal.

2. Meanwhile, combine paprika, garlic salt, thyme and white, red and black peppers in small bowl; mix well. Set aside. Melt butter in small saucepan over medium heat. Pour melted butter into pie plate or shallow bowl. Cool slightly.

3. Dip sea bass into melted butter, evenly coating both sides. Sprinkle both sides of sea bass evenly with paprika mixture.

4. Place sea bass on grid. (Fire will flare up when sea bass is placed on grid, but will subside when grill is covered.) Grill sea bass, on covered grill, over hot coals 4 to 6 minutes or until sea bass is blackened and flakes easily when tested with fork, turning halfway through grilling time. Serve with lemon halves. Garnish, if desired.

Makes 4 servings

Cook's Nook: A lean to moderately fatty saltwater fish, sea bass is generally available year-round. And don't worry about the salt! Saltwater fish are quite low in sodium—- they have a special structure that prevents them from becoming as salty as the sea.

Blackened Sea Bass

Grilled Five-Spice Fish with Garlic Spinach

1½ teaspoons finely shredded lime peel

3 tablespoons fresh lime juice

4 teaspoons minced fresh ginger

½ to 1 teaspoon Chinese 5-spice powder

½ teaspoon sugar

½ teaspoon salt

⅛ teaspoon black pepper

2 teaspoons vegetable oil, divided

1 pound salmon steaks

½ pound fresh baby spinach leaves (about 8 cups lightly packed), washed

2 large cloves garlic, pressed through garlic press

1. Combine lime peel, lime juice, ginger, 5-spice powder, sugar, salt, pepper and 1 teaspoon oil in 2-quart dish. Add salmon; turn to coat. Cover; refrigerate 2 to 3 hours.

2. Combine spinach, garlic and remaining 1 teaspoon oil in 3-quart microwavable dish; toss. Cover; microwave at HIGH (100% power) 2 minutes or until spinach is wilted. Drain; keep warm.

3. Meanwhile, prepare barbecue grill for direct cooking.

4. Remove salmon from marinade and place on oiled grid. Brush salmon with portion of marinade. Grill salmon, covered, over medium-hot coals 4 minutes. Turn salmon; brush with marinade and grill 4 minutes or until salmon flakes easily with fork. Discard marinade.

5. Serve fish over bed of spinach.

Makes 4 servings

Grilled Grouper

2 pounds Florida grouper fillets (or substitute snapper, shark or tilefish)

1 bottle Italian dressing

2 tablespoons lemon juice

1 teaspoon salt

Cut fish into serving size pieces and place in shallow dish. Combine Italian dressing, lemon juice and salt; pour over fish. Marinate in refrigerator 30 minutes. Brush grill with oil, then place grouper on grill over hot coals. Measure thickness of fish. Grill 10 minutes for each inch of thickness or until fish flakes when tested with fork. Turn fish halfway through cooking (unless it is less than 1 inch thick).   *Makes 6 servings*

Favorite recipe from **Florida Department of Agriculture and Consumer Services, Bureau of Seafood and Aquaculture**

Grilled Five-Spice Fish with Garlic Spinach

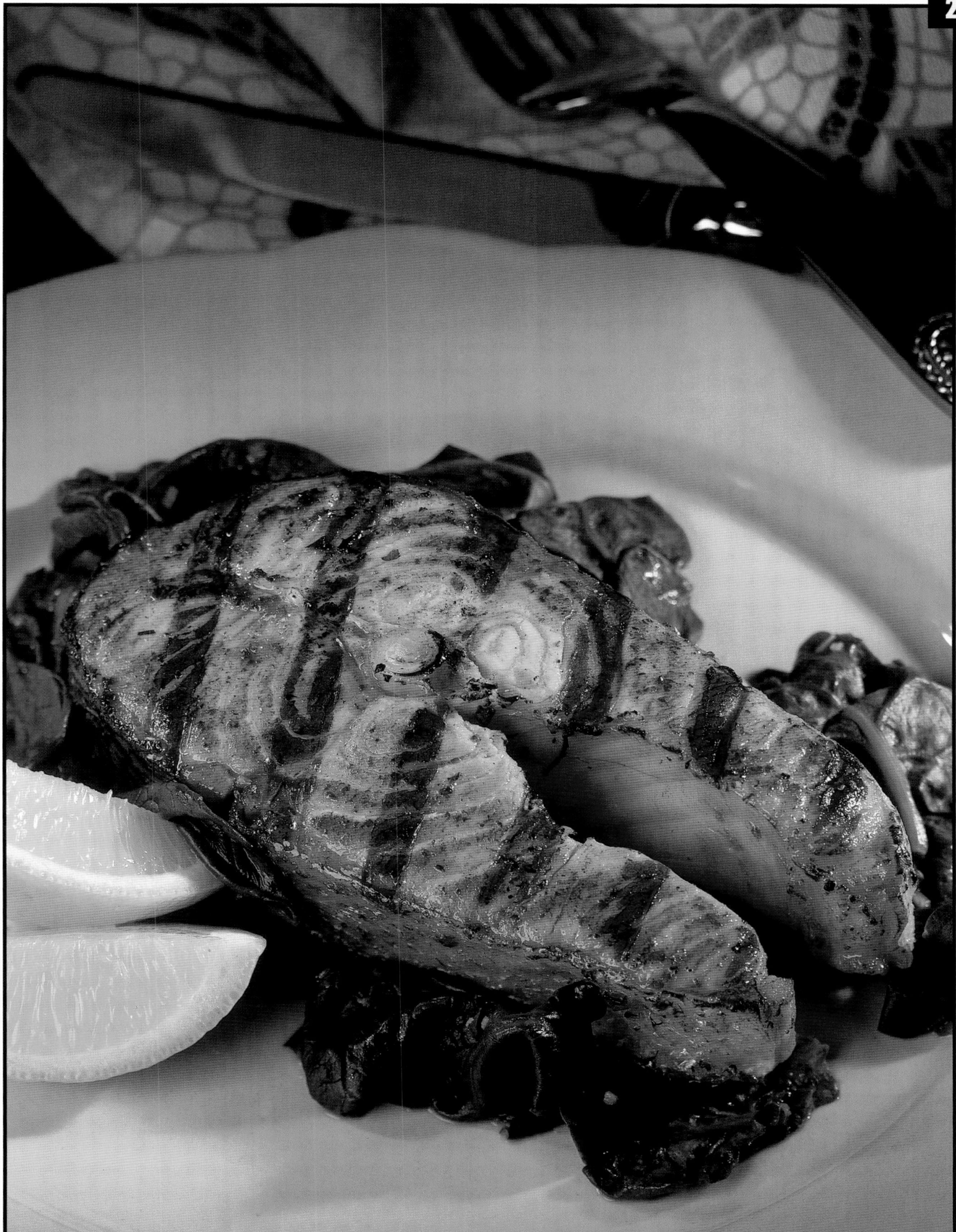

Pineapple Salsa Topped Halibut

Pineapple Salsa

¾ cup diced fresh pineapple *or*
1 can (8 ounces)
unsweetened pineapple
tidbits, drained

2 tablespoons finely chopped
red bell pepper

2 tablespoons chopped fresh
cilantro

2 teaspoons vegetable oil

1 teaspoon bottled minced
ginger or finely shredded
fresh ginger

1 teaspoon bottled minced
jalapeño pepper or fresh
jalapeño pepper*

Halibut

4 halibut or swordfish steaks
(6 ounces each), cut
about ¾-inch thick

1 tablespoon garlic-flavored
olive oil**

¼ teaspoon salt

*Jalapeño peppers can sting and irritate the
skin; wear rubber gloves when handling peppers
and do not touch eyes. Wash hands after
handling.*

**Or, add ¼ teaspoon bottled minced garlic to
1 tablespoon olive oil.*

1. For salsa, combine pineapple, bell pepper,
cilantro, oil, ginger and jalapeño pepper in small
bowl; mix well. Cover; refrigerate up to 2 days.

2. To complete recipe, prepare barbecue grill for
direct cooking. Brush halibut with oil; sprinkle
with salt.

3. Grill halibut, on uncovered grill, over
medium-hot coals 8 minutes or until halibut flakes
easily when tested with fork, turning once.

4. Top halibut with salsa; serve immediately.

Makes 4 servings

Serving suggestion: Serve with rice pilaf.

Make-Ahead Time: up to 2 days in refrigerator
Final Prep and Cook Time: 11 minutes

Pineapple Salsa Topped Halibut

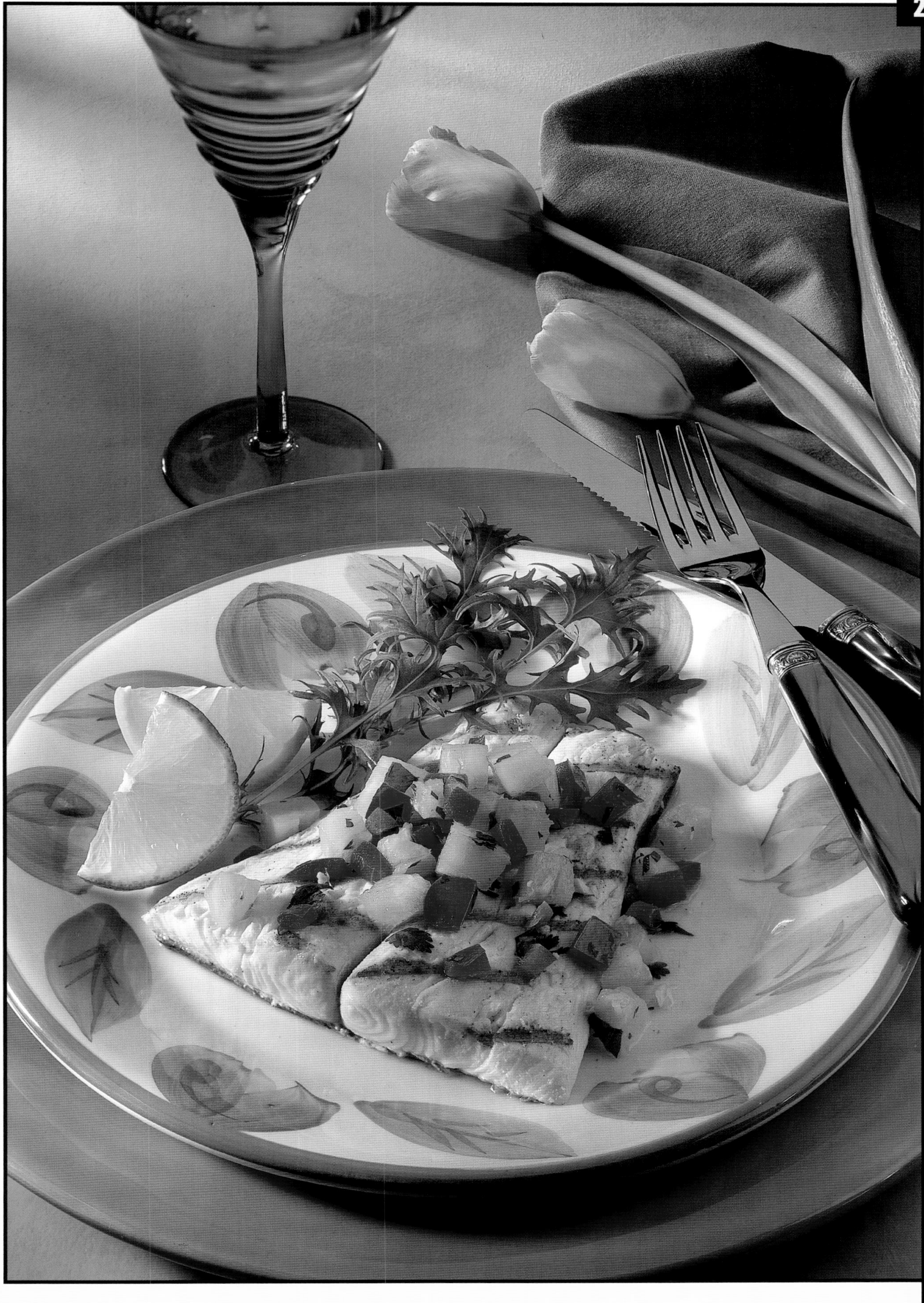

Grilled Fish, Vegetable & Rice Packets

1 box UNCLE BEN'S® Long
  Grain & Wild Rice
  Original Recipe
4 orange roughy or tilapia fish
  fillets (4 ounces each)
3 tablespoons olive oil
3 tablespoons balsamic
  vinegar or fresh lemon
  juice
1 medium red bell pepper, cut
  into thin 2-inch strips
1 cup thinly sliced zucchini
½ cup thinly sliced red onion
8 button mushrooms,
  quartered

1. Prepare rice according to package directions. Divide cooked rice evenly between four 15×12-inch pieces of heavy-duty foil; spread out rice slightly in center of foil. Place 1 fish fillet over each portion of rice; season fish with salt and pepper, if desired.

2. In medium bowl, gradually whisk oil into vinegar until combined. Add vegetables; toss gently until coated. Divide vegetables evenly over fish and rice; drizzle any remaining oil mixture over fish.

3. Seal foil packets by bringing the two long sides together above food and folding down in several tight folds, then tightly fold in the short ends.

4. Place foil packets, seam side up, on grid over medium coals. Grill, covered, 15 to 20 minutes or until fish flakes easily when tested with fork.

Makes 4 servings

Cook's Tip: Packets can be placed on a baking sheet and baked in a preheated 400°F oven for 20 to 25 minutes or until the fish flakes easily when tested with fork.

Salmon en Papillote

⅔ cup *French's®* Napa Valley
    Style Dijon Mustard
½ cup (1 stick) butter or
    margarine, melted
3 cloves garlic, minced
¼ cup minced fresh dill weed
    or 1 tablespoon dried dill
    weed
4 pieces (2 pounds)
    salmon fillet, cut into
    4×3×1½-inch portions
Salt
Ground black pepper
Vegetable cooking spray
2 cups very thin vegetable
    strips, such as bell
    peppers, carrots, leek,
    celery or fennel bulb
2 tablespoons capers, drained

Combine mustard, butter, garlic and dill weed in medium microwave-safe bowl. Cover loosely with vented plastic wrap. Microwave on HIGH (100%) 1 minute. Whisk sauce until smooth; set aside.

Sprinkle salmon with salt and black pepper. Cut four 12-inch circles of heavy-duty foil. Coat one side of foil with vegetable cooking spray. Place 1 piece salmon in center of each piece of foil. Spoon about 2 tablespoons mustard sauce over each piece of fish. Reserve remaining sauce. Top fish with vegetables and capers, dividing evenly. Fold foil in half over salmon and vegetables. Seal edges securely with tight double folds.

Place packets on grid. Cook over hot coals 15 to 20 minutes until fish flakes easily with a fork, opening foil packets carefully. Serve with reserved mustard sauce. *Makes 4 servings*

Prep Time: 30 minutes
Cook Time: 20 minutes

Lemon Tarragon Fish

½ cup CRISCO® Oil*
1 teaspoon grated lemon peel
    (optional)
½ cup lemon juice
1 tablespoon chopped parsley
2 teaspoons dried tarragon
    leaves
½ teaspoon salt
¼ teaspoon pepper
4 cod, halibut or haddock
    steaks (about 1 pound)
2⅔ cups hot cooked rice
    (cooked without salt or
    fat)

*Use your favorite Crisco Oil product.

1. Combine oil, lemon peel, if desired, lemon juice, parsley, tarragon, salt and pepper in shallow baking dish. Stir to mix well.

2. Place fish in lemon juice mixture. Turn to coat. Refrigerate 30 minutes, turning after 15 minutes.

3. Prepare grill or heat broiler.

4. Remove fish from marinade; discard marinade. Grill or broil 3 to 5 minutes per side or until fish flakes easily with fork. Serve with hot rice.

Makes 4 servings

Mediterranean Grilled Snapper

1 whole red snapper (about
    4½ pounds), scaled,
    gutted and cavity cut
    open*
2 tablespoons fresh lemon
    juice
    Salt and pepper
3 tablespoons olive oil,
    divided
2 tablespoons chopped fresh
    oregano leaves *or*
    2 teaspoons dried
    oregano leaves, crushed
2 tablespoons chopped fresh
    basil leaves *or*
    2 teaspoons dried basil
    leaves, crushed
4 slices lemon
3 whole heads garlic**
    Fresh oregano sprigs
    (optional)
6 slices Italian bread, cut
    1 inch thick
    Additional olive oil
    (optional)

This can be done by your fish retailer at the time of purchase or you may wish to do this yourself.

**The whole garlic bulb is called a head.*

1. Prepare grill for direct cooking. Rinse snapper under cold running water; pat dry with paper towels. Open cavity of snapper; brush with lemon juice. Sprinkle lightly with salt and pepper. Combine 1 tablespoon oil, chopped oregano and basil in small bowl. Using small spatula, spread mixture inside cavity of snapper. Place lemon slices in cavity; close snapper. Secure opening by threading 6-inch metal skewer lengthwise through outside edge of cavity.

2. Cut off top third of garlic heads to expose cloves; discard. Place each head on small sheet of heavy-duty foil; drizzle evenly with remaining 2 tablespoons oil. Wrap in foil. Place packets directly on medium-hot coals.

3. Place snapper in oiled, hinged fish basket or directly on oiled grid. Grill snapper and garlic, on uncovered grill, over medium-hot coals 20 to 25 minutes or until snapper flakes easily when tested with fork, turning halfway through grilling time.

4. Soak oregano sprigs in water. Place oregano sprigs directly on coals during last 10 minutes of grilling.

5. Brush bread lightly with additional oil. During last 5 minutes of grilling, place bread around outer edges of grid to toast, about 4 minutes, turning once.

6. Transfer snapper to carving board. Carefully unwrap garlic. Peel off any charred papery outer skin. Using pot holder, squeeze softened garlic from heads into small bowl; mash to a paste with wooden spoon or potato masher, adding additional oil. Spread bread lightly with garlic paste.

Continued on page 274

Mediterranean Grilled Snapper

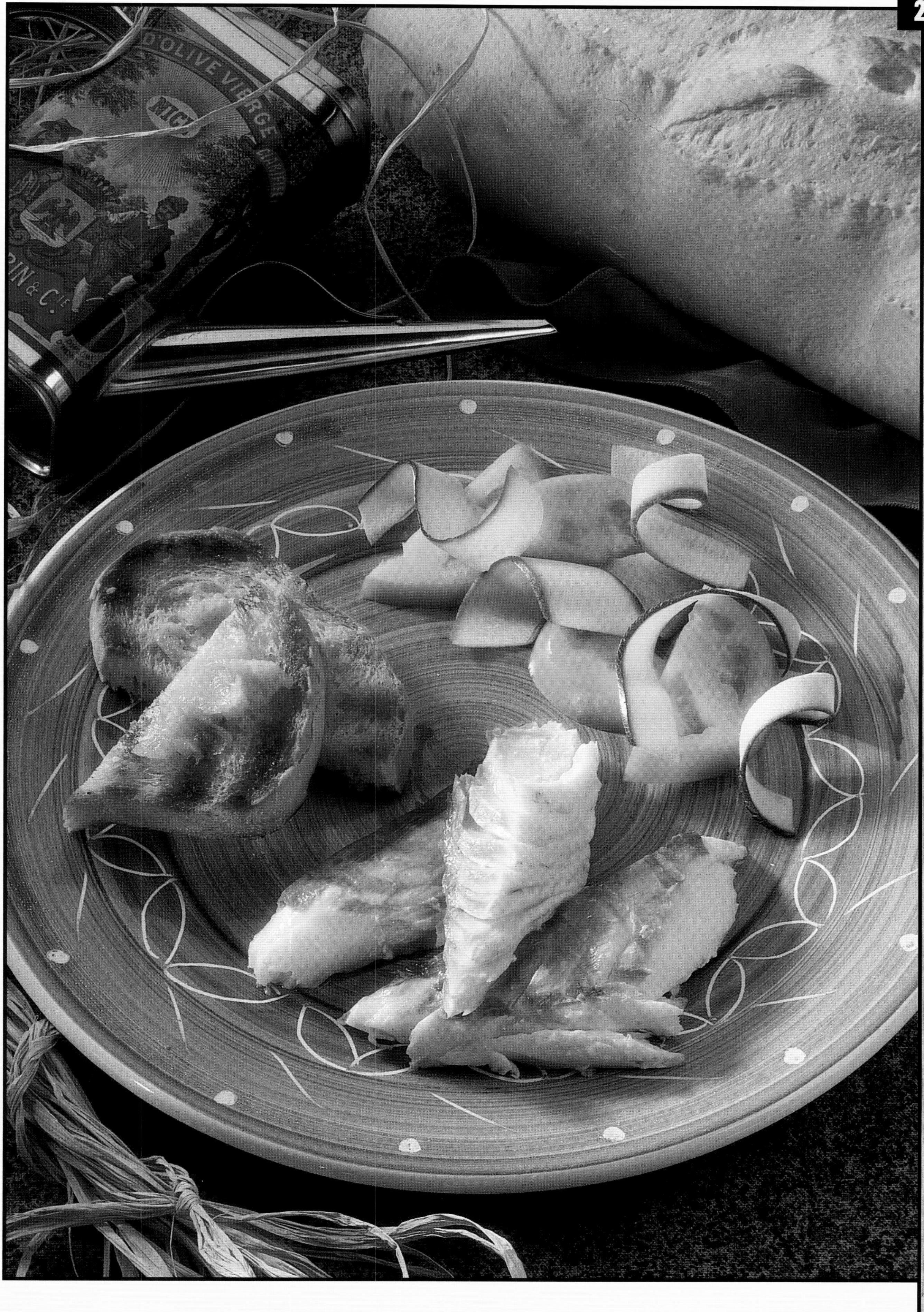
D'OLIVE VIERGE

7. Remove skewer from snapper. Slit skin from head to tail along back and belly of snapper; pull skin from top side of snapper with fingers. Discard skin. Using utility knife, separate top fillet from backbone; cut into serving-size pieces. Lift up tail; pull forward to free backbone from lower fillet. Cut lower fillet into serving-size pieces. Remove skin, if desired. *Makes 6 servings*

Note: A whole red snapper may not fit in hinged fish basket. If desired, remove head and tail from snapper.

Grilled Salmon with Cilantro Butter

 1 clove garlic, peeled
⅓ cup fresh cilantro leaves
¼ cup butter or margarine,
　　softened
½ teaspoon grated lime or
　　lemon peel
¼ teaspoon black pepper
 4 salmon fillets (about
　　6 ounces each)
　　Salt (optional)
　　Lime or lemon wedges

1. Drop garlic through feed tube of food processor with motor running. Add cilantro leaves; process until cilantro is coarsely chopped. Add butter, lime peel and pepper; process until well combined and cilantro is finely chopped.

2. Place butter mixture on sheet of waxed paper. Using waxed paper as a guide, roll mixture back and forth into 1-inch-diameter log, 2 inches long. Wrap waxed paper around butter mixture to seal; refrigerate until firm, about 30 minutes.

3. Meanwhile, prepare grill for direct cooking.

4. Lightly sprinkle salmon with salt. Place salmon, skin side down, on grid. Grill salmon, on covered grill, over medium coals 8 to 10 minutes or until salmon flakes easily when tested with fork.

5. Transfer salmon to serving plates. Cut butter log crosswise into 8 slices; top each fillet with 2 slices. Serve with lime or lemon wedges.

Makes 4 servings

Salmon Steaks and Linguine with Cilantro Pesto

Nonstick cooking spray
1½ cups halved Brussels
    sprouts, cooked crisp-
    tender
2 cups sliced mushrooms
1 cup frozen tiny peas,
    thawed
½ cup thinly sliced celery
2 tablespoons lemon juice,
    divided
1½ teaspoons dried dill weed,
    divided
4 small salmon steaks (3 to
    4 ounces each)
8 ounces linguine, cooked and
    kept warm
Cilantro Pesto (recipe
    follows)
Salt and black pepper

1. Spray large skillet with cooking spray. Heat over medium heat until hot. Add Brussels sprouts, mushrooms, peas and celery; cook and stir about 5 minutes or until mushrooms are tender. Sprinkle with 1 tablespoon lemon juice and ½ teaspoon dill weed; remove from heat and keep warm.

2. Sprinkle both sides of salmon with remaining 1 tablespoon lemon juice and remaining 1 teaspoon dill weed. Grill over medium-hot coals or broil 6 inches from heat source about 5 minutes on each side or until fish flakes easily when tested with fork.

3. Mix linguine and Cilantro Pesto in bowl; add vegetable mixture and toss. Season to taste with salt and pepper. Spoon pasta onto serving plates; top with salmon. Garnish with lemon wedges, if desired. *Makes 4 servings*

Cilantro Pesto

1 cup loosely packed fresh cilantro leaves
1 clove garlic, minced
2 tablespoons grated Parmesan cheese
1 tablespoon pine nuts or slivered almonds
1 tablespoon olive oil
1 tablespoon lemon juice
¼ teaspoon fennel seeds

1. Combine all ingredients in food processor or blender; process until almost smooth, adding 1 teaspoon water at a time, if necessary, until mixture is medium to thick consistency.
Makes 4 servings (1 tablespoon each)

Salmon with Fresh Pineapple Salsa

1 cup plus 1½ tablespoons LAWRY'S® Teriyaki Marinade with Pineapple Juice, divided
1¼ pounds fresh salmon fillets or steaks
1 cup chopped fresh or canned pineapple, drained
¼ cup finely chopped red onion
2 tablespoons chopped red bell pepper
1 tablespoon chopped fresh cilantro
1 tablespoon minced fresh jalapeño chile pepper

In large resealable plastic food storage bag, combine 1 cup Teriyaki Marinade and salmon; seal bag. Marinate in refrigerator at least 30 minutes. In small bowl, combine pineapple, onion, bell pepper, additional 1½ tablespoons Teriyaki Marinade, cilantro and jalapeño; mix gently. Let stand at room temperature 30 minutes to allow flavors to blend. Remove salmon; discard used marinade. Grill or broil salmon 10 to 12 minutes or until fish flakes easily when tested with fork, turning halfway through grilling time. Top with pineapple salsa. *Makes 4 servings*

Serving Suggestion: Serve with herbed rice pilaf and sugar snap peas.

Hint: Jalapeño peppers can sting and irritate the skin; wear rubber gloves when handling and do not touch eyes.

Szechuan Tuna Steaks

4 tuna steaks (6 ounces each), cut 1 inch thick
¼ cup soy sauce
¼ cup dry sherry or sake
1 tablespoon dark sesame oil
1 teaspoon hot chili oil *or* ¼ teaspoon red pepper flakes
1 clove garlic, minced
3 tablespoons chopped fresh cilantro

Place tuna in single layer in large shallow glass dish. Combine soy sauce, sherry, sesame oil, hot chili oil and garlic in small bowl. Reserve ¼ cup soy sauce mixture at room temperature. Pour remaining soy sauce mixture over tuna. Cover and marinate in refrigerator 40 minutes, turning once.

Prepare grill. Drain tuna, discarding marinade. Place tuna on grid. Grill, uncovered, over medium-hot coals 6 minutes or until tuna is opaque, but still feels somewhat soft in center,* turning halfway through grilling time. Transfer tuna to carving board. Cut each tuna steak into thin slices; fan out slices onto serving plates. Drizzle tuna slices with reserved soy sauce mixture; sprinkle with cilantro.

Makes 4 servings

Tuna becomes dry and tough if overcooked. Cook it as if it were beef.

Salmon with Fresh Pineapple Salsa

Grilled Snapper with Pesto

1½ cups packed fresh basil leaves

1½ cups packed fresh cilantro or parsley

¼ cup packed fresh mint leaves

¼ cup olive oil

3 tablespoons lime juice

3 cloves garlic, chopped

1 tablespoon sugar

½ teaspoon salt

4 (6-ounce) snapper or grouper fillets

Black pepper

1. Combine basil, cilantro, mint, oil, lime juice, garlic, sugar and salt in food processor or blender; process until smooth.

2. Spread about ½ teaspoon pesto on each side of fillets. Sprinkle both sides with pepper to taste. Arrange fish in single layer in grill basket coated with nonstick cooking spray. Grill, covered, over medium-hot coals 3 to 4 minutes per side or until fish flakes easily when tested with fork. Serve with remaining pesto. Garnish with lime wedges if desired. *Makes 4 servings*

Prep and Cook Time: 20 minutes

Grilled Salmon Fillets, Asparagus and Onions

½ teaspoon paprika

6 salmon fillets (6 to 8 ounces each)

⅓ cup bottled honey-Dijon marinade or barbecue sauce

1 bunch (about 1 pound) fresh asparagus spears, ends trimmed

1 large red or sweet onion, cut into ¼-inch slices

1 tablespoon olive oil

Salt and black pepper

1. Prepare grill for direct grilling. Sprinkle paprika over salmon fillets. Brush marinade over salmon; let stand at room temperature 15 minutes.

2. Brush asparagus and onion slices with olive oil; season to taste with salt and pepper.

3. Place salmon, skin side down, in center of grid over medium coals. Arrange asparagus spears and onion slices around salmon. Grill salmon and vegetables on covered grill 5 minutes. Turn salmon, asparagus and onion slices. Grill 5 to 6 minutes more or until salmon flakes easily when tested with a fork and vegetables are crisp-tender. Separate onion slices into rings; arrange over asparagus. *Makes 6 servings*

Prep and Cook Time: 26 minutes

Grilled Snapper with Pesto

Moroccan Swordfish

4 swordfish steaks (4 ounces each), about 1 inch thick
1 tablespoon fresh lemon juice
1 tablespoon apple cider vinegar
2½ teaspoons garlic-flavored vegetable oil
1 teaspoon ground ginger
1 teaspoon paprika
½ teaspoon ground cumin
½ teaspoon hot chili oil
¼ teaspoon salt
¼ teaspoon ground coriander
⅛ teaspoon black pepper
2⅔ cups prepared couscous

1. Place swordfish in single layer in medium shallow dish. Combine lemon juice, vinegar, garlic-flavored oil, ginger, paprika, cumin, chili oil, salt, coriander and pepper in small bowl; pour over swordfish and turn to coat both sides. Cover and refrigerate 40 minutes, turning once.

2. Discard marinade; grill swordfish on uncovered grill over medium-hot coals 8 to 10 minutes or until swordfish is opaque and flakes easily when tested with fork, turning once. Serve with couscous. *Makes 4 servings*

Grilled Trout with Walnut Butter Sauce

Walnut Butter Sauce (recipe follows)
4 whole, cleaned trout or other small whole fish, about 12 ounces each

Prepare Walnut Butter Sauce. Place fish on well-oiled grill rack or in well-oiled wire grill basket positioned on grill rack, over medium-hot KINGSFORD® with Mesquite Charcoal Briquets. Grill 13 to 15 minutes, turning after 6 minutes or until fish flakes easily when tested with fork. Serve trout topped with Walnut Butter Sauce.

Makes 4 servings

Walnut Butter Sauce

½ cup butter, divided
½ cup chopped walnuts
3 tablespoons Madeira wine

Heat 2 tablespoons butter in large skillet over medium heat until butter is melted. Add walnuts; cook and stir until walnuts are golden and fragrant. Reduce heat to low. Add remaining 6 tablespoons butter; stir until melted. Stir in Madeira. Serve warm. *Makes about ¾ cup*

Moroccan Swordfish

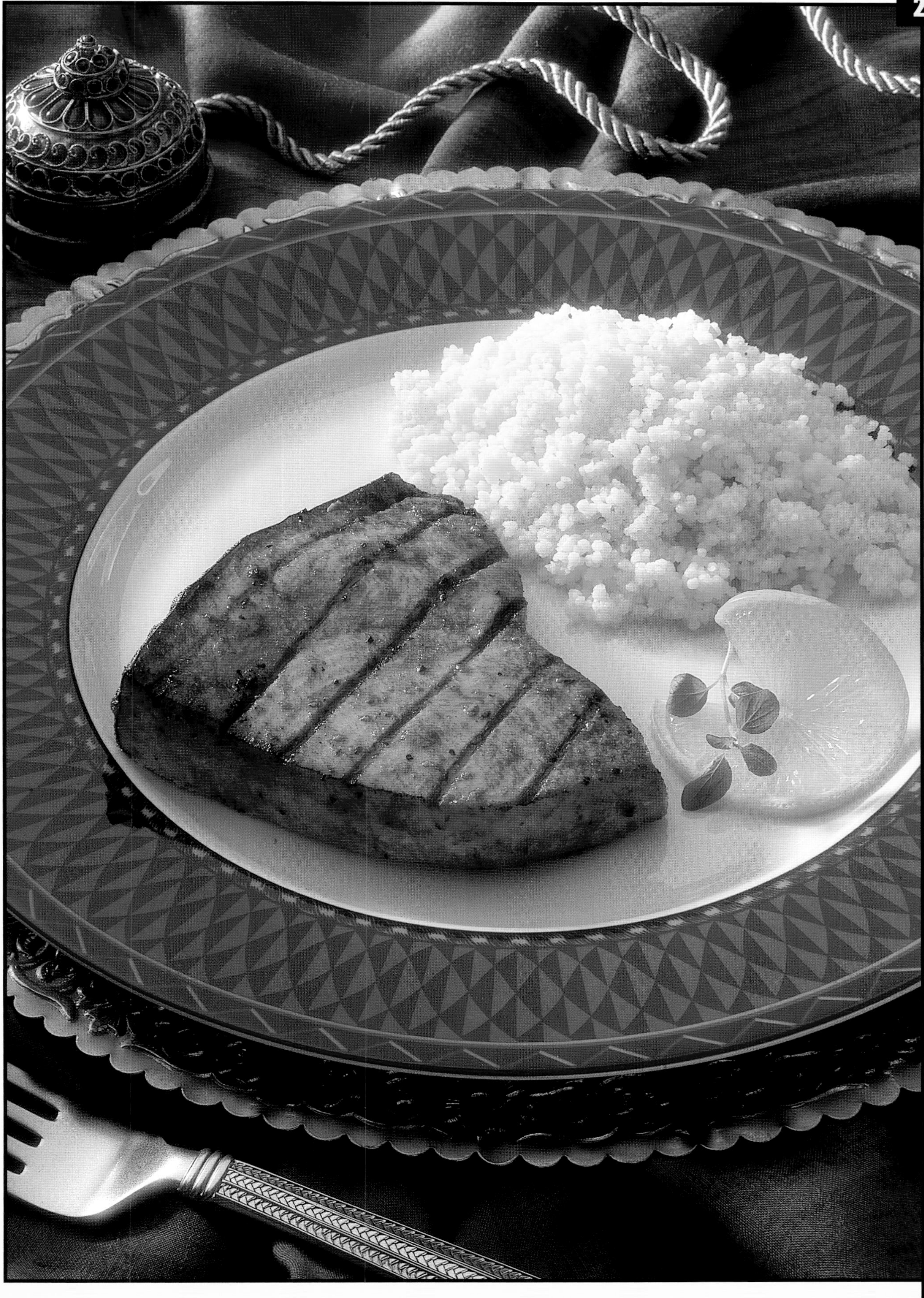

Grilled Tuna Niçoise with Citrus Marinade

Citrus Marinade (recipe
   follows)
1 tuna steak (about 1 pound)
2 cups green beans, trimmed,
   halved
4 cups romaine lettuce leaves,
   washed, torn into small
   pieces
8 small cooked red potatoes,
   quartered
1 cup chopped seeded tomato
4 cooked egg whites, chopped
¼ cup sliced red onion, halved
2 teaspoons chopped black
   olives

1. Prepare Citrus Marinade; combine with tuna in large resealable plastic food storage bag. Seal bag; turn to coat. Marinate in refrigerator 1 hour, turning occasionally.* Drain tuna; discard marinade.

2. To prevent sticking, spray grill with nonstick cooking spray. Prepare coals for grilling.

3. Place tuna on grill, 4 inches from hot coals. Grill 8 to 10 minutes or until tuna flakes easily when tested with fork, turning once. Or, place tuna on rack of broiler pan coated with nonstick cooking spray. Broil 4 inches from heat, 8 to 10 minutes or until tuna flakes easily when tested with fork. Slice tuna into ¼-inch-thick slices; set aside.

4. Place 2 cups water in large saucepan; bring to a boil over high heat. Add beans; cook 2 minutes. Drain; rinse with cold water and drain again.

5. Place lettuce on large serving platter. Arrange tuna, beans, potatoes, tomato, egg whites and onion on lettuce. Sprinkle servings with olives. Serve with low calorie salad dressing, if desired.

Makes 4 servings

Marinate in refrigerator 1 hour for each inch of thickness.

Citrus Marinade

½ cup fresh lime juice
¼ cup vegetable oil
2 green onions, chopped
1 teaspoon dried tarragon leaves
¼ teaspoon garlic powder
¼ teaspoon black pepper

Blend all ingredients in small bowl.

Shanghai Fish Packets

4 orange roughy or tilefish
    fillets (4 to 6 ounces
    each)
¼ cup mirin* or Rhine wine
3 tablespoons soy sauce
1 tablespoon dark sesame oil
1½ teaspoons grated fresh
    ginger
¼ teaspoon red pepper flakes
1 tablespoon peanut or
    vegetable oil
1 clove garlic, minced
1 package (10 ounces) fresh
    spinach leaves,
    destemmed

*Mirin is a Japanese sweet wine available in
Japanese markets and the gourmet section of
large supermarkets.*

1. Prepare barbecue grill for direct cooking.

2. Place orange roughy in single layer in large
shallow dish. Combine mirin, soy sauce, sesame
oil, ginger and red pepper flakes in small bowl;
pour over orange roughy. Cover; marinate in
refrigerator 20 minutes.

3. Heat peanut oil in large skillet over medium
heat. Add garlic; cook and stir 1 minute. Add
spinach; cook and stir until wilted, about
3 minutes, tossing with 2 wooden spoons.

4. Place spinach mixture in center of four 12-inch
squares of heavy-duty foil. Remove orange roughy
from marinade; reserve marinade. Place 1 orange
roughy fillet over each mound of spinach. Drizzle
reserved marinade evenly over orange roughy.
Wrap in foil.

5. Place packets on grid. Grill packets, on covered
grill, over medium coals 15 to 18 minutes or until
orange roughy flakes easily when tested with fork.

Makes 4 servings

Marinated Salmon with Lemon Tarragon Sauce

¼ cup lemon juice
¼ cup olive oil
2 cloves garlic, crushed
½ teaspoon salt
¼ teaspoon black pepper
1 pound fresh 1-inch thick
    salmon fillet
⅔ cup sour cream
¼ cup milk
¼ cup minced green onions
1 teaspoon dried tarragon
    leaves *or* 1 tablespoon
    fresh tarragon leaves
¼ teaspoon salt

Combine lemon juice, olive oil, garlic, pepper and
salt in shallow, nonreactive 11×7-inch baking dish.
Mix well. Add salmon; turn twice to coat with
marinade. With salmon skin-side up in baking
dish, cover tightly and refrigerate 2 hours. Combine
remaining ingredients in small bowl; mix well.
Cover and refrigerate until ready to serve.

Cut salmon into 4 pieces. Preheat grill or broiler. If
grilling, cook over medium-hot coals 5 minutes
per side or until fish begins to flake when tested
with fork. If broiling, place skin side down on
broiling pan. Cook 6 inches from heat 8 to
10 minutes or until fish just begins to flake when
tested with fork. Serve hot with chilled sauce
spooned over each piece. *Makes 4 servings*

Grilled Fish with Chili-Corn Salsa

1 cup cooked corn
1 large tomato, seeded and diced
¼ cup thinly sliced green onions with tops
¼ cup canned diced green chilies
1 tablespoon coarsely chopped fresh cilantro
⅛ teaspoon ground cumin
1 tablespoon lime juice
4 teaspoons olive oil, divided
Salt and black pepper
1½ pounds firm-textured fish steaks or fillets such as salmon, halibut, sea bass or swordfish, each 1 inch thick
Cilantro sprigs for garnish

Combine corn, tomato, green onions, green chilies, cilantro, cumin, lime juice and 2 teaspoons of oil in small bowl; mix well. Add salt and pepper to taste. Let stand at room temperature 30 minutes for flavors to blend. Brush fish with remaining 2 teaspoons oil; season with salt and pepper. Preheat charcoal grill and grease grill rack. Place fish on grill 4 to 6 inches above solid bed of coals (coals should be evenly covered with grey ashes). Cook, turning once, 4 to 5 minutes on each side or until fish turns opaque and just begins to flake. Serve with salsa. Garnish with cilantro.

Makes 4 servings

Mesquite-Grilled Salmon Fillets

2 tablespoons olive oil
1 clove garlic, minced
2 tablespoons lemon juice
1 teaspoon grated lemon peel
½ teaspoon dried dill weed
½ teaspoon dried thyme leaves
¼ teaspoon salt
¼ teaspoon black pepper
4 salmon fillets, ¾ to 1 inch thick (about 5 ounces each)

Cover 1 cup mesquite chips with cold water; soak 20 to 30 minutes. Prepare grill for direct cooking.

Combine oil and garlic in small microwavable bowl. Microwave at HIGH (100%) 1 minute or until garlic is tender. Add lemon juice, lemon peel, dill, thyme, salt and pepper; whisk until blended. Brush skinless sides of salmon with half of lemon mixture.

Drain mesquite chips; sprinkle chips over coals. Place salmon, skin side up, on grid. Grill, covered, over medium-high heat 4 to 5 minutes; turn and brush with remaining lemon mixture. Grill 4 to 5 minutes or until salmon flakes easily when tested with fork.

Makes 4 servings

Grilled Fish with Chili-Corn Salsa

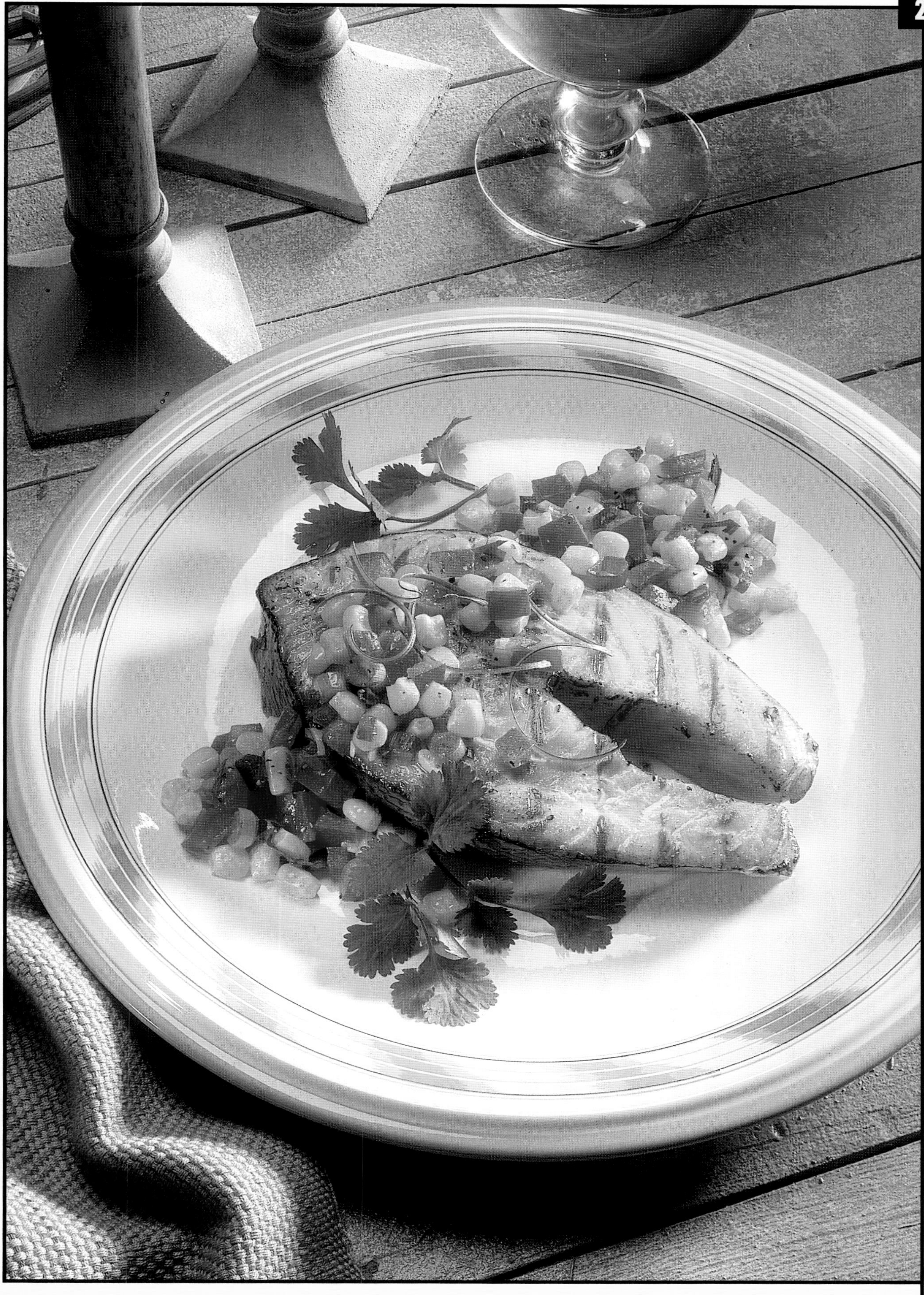

Grilled Swordfish à l'Orange

4 swordfish, halibut or shark
    steaks (about
    1½ pounds)
1 orange
¾ cup orange juice
1 tablespoon lemon juice
1 tablespoon sesame oil
1 tablespoon soy sauce
1 teaspoon cornstarch
    Salt and black pepper to
    taste

Rinse swordfish and pat dry with paper towels. Grate enough orange peel to measure 1 teaspoon; set aside. Peel orange and cut into sections; set aside. Combine orange juice, lemon juice, oil and soy sauce in small bowl. Pour half of orange juice mixture into shallow glass dish. Add ½ teaspoon grated orange peel to orange juice mixture. Place fish in dish; turn to coat in mixture. Cover and allow to marinate in refrigerator up to 1 hour.

Place remaining half of orange juice mixture in small saucepan. Stir in cornstarch and remaining ½ teaspoon orange peel. Heat over medium-high heat, stirring constantly, 3 to 5 minutes or until sauce thickens; set aside.

Remove fish from marinade; discard remaining marinade. Lightly sprinkle fish with salt and pepper. Grill over medium coals 3 to 4 minutes per side or until fish is opaque and flakes easily when tested with fork. Top with reserved orange sections and orange sauce. Serve immediately.

Makes 4 servings

FOOD FACT

Swordfish are large, saltwater game fish that are found in warm waters. Their firm, coarse-textured and slightly oily flesh is usually cut into steaks and then broiled or baked.

Mediterranean Mahi Mahi with Creamy Herb Sauce

Creamy Herb Sauce (recipe follows)
¼ cup lemon juice
2 tablespoons olive oil
1½ teaspoons grated lemon peel
½ teaspoon dried oregano leaves
¼ teaspoon salt
¼ teaspoon black pepper
1¼ pounds mahi mahi, ½ to ¾ inch thick, cut into 4 or 5 pieces

Prepare Creamy Herb Sauce; cover and refrigerate.

Combine lemon juice, oil, lemon peel, oregano, salt and pepper in small bowl until blended. Place juice mixture and mahi mahi in large resealable plastic food storage bag. Close bag securely, turning to coat. Marinate in refrigerator 30 minutes, turning after 15 minutes.

Prepare grill for direct cooking.

Drain mahi mahi; reserve marinade. Place mahi mahi on grid. Grill, covered, over medium-high heat 4 to 5 minutes; turn and brush with reserved marinade. Grill 4 to 5 minutes or until mahi mahi flakes easily when tested with fork. Serve with Creamy Herb Sauce. *Makes 4 to 5 servings*

Creamy Herb Sauce

½ cup plain yogurt
½ cup chopped peeled cucumber
1 tablespoon chopped fresh basil
1 teaspoon dried oregano leaves
½ teaspoon dried mint leaves
¼ teaspoon minced garlic
3 dashes ground red pepper

Combine all ingredients in small bowl until blended. Cover and refrigerate 1 hour before serving. *Makes about 1 cup*

Mediterranean Mahi Mahi with Creamy Herb Sauce

Grilled Chinese Salmon

3 tablespoons soy sauce
2 tablespoons dry sherry
2 cloves garlic, minced
1 pound salmon steaks or
    fillets
2 tablespoons finely chopped
    fresh cilantro

1. Combine soy sauce, sherry and garlic in shallow dish. Add salmon; turn to coat. Cover and refrigerate at least 30 minutes or up to 2 hours.

2. Drain salmon; reserve marinade. Arrange steaks (arrange fillets skin side down) on oiled rack of broiler pan or oiled grid over hot coals. Broil or grill 5 to 6 inches from heat 10 minutes. Baste with reserved marinade after 5 minutes of broiling; discard any remaining marinade. Sprinkle with cilantro. *Makes 4 servings*

Halibut with Red Pepper Sauce

1 cup LAWRY'S® Herb &
    Garlic Marinade with
    Lemon Juice
1 to 1½ pounds halibut fillets,
    cut into 4 (1-inch) steaks
    Red Pepper Sauce (recipe
    follows)

In large resealable plastic food storage bag, combine Herb & Garlic Marinade and halibut; seal bag. Marinate in refrigerator at least 30 minutes. Remove halibut from marinade; discard used marinade. Grill or broil halibut 10 minutes or until fish flakes easily when tested with fork, turning halfway through grilling time. Serve with Red Pepper Sauce. *Makes 4 servings*

Red Pepper Sauce

2 red bell peppers, roasted, peeled and seeded
¾ cup fresh bread crumbs
¼ cup fish or chicken broth
2 tablespoons olive oil
1 teaspoon LAWRY'S® Garlic Powder with
    Parsley
1 teaspoon LAWRY'S® Seasoned Salt
½ teaspoon LAWRY'S® Seasoned Pepper

In blender or food processor, combine all ingredients. Blend or process until sauce is smooth. *Makes about 2 cups*

Grilled Chinese Salmon

SHELLFISH

ON THE BARBIE

Want grilled shrimp and more? From seafood kabobs with speared scallops, cherry tomatoes and pineapple to lobster tail with a spicy butter, it's all here.

Thai Seafood Kabobs with Spicy Peanut Rice

1¼ cups UNCLE BEN'S®
    ORIGINAL
    CONVERTED® Brand
    Rice
 1 pound medium raw shrimp,
    peeled and deveined, with
    tails intact
½ pound bay scallops
¼ cup soy sauce
 2 tablespoons sesame oil
 1 large red bell pepper, cut
    into 1-inch squares
 6 green onions with tops, cut
    into 1-inch pieces
½ cup prepared Thai peanut
    sauce*
½ cup chopped peanuts

Thai peanut sauce can be found in the Asian section of large supermarket.

1. Cook rice according to package directions.

2. Meanwhile, place shrimp and scallops in medium bowl. Combine soy sauce and sesame oil; pour half of mixture over shellfish, tossing to coat. Let stand 15 minutes. Reserve remaining soy sauce mixture for basting.

3. Alternately thread shrimp, scallops, bell pepper and green onions onto twelve 12-inch metal skewers. Brush with half the reserved soy sauce mixture. Spoon Thai peanut sauce over each skewer, coating evenly. Grill or broil 8 minutes or until shrimp are pink and scallops are opaque, turning and brushing once with remaining soy sauce mixture and Thai peanut sauce.

4. Stir peanuts into cooked rice; place on serving platter. Top with seafood kabobs. Serve immediately.   *Makes 6 servings*

Serving Suggestion: Garnish with minced fresh cilantro, if desired.

**Thai Seafood Kabobs
with Spicy Peanut Rice**

Grilled Squid with Pasta and Mushrooms

2 pounds (about 20) frozen squid, thawed

⅓ cup prepared pesto

1 pound pasta, such as bow ties, radiatore or rotini

3 to 4 tablespoons olive oil, divided

½ pound wild mushrooms, such as shiitake, cremini, oyster or morel, sliced

2 cloves garlic, minced

½ teaspoon salt

½ teaspoon black pepper

½ cup fresh basil leaves, cut into narrow strips

½ cup grated Parmesan cheese

Cut off tentacles of squid just above eyes; reserve tentacles. Cut back side of body lengthwise with kitchen shears. Remove and discard entrails. Remove and discard transparent quill. With a knife, score the inside (dull side) of body lengthwise to a depth of about ¹⁄₁₆-inch at ¼-inch intervals. Repeat with remaining squid. Brush each side of bodies and tentacles liberally with pesto.

Prepare grill for direct cooking.

Cook pasta al dente according to package directions in large saucepan; drain. Set aside and keep warm.

Place 2 tablespoons oil in medium skillet over medium heat. Add mushrooms and garlic; cook and stir 2 to 3 minutes or until tender. Add salt and pepper; stir. Cover; set aside.

Place squid on grid. Grill over high heat 3 minutes or until tender, turning halfway through grilling time. Cut squid bodies into strips through score lines; cover with foil and set aside.

Combine pasta, mushroom mixture, basil, cheese and 1 to 2 tablespoons remaining oil in large serving bowl. (Add just enough oil to moisten.) Top with squid. *Makes 5 to 6 servings*

Grilled Squid with Pasta and Mushrooms

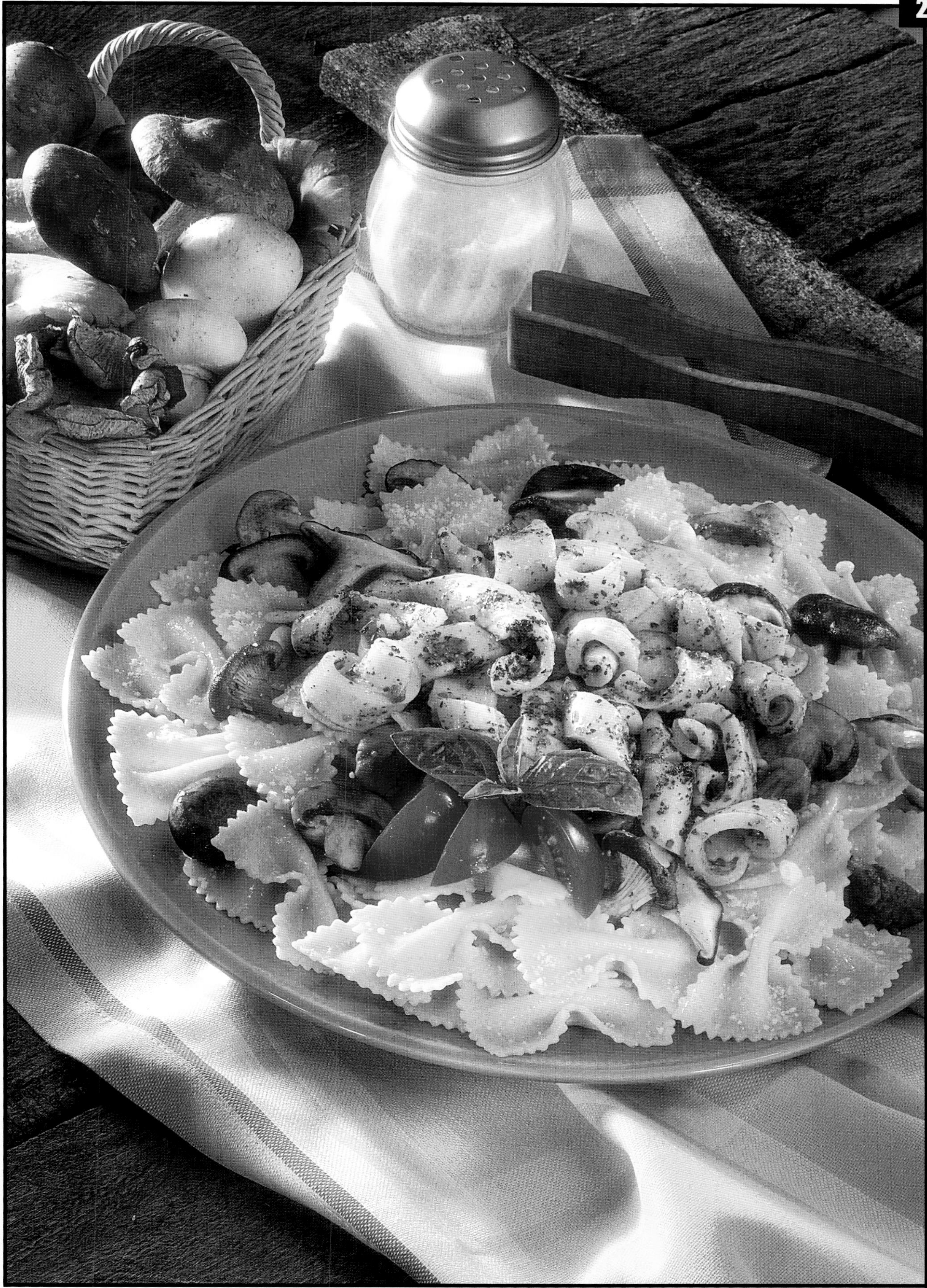

Barbecued Shrimp with Spicy Rice

1 pound large shrimp, peeled
  and deveined
4 wooden* or metal skewers
  Vegetable cooking spray
⅓ cup prepared barbecue
  sauce
  Spicy Rice (recipe follows)

*Soak wooden skewers in water 20 minutes before using to prevent burning.

Thread shrimp on skewers. To broil in oven, place on broiler rack coated with cooking spray. Broil 4 to 5 inches from heat 4 minutes. Brush with barbecue sauce. Turn and brush with remaining barbecue sauce. Broil 2 to 4 minutes longer or until shrimp are done. To cook on outdoor grill, cook skewered shrimp over hot coals 4 minutes. Brush with barbecue sauce. Turn and brush with remaining barbecue sauce. Grill 4 to 5 minutes longer or until shrimp are done. Serve with Spicy Rice. *Makes 4 servings*

Favorite recipe from **USA Rice Federation**

Spicy Rice

½ cup sliced green onions
½ cup minced carrots
½ cup minced red bell pepper
1 jalapeño or serrano pepper, minced
1 tablespoon vegetable oil
2 cups cooked rice (cooked in chicken broth)
2 tablespoons chopped cilantro
1 tablespoon lime juice
1 teaspoon soy sauce
  Hot pepper sauce to taste

Cook onions, carrots, bell pepper and jalapeño pepper in oil in large skillet over medium-high heat until tender crisp. Stir in rice, cilantro, lime juice, soy sauce and pepper sauce; cook until thoroughly heated. *Makes 4 servings*

Microwave Directions: Combine onions, carrots, bell pepper, jalapeño pepper and oil in 2-quart microproof baking dish. Cook on HIGH (100% power) 2 to 3 minutes or until vegetables are tender crisp. Add rice, cilantro, lime juice, soy sauce and pepper sauce. Cook on HIGH 3 to 4 minutes, stirring after 2 minutes, or until thoroughly heated.

Favorite recipe from **USA Rice Federation**

Grilled Prawns with Salsa Vera Cruz

1 can (14½ ounces) DEL
  MONTE® Diced
  Tomatoes, drained
1 orange, peeled and chopped
¼ cup sliced green onions
¼ cup chopped cilantro or
  parsley
1 small clove garlic, crushed
1 pound medium shrimp,
  peeled and deveined

1. Combine tomatoes, orange, green onions, cilantro and garlic in medium bowl.

2. Thread shrimp onto skewers; season with salt and pepper, if desired.

3. Brush grill with oil. Cook shrimp over hot coals about 3 minutes on each side or until shrimp turn pink. Top with salsa. Serve over rice and garnish, if desired. *Makes 4 servings*

Hint: Thoroughly rinse shrimp in cold water before cooking.

Prep Time: 25 minutes
Cook Time: 6 minutes

FOOD FACT

The terms barbecue and grill are usually used interchangeably. When a distinction is made, barbecue refers to long, slow cooking, sometimes on a spit or in a pit, of large pieces of meat kept moist with a highly seasoned sauce. Barbecuing in this form is likely done for large groups or gatherings. By contrast, grilling implies quicker, lighter cooking of a wider variety of foods including poultry, seafood, vegetables and fruits, using seasonings, spice rubs, marinades and light sauces.

Grilled Jumbo Shrimp

24 raw jumbo shrimp, shelled
and deveined
1 cup WESSON® Canola Oil
½ cup minced fresh onion
2 teaspoons dried oregano
1 teaspoon salt
1 teaspoon crushed fresh
garlic
½ teaspoon dried basil
½ teaspoon dried thyme
3 tablespoons fresh lemon
juice
6 long bamboo skewers,
soaked in water for
20 minutes

Rinse shrimp and pat dry; set aside. In a large bowl, whisk together Wesson® Oil and *next* 6 ingredients, ending with thyme. Reserve ⅓ cup marinade; set aside. Toss shrimp in remaining marinade; cover and refrigerate 3 hours, tossing occasionally. Stir in lemon juice; let stand at room temperature for 30 minutes. Meanwhile, preheat grill or broiler. Drain shrimp; discard marinade. Thread 4 shrimp per skewer. Grill shrimp, 4 inches over hot coals, 3 minutes per side or until pink, basting with reserved ⅓ cup marinade.

Makes 6 servings

Grilled Jumbo Shrimp

Scallop Kabobs

1 pound Florida calico
    scallops, fresh or frozen
2 cups cherry tomatoes
2 cups fresh small
    mushrooms
1 can (13½ ounces) pineapple
    chunks, drained
1 green pepper, cut into
    1-inch squares
¼ cup vegetable oil
¼ cup lemon juice
¼ cup chopped parsley
¼ cup soy sauce
½ teaspoon salt
⅛ teaspoon black pepper

Thaw scallops, if frozen. Rinse scallops with cold running water to remove any remaining shell particles. Place tomatoes, mushrooms, pineapple, green pepper and scallops in a bowl. Combine oil, lemon juice, parsley, soy sauce, salt and black pepper. Pour sauce over scallop mixture and let stand for 30 minutes, stirring occasionally. Using long skewers, alternate scallops, tomatoes, mushrooms, pineapple and green pepper until skewers are filled. Cook about 4 minutes over moderately hot coals. Baste with sauce. Turn and cook for 3 to 4 minutes longer.

Makes 6 servings

*Favorite recipe from **Florida Department of Agriculture and Consumer Services, Bureau of Seafood and Aquaculture***

FOOD FACT

There are two common varieties of scallops. Bay scallops, called calico when harvested from the deep sea, are tiny scallops that are harvested mainly from the East Coast; they tend to cost more than sea scallops, which are about three times as large. If cut into halves or thirds, sea scallops make an economical alternative to bay scallops.

Scallop Kabobs

Sweet Citrus and Dijon Grilled Shrimp

½ cup LAWRY'S® Dijon &
    Honey Marinade with
    Lemon Juice
½ cup orange juice
½ teaspoon LAWRY'S® Garlic
    Salt
1 pound raw large shrimp,
    peeled and deveined
1 onion, cut into wedges
8 cherry tomatoes
2 limes, cut into wedges

In medium bowl, combine Dijon & Honey Marinade, orange juice and Garlic Salt; mix well. Arrange shrimp, onion, tomatoes and limes in well-oiled wire grill basket; brush with marinade mixture. Grill 4 to 6 minutes or until shrimp are pink, turning once and basting often with marinade mixture. *Makes 4 servings*

Serving Suggestion: Serve with hot cooked orzo. Garnish with fresh thyme, if desired.

Shrimp and Pineapple Kabobs

8 ounces medium shrimp,
    peeled and deveined
½ cup pineapple juice
¼ teaspoon garlic powder
12 chunks canned pineapple
1 green bell pepper, cut into
    1-inch pieces
¼ cup prepared chili sauce

1. Combine shrimp, juice and garlic powder in bowl; toss to coat. Marinate in refrigerator 30 minutes. Drain shrimp; discard marinade.

2. Alternately thread pineapple, pepper and shrimp onto 4 (10-inch) skewers. Brush with chili sauce. Grill, 4 inches from hot coals, 5 minutes or until shrimp are opaque, turning once and basting with chili sauce. *Makes 4 servings*

Sweet Citrus and Dijon Grilled Shrimp

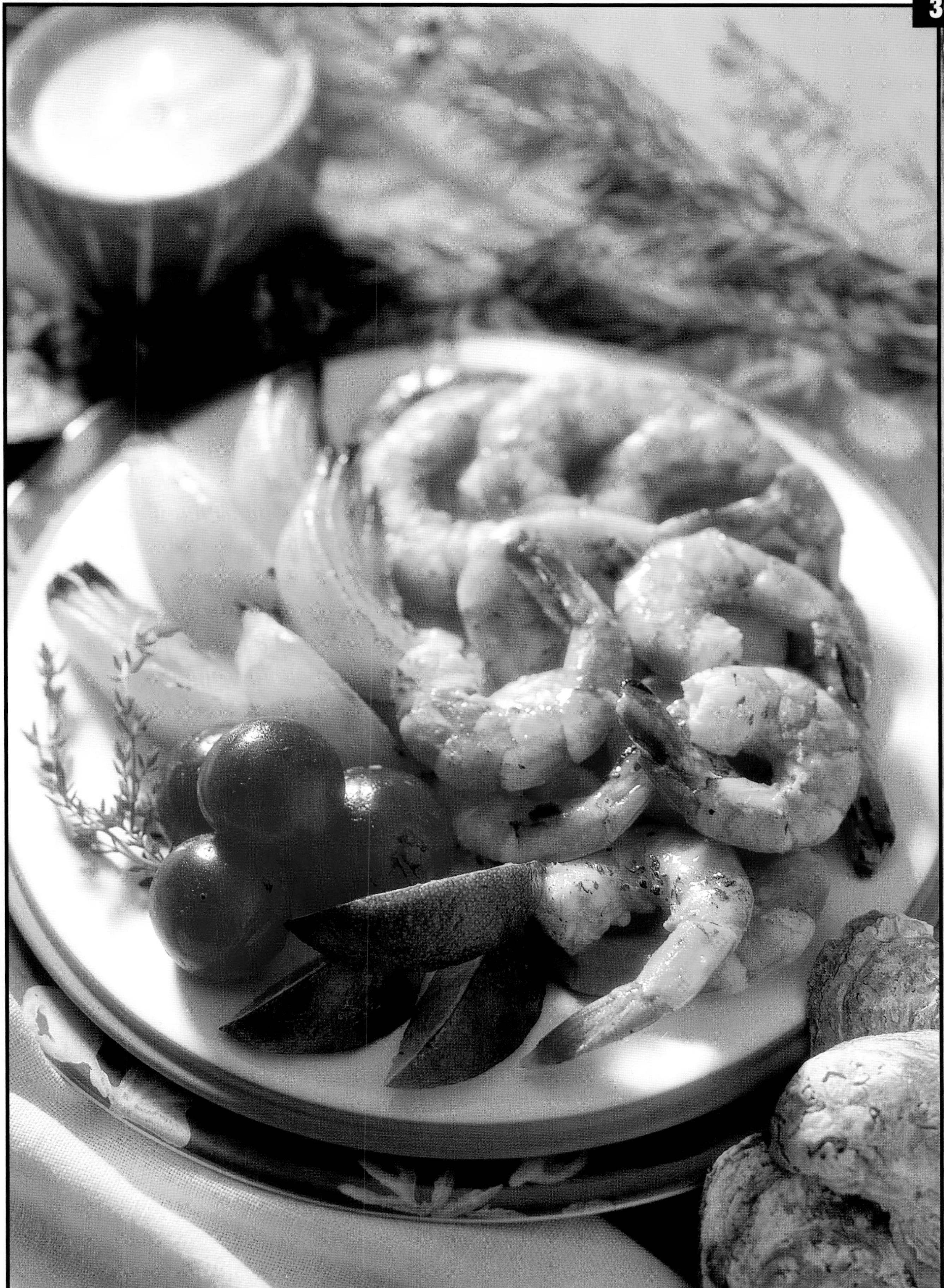

Shrimp Skewers with Tropical Fruit Salsa

½ cup soy sauce
¼ cup lime juice
2 cloves garlic, minced
1½ pounds large shrimp,
    shelled and deveined
Tropical Fruit Salsa (recipe
    follows)
Vegetable oil
Salt and black pepper

Combine soy sauce, lime juice and garlic in shallow glass dish or large heavy plastic food storage bag. Add shrimp; cover dish or close bag. Marinate in refrigerator no longer than 30 minutes.

Meanwhile, prepare Tropical Fruit Salsa. (Salsa should not be made more than two hours before serving.)

Remove shrimp from marinade; discard marinade. Thread shrimp on metal or bamboo skewers. (Soak bamboo skewers in water at least 20 minutes to keep them from burning.) Brush one side of shrimp lightly with oil; season with salt and pepper.

Oil hot grid to help prevent sticking. Grill shrimp, oil side down, on covered grill, over medium-hot KINGSFORD® Briquets, 6 to 8 minutes. Halfway through cooking time, brush top with oil, season with salt and pepper, then turn and continue grilling until shrimp firm up and turn opaque throughout. Serve with Tropical Fruit Salsa.

Makes 4 servings

Tropical Fruit Salsa

2 mangos*
2 kiwifruit
3 tablespoons finely chopped or finely slivered
    red onion
3 tablespoons lime juice
¼ teaspoon salt
⅓ teaspoon crushed red pepper flakes
1 teaspoon sugar
1 tablespoon finely chopped fresh mint leaves
1 tablespoon finely chopped fresh cilantro

Substitute 1 papaya or 2 large or 3 medium peaches for mangos.

Peel fruit. Cut mango into ¼-inch pieces; cut kiwifruit into wedges. Combine with remaining ingredients in medium bowl; adjust flavors to taste. Cover and refrigerate 2 hours.

Makes about 1 cup

Seafood Paella

¼ cup *Frank's® RedHot®* Cayenne Pepper Sauce
3 tablespoons olive oil
2 cloves garlic, minced
1 teaspoon dried thyme leaves
1 pound jumbo raw shrimp, shelled and deveined
1 pound boneless skinless chicken thighs or breasts, cut into 1-inch cubes
½ pound Spanish chorizo sausage or Polish kielbasa, cut into 1-inch slices
1 bag (2 pounds) mussels, well scrubbed
Spicy Rice (recipe follows)

Combine *Frank's RedHot* Sauce, oil, garlic and thyme in large bowl; mix well. Add shrimp, chicken and sausage; toss well to coat evenly.

Cut six 14-inch circles of heavy-duty foil. Spoon about 1½ cups seafood and chicken mixture in center of each piece of foil. Divide mussels evenly on top of each portion. Fold foil in half over seafood mixture. Seal edges securely with tight double folds.

Place packets on grid. Cook over medium coals 15 minutes or until chicken is no longer pink in center, shrimp are pink and mussels open, opening foil packets carefully. (Discard any shells that do not open.) Serve with Spicy Rice.

Makes 6 servings

Prep Time: 20 minutes
Cook Time: 15 minutes

Spicy Rice

2 tablespoons olive oil
½ cup finely chopped onion
2 cloves garlic, minced
1 cup uncooked long grain white rice
1 can (13¾ ounces) chicken broth
2 tablespoons *French's®* Worcestershire Sauce
1 package (9 ounces) frozen peas, thawed
1 jar (7 ounces) roasted red peppers, drained and sliced

Combine oil, onion and garilc in 3-quart microwave-safe bowl. Cover with vented plastic wrap and microwave on HIGH (100% power) 2 minutes. Stir in rice, broth and Worcestershire. Cover tightly with plastic wrap. Microwave on HIGH (100% power) 7 minutes, stirring once. Cover and microwave on MEDIUM (50% power) 10 minutes or until rice is just tender. Stir in peas and peppers. Cover and let stand 5 minutes before serving. *Makes 6 side-dish servings*

Prep Time: 15 minutes
Cook Time: 19 minutes

Lobster Tail with Tasty Butters

Hot & Spicy Butter or
   Scallion Butter or Chili-
   Mustard Butter (recipes
   follow)
4 fresh or thawed frozen
   lobster tails (about
   5 ounces each)

Prepare grill for direct cooking. Prepare butter mixture.

Rinse lobster tails in cold water. Butterfly tails by cutting lengthwise through centers of hard top shells and meat. Cut to, but not through, bottoms of shells. Press shell halves of tails apart with fingers. Brush lobster meat with butter mixture.

Place tails on grid, meat side down. Grill over medium-high heat 4 minutes. Turn tails meat side up. Brush with butter mixture and grill 4 to 5 minutes or until lobster meat turns opaque.

Heat remaining butter mixture, stirring occasionally. Serve butter sauce for dipping.

Makes 4 servings

Tasty Butters

Hot & Spicy Butter
   ⅓ cup butter or margarine, melted
   1 tablespoon chopped onion
   1 teaspoon dried thyme leaves
   ¼ teaspoon ground allspice
   2 to 3 teaspoons hot pepper sauce

Scallion Butter
   ⅓ cup butter or margarine, melted
   1 tablespoon finely chopped green onion tops
   1 tablespoon lemon juice
   1 teaspoon grated lemon peel
   ¼ teaspoon black pepper

Chili-Mustard Butter
   ⅓ cup butter or margarine, melted
   1 tablespoon chopped onion
   1 tablespoon Dijon mustard
   1 teaspoon chili powder

For each butter sauce, combine ingredients in small bowl.

Lobster Tail with Tasty Butters

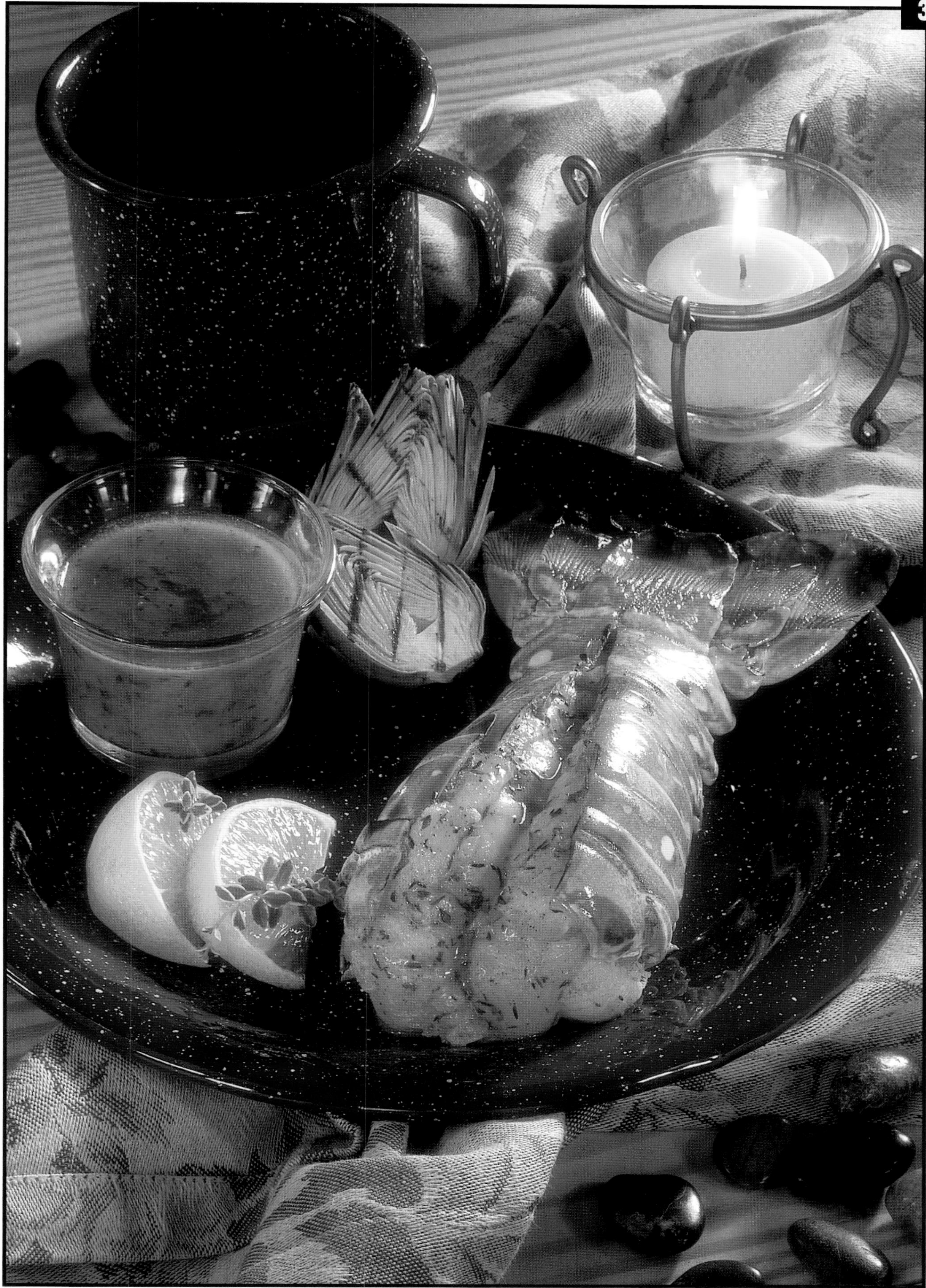

Cajun Grilled Shrimp

3 green onions, minced
2 tablespoons lemon juice
3 cloves garlic, minced
2 teaspoons paprika
1 teaspoon salt
¼ to ½ teaspoon black pepper
¼ to ½ teaspoon cayenne
    pepper
1 tablespoon olive oil
1½ pounds shrimp, shelled with
    tails intact, deveined
Lemon wedges

Combine onions, lemon juice, garlic, paprika, salt and peppers in 2-quart glass dish; stir in oil. Add shrimp; turn to coat. Cover and refrigerate at least 15 minutes. Thread shrimp onto metal or wooden skewers. (Soak wooden skewers in hot water 30 minutes to prevent burning.) Grill shrimp over medium-hot KINGSFORD® Briquets about 2 minutes per side until opaque. Serve immediately with lemon wedges.

Makes 4 servings

Sizzling Florida Shrimp

1½ pounds Florida Shrimp,
    peeled and deveined
1 cup Florida mushrooms, cut
    in halves
½ cup Florida red bell pepper
    pieces (1-inch pieces)
½ cup Florida onion pieces
    (1-inch pieces)
1 (8½-ounce) jar lemon
    pepper sauce

Arrange shrimp on wooden skewers with mushroom, red bell pepper and onion. Place skewers in a glass dish and cover with sauce, reserving about 2 tablespoons for basting during cooking. Cover dish and refrigerate for 1 hour. Prepare grill surface by cleaning and coating with oil. Coals are ready when coals are no longer flaming but are covered with gray ash. Place skewers on grill about 6 inches from the coals. Let shrimp grill for about 3 to 4 minutes on each side, basting before turning once. Serve with sautéed asparagus and grilled garlic bread.

Makes 4 servings

Favorite recipe from **Florida Department of Agriculture and Consumer Services, Bureau of Seafood and Aquaculture**

Cajun Grilled Shrimp

Grilled Scallops and Vegetables with Cilantro Sauce

1 teaspoon hot chili oil

1 teaspoon dark sesame oil

1 green onion, chopped

1 tablespoon finely chopped fresh ginger

1 cup fat-free reduced-sodium chicken broth

1 cup chopped fresh cilantro

1 pound sea scallops

2 medium zucchini, cut into ½-inch slices

2 medium yellow squash, cut into ½-inch slices

1 medium yellow onion, cut into wedges

8 large mushrooms

1. Spray cold grid with nonstick cooking spray. Preheat grill to medium-high heat. Heat chili oil and sesame oil in small saucepan over medium-low heat. Add green onion; cook about 15 seconds or just until fragrant. Add ginger; cook 1 minute.

2. Add chicken broth; bring mixture to a boil. Cook until liquid is reduced by half. Cool slightly. Place mixture in blender or food processor with cilantro; blend until smooth. Set aside.

3. Thread scallops and vegetables onto 4 (12-inch) skewers. (If using wooden skewers, soak in water 25 to 30 minutes before using, to prevent skewers from burning.) Grill about 8 minutes per side or until scallops turn opaque. Serve hot with cilantro sauce. Garnish, if desired.

Makes 4 servings

Grilled Scallops and Vegetables with Cilantro Sauce

South Seas Shrimp & Mango

1 pound raw jumbo shrimp, shelled and deveined
3 tablespoons *French's*® Napa Valley Style Dijon Mustard
2 tablespoons olive oil
2 tablespoons fresh orange juice
1 tablespoon *Frank's*® *RedHot*® Cayenne Pepper Sauce
1 teaspoon grated orange peel
1 large ripe mango, peeled cut into 1-inch pieces
1 red bell pepper, cut into 1-inch pieces
4 green onions, cut into 1½-inch pieces

1. Place shrimp in large resealable plastic food storage bag. Combine mustard, oil, juice, *Frank's RedHot* Sauce and orange peel in small bowl; pour over shrimp. Seal bag; marinate in refrigerator 20 minutes.

2. Alternately thread shrimp, mango, bell pepper and onions onto 4 (10-inch) metal skewers. Place skewers on oiled grid. Grill over high heat 7 minutes or until shrimp are opaque, turning and basting once with mustard mixture. Discard any remaining marinade. *Makes 4 servings*

Prep Time: 15 minutes
Marinate Time: 20 minutes
Cook Time: 7 minutes

GRILLING TIP

Mangoes have a large central seed that clings tenaciously to the flesh. Do not try to cut the mango in half and twist the two halves apart, as is often directed.

To prepare a mango, hold it, stem end up, on a cutting board. Using a long knife, make a vertical cut on the flat side of the mango from the top to the bottom about 1/2 inch to the right of the stem and seed. Repeat on the opposite flat side of the mango.

To cube a mango, do not peel the skin from the cut sections. Score the flesh, but not the skin, with the tip of a paring knife. Holding the scored section in two hands, gently push from the skin side toward you so that the flesh separates.

To separate the cubes from the skin, gently run a table knife or the edge of a spoon between the skin and the flesh. Peel the sections still attached to the mango and slice the flesh from the seed. Cut the flesh into cubes.

South Seas Shrimp & Mango

Bacon-Wrapped Shrimp

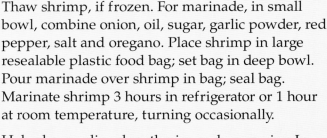

1 pound fresh or frozen large
    raw shrimp, shelled and
    deveined
1 small onion, finely chopped
½ cup olive oil
½ teaspoon sugar
½ teaspoon garlic powder
½ teaspoon ground red
    pepper
¼ teaspoon salt
¼ teaspoon dried oregano
    leaves, crushed
½ pound bacon
    Mexican Fried Rice (recipe
    follows)

Thaw shrimp, if frozen. For marinade, in small bowl, combine onion, oil, sugar, garlic powder, red pepper, salt and oregano. Place shrimp in large resealable plastic food bag; set bag in deep bowl. Pour marinade over shrimp in bag; seal bag. Marinate shrimp 3 hours in refrigerator or 1 hour at room temperature, turning occasionally.

Halve bacon slices lengthwise and crosswise. In large skillet, partially cook bacon. Drain on paper towels. Drain shrimp; discard marinade. Wrap bacon strips around shrimp; secure with wooden toothpicks. Place wrapped shrimp in wire grill basket or on 12×9-inch piece of heavy-duty aluminum foil. (If using foil, puncture foil in several places.)

Grill shrimp on uncovered grill directly over medium-hot KINGSFORD® Briquets 12 minutes or until bacon is done and shrimp are opaque, turning basket or individual shrimp once. Serve with Mexican Fried Rice.   *Makes 6 servings*

Mexican Fried Rice

3 tablespoons vegetable oil
1 cup long-grain rice
1 (8-ounce) package frozen raw shrimp, shelled
    and deveined (optional)
1 cup salsa
½ cup chopped green bell pepper
1 small onion, chopped
1 clove garlic, minced

Heat oil in large skillet over medium heat. Add rice; cook until golden brown, stirring frequently. Stir in shrimp, salsa, bell pepper, onion, garlic and 2 cups water. Bring mixture to a boil; reduce heat to low. Cover; simmer 15 to 20 minutes or until rice is tender. Season to taste; serve with additional salsa, if desired.   *Makes 6 servings*

Grilled Oriental Shrimp Kabobs

3 tablespoons reduced-
    sodium soy sauce or
    regular soy sauce
1 tablespoon regular or
    seasoned rice vinegar
1 tablespoon dark sesame oil
2 cloves garlic, minced
¼ teaspoon red pepper flakes
1 pound uncooked large
    shrimp, peeled and
    deveined

1. For marinade, combine soy sauce, vinegar, oil, garlic and pepper flakes in small bowl; mix well. Cover; refrigerate up to 3 days.

2. To complete recipe, combine marinade and shrimp in resealable plastic food storage bag. Seal bag securely. Refrigerate at least 30 minutes or up to 2 hours, turning bag once.

3. Spray barbecue grid with nonstick cooking spray. Prepare barbecue grill for direct cooking.

4. Drain shrimp, reserving marinade. Thread shrimp onto 12-inch-long skewers. Place skewers on prepared grid; brush with half of reserved marinade.

5. Grill skewers, on covered grill, over medium coals 5 minutes. Turn skewers over; brush with remaining half of marinade. Grill 3 to 5 minutes or until shrimp are opaque. *Makes 4 servings*

Serving Suggestion: Serve with fried rice and fresh pineapple spears.

Make-Ahead Time: up to 3 days in refrigerator
Final Prep and Cook Time: 20 minutes

Asian Honey-Tea Grilled Prawns

Marinade
- 1 cup brewed double-strength orange-spice tea, cooled
- ¼ cup honey
- ¼ cup rice vinegar
- ¼ cup soy sauce
- 1 tablespoon fresh ginger, peeled and finely chopped
- ½ teaspoon ground black pepper

Prawns
- 1½ pounds medium shrimp, peeled and deveined
- Salt
- 2 green onions, thinly sliced

In plastic bag, combine marinade ingredients. Remove ½ cup marinade; set aside for dipping sauce. Add shrimp to marinade in bag, turning to coat. Close bag securely and marinate in refrigerator 30 minutes or up to 12 hours.

Remove shrimp from marinade; discard marinade. Thread shrimp onto 8 skewers, dividing evenly. Grill over medium coals 4 to 6 minutes or until shrimp turn pink and are just firm to the touch, turning once. Season with salt, as desired.

Meanwhile prepare dipping sauce by placing reserved ½ cup marinade in small saucepan. Bring to a boil over medium-high heat. Boil 3 to 5 minutes or until slightly reduced. Stir in green onions. *Makes 4 servings*

Favorite recipe from **National Honey Board**

FOOD FACT

The term prawn is often used in place of shrimp, especially when referring to larger varieties, usually 12 to 15 per pound. However, all prawns are not necessarily considered shrimp. Some are called lobsterettes, scampi, and langoustine, all considerably larger than even the largest shrimp.

Asian Honey-Tea Grilled Prawns

Grilled Paella

1½ to 2 pounds chicken wings or thighs
2 tablespoons plus ¼ cup extra-virgin olive oil, divided
Salt and black pepper
1 pound garlicky sausage links, such as linguisa, chorizo or Italian
1 large onion, chopped
2 large red bell peppers, seeded and cut into thin strips
4 cloves garlic, minced
1 can (14 ounces) diced tomatoes, undrained
4 cups uncooked rice
16 tightly closed live mussels or clams,* scrubbed
½ pound large shrimp,* peeled and deveined with tails intact
1½ cups frozen peas
1 can (about 14 ounces) chicken broth
2 lemons, cut into wedges
1 oval disposable foil pan (about 17×13×3 inches)

*Seafood can be omitted; add an additional 1¼ to 1½ pounds chicken.

Brush chicken with 2 tablespoons oil; season with salt and black pepper. Grill chicken and sausage on covered grill over medium KINGSFORD® Briquets 15 to 20 minutes or until chicken juices run clear and sausage is no longer pink, turning every 5 minutes. Cut sausage into 2-inch pieces.

Heat remaining ¼ cup oil in large skillet over medium-high heat. Add onion, bell peppers and garlic; cook and stir 5 minutes or until vegetables are tender. Add tomatoes, 1½ teaspoons salt and ½ teaspoon black pepper; cook about 8 minutes until thick, stirring frequently. Combine onion mixture and rice in foil pan; spread evenly. Arrange chicken, sausage, seafood and peas over rice. Bring broth and 6 cups water to a boil in 3 quart saucepan. Place foil pan on grid over medium KINGSFORD® briquets; immediately pour boiling broth mixture over rice. Grill on covered grill about 20 minutes until liquid is absorbed. *Do not stir.* Cover with foil; let stand 10 minutes. Garnish with lemon wedges.

Makes 8 to 10 servings

Grilled Paella

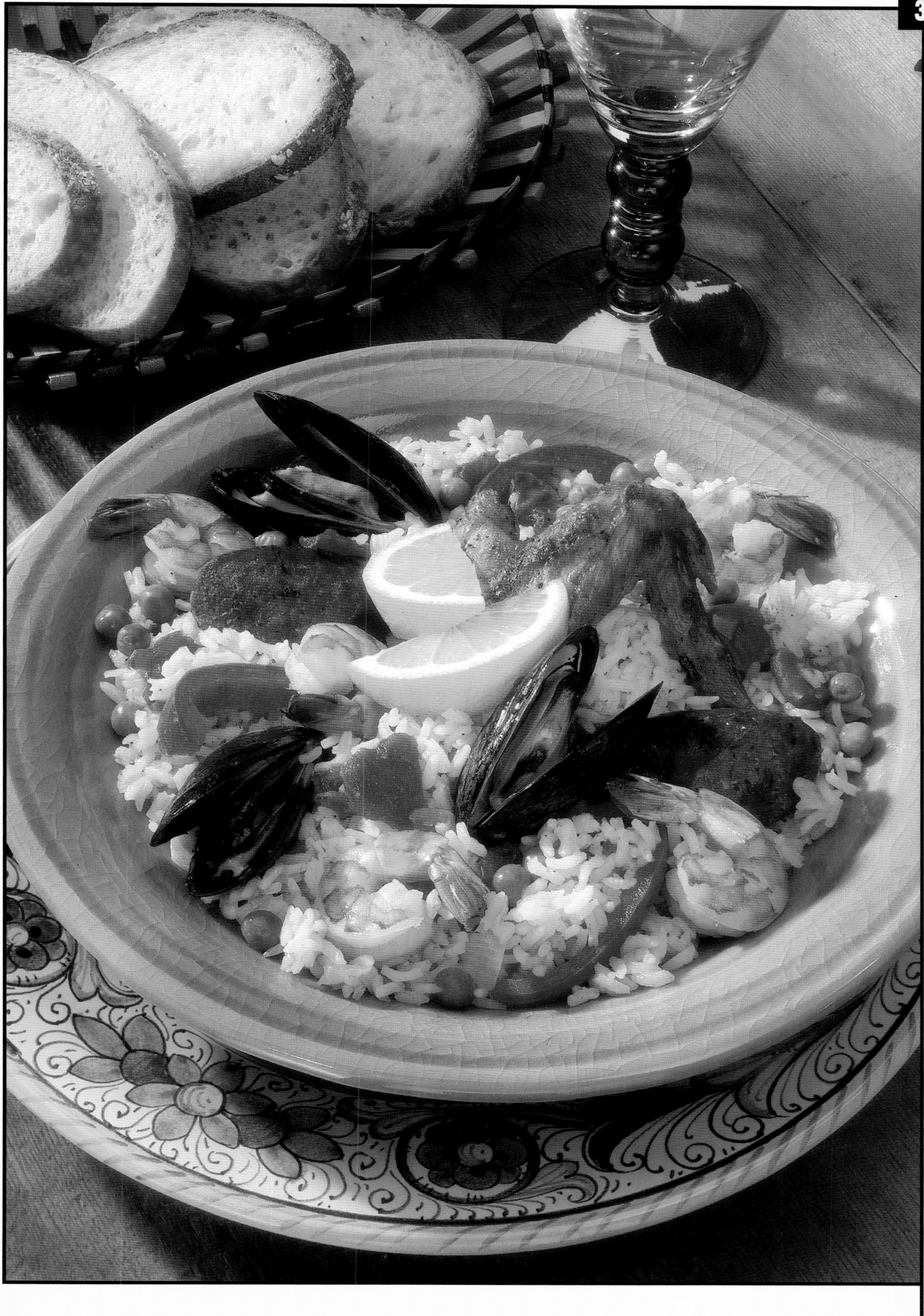

Beach Grill

1 cup vegetable oil
2 teaspoons LAWRY'S®
　　Seasoned Salt
1 teaspoon LAWRY'S® Garlic
　　Powder with Parsley
½ teaspoon hot pepper sauce
　　(optional)
12 raw medium shrimp, peeled
　　and deveined
12 sea scallops
1 small red onion, cut into
　　12 wedges
　　Skewers

In large resealable plastic food storage bag, combine oil, Seasoned Salt, Garlic Powder with Parsley and hot pepper sauce, if desired; mix well. Add shrimp, scallops and onion; seal bag. Marinate in refrigerator at least 1 hour. Remove shrimp, scallops and onion from marinade; discard used marinade. Alternately thread shrimp, scallops and onion onto skewers. Grill or broil skewers 4 to 6 minutes or until shrimp are pink and scallops are opaque, turning halfway through grilling time.　　*Makes 6 servings*

Serving Suggestion: Serve with lime wedges and crusty French bread.

Hint: If using wooden skewers, soak in water overnight before using to prevent scorching.

FOOD FACT

Does chopping or slicing onions make you cry? It is probably due to an enzyme called alliinase. When exposed to the air through peeling or chopping it can irritate the tear ducts causing your eyes to water. Sometimes chilling the onion before cutting can reduce the effects of alliinase.

Hot Shrimp with Cool Salsa

¼ cup prepared salsa

4 tablespoons fresh lime juice, divided

1 teaspoon honey

1 clove garlic, minced

2 to 4 drops hot pepper sauce

1 pound large shrimp, peeled and deveined, with tails intact

1 cup finely diced honeydew melon

½ cup finely diced unpeeled cucumber

2 tablespoons minced parsley

1 green onion, finely chopped

1½ teaspoons sugar

1 teaspoon olive oil

¼ teaspoon salt

1. To make marinade, combine prepared salsa, 2 tablespoons lime juice, honey, garlic and hot pepper sauce in small bowl. Thread shrimp onto skewers. Brush shrimp with marinade; set aside.

2. To make salsa, combine remaining 2 tablespoons lime juice, melon, cucumber, parsley, onion, sugar, oil and salt in medium bowl; mix well.

3. Grill shrimp over medium coals 4 to 5 minutes or until shrimp are opaque, turning once. Serve with salsa. *Makes 4 servings*

Garlic Skewered Shrimp

1 pound large shrimp, peeled
    and deveined
2 tablespoons reduced-
    sodium soy sauce
1 tablespoon vegetable oil
3 cloves garlic, minced
¼ teaspoon red pepper flakes
    (optional)
3 green onions, cut into
    1-inch pieces

Prepare grill or preheat broiler. Soak 4 (12-inch) skewers in water 20 minutes. Meanwhile, place shrimp in large plastic bag. Combine soy sauce, oil, garlic and red pepper in cup; mix well. Pour over shrimp. Close bag securely; turn to coat. Marinate at room temperature 15 minutes.

Drain shrimp; reserve marinade. Alternately thread shrimp and onions onto skewers. Place skewers on grid or rack of broiler pan. Brush with reserved marinade; discard any remaining marinade. Grill, covered, over medium-hot coals or broil 5 to 6 inches from heat 5 minutes on each side or until shrimp are pink and opaque. Serve on lettuce-lined plate. *Makes 4 servings*

Tip: For a more attractive presentation, leave the tails on the shrimp.

Grilled Tropical Shrimp

¼ cup barbecue sauce
2 tablespoons pineapple juice
    or orange juice
10 ounces medium shrimp in
    shells
2 medium firm nectarines
1 yellow onion, cut into
    8 wedges, or 6 green
    onions, cut into 2-inch
    lengths

1. Stir together barbecue sauce and pineapple juice. Set aside.

2. Peel and devein shrimp. Cut each nectarine into 6 wedges. Thread shrimp, nectarines and onion wedges onto 4 long metal skewers.

3. Spray grill grid with nonstick cooking spray. Prepare grill for direct grilling. Grill skewers over medium coals 4 to 5 minutes or until shrimp are opaque, turning once and brushing frequently with barbecue sauce. *Makes 2 servings*

Tip: Although shrimp are high in cholesterol, they are naturally low in total fat and saturated fat, making them a good choice for a low-fat diet.

Shrimp on the Barbie

1 pound large raw shrimp,
   shelled and deveined
1 *each* red and yellow bell
   pepper, seeded and cut
   into 1-inch chunks
4 slices lime (optional)
½ cup prepared smoky-flavor
   barbecue sauce
2 tablespoons *French's®*
   Worcestershire Sauce
2 tablespoons *Frank's®*
   RedHot® Cayenne Pepper
   Sauce
1 clove garlic, minced

Thread shrimp, peppers and lime, if desired, alternately onto metal skewers. Combine barbecue sauce, Worcestershire, *Frank's RedHot* Sauce and garlic in small bowl; mix well. Brush on skewers.

Place skewers on grid, reserving sauce mixture. Grill over hot coals 15 minutes or until shrimp turn pink, turning and basting often with sauce mixture. (Do not baste during last 5 minutes of cooking.) Serve warm.   *Makes 4 servings*

Prep Time: 10 minutes
Cook Time: 15 minutes

Hot & Spicy Shrimp

1 teaspoon LAWRY'S®
   Seasoned Salt
1 pound raw large shrimp,
   peeled, deveined and
   butterflied
½ cup butter
2 tablespoons vegetable oil
1 bay leaf, crushed
1 teaspoon dried rosemary,
   crushed
½ to 1 teaspoon hot pepper
   sauce
¼ teaspoon LAWRY'S® Garlic
   Powder with Parsley
¼ teaspoon dried basil,
   crushed
⅛ teaspoon dried oregano,
   crushed

Sprinkle Seasoned Salt over shrimp; let stand 10 minutes. In small saucepan, heat butter. Add remaining ingredients except shrimp and cook over low heat 5 minutes. Arrange shrimp in well-oiled grill basket or on broiler pan; brush generously with butter mixture. Grill or broil until shrimp are pink, basting often with butter mixture.   *Makes 2 to 3 servings*

Serving Suggestion: Serve with hot cooked rice mixed with chopped fresh parsley and lemon wedges on the side.

Shrimp on the Barbie

Italian Mixed Seafood

½ pound large raw shrimp, peeled and deveined

½ pound sea scallops

1 small zucchini, cut into ½-inch pieces

1 small red bell pepper, cut into ½-inch pieces

1 small red onion, cut into wedges

12 large mushrooms

1 bottle (8 ounces) Italian salad dressing

2 teaspoons dried Italian seasoning, divided

1½ cups brown rice

2 cans (about 14 ounces each) chicken broth

Place shrimp, scallops, zucchini, pepper, onion, mushrooms, salad dressing and 1 teaspoon Italian seasoning in large resealable plastic food storage bag. Close bag securely, turning to coat. Marinate in refrigerator 30 minutes, turning after 15 minutes.

Meanwhile, place rice, chicken broth and remaining 1 teaspoon Italian seasoning in medium saucepan over high heat. Bring to a boil; cover and reduce heat to low. Simmer 35 minutes or until liquid is absorbed.

Prepare grill for direct cooking.

Drain seafood and vegetables; reserve marinade.

Place seafood and vegetables in lightly oiled grill basket or on vegetable grilling grid. Grill, covered, over medium-high heat 4 to 5 minutes; turn and baste with marinade. Grill 4 to 5 minutes or until shrimp are opaque.

Serve seafood and vegetables over rice.

Makes 4 to 6 servings

Italian Mixed Seafood

Jamaican Shrimp & Pineapple Kabobs

½ cup prepared jerk sauce

¼ cup pineapple preserves

2 tablespoons minced fresh chives

1 pound large shrimp, peeled and deveined

½ medium pineapple, peeled, cored and cut into 1-inch cubes

2 large red, green or yellow bell peppers, cut into 1-inch squares

1. Combine jerk sauce, preserves and chives in small bowl; mix well. Thread shrimp, pineapple and peppers onto 4 skewers; brush with jerk sauce mixture.

2. Grill kabobs over medium-hot coals 6 to 10 minutes or until shrimp turn pink and opaque, turning once. Serve with remaining jerk sauce mixture. *Makes 4 servings*

Cutting Corners: Purchase pineapple already trimmed and cored in the produce section of your local supermarket.

Serving Suggestion: Serve kabobs with hot cooked rice.

Prep and Cook Time: 25 minutes

FOOD FACT

Jamaican jerk seasoning is typically a combination of garlic, chilies, cinnamon, ginger, thyme, allspice and cloves, though exact quantities vary from cook to cook. Jerk is usually used on pork or chicken.

Shellfish on the Barbie

Oriental Shrimp & Steak Kabobs

1 envelope LIPTON® RECIPE SECRETS® Savory Herb with Garlic or Onion Soup Mix

¼ cup soy sauce

¼ cup lemon juice

¼ cup BERTOLLI® Olive Oil

¼ cup honey

½ pound uncooked medium shrimp, peeled and deveined

½ pound boneless sirloin steak, cut into 1-inch cubes

16 cherry tomatoes

2 cups mushroom caps

1 medium green bell pepper, cut into chunks

In 13×9-inch glass baking dish, blend savory herb with garlic soup mix, soy sauce, lemon juice, oil and honey; set aside. On skewers, alternately thread shrimp, steak, tomatoes, mushrooms and green pepper. Add prepared skewers to baking dish; turn to coat. Cover and marinate in refrigerator, turning skewers occasionally, at least 2 hours. Remove prepared skewers, reserving marinade. Grill or broil, turning and basting frequently with reserved marinade, until shrimp turn pink and steak is cooked to desired doneness. Do not brush with marinade during last 5 minutes of cooking. *Makes about 8 servings*

Menu Suggestion: Serve with corn-on-the-cob, a mixed green salad and grilled garlic bread.

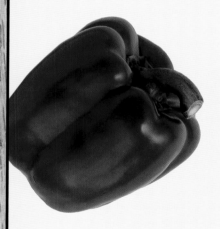

Oriental Shrimp & Steak Kabobs

SCINTILLATING
SIDES

This wonderful collection of side dishes is filled with delicious classic recipes. Choose two or three to round out your next barbecue menu.

Barbecued Corn with Three Savory Butters

12 ears corn, unhusked

Horseradish Butter
  ½ cup (1 stick) butter or margarine, softened
  3 tablespoons *French's®* Bold n' Spicy Brown Mustard
  1 tablespoon horseradish

RedHot® Chili Butter
  ½ cup (1 stick) butter or margarine, softened
  2 tablespoons *Frank's® RedHot®* Cayenne Pepper Sauce
  1 teaspoon chili powder
  1 clove garlic, minced

Herb Butter
  ½ cup (1 stick) butter or margarine, softened
  2 tablespoons snipped fresh chives
  1 tablespoon *French's®* Worcestershire Sauce
  1 tablespoon minced fresh parsley
  ½ teaspoon dried thyme leaves
  ½ teaspoon salt (optional)

Carefully peel back husks; remove corn silk. Bring husks up and tie securely with kitchen string. Soak corn in cold water to cover 30 minutes.

Place ingredients for each flavored butter in separate small bowls; beat until smooth. Serve at room temperature.

Place corn on grid. Grill over medium-high coals 25 minutes or until corn is tender, turning often. Remove string and husks. Serve with your choice of savory butter.   *Makes 12 side-dish servings*

Prep Time: 40 minutes
Cook Time: 25 minutes

Barbecued Corn with
Three Savory Butters

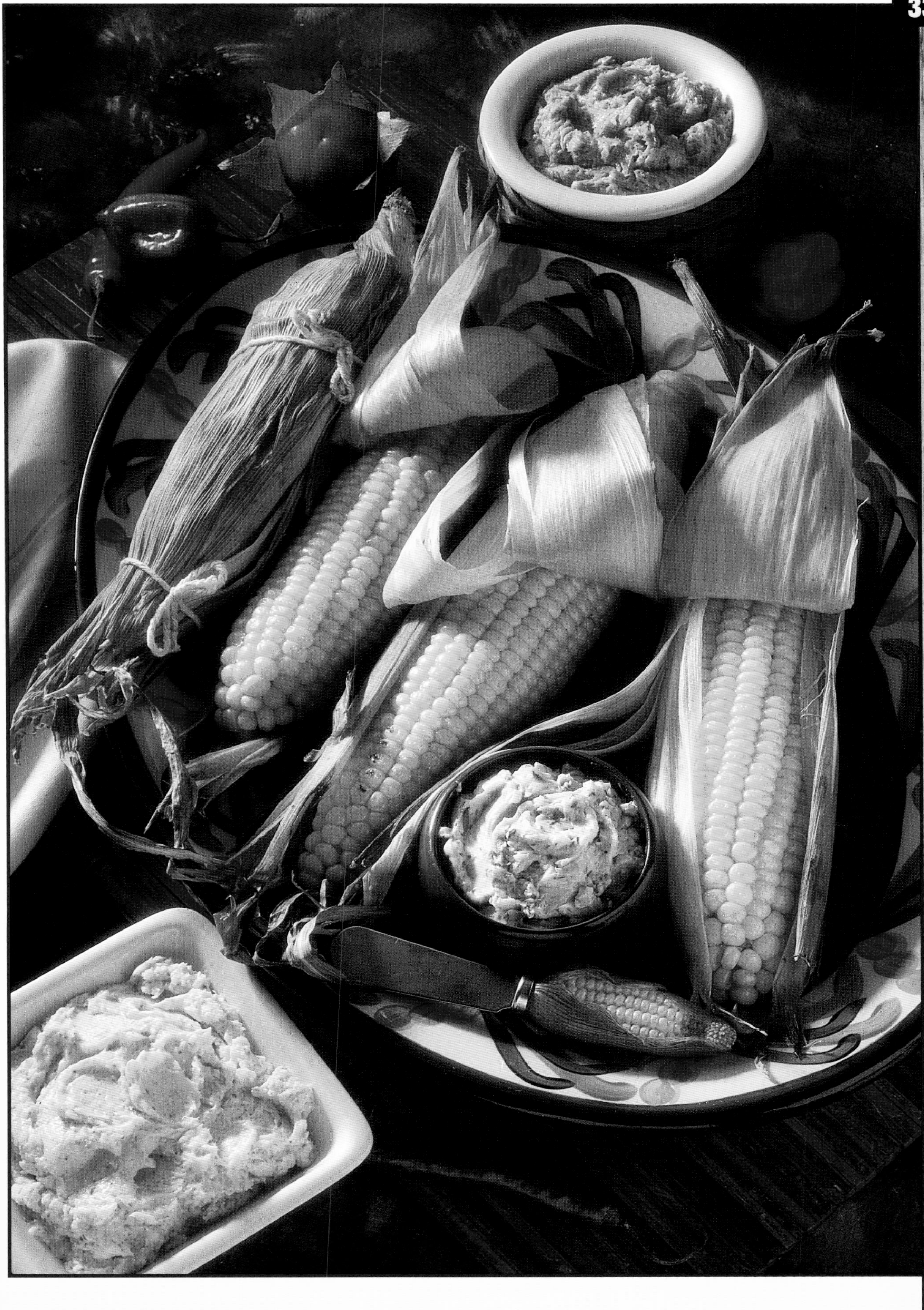

Grilled Cajun Potato Wedges

3 large russet potatoes,
    washed and scrubbed
    (do not peel) (about
    2¼ pounds)
¼ cup olive oil
2 cloves garlic, minced
1 teaspoon salt
1 teaspoon paprika
½ teaspoon dried thyme leaves
½ teaspoon dried oregano
    leaves
¼ teaspoon black pepper
⅛ to ¼ teaspoon ground red
    pepper
2 cups mesquite chips

1. Prepare barbecue grill for direct cooking. Preheat oven to 425°F.

2. Cut potatoes in half lengthwise; then cut each half lengthwise into 4 wedges. Place potatoes in large bowl. Add oil and garlic; toss to coat well.

3. Combine salt, paprika, thyme, oregano, black pepper and ground red pepper in small bowl. Sprinkle over potatoes; toss to coat well. Place potato wedges in single layer in shallow roasting pan. (Reserve remaining oil mixture left in large bowl.) Bake 20 minutes.

4. Meanwhile, cover mesquite chips with cold water; soak 20 minutes. Drain mesquite chips; sprinkle over coals. Place potato wedges on their sides on grid. Grill potato wedges, on covered grill, over medium coals 15 to 20 minutes or until potatoes are browned and fork-tender, brushing with reserved oil mixture halfway through grilling time and turning once with tongs.

Makes 4 to 6 servings

Grilled Pineapple

1 pineapple
  Dark rum
  Brown sugar
  Ice cream, frozen yogurt or
    sorbet
  Toasted shredded coconut

Peel, core and cut pineapple into ¾-inch-thick rings or thin wedges. Brush generously with dark rum; sprinkle with brown sugar. Lightly oil grid to prevent sticking. Grill 8 to 10 minutes over medium-hot KINGSFORD® Briquets until warm and golden brown, turning once. Top each ring with 1 scoop of ice cream, frozen yogurt or sorbet and a sprinkling of toasted coconut.

Coal-Roasted Potato Salad

Lemon Dijon Dressing
(recipe follows)
1½ pounds small red or white
potatoes, cut into 1-inch
chunks
Olive oil
1½ teaspoons dried thyme
leaves
Salt and black pepper
2 medium yellow onions, cut
into ½-inch-thick slices

Prepare Lemon Dijon Dressing. Toss potatoes with 1 tablespoon oil, thyme, salt and pepper. Insert wooden picks into onion slices from edges to prevent separating into rings. (Soak wooden picks in hot water 15 minutes to prevent burning.) Brush lightly with oil. Grill potatoes and onions on covered grill over medium KINGSFORD® Briquets about 30 minutes until golden brown and tender, turning occasionally. Remove picks from onions; separate into rings. Place potatoes and onions in large bowl; toss with dressing. Serve warm. *Makes 4 servings*

Lemon Dijon Dressing: Whisk together 3 tablespoons olive oil, 1 tablespoon white wine vinegar, 1 tablespoon *each* chopped green onion and parsley, 1½ teaspoons lemon juice and ½ teaspoon Dijon mustard. Season to taste with salt and pepper.

Avocado Salsa

1 large ripe avocado, coarsely
chopped
1 large tomato, seeded and
diced
3 tablespoons chopped fresh
cilantro
1 tablespoon vegetable oil
1 tablespoon fresh lime juice
2 teaspoons minced fresh or
drained, bottled jalapeño
pepper*
1 clove garlic, minced
½ teaspoon salt

*Jalapeño peppers can sting and irritate the skin; wear rubber gloves when handling peppers and do not touch eyes. Wash hands after handling.

1. Place avocado in medium bowl.

2. Gently stir in tomato, cilantro, oil, lime juice, jalapeño, garlic and salt until well combined. Let stand at room temperature. Cover; refrigerate if preparing in advance. Bring to room temperature before serving. *Makes about 1½ cups*

Mesquite Summer Vegetable Medley

2 red potatoes, cut into thin
    wedges
2 medium carrots, diagonally
    sliced
3 zucchini, diagonally sliced
1 medium onion, cut into
    chunks
1 small head cauliflower,
    broken into flowerettes
½ cup LAWRY'S® Mesquite
    Marinade with Lime Juice
¾ teaspoon LAWRY'S® Lemon
    Pepper
½ teaspoon LAWRY'S® Garlic
    Powder with Parsley
2 bacon slices, cooked and
    crumbled

In large bowl, combine all ingredients except bacon; mix well. Place vegetable mixture evenly on 4 (20×12-inch) pieces heavy-duty aluminum foil. Fold foil to enclose; seal tightly. Grill packets seam side up 20 to 30 minutes or until vegetables are tender. To serve, carefully remove vegetables—they will be very hot. Sprinkle with bacon.

Makes 4 servings

Serving Suggestion: Serve with grilled meat, chicken or fish.

Honey Strawberry Salsa

1½ cups diced red bell pepper
1 cup sliced fresh strawberries
1 cup diced green bell pepper
1 cup diced fresh tomato
¼ cup chopped Anaheim
    pepper
2 tablespoons finely chopped
    fresh cilantro
⅓ cup honey
¼ cup lemon juice
1 tablespoon tequila
    (optional)
½ teaspoon crushed dried red
    chili pepper
½ teaspoon salt
¼ teaspoon pepper

Combine ingredients in glass container; mix well. Cover tightly and refrigerate overnight to allow flavors to blend. Serve on grilled fish or chicken.

Makes 3 to 4 cups

Favorite recipe from **National Honey Board**

Mesquite Summer Vegetable Medley

Parmesan Polenta

4 cups chicken broth
1¼ cups yellow cornmeal
1 small onion, minced
4 cloves garlic, minced
1 tablespoon minced fresh
 rosemary *or* 1 teaspoon
 dried rosemary
½ teaspoon salt
6 tablespoons grated
 Parmesan cheese
1 tablespoon olive oil, divided

1. Spray 11×7-inch baking pan with nonstick cooking spray; set aside. Spray one side of 7-inch-long sheet of waxed paper with cooking spray; set aside. Combine chicken broth, onion, garlic, rosemary and salt in medium saucepan. Bring to a boil over high heat; add cornmeal gradually, stirring constantly. Reduce heat to medium and simmer 30 minutes or until mixture has consistency of thick mashed potatoes. Remove from heat and stir in cheese.

2. Spread polenta evenly in prepared pan; place waxed paper, sprayed-side down, on polenta and smooth. (If surface is bumpy, it is more likely to stick to grill.) Cool on wire rack 15 minutes or until firm. Remove waxed paper; cut into 6 squares. Remove squares from pan.

3. To prevent sticking, spray grid with cooking spray. Prepare coals for grilling. Brush tops of squares with half the oil. Grill oil-side down on covered grill over medium to low coals for 6 to 8 minutes or until golden. Brush with remaining oil and gently turn over. Grill 6 to 8 minutes more or until golden. Serve warm. *Makes 6 servings*

Onion-Roasted Potatoes

1 envelope LIPTON® RECIPE
 SECRETS® Onion Soup
 Mix*
4 medium all-purpose
 potatoes, cut into large
 chunks (about 2 pounds)
⅓ cup BERTOLLI® Olive Oil

Also terrific with LIPTON® RECIPE SECRETS® Onion-Mushroom, Golden Onion or Savory Herb with Garlic Soup Mix.

1. Preheat oven to 450°F. In large plastic bag or bowl, add all ingredients. Close bag and shake, or toss in bowl, until potatoes are evenly coated.

2. In 13×9-inch baking or roasting pan, arrange potatoes; discard bag.

3. Bake uncovered, stirring occasionally, 40 minutes or until potatoes are tender and golden brown. *Makes 4 servings*

Prep Time: 10 minutes
Cook Time: 40 minutes

Parmesan Polenta

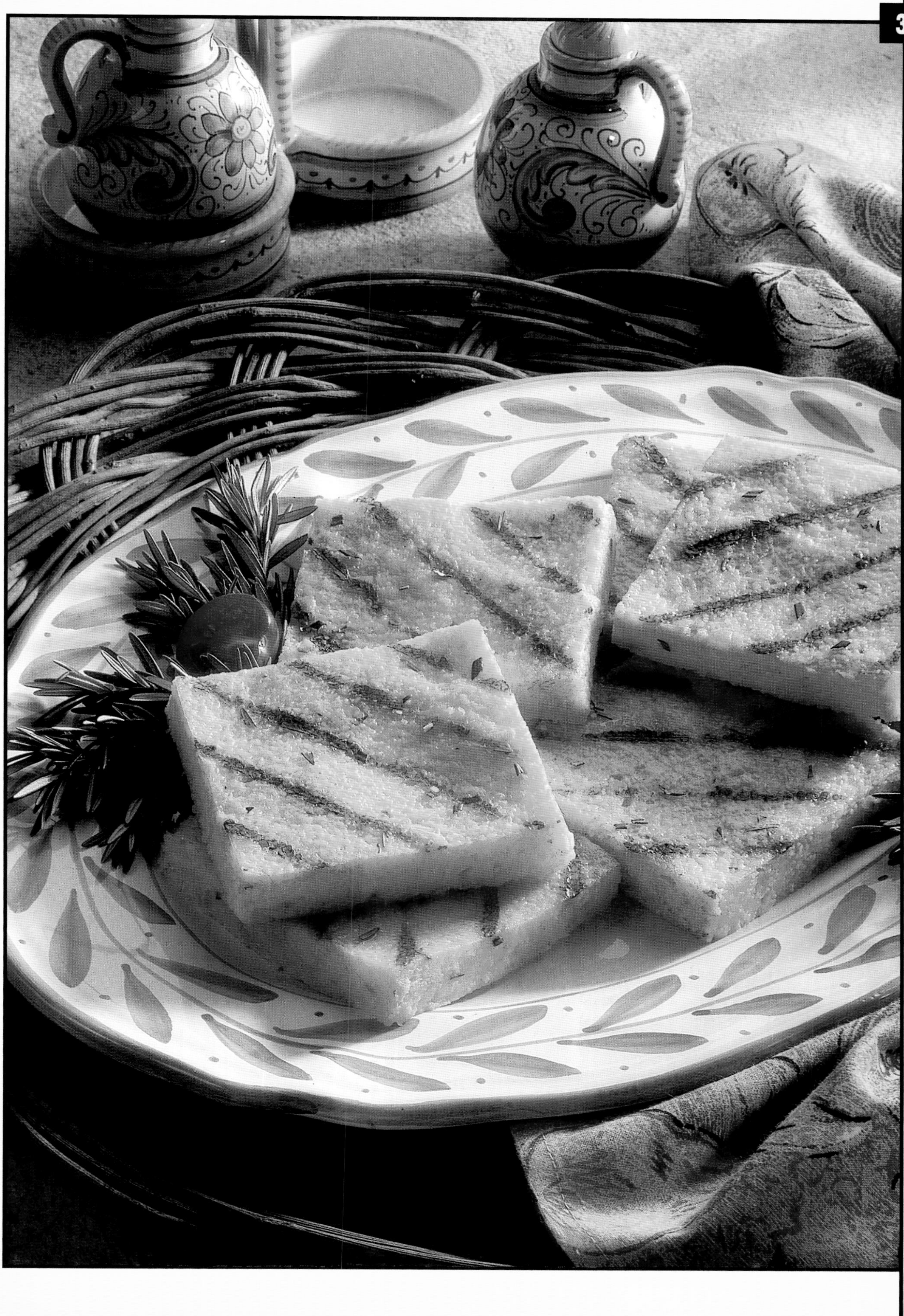

Balsamic-Herb Ratatouille

4 tablespoons balsamic
   vinegar, divided
1 tablespoon olive oil
2 yellow or red Grilled Bell
   Peppers (recipe
   page 342)
1 medium eggplant (about
   1 pound)
1 small onion, peeled and
   quartered
   Balsamic-Herb Vinaigrette
   (recipe page 342)
½ pint cherry tomatoes,
   grilled*
12 mushrooms
2 small yellow zucchini, halved
   lengthwise
⅓ cup slivered fresh basil
   leaves

*To grill cherry tomatoes, thread tomatoes onto
prepared skewers. Grill on covered grill over
medium coals 5 minutes or until blistered and
browned, basting and turning once.

1. Spray medium nonmetallic grillproof casserole with nonstick cooking spray; set aside. To make basting mixture, combine 2 tablespoons vinegar with oil in small bowl; set aside.

2. Prepare Grilled Bell Peppers; set aside. Remove strips of peel from eggplant lengthwise at 1-inch intervals and remove ends. Slice eggplant into ½-inch-thick rounds; thread with onion quarters onto metal skewers. Baste eggplant and onion. Grill on covered grill over medium coals 20 to 30 minutes or until grill marked and tender, basting and turning every 10 minutes.

3. Meanwhile, heat oven to 325°F. Prepare Balsamic-Herb Vinaigrette. Remove eggplant and onion from grill. Cut eggplant into ½-inch strips; place eggplant and onion in prepared casserole with Balsamic-Herb Vinaigrette. Cover loosely and place in oven to hold. Or, place casserole on upper rack of grill to hold.

4. Grill cherry tomatoes. To grill mushrooms, thread whole mushrooms onto 2 or 3 metal skewers; baste mushrooms and cut sides of zucchini. Grill mushrooms and zucchini on covered grill over medium coals 10 to 15 minutes or until browned and tender, basting and turning once. Remove; cut zucchini into ½-inch slices and add to eggplant mixture with mushrooms.

5. Dice bell peppers; add to eggplant mixture with tomatoes. Stir in remaining 2 tablespoons vinegar and basil. *Makes 6 servings*

Continued on page 342

Grilled Bell Pepper

1 bell pepper (any color), stemmed, seeded and halved

Grill bell pepper halves skin-side down on covered grill over medium to hot coals 15 to 25 minutes or until skin is charred, without turning. Remove from grill and place in plastic bag until cool enough to handle, about 10 minutes. Remove skin with paring knife and discard.

Balsamic-Herb Vinaigrette

4 cloves garlic, minced
3 tablespoons balsamic vinegar
1 teaspoon dried oregano leaves *or* 1 tablespoon minced fresh oregano
1 teaspoon dried thyme leaves *or* 1 tablespoon minced fresh thyme
1 teaspoon Dijon mustard
1 teaspoon black pepper

Whisk together all ingredients in small bowl; set aside.

Grilled Asparagus

1 pound fresh asparagus
   CRISCO® No-Stick Cooking Spray
½ teaspoon salt
¼ teaspoon freshly ground black pepper

1. Prepare charcoal or gas grill. Trim woody stems off asparagus by breaking stalks. Spray asparagus with Crisco No-Stick Cooking Spray.

2. Grill asparagus for 3 minutes. Turn spears with tongs. Grill 3 to 4 minutes. Sprinkle with salt and pepper. Serve immediately.

Makes 4 servings

Goat Cheese & Corn Chiles Rellenos

4 large plum tomatoes,
    seeded and diced
1 small red onion, diced and
    divided
3 tablespoons extra-virgin
    olive oil, divided
2 cloves garlic, minced and
    divided
1 teaspoon balsamic vinegar
¼ teaspoon salt
¼ teaspoon black pepper
6 poblano *or* 8 Anaheim
    peppers
2 ears corn, husked*
¾ cup crumbled goat or feta
    cheese
½ cup (2 ounces) shredded
    hot pepper Jack,
    Monterey Jack or sharp
    Cheddar cheese
½ cup minced fresh cilantro
    Fresh cilantro sprigs

*Substitute 1 can (17 ounces) corn, drained, or
1½ cups frozen corn, thawed, for fresh corn, if
desired. Add to filling as directed above.*

Combine tomatoes, ½ onion, 2 tablespoons oil,
1 clove garlic, vinegar, salt and black pepper in
medium bowl; let salsa stand 15 minutes. Remove
stems from poblano peppers by cutting each
pepper about ½ inch from stem; remove seeds.
Grill peppers over medium-hot KINGSFORD®
Briquets until skins are charred on all sides. Place
peppers in large resealable plastic food storage
bag; seal. Let stand 5 minutes; remove skin. Grill
corn over medium-hot briquets 6 to 10 minutes or
until tender, turning every minute; cut kernels
from cob. Combine corn, cheeses, minced cilantro,
remaining ½ onion and 1 clove garlic in medium
bowl; mix well. Carefully fill each pepper with
cheese mixture, making cut in side of pepper, if
necessary. Secure opening with wooden pick.
(Soak wooden picks in hot water 15 minutes to
prevent burning.) Brush peppers with remaining
1 tablespoon oil; grill over medium briquets
1 minute per side until cheese melts. Serve with
salsa. Garnish with cilantro sprigs.

Makes 6 servings

Herbed Corn on the Cob

1 tablespoon butter or
    margarine
1 teaspoon mixed dried herb
    leaves, such as basil,
    oregano, sage and
    rosemary
⅛ teaspoon salt
    Black pepper
4 ears corn, husks removed

Microwave Directions

1. Combine butter, herbs, salt and pepper in
small microwavable bowl. Microwave at MEDIUM
(50%) 30 to 45 seconds or until butter is melted.

2. With pastry brush, coat corn with butter
mixture. Place corn on microwavable plate;
microwave at HIGH (100%) 5 to 6 minutes. Turn
corn over and microwave at HIGH (100%) 5 to
6 minutes until tender.

Makes 4 servings

Grilled Vegetables with Balsamic Vinaigrette

1 medium eggplant (about
    1¼ pounds)
2 medium zucchini
2 to 3 medium yellow squash
2 medium red bell peppers
¾ cup olive oil
¼ cup balsamic vinegar
1 teaspoon salt
¼ teaspoon black pepper
1 clove garlic, minced
2 to 3 tablespoons finely
    chopped mixed fresh
    herbs

Trim, then slice eggplant, zucchini and yellow squash lengthwise into ¼- to ½-inch-thick slices. Core, seed and cut red peppers into 1 inch-wide strips. Place vegetables in deep serving platter or wide shallow casserole. Combine oil, vinegar, salt, pepper, garlic and herbs in small bowl. Pour vinaigrette over vegetables; turn to coat. Let stand 30 minutes or longer. Lift vegetables from vinaigrette, leaving vinaigrette that does not cling to the vegetables in the dish.

Oil hot grid to help prevent sticking. Grill vegetables, on covered grill, over medium KINGSFORD® Briquets, 8 to 16 minutes until fork-tender, turning once or twice. (Time will depend on the vegetable; eggplant takes the longest.) As vegetables are done, return them to the platter, then turn to coat with vinaigrette. (Or, cut eggplant, zucchini and yellow squash into cubes, then toss with red peppers and vinaigrette.) Serve warm or at room temperature.

Makes 6 servings

Mango Pineapple Chutney

2 cups diced fresh pineapple
2 kiwi, peeled and diced
1 navel orange, peeled and
    diced
2 green onions, thinly sliced
½ cup mango chutney, large
    pieces chopped
2 tablespoons *Frank's®*
    RedHot® Cayenne Pepper
    Sauce
2 tablespoons chopped fresh
    mint or cilantro
1 tablespoon red wine vinegar
½ teaspoon salt

Combine all ingredients in large bowl; toss to coat evenly. Cover; refrigerate 30 minutes.

Makes 3 cups chutney

Prep Time: 20 minutes
Chill Time: 30 minutes

**Grilled Vegetables
with Balsamic Vinaigrette**

Glazed Fruit Kabobs

2 fresh California nectarines,
    halved, pitted and cut
    into 6 wedges
3 fresh California plums,
    halved, pitted and
    quartered
½ fresh pineapple, peeled and
    cut into 2-inch cubes
¼ cup packed brown sugar
2 tablespoons water
1½ teaspoons cornstarch
¾ teaspoon rum extract

Alternately thread fruit onto skewers. Combine sugar, water, cornstarch and rum extract in small saucepan. Bring to a boil, stirring constantly, until thickened and clear. Place fruit kabobs in shallow pan. Brush with glaze mixture. (This may be done ahead.) Grill kabobs about 4 to 5 inches from heat 6 to 8 minutes or until hot, turning once, brushing occasionally with glaze. *Makes 4 servings*

Favorite recipe from **California Tree Fruit Agreement**

Honey-Dijon Fresh Fruit Chutney

1 cup coarsely chopped fruit,
    such as mango, peaches,
    pineapple and kiwifruit
½ cup unsweetened
    applesauce
½ cup chopped celery
5 tablespoons honey
¼ cup finely chopped red
    onion
3 tablespoons Dijon mustard
2 tablespoons chopped fresh
    mint or cilantro
1 tablespoon lime or lemon
    juice
2 teaspoons grated fresh
    gingerroot
    Crushed red pepper flakes
    to taste
    Salt to taste

Combine all ingredients in medium bowl; stir until well blended. Chill until ready to serve. Serve with sliced grilled turkey or pork tenderloin. Also a great relish on sandwiches.

Makes about 2 cups

Favorite recipe from **National Honey Board**

Glazed Fruit Kabobs

Grilled Vegetables & Brown Rice

1 medium zucchini
1 medium red or yellow bell
    pepper, quartered
    lengthwise
1 small onion, cut crosswise
    into 1-inch-thick slices
¾ cup Italian dressing
4 cups hot cooked UNCLE
    BEN'S® Original Brown
    Rice

1. Cut zucchini lengthwise into thirds. Place all vegetables in large resealable plastic food storage bag; add dressing. Seal bag; refrigerate several hours or overnight.

2. Remove vegetables from marinade, reserving marinade. Place bell peppers and onion on grill over medium coals; brush with marinade. Grill 5 minutes. Turn vegetables over; add zucchini. Brush with marinade. Continue grilling until vegetables are crisp-tender, about 5 minutes, turning zucchini over after 3 minutes.

3. Remove vegetables from grill; coarsely chop. Add to hot rice; mix lightly. Season with salt and black pepper, if desired.   *Makes 6 to 8 servings*

Cook's Tip: Grilling adds a unique smoky flavor to vegetables and brings out their natural sweetness. The easiest way to grill vegetables is to cut them into large pieces and toss them in salad dressing or seasoned oil before grilling. Seasoned raw vegetables may also be wrapped tightly in foil packets and grilled until tender.

Sassy Corn on the Cob

1 cup (2 sticks) unsalted
    butter or margarine,
    softened
2 teaspoons TABASCO®
    brand Pepper Sauce
8 ears unhusked fresh corn

Preheat grill. Combine butter and TABASCO® Sauce in small bowl; mix well. Peel one side of corn husk away from cob without removing completely, and loosen remaining husk. Do not remove silk. Brush butter mixture over kernels and smooth back husk to original shape.

Place corn on oiled grid over medium heat and grill 15 to 20 minutes, turning every 5 minutes. (Outside husk will be charred.)

Makes 8 servings

Grilled Vegetables & Brown Rice

Mesquite Baked Beans

4 strips 50% less salt bacon
1 large red onion, minced
1 (28-ounce) can low sodium
  baked beans in tomato
  sauce
2 tablespoons MRS. DASH®
  Mesquite Grilling Blend
1 teaspoon dry mustard
½ cup maple syrup

Preheat oven to 350°F. Fry bacon in large skillet over medium-high heat. Cook until lightly browned and crisp. Remove from skillet and set aside. Add onion to skillet and cook until soft. Dice bacon. Place beans, bacon and onion in 2-quart casserole. Combine Mrs. Dash® Mesquite Grilling Blend, dry mustard and maple syrup in bowl and mix well; add to beans and stir. Cover and bake for 25 minutes or until beans are bubbling and heated through. *Makes 6 servings*

Note: This casserole can be made ahead and heated when ready to serve.

Serving Suggestion: This is a natural side dish for any barbecue. Serve it with ribs or chicken.

Preparation Time: 10 minutes
Cooking Time: 25 minutes

Portobello Mushrooms Sesame

4 large portobello
  mushrooms
2 tablespoons sweet rice wine
2 tablespoons reduced-
  sodium soy sauce
2 cloves garlic, minced
1 teaspoon dark sesame oil

1. Remove and discard stems from mushrooms; set caps aside. Combine remaining ingredients in small bowl.

2. Brush both sides of mushrooms with soy sauce mixture. Grill mushrooms top side up on covered grill over medium coals 3 to 4 minutes. Brush tops with soy sauce mixture and turn over; grill 2 minutes more or until mushrooms are lightly browned. Turn again and grill, basting frequently, 4 to 5 minutes or until tender when pressed with back of spatula. Remove mushrooms and cut diagonally into ½-inch-thick slices.

Makes 4 servings

Polenta Triangles

½ cup yellow corn grits
1½ cups chicken broth, divided
2 cloves garlic, minced
½ cup (2 ounces) crumbled
    feta cheese
1 red bell pepper, roasted,*
    peeled and finely chopped

*Place pepper on foil-lined broiler pan; broil 15 minutes or until blackened on all sides, turning every 5 minutes. Place pepper in paper bag; close bag and let stand 15 minutes before peeling.

1. Combine grits and ½ cup chicken broth; mix well and set aside. Pour remaining 1 cup broth into large heavy saucepan; bring to a boil. Add garlic and moistened grits; mix well and return to a boil. Reduce heat to low; cover and cook 20 minutes. Remove from heat; add feta cheese. Stir until cheese is completely melted. Add pepper; mix well.

2. Spray 8-inch square pan with nonstick cooking spray. Spoon grits mixture into prepared pan. Press grits evenly into pan with wet fingertips. Refrigerate until cold.

3. Spray grid with nonstick cooking spray. Prepare grill for direct cooking. Turn polenta out onto cutting board and cut into 2-inch squares. Cut each square diagonally into 2 triangles.

4. Place polenta triangles on grid. Grill over medium-high heat 1 minute or until bottoms are lightly browned. Turn triangles over and grill until browned and crisp. Serve warm or at room temperature. *Makes 8 servings*

Grilled Banana Squash with Rum & Brown Sugar

2 pounds banana squash or
    butternut squash
2 tablespoons dark rum or
    apple juice
2 tablespoons melted butter
2 tablespoons brown sugar

Cut squash into 4 pieces; discard seeds. Place squash in microwavable baking dish. Cover with vented plastic wrap. Microwave at HIGH (100%) 5 to 7 minutes, turning once. Discard plastic wrap; pierce flesh of squash with fork at 1-inch intervals. Place squash in foil pan. Combine rum and butter; brush over squash. Sprinkle with sugar. Grill squash on covered grill over medium KINGSFORD® Briquets 20 to 30 minutes until squash is tender. *Makes 4 servings*

Buffalo Chili Onions

½ cup *Frank's® RedHot®*
  Cayenne Pepper Sauce
½ cup (1 stick) butter or
  margarine, melted or
  olive oil
¼ cup chili sauce
1 tablespoon chili powder
4 large sweet onions, cut into
  ½-inch-thick slices

Whisk together *Frank's RedHot* Sauce, butter, chili sauce and chili powder in medium bowl until blended; brush on onion slices.

Place onions on grid. Grill over medium-high coals 10 minutes or until tender, turning and basting often with the chili mixture. Serve warm.

Makes 6 side-dish servings

Tip: Onions may be prepared ahead and grilled just before serving.

Prep Time: 10 minutes
Cook Time: 10 minutes

Jamaican Grilled Sweet Potatoes

2 large (about 1½ pounds)
  sweet potatoes or yams
3 tablespoons packed brown
  sugar
2 tablespoons softened
  margarine, divided
1 teaspoon ground ginger
2 teaspoons dark rum
1 tablespoon chopped fresh
  cilantro

1. Pierce potatoes in several places with fork. Place on paper towel in microwave. Microwave at HIGH (100%) 5 to 6 minutes or until crisp-tender, rotating ¼ turn halfway through cooking. Let stand 10 minutes. Diagonally slice about ½ inch off ends of potatoes. Continue cutting potatoes diagonally into ¾-inch-thick slices.

2. Combine brown sugar, 1 tablespoon margarine and ginger in small bowl; mix well. Stir in rum and cilantro; set aside.

3. Melt remaining 1 tablespoon margarine. With half of melted margarine, lightly brush one side of each potato slice. Grill slices margarine-side down on covered grill over medium coals 4 to 6 minutes or until grillmarked. Brush tops with remaining melted margarine; turn over and grill 3 to 5 minutes or until grillmarked. To serve, spoon rum mixture equally over potato slices.

Makes 6 servings

Prep and Cook Time: 30 minutes

Buffalo Chili Onions

THIRST
QUENCHERS

Refreshing and delicious drinks will help you cool down as you toil away over your hot grill. So, whip up a pitcher and pour yourself a tall one.

Caribbean Dream

¾ cup vanilla ice cream
¾ cup pineapple sherbet
¾ cup tropical fruit salad, drained
¼ cup frozen banana-orange juice concentrate
¼ teaspoon rum-flavored extract

Place ice cream, sherbet, fruit salad, concentrate and extract in blender. Blend on medium speed 1 to 2 minutes or until smooth and well blended. Pour into 2 serving glasses. Serve immediately.

Makes 2 servings

Serve It With Style!: Try adding a tablespoon of rum instead of rum-flavored extract for a more mature flavor.

Lighten Up: To reduce the fat, replace vanilla ice cream with reduced-fat or fat-free ice cream or frozen yogurt.

Prep time: 10 minutes

Honey Tea Cooler

1 pint fresh strawberries, stemmed and cleaned
¼ cup honey
1 can (6 ounces) frozen orange juice concentrate
2 cups brewed green tea, cooled

In a blender or food processor container, combine strawberries and honey; process until smooth. Add orange juice concentrate; process until well blended. Stir into cooled tea. Serve over ice.

Makes 4 servings

*Favorite recipe from **National Honey Board***

Caribbean Dream

354

Sunrise Punch

1 tub CRYSTAL LIGHT
    TROPICAL PASSIONS®
    Strawberry Kiwi Flavor
    Low Calorie Soft Drink
    Mix
2 cups cold water
2 cups chilled unsweetened
    pineapple juice
1 bottle (1 liter) chilled seltzer
   Ice cubes

PLACE drink mix in large plastic or glass pitcher. Add water and juice; stir to dissolve. Refrigerate.

JUST before serving, pour into large punch bowl. Stir in seltzer. Serve over ice.

Makes 2 quarts or 8 (1-cup) servings

Prep Time: 5 minutes plus refrigerating

Icy Fruit Tea

CONCENTRATE
   4 tea bags
   1 cup boiling water
   ½ cup honey
   ¼ cup crushed packed fresh
     mint leaves
   1 cup orange juice
   ¾ cup pineapple juice
   ¼ cup fresh lime juice

MIXER
   Ice cubes
  1½ quarts carbonated water

For concentrate, place tea bags in medium bowl. Add boiling water and steep 10 minutes. Remove tea bags. Add honey and mint; mix well. Mix fruit juices in 1-quart container. Add tea mixture and refrigerate until ready to use.

For tea, fill 12-ounce glass with ice cubes. Add ½ cup tea concentrate and fill glass with carbonated water.   *Makes 6 servings*

Tip: Garnish with a pineapple spear and mint sprig.

*Favorite recipe from **National Honey Board***

Dole® Juice Spritzer

½ cup DOLE® Country
   Raspberry Juice or
   Pineapple Juice
½ cup mineral or sparkling
   water

• Pour juice and mineral water over ice cubes in large glass. Garnish with lime wedge and citrus curl, if desired.   *Makes 1 serving*

Prep Time: 5 minutes

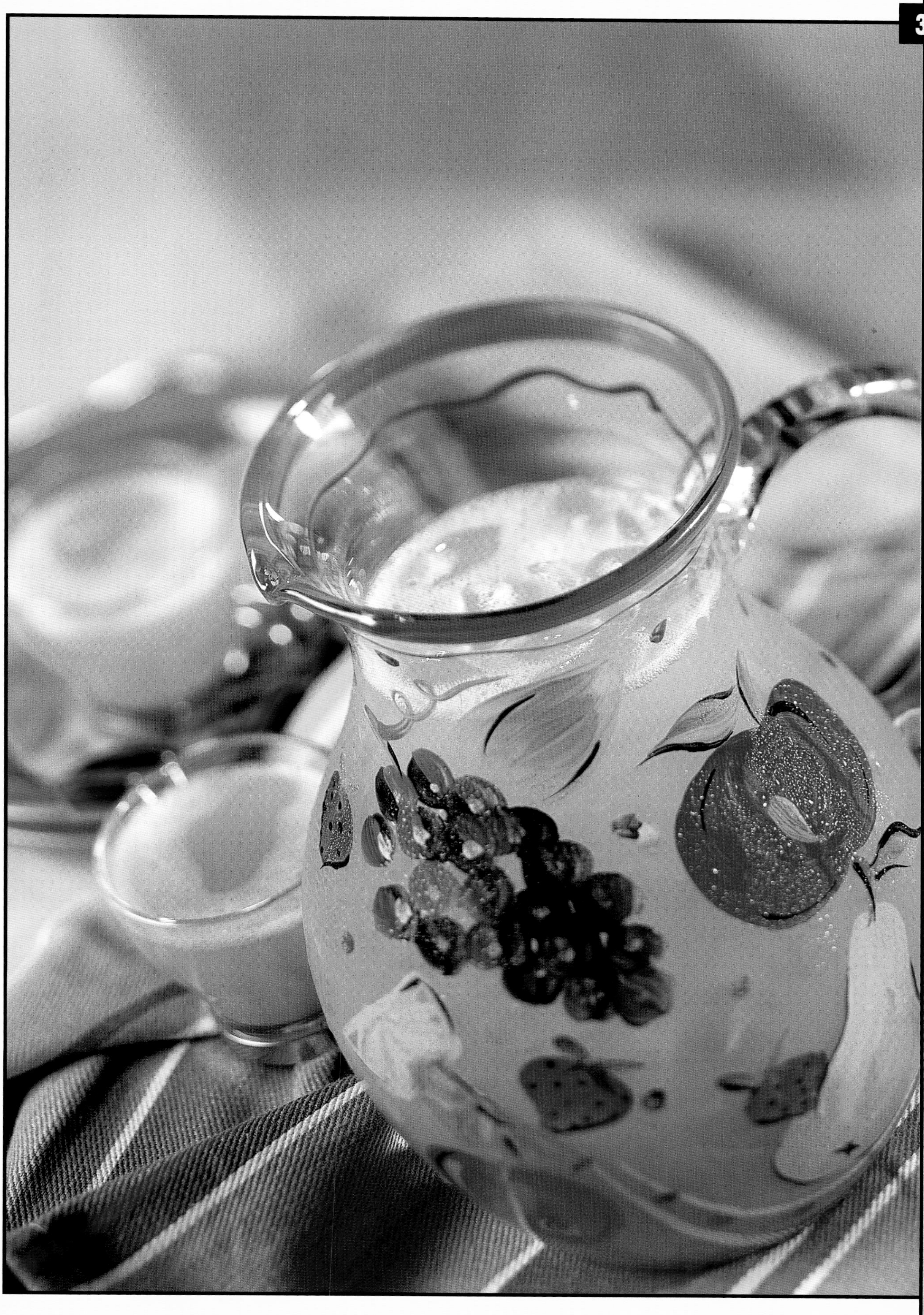

Country Time® Lemon Creamy Frosty

1 cup prepared COUNTRY
   TIME® Lemonade Flavor
   Sugar Free Low Calorie
   Drink Mix
1 cup no-sugar-added vanilla
   ice cream
½ cup ice cubes or crushed ice

PLACE all ingredients in blender container; cover. Blend on high speed about 30 seconds or until thickened and smooth. Serve immediately.

Makes 2 (1-cup) servings

Prep: 5 minutes

Country Time® Lemon Berry Cooler

1 cup prepared COUNTRY
   TIME® Lemonade Flavor
   Sugar Free Low Calorie
   Drink Mix
½ cup cold 2% reduced-fat
   milk
½ cup strawberry or raspberry
   sorbet or sherbet
½ cup ice cubes or crushed ice

PLACE all ingredients in blender container; cover. Blend on high speed until smooth. Serve immediately. *Makes 2 (1-cup) servings*

Prep: 5 minutes

Honey Coffee Cooler

2 tablespoons instant coffee
   granules
¼ cup boiling water
¼ cup honey
1 cinnamon stick
¼ cup cold water
   Ice cubes
4 cups 2% low-fat milk

Dissolve coffee granules in boiling water in medium bowl; add honey and mix well. Add cinnamon stick and stir in cold water; refrigerate. Fill 4 tall glasses with ice cubes. Add 3 tablespoons coffee concentrate and fill each glass with 1 cup milk. *Makes 4 servings*

*Favorite recipe from **National Honey Board***

Top to Bottom:
COUNTRY TIME® Lemon Creamy Frosty,
COUNTRY TIME® Lemon Berry Cooler

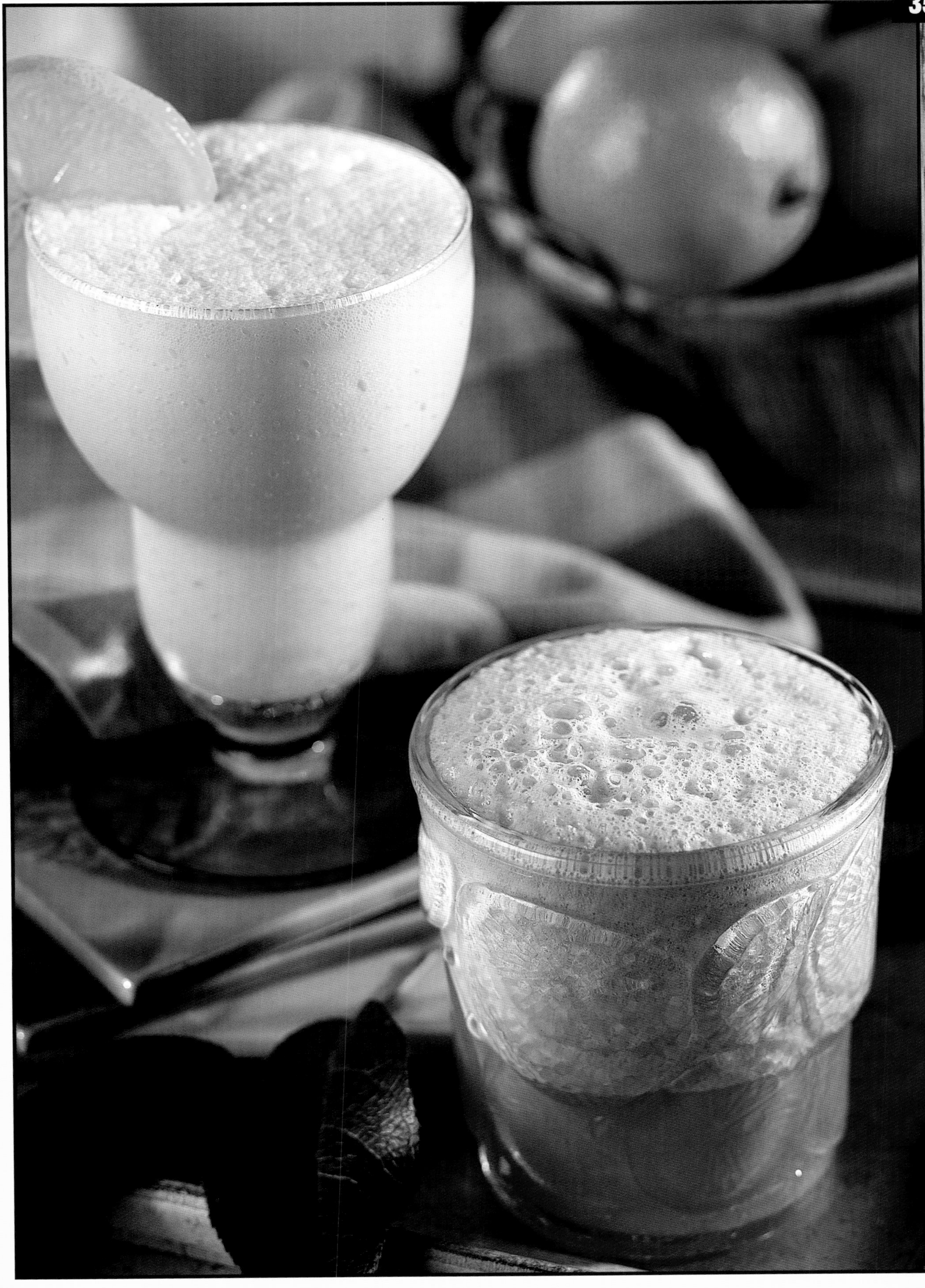

Cardamom-Spiked Fresh Lemonade Spritzer

40 whole white cardamom
    pods, cracked
1¼ cups sugar
3 cups water
2 cups fresh lemon juice
1 bottle (750 ml) Asti
    Spumante or club soda
    Additional sugar (optional)
    Ice
    Mint leaves for garnish

Combine cardamom pods with 1¼ cups sugar and water in medium saucepan. Cook and stir over high heat until mixture comes to a boil and sugar dissolves. Reduce heat to low; cover and simmer 30 minutes. Remove from heat; cool completely. Refrigerate 2 hours or up to 3 days.

Pour mixture through strainer into 3-quart pitcher; discard pods. Stir in lemon juice and Asti Spumante. Stir in additional sugar to taste. Serve over ice. Garnish, if desired. *Makes 6 servings*

Raspberry Wine Punch

1 package (10 ounces) frozen
    red raspberries in syrup,
    thawed
1 bottle (750 ml) white
    Zinfandel or blush wine
¼ cup raspberry-flavored
    liqueur
    Empty half-gallon milk or
    juice carton
3 to 4 cups distilled water,
    divided
    Sprigs of pine and tinsel
    Fresh cranberries

Process raspberries with syrup in food processor or blender until smooth; press through strainer, discarding seeds. Combine wine, raspberry purée and liqueur in pitcher; refrigerate until serving time. Rinse out wine bottle and remove label.

Fully open top of carton. Place wine bottle in center of carton. Tape bottle securely to carton so bottle will not move when adding water. Pour 2 cups distilled water into carton. Carefully push pine sprigs, cranberries and tinsel into water between bottle and carton to form decorative design. Add remaining water to almost fill carton. Freeze until firm, 8 hours or overnight.

Just before serving, peel carton from ice block. Using funnel, pour punch back into wine bottle. Wrap bottom of ice block with white cotton napkin or towel to hold while serving.

Makes 8 servings

Note: Punch may also be served in punch bowl if desired.

Mojito

6 packets NatraTaste® Brand
   Sugar Substitute
2 cups very hot water
4 to 6 mint leaves
¼ cup fresh lime juice
2 ounces light or dark rum
½ cup seltzer or club soda
   Ice cubes

1. Combine the NatraTaste® and water in a jar or container with a lid, shake.

2. Place the mint leaves in the bottom of two glasses and press down with a spoon to release the flavor. Divide lime juice and rum between glasses. Add ¼ cup *each* sweetened water and seltzer to each glass. Add ice cubes and stir.

Makes 2 servings

Note: Refrigerate remaining sweetened water for future use.

Orange Iced Tea

2 SUNKIST® oranges
4 cups boiling water
5 tea bags
   Ice cubes
   Honey or brown sugar to
      taste

With vegetable peeler, peel each orange in continuous spiral, removing only outer colored layer of peel (eat peeled fruit or save for other uses). In large pitcher, pour boiling water over tea bags and orange peel. Cover and steep 5 minutes. Remove tea bags; chill tea mixture with peel in covered container. To serve, remove peel and pour over ice cubes in tall glasses. Sweeten to taste with honey. Garnish with orange quarter-cartwheel slices and fresh mint leaves, if desired.

Makes 4 (8-ounce) servings

Crabby Bob's Secret Drink

½ cup MAUNA LA'I® Paradise
   Passion® Juice Drink
½ cup MAUNA LA'I® ¡Mango
   Mango!® Juice Drink
⅛ cup lemon-lime flavored
   rum
   Splash peach brandy
   Lime wedge, as needed
   Ice, as needed

Combine Mauna La'i Paradise Passion Juice Drink, Mauna La'i ¡Mango Mango! Juice Drink, rum, and peach brandy in shaker with ice. Pour into glass filled with ice. Garnish with lime wedge.

Makes 1 drink

Bloody Marys

1 quart tomato juice
½ cup vodka
2 tablespoons *Frank's®*
    RedHot® Cayenne Pepper
    Sauce
2 tablespoons *French's®*
    Worcestershire Sauce
2 tablespoons prepared
    horseradish
1 tablespoon lemon juice
1 teaspoon celery salt

Combine all ingredients in large pitcher; refrigerate. Serve over ice.   *Makes 4 servings*

Prep Time: 5 minutes
Chill Time: 30 minutes

Honeydew Melon Shake

1 cup honeydew melon
    chunks, chilled
½ cup vanilla low-fat yogurt
2 teaspoons sugar

Combine all ingredients in blender or food processor. Blend thoroughly. Pour and serve.
    Makes 2 servings

Variation: For strawberry melon flavor, blend in 1 cup frozen strawberries and add another teaspoon sugar.

Favorite recipe from **The Sugar Association, Inc.**

"Lemon Float" Punch

Juice of 10 to 12 SUNKIST®
    lemons (2 cups)
¾ cup sugar
4 cups water
1 bottle (2 liters) ginger ale,
    chilled
1 pint lemon sherbet or
    frozen vanilla yogurt
Lemon half-cartwheel slices
    and fresh mint leaves
    (optional) for garnish

Combine lemon juice and sugar; stir to dissolve sugar. Add water; chill. To serve, in large punch bowl, combine lemon mixture and ginger ale. Add small scoops of sherbet, lemon slices and mint.
    Makes about 15 cups (thirty 6-ounce servings)

Bloody Marys

Strawberry-Peach Cooler

1 cup sliced strawberries
1 cup chopped peaches
2 tablespoons sugar
1 bottle (750 ml) white wine, chilled
1 bottle (1 quart) sparkling water, chilled
Mint sprigs
Ice

Combine strawberries and peaches in small bowl. Sprinkle with sugar; stir gently. Let stand at room temperature 30 minutes. Pour fruit into punch bowl. Gently pour in wine and water. Add mint sprigs and ice. *Makes about 2 quarts*

Nonalcoholic Cooler: Use only 1 tablespoon sugar. Substitute 1 quart apple juice for wine.

The Hangover Concoction

1 can spicy CLAMATO® drink
½ can of beer
Juice from ½ lemon
Hot pepper sauce, to taste
Pinch of salt and black pepper
1 celery stalk, for garnish

Combine all ingredients except celery stalk in large glass. Stir and garnish with celery stalk.
Makes 1 drink

Sunny Orange Delight

1 envelope KOOL-AID® Sugar Free Lemonade Flavor Low Calorie Soft Drink Mix
8 cups (2 quarts) cold water
1 can (6 ounces) frozen orange juice concentrate, thawed
Ice cubes

PLACE drink mix in large plastic or glass pitcher. Add water; stir to dissolve. Stir in juice concentrate. Refrigerate. Serve over ice.
Makes 8 (1-cup) servings

Prep: 10 minutes plus refrigerating

Cranberry-Lime Margarita Punch

6 cups water
1 container (12 ounces)
    frozen cranberry juice
    cocktail
½ cup fresh lime juice
¼ cup sugar
2 cups ice cubes
1 cup ginger ale or tequila
1 lime, sliced

1. Combine water, cranberry juice, lime juice and sugar in punch bowl; stir until sugar dissolves.

2. Stir in ice cubes, ginger ale and lime; garnish with fresh cranberries, if desired.

Makes 10 (8-ounce) servings

Honey Lemonade

Concentrate
    6 tablespoons honey
    1 cup lemon juice
    1 lemon, thinly sliced

Mixer
    Ice cubes
    1 quart carbonated water

For concentrate, dissolve honey in lemon juice in 1-quart jar or glass bowl. Add lemon slices and refrigerate until ready to use.

For mixer, fill 12-ounce glass with ice cubes. Add ¼ cup lemon juice concentrate and fill glass with carbonated water. *Makes 4 servings*

Tip: Garnish with a lemon wedge.

Favorite recipe from **National Honey Board**

Lemon Herbal Iced Tea

2 SUNKIST® lemons
4 cups boiling water
6 herbal tea bags
    (peppermint and
    spearmint blend or
    ginger-flavored)
Ice cubes
Honey or sugar to taste

With vegetable peeler, peel each lemon in continuous spiral, removing only outer colored layer of peel (save peeled fruit for other uses). In large pitcher, pour boiling water over tea bags and lemon peel. Cover and steep 10 minutes. Remove tea bags; chill tea mixture with peel in covered container. To serve, remove peel and pour over ice cubes in tall glasses. Sweeten to taste with honey. Garnish with lemon half-cartwheel slices, if desired. *Makes 4 (8-ounce) servings*

"M&M's"® Brain Freezer Shake

2 cups any flavor ice cream
1 cup milk
¾ cup "M&M's"® Chocolate
    Mini Baking Bits, divided
Aerosol whipped topping
Additional "M&M's"®
    Chocolate Mini Baking
    Bits for garnish

In blender container combine ice cream and milk; blend until smooth. Add ½ cup "M&M's"® Chocolate Mini Baking Bits; blend just until mixed. Pour into 2 glasses. Top each glass with whipped topping; sprinkle with remaining ¼ cup "M&M's"® Chocolate Mini Baking Bits. Serve immediately. *Makes 2 (1¼-cup) servings*

Piña Colada Punch

3 cups water
10 whole cloves
4 cardamom pods
2 sticks cinnamon
1 can (12 ounces) frozen
    pineapple juice
    concentrate, thawed
1 pint low-fat piña colada
    frozen yogurt, softened*
1¼ cups lemon seltzer water
1¼ teaspoons rum extract
¾ teaspoon coconut extract
    (optional)

Can substitute pineapple sherbet for low-fat piña colada frozen yogurt. When using pineapple sherbet, use coconut extract for more authentic flavor.

1. Combine water, cloves, cardamom and cinnamon in small saucepan. Bring to a boil over high heat; reduce heat to low. Simmer, covered, 5 minutes; cool. Strain and discard spices.

2. Combine spiced water, pineapple juice concentrate and frozen yogurt in small punch bowl or pitcher. Stir until frozen yogurt is melted. Stir in seltzer water, rum extract and coconut extract, if desired. Garnish with mint sprigs, if desired. *Makes 12 (4-ounce) servings*

Sunlight Sipper

1½ cups DOLE® Pine-Orange
    Banana Juice, chilled
1 tablespoon peach schnapps
1 tablespoon light rum
1 tablespoon orange liqueur
    Cracked ice

• Pour juice, schnapps, rum and liqueur in 2 glasses. Add ice. Garnish as desired.
Makes 2 servings

"M&M's"® Brain Freezer Shakes

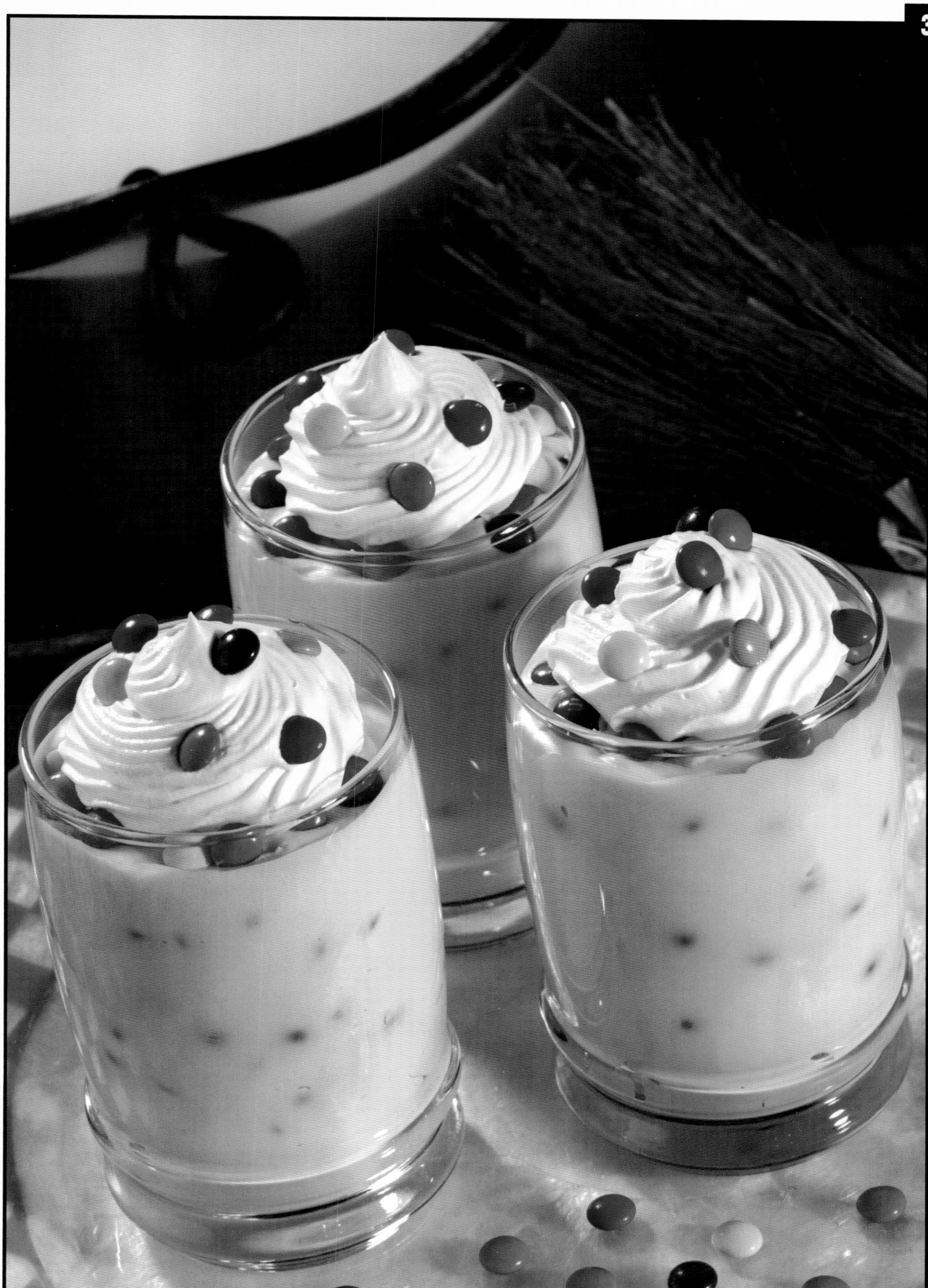

Citrus Cooler

2 cups fresh squeezed orange
    juice
2 cups unsweetened
    pineapple juice
1 teaspoon fresh lemon juice
¾ teaspoon vanilla extract
¾ teaspoon coconut extract
2 cups cold sparkling water

Combine juices and extracts in large pitcher; refrigerate until cold. Stir in sparkling water. Serve over ice.

Makes 9 servings

Toasted Almond Horchata

3½ cups water, divided
2 (3-inch) cinnamon sticks
1 cup uncooked instant white
    rice
1 cup slivered almonds,
    toasted
3 cups cold water
¾ to 1 cup sugar
½ teaspoon vanilla
    Lime wedges for garnish

Combine 3 cups water and cinnamon sticks in medium saucepan. Cover and bring to a boil over high heat. Reduce heat to medium-low. Simmer 15 minutes. Remove from heat; let cool to temperature of hot tap water. Measure cinnamon water to equal 3 cups, adding additional hot water if needed.

Place rice in food processor; process using on/off pulsing action 1 to 2 minutes or until rice is powdery. Add almonds; process until finely ground (mixture will begin to stick together). Remove rice mixture to medium bowl; stir in cinnamon water. Let stand 1 hour or until mixture is thick and rice grains are soft.

Remove cinnamon sticks; discard. Pour mixture into food processor. Add remaining ½ cup water; process 2 to 4 minutes or until mixture is very creamy. Strain mixture through fine-meshed sieve or several layers of dampened cheesecloth into half-gallon pitcher. Stir in 3 cups cold water, sugar and vanilla; stir until sugar is completely dissolved.

To serve, pour over ice cubes, if desired. Garnish, if desired.

Makes 8 to 10 servings

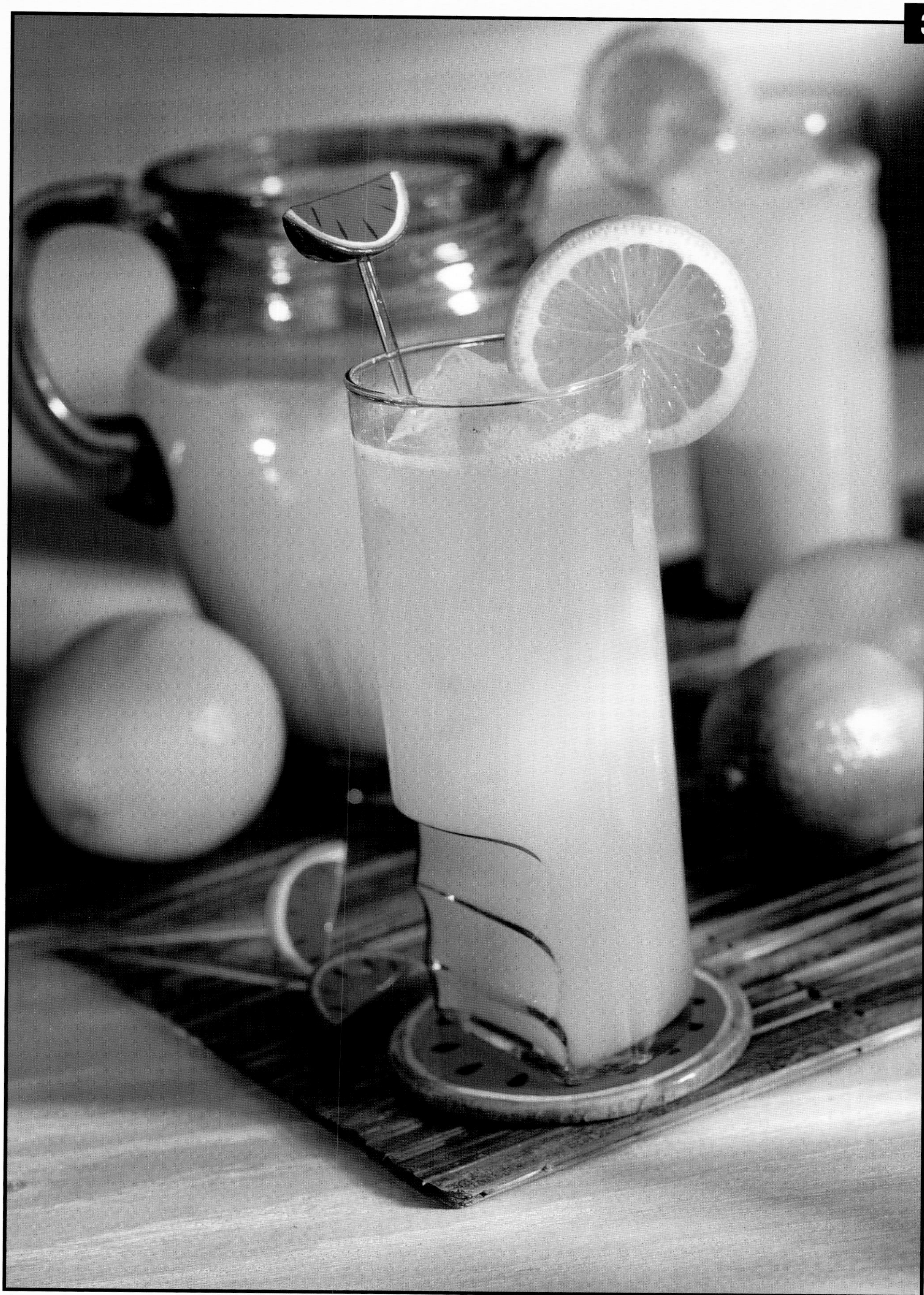

Peach-Lemon Frost

3 fresh California peaches, peeled, halved, pitted and quartered
1 cup 2% low-fat milk
½ cup fresh lemon juice
3 ice cubes, crushed
2 teaspoons grated lemon peel
½ pint vanilla ice milk

Add peaches to food processor or blender. Process until smooth to measure 2 cups. Add low-fat milk, lemon juice, ice cubes and lemon peel. Process until smooth. Continue processing at low speed; slowly add ice milk until well blended. Pour into glasses. Serve immediately. *Makes 4 servings*

Favorite recipe from California Tree Fruit Agreement

Raspberry Watermelon Slush

1 cup frozen raspberries
1 cup watermelon, seeded
1 cup lemon-lime seltzer
1 tablespoon sugar

Combine all ingredients in blender or food processor. Blend thoroughly. Serve immediately.

Makes 2 servings

Favorite recipe from The Sugar Association, Inc.

Margaritas, Albuquerque Style

1 lime, cut into wedges
  Coarse salt
1 can (6 ounces) frozen lime concentrate
¾ cup tequila
6 tablespoons Triple Sec
1 can (12 ounces) lemon-lime or grapefruit soda
3 to 4 cups ice cubes
  Lime twist for garnish
  Lime peel for garnish

Rub rim of each cocktail glass with lime wedge; swirl glass in salt to coat rim. Combine half of each of the remaining ingredients, except garnishes, in blender container; blend until ice is finely chopped and mixture is slushy. Pour into salt-rimmed glasses. Repeat with remaining ingredients. Garnish, if desired.

Makes 7 to 8 servings

Top to bottom: Peach-Lemon Frosts and Raspberry Watermelon Slush

Mimosa Cocktail

1 bottle (750 mL)
    champagne, chilled
3 cups Florida orange juice,
    chilled

Combine equal parts of champagne and orange juice in champagne glasses. Serve immediately.

Makes 12 servings

*Favorite recipe from **Florida Department of Citrus***

Honey Lemonade with Frozen Fruit Cubes

1½ cups lemon juice
¾ cup honey
9 cups water
48 small pieces assorted fruit

Combine lemon juice and honey in large pitcher; stir until honey is dissolved. Stir in water. Place 1 to 2 pieces of fruit in each compartment of 2 ice cube trays. Fill each compartment with honey lemonade and freeze until firm. Chill remaining lemonade. To serve, divide frozen fruit cubes between tall glasses and fill with remaining lemonade. *Makes 9 cups*

*Favorite recipe from **National Honey Board***

Chili-Spiked Fresh Lemonade Spritzer

3 cups water
1¼ cups sugar
5 to 10 small dried hot red
    chilies*
2 cups fresh lemon juice
1 bottle (750 ml) Asti
    Spumante or club soda
    Additional sugar (optional)
    Ice
    Lime wedges and dried hot
    red chilies for garnish

Use chilies according to taste.

Combine water, 1¼ cups sugar and chilies in medium saucepan. Cook and stir over high heat until mixture comes to a boil and sugar dissolves. Reduce heat to low; cover and simmer 30 minutes. Remove from heat and cool completely. Refrigerate 2 hours or up to 3 days.

Pour mixture through strainer into 3-quart pitcher; discard chilies. Stir in lemon juice and Asti Spumante. Stir in additional sugar to taste. Serve over ice. Garnish, if desired.

Makes 6 servings

Pineapple-Champagne Punch

1 quart pineapple sherbet
1 quart unsweetened
   pineapple juice, chilled
1 bottle (750 ml) dry
   champagne, chilled
2 fresh or canned pineapple
   slices, each cut into
   6 wedges
Mint sprigs

Process sherbet and pineapple juice in blender until smooth and frothy. Pour into punch bowl. Stir in champagne.

Float pineapple wedges in punch in groups of 3 or 4 to form flowers; garnish with mint sprigs. Serve immediately.   *Makes 20 (4-ounce) servings*

Raspberry Mint Cooler

1 to 2 cups fresh mint leaves
5 cups DOLE® Pineapple
   Juice, chilled
2 cups fresh or frozen
   raspberries
1 bottle (32 ounces) lemon-
   lime soda, chilled
1 can (6 ounces) frozen
   limeade concentrate,
   thawed
1 lime, thinly sliced for
   garnish (optional)

• Rub mint leaves around sides of punch bowl, then drop the bruised leaves in bottom of bowl.

• Combine remaining ingredients in punch bowl.
                                    Makes 15 servings

Chesapeake Bay Bloody Mary

1 cup ice
4 ounces MR & MRS T®
   Bloody Mary Mix
1½ ounces vodka
½ ounce ROSE'S® Lime Juice
¼ teaspoon crab boil
   seasoning (or favorite
   seafood spice blend)
Lime wedge (for garnish)
Celery stick (for garnish)

Fill a tall glass with ice; add next 4 ingredients. Stir well and garnish with lime wedge or celery stick.   *Makes 1 serving*

Sangrita

3 cups DEL MONTE® Tomato
    Juice
1½ cups orange juice
½ cup salsa
    Juice of 1 medium lime

1. Mix all ingredients in large pitcher; chill.

2. Serve over ice with fruit garnishes, if desired.

Makes 6 (6-ounce) servings

Prep Time: 3 minutes

Snappy Cooler

3 to 6 ounces SNAP-E-TOM®
    Tomato and Chile
    Cocktail, chilled
3 ounces orange juice, chilled

1. Combine ingredients. Serve over ice, if desired.

Makes 1 serving

Prep Time: 2 minutes

Pineapple-Mint Lemonade

1 cup sugar
⅔ cup water*
1 can (46 ounces) DOLE®
    Pineapple Juice
1 cup lemon juice
⅓ cup chopped fresh mint
    Fresh mint sprigs (optional)

**For less tart lemonade, use 1 cup water
instead of ⅔ cup.*

• Combine sugar and water in large saucepan; bring to boil. Boil 1 minute; remove from heat.

• Stir in pineapple juice, lemon juice and chopped mint; let stand 15 minutes.

• Strain lemonade into large pitcher; discard chopped mint. Serve over ice cubes in tall glasses. Garnish with mint sprigs.   *Makes 8 servings*

Summer Spritzer: Combine 2 cups Pineapple-Mint Lemonade with 2 cups mineral or sparkling water. Serve over ice. Makes 4 servings.

Prep Time: 15 minutes
Cook/Stand Time: 20 minutes

Sangrita, Snappy Cooler

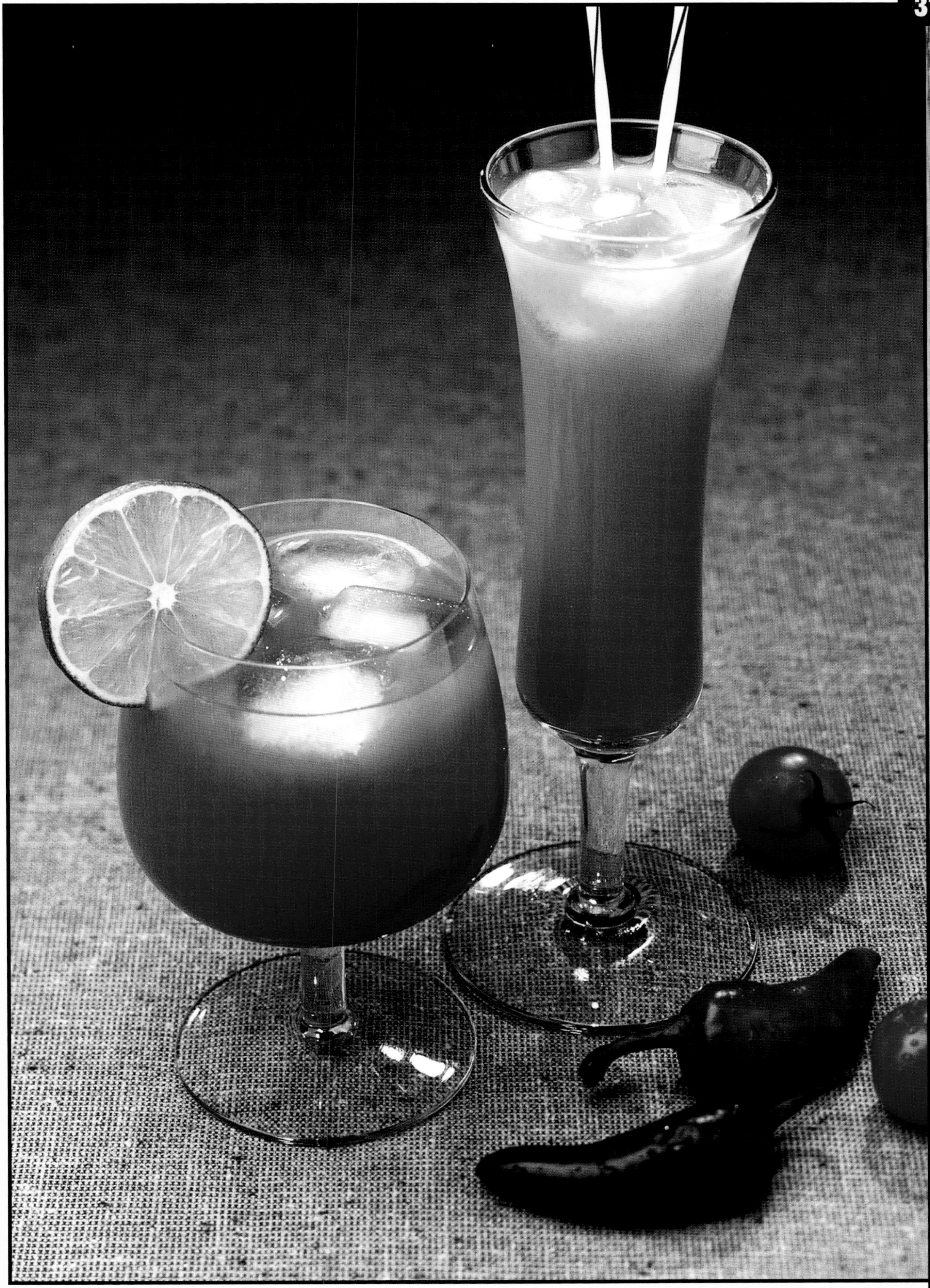

Acknowledgments

The publisher would like to thank the companies and organizations listed below for the use of their recipes and photographs in this publication.

A.1.® Steak Sauce

BC-USA, Inc.

Bob Evans®

Butterball® Turkey

California Tree Fruit Agreement

Chef Paul Prudhomme's Magic Seasoning Blends®

Clamato® is a registered trademark of Mott's, Inc.

Colorado Potato Administrative Committee

ConAgra Foods®

Delmarva Poultry Industry, Inc.

Del Monte Corporation

Dole Food Company, Inc.

Filippo Berio® Olive Oil

Florida Department of Agriculture and Consumer Services, Bureau of Seafood and Aquaculture

Florida's Citrus Growers

Grandma's® is a registered trademark of Mott's, Inc.

Grey Poupon® Dijon Mustard

Heinz North America

Holland House® is a registered trademark of Mott's, Inc.

The Kingsford Products Company

Kraft Foods Holdings

Lawry's® Foods

© Mars, Incorporated 2003

Mauna La'i® is a registered trademark of Mott's, Inc.

McCormick®

McIlhenny Company (TABASCO® brand Pepper Sauce)

Mr & Mrs T® is a registered trademark of Mott's, Inc.

Mrs. Dash®

National Chicken Council / US Poultry & Egg Association

National Honey Board

National Pork Board

National Turkey Federation

NatraTaste® is a registered trademark of Stadt Corporation

North Dakota Beef Commission

Perdue Farms Incorporated

Plochman, Inc.

Reckitt Benckiser Inc.

The J.M. Smucker Company

The Sugar Association, Inc.

Property of © 2003 Sunkist Growers, Inc. All rights reserved.

Uncle Ben's Inc.

Unilever Bestfoods North America

USA Rice Federation

Washington Apple Commission

Wisconsin Milk Marketing Board

Index

METRIC CONVERSION CHART

VOLUME MEASUREMENTS (dry)

$1/8$ teaspoon = 0.5 mL
$1/4$ teaspoon = 1 mL
$1/2$ teaspoon = 2 mL
$3/4$ teaspoon = 4 mL
1 teaspoon = 5 mL
1 tablespoon = 15 mL
2 tablespoons = 30 mL
$1/4$ cup = 60 mL
$1/3$ cup = 75 mL
$1/2$ cup = 125 mL
$2/3$ cup = 150 mL
$3/4$ cup = 175 mL
1 cup = 250 mL
2 cups = 1 pint = 500 mL
3 cups = 750 mL
4 cups = 1 quart = 1 L

VOLUME MEASUREMENTS (fluid)

1 fluid ounce (2 tablespoons) = 30 mL
4 fluid ounces ($1/2$ cup) = 125 mL
8 fluid ounces (1 cup) = 250 mL
12 fluid ounces ($1 1/2$ cups) = 375 mL
16 fluid ounces (2 cups) = 500 mL

WEIGHTS (mass)

$1/2$ ounce = 15 g
1 ounce = 30 g
3 ounces = 90 g
4 ounces = 120 g
8 ounces = 225 g
10 ounces = 285 g
12 ounces = 360 g
16 ounces = 1 pound = 450 g

DIMENSIONS

$1/16$ inch = 2 mm
$1/8$ inch = 3 mm
$1/4$ inch = 6 mm
$1/2$ inch = 1.5 cm
$3/4$ inch = 2 cm
1 inch = 2.5 cm

OVEN TEMPERATURES

250°F = 120°C
275°F = 140°C
300°F = 150°C
325°F = 160°C
350°F = 180°C
375°F = 190°C
400°F = 200°C
425°F = 220°C
450°F = 230°C

BAKING PAN SIZES

Utensil	Size in Inches/Quarts	Metric Volume	Size in Centimeters
Baking or Cake Pan (square or rectangular)	$8 \times 8 \times 2$	2 L	$20 \times 20 \times 5$
	$9 \times 9 \times 2$	2.5 L	$23 \times 23 \times 5$
	$12 \times 8 \times 2$	3 L	$30 \times 20 \times 5$
	$13 \times 9 \times 2$	3.5 L	$33 \times 23 \times 5$
Loaf Pan	$8 \times 4 \times 3$	1.5 L	$20 \times 10 \times 7$
	$9 \times 5 \times 3$	2 L	$23 \times 13 \times 7$
Round Layer Cake Pan	$8 \times 1 1/2$	1.2 L	20×4
	$9 \times 1 1/2$	1.5 L	23×4
Pie Plate	$8 \times 1 1/4$	750 mL	20×3
	$9 \times 1 1/4$	1 L	23×3
Baking Dish or Casserole	1 quart	1 L	—
	$1 1/2$ quart	1.5 L	—
	2 quart	2 L	—